Social Work Prac
Individuals and Families

Social Work Practice With Individuals and Families

Evidence-Informed Assessments and Interventions

Edited by

**Michael J. Holosko
Catherine N. Dulmus
Karen M. Sowers**

WILEY

JOHN WILEY & SONS, INC.

Cover Design: Andrew Liefer
Cover Images: Background bottom image: © javarman3/iStockphoto, Inset left: © Miodrag Gagic/iStockphoto,
          Inset middle: © Aldo Murillo/iStockphoto, Inset right: © Christopher Futcher/iStockphoto

Library of Congress Cataloging-in-Publication Data:

Holosko, Michael J.
  Social work practice with individuals and families : evidence-informed assessments and interventions /
Michael J. Holosko, Catherine N. Dulmus, Karen M. Sowers.
      p. cm.
  Includes bibliographical references and index.
  ISBN 978-1-118-17697-9 (pbk.)
  ISBN 978-1-118-41935-9 (ebk.)
  ISBN 978-1-118-42091-1 (ebk.)
  ISBN 978-1-118-43378-2 (ebk.)
  1. Family social work. 2. Social work with children. 3. Evidence-based social work. 4. Social case work.
I. Dulmus, Catherine N. II. Sowers, Karen M. (Karen Marlaine) III. Title.
  HV697.H66 2013
  361.3'2—dc23
                                                                2012022694

Printed in the United States of America
V10014475_100319

We have many blessings to be thankful for each day of our lives.
The extent to which we actually count our blessings and give thanks
is less well certain.

I dedicate this volume to
my life partner, spiritual anchor, ego-validity checker, and reality-grounded spouse,
Deborah Ann Holosko,
whose support, love, and inspiration
are what drives me to be me.
Thank you for being you, Ann.

—Michael J. Holosko

Contents

Chapter 9   **Assessment of Families 237**
Robyn Munford and Jackie Sanders

Chapter 10   **Intervention With Families 265**
*Cynthia Franklin, Catheleen Jordan,
    and Laura Hopson*

Preface

North American social welfare and social work as we know it today evolved in the United Kingdom from the Elizabethan Poor Laws of 1601, more specifically the Act for the Relief of the Poor. Thus, it was social policy that set the framework for the provision of goods and services doled out to the have-nots of society. Since its inception then, social policy has directed social work practice and from the 19th century onward, social research has informed social work practice.

Social Work Practice With Individuals and Families: Evidence-Informed Assessments and Interventions reiterates that these two cornerstone principles of social work have never wavered. What has changed, however, are our societies, economies, and the social/political context that shape how social workers deliver services to those in need, or the vulnerable populations who are our clients. Thus, this volume links policy-practice to research and evaluation in each chapter within it.

The point of departure for each chapter is how research and evaluation document, critically appraise, assess, and provide empirical evidence for our day-to-day activities in direct practice—that being face-to-face interactions with individuals and families, or the lifeblood of social work practice. The chapters cut across the life span from children to adults, to the elderly. For each of these cohorts, material is presented that shows how to both assess and use intervention evidence judiciously. This volume shows clearly how our profession has matured, by continually making the aforementioned connections throughout research and evaluation ↔ policy-practice, and assessment ↔ intervention, and the mechanism to achieve these intersecting areas is empirical evidence.

Indeed, our profession's use of evidence has moved from: case wisdom → empirical practice → evidence-based practice → evidence-informed practice. The latter emphasizes the incorporation of wider forms of systemically collected data, for example, case studies; findings from research studies; synthesized reviews of literature; best or promising practices; and data and evidence from the experiences of consumers, service users, professional practitioners, administrators, and policy makers. As such, the evidence-informed practice offered in this volume is an effort to be the first link in a knowledge-sharing chain-of-events system involving: the evidence itself to → assessment of the evidence to → the self-appraisal of how the evidence can be used to → transparency between all stakeholders in this process (i.e., clients, practitioners, administrators, etc.) to → disseminating the evidence to → utilization, or applying the evidence to inform practice decisions. Thus, each chapter in this text is judiciously anchored in this chain of evidence.

In an effort to stylistically address this chain-of-evidence idea, all contributors were asked to first construct succinct text boxes to establish the chapter's overall purpose and rationale, as well as to explain how examples of evidence were used within the chapter. They then presented an overarching question that students could think about while reading the chapter. At the end of each chapter, contributors then identified a set of key chapter terms and three to six field-tested websites that students or practitioners could access for additional readings, as well as five critical thinking questions to further probe the content of the chapter. This uniformity of style to address these important evidence-informed issues are presented consistently in the writing and reading of the chapters. We hope these elements also made the chapters more student and practitioner friendly.

This book is designed as a foundation social work practice text with individuals and families for undergraduate and graduate students in social work programs. The text provides the foundation of skills required for beginning social work practice with individuals and families. This book addresses Council on Social Work Education (CSWE) required competencies for accreditation. Specifically, the book addresses the following required accreditation competencies:

- Educational Policy 2.1.2 – Apply social work ethical principles to guide professional practice.
- Educational Policy 2.1.3 – Apply critical thinking to inform and communicate professional judgments.
- Educational Policy 2.1.4 – Engage diversity and difference in practice.
- Educational Policy 2.1.6 – Engage in research-informed practice and practice-informed research.
- Educational Policy 2.1.7 – Apply knowledge of human behavior and the social environment.
- Educational Policy 2.1.9 – Respond to contexts that shape practice.
- Educational Policy 2.1.10 – Engage, assess, and intervene with individuals and families.

As our profession develops and uses evidence more routinely and effectively, as such, it will not only fare well in this competitive era of legitimacy, but it will be better prepared to more effectively and ethically serve the unique needs of our diverse and marginalized clients.

—MJH, CND, KMS

Acknowledgments

A text of this nature could not have come to fruition without the support of many. This collective group is the real story behind the book, and they need recognition. First, I would like to acknowledge both of my co-editors for pushing this well-conceptualized and well-crafted book forward for publication in our field. Catherine N. Dulmus, one co-editor, spent much appreciated time shepherding, marshalling, and empowering my ability to write, edit, tweak, and freshen-up this well-written set of chapters; I thank you for this, Catherine. In regard to the chapter contributors, thank you for sharing your poignant ideas on evidence-informed assessments and intervention from your practice wisdom and research. Your professionalism and commitment to promoting this leading edge topic in order to advance our practice reality was much appreciated.

At John Wiley, a special acknowledgment goes to Rachel Livsey, Senior Editor for Social Work and Counseling and particularly Amanda Orenstein, Editorial Assistant for supporting this work from A to Z, through numerous phone calls, e-mails, long telephone messages, and edited PDF files. At the University of Georgia, I would like to acknowledge and thank Dr. Israel Berger who endowed my chair in family and child welfare in the School of Social Work. This allowed me to obtain the much needed resources and additional time to dedicate to this project. Finally, I would like to thank Catherine A. Patterson, Tisha Abolt Graduate Assistant, MSW, who not only spent countless hours on this manuscript as a research and editorial assistant, but who also found the time to co-author a chapter in the text itself. I very much appreciated your professionalism, diligence, sense of humor, and student voice in reviewing and working on countless renditions of this manuscript during this past year.

In sum, I sincerely appreciate all your help with this endeavor and I enjoyed working with all of you on this journey very much.

—MJH

About the Editors

Michael J. Holosko, PhD, MSW, is the Pauline M. Berger Professor of Family and Child Welfare at the University of Georgia, School of Social Work. He has taught across the undergraduate and graduate curriculum in schools of: social work (primarily), nursing, public administration, and applied social science in Canada, the United States, Hong Kong, Sweden, Australia, and the U.S. Virgin Islands. He has published extensively in the areas of evaluation, health care, gerontology, social policy, research, music intervention, and spirituality. For the past 33 years, he has been a consultant to a variety of large and small health and human service organizations in the areas of: program evaluation, outcomes, accreditation, organizational development, communication, leadership, visioning, organizational alignment, and stress management. He serves on the editorial boards of: *Research on Social Work Practice*; *Journal of Health and Social Policy*; *Journal of Human Behavior and Social Environment*; the *Hong Kong Journal of Social Work*; *Journal of Social Service Research*; and the *Journal of Evidence-Based Social Work Practice*.

Catherine N. Dulmus, PhD, LCSW, is Professor, Associate Dean for Research, and Director of the Buffalo Center for Social Research at the University at Buffalo and Research Director at Hillside Family of Agencies in Rochester, New York. She received her baccalaureate degree in Social Work from Buffalo State College in 1989, the master's degree in Social Work from the University at Buffalo in 1991, and a doctoral degree in Social Welfare from the University at Buffalo in 1999. As a researcher with interests that include community-based research, child and adolescent mental health, evidence-based practice, and university-community partnerships, Dr. Dulmus' recent contributions have focused on fostering interdependent collaborations among practitioners, researchers, schools, and agencies critical in the advancement and dissemination of new and meaningful knowledge. She has authored or co-authored several journal articles and books and has presented her research nationally and internationally. Prior to obtaining the PhD, her social work practice background encompassed almost a decade of experience in the fields of mental health and school social work.

Karen M. Sowers, PhD, is Dean and Beaman Professor in the College of Social Work at University of Tennessee, Knoxville. She is the University of Tennessee Beaman Professor for Outstanding Research and Service. Dr. Sowers received her baccalaureate degree in sociology from the University of Central Florida, and her master's degree and PhD degree in social work from Florida State University. Dr. Sowers serves on several local, national, and international boards. Dr. Sowers is nationally known for her research and scholarship in the areas of international practice, juvenile justice, child welfare, cultural diversity, and culturally effective intervention strategies for social work practice, evidence-based social work practice, and social work education.

Contributors

Paula Allen-Meares, PhD
School of Social Work
University of Michigan
Ann Arbor, Michigan

Kimberly A. Brisebois, BSW, MSW
School of Social Work
Wayne State University
Detroit, Michigan

Elaine Congress, PhD, DSW, LCSW
Fordham University Graduate School
of Social Service
New York, New York

Cynthia Franklin, PhD, LCSW, LMFT
School of Social Work
University of Texas–Austin
Austin, Texas

Michael J. Holosko, PhD
School of Social Work
University of Georgia
Athens, Georgia

Laura Hopson, PhD
School of Social Welfare
University at Albany
Albany, New York

Catheleen Jordan, PhD, LCSW
School of Social Work
University of Texas–Arlington
Arlington, Texas

Craig Winston LeCroy, PhD
School of Social Work
Arizona State University
Tucson, Arizona

Robyn Munford, PhD
School of Health and Social Services
Massey University
Palmerston North, New Zealand

Catherine A. Patterson, MSW
School of Social Work
University of Georgia
Athens, Georgia

Gregory J. Paveza, MSW, PhD
School of Health and Human Services
Southern Connecticut State University
New Haven, Connecticut

Tara M. Powell, MSW, MPH
Austin, Texas

Mary C. Ruffolo, PhD, LMSW
School of Social Work
University of Michigan
Ann Arbor, Michigan

Jackie Sanders, PhD
School of Health and Social Services
Massey University
Palmerston North, New Zealand

Jeffrey F. Skinner, LCSW, MDiv
School of Social Work
University of Georgia
Athens, Georgia

David W. Springer, PhD, LCSW
School of Social Work
Portland State University
Portland, Oregon

Bruce A. Thyer, PhD
College of Social Work
Florida State University
Tallahassee, Florida

Lela Rankin Williams, PhD
School of Social Work
Arizona State University
Tucson, Arizona

Michael E. Woolley, MSW, DCSW, PhD
School of Social Work
University of Maryland
Baltimore, Maryland

Chapter 1
Assessment of Children

Michael E. Woolley

Purpose: This chapter details and discusses the historical evolution and current trends in social work in the systematic, ecological, and evidenced-informed assessment of children. It includes the myriad struggles impacting children and the broad range of settings in which social workers serve children and their families.

Rationale: Whether in schools, child protective services, juvenile justice, family or community centers, mental-health agencies, or hospitals, social workers assume many roles in providing services for children. A critical part of providing effective services is a comprehensive assessment informed by social work values, ethics, interfacing with our evolving professional orientation, knowledge, skills, and tools.

How evidence-informed practice is presented: One current trend is the increasing use of quantitative survey instruments in child assessment, and there is an increasing number of such assessment tools being developed by social work researchers. A second trend is the increasingly widespread need for the evaluation of the effects of interventions. In order to offer such evaluations, valid and reliable assessment tools are needed that can show changes in the assessed struggles and targeted outcomes of those interventions.

Overarching questions: Within specific social work practice settings serving children, in order to complete an ecologically oriented and comprehensive assessment of a child and family, what information would be needed, from whom should that information be gathered, and by what means or methods should that information be collected?

Social workers are vital members of teams delivering services to children across a variety of settings, including, but not limited to, child welfare agencies, family service organizations, schools, health-care providers, and mental-health settings. The struggles and challenges faced by children served by those social workers covers a broad spectrum from day-to-day struggles to life-altering trauma. In all those settings and struggles, beginning the social work intervention process with a systematic and comprehensive effort to gather information about the child, the social contexts of the child, and the presenting struggle or challenge is a critical first step to providing professional, appropriate, and effective services to children who have been impacted by issues ranging from sexual abuse or mental illness to brain tumors or learning disabilities.

Social work has been increasingly called on, from both outside and inside the profession, to demonstrate the effectiveness of its practices. This scrutiny provides the impetus to engage in research to develop evidence-based practice (EBP) strategies and approaches (Gambrill, 1999). The needs for quality assessment tools and strategies as a fundamental task within that effort are twofold. First, all practice activities should start with and be informed by an assessment process. Second, gathering evidence as to the effectiveness of an intervention requires assessing the target of that intervention before and after that intervention is delivered; therefore, reliable and valid assessment measures are a fundamental tool in the pursuit of evidence to support practice.

This chapter first defines what is involved in performing a systematic and comprehensive social work child-assessment process. The accumulated social work practice knowledge in the area of child assessment emerging across the first 100 years of professional social work is discussed. We then outline the current prevailing framework used to gather, organize, and present assessment information about children. More recent developments in the assessment of children are then added to that framework—for example, the necessity of gathering information from multiple informants and using multiple information-gathering tools when assessing children. Within that evolving assessment framework, a growing effort in social work (and other helping professions) is to strive to utilize evidence-based strategies and tools in practice. What is meant by evidence-based practice and how that effort can inform the most effective and efficient assessment of children is explored. The limitations to the evidence in support of our current assessment strategies with children, as well as promising ways to reduce those limitations, are detailed. Finally, current trends and developments in the assessment of children in social work practice settings, including child protection, schools, and mental health, are presented.

Defining Assessment

Assessment is used to describe an assortment of activities and processes in the social sciences and human services that involve gathering information about a client(s) and the presenting circumstances leading to an evaluation, determination, or plan of action focused on that client or client system. In social work practice, some aspects of assessment are driven by the practice setting, the population being served, and the practice model being applied by the social worker. However, this chapter offers a framework for social work assessment with children that, although embedded within the evolution of the social work perspective and the current effort to situate social work practice on an evidence base, can be applied by any direct practitioner regardless of setting, population, practice level, or model. In this chapter, a descriptive and evolving definition of assessment in the context of providing social work services to children is offered. As a starting framework, assessment in social work with children is defined as including three key components: (1) collecting data, (2) being informed by a contextual perspective, (3) leading to a prevention or intervention plan.

Data Collection

First, assessment of children is, in large part, defined by a range of activities used to gather information about a child, a struggle or challenge confronting that child, and relevant information about that child's social environments. Those activities can include but are not limited to (a) clinical interviews, (b) structured interviews, (c) self-report instruments, (d) direct observations, and (e) reviews of existing records. Those data-collection activities may elicit information from multiple informants, including the child, parents/guardians, other family members, key individuals in the child's life, and professionals who have direct experience with the child.

Contextual Perspective

The second component is illustrated by an enlightening distinction about assessment in social work practice made by Clifford (1998). He referred to "social assessment," as opposed to psychological or medical assessment, in that social assessment "is centered on a social explanation—and will draw on social research and social science concepts" in identifying the service needs of an individual, small group, or community. Although social workers clearly also draw on and are informed by psychological and medical aspects of and explanations for client struggles, Clifford's focus on the social aspects of the client and his or her struggles distinguishes assessment in social work from assessment in other disciplines. This focus on contextual factors in social work can be seen in many assessment orientations in social work, such as the person-in-environment perspective, psychosocial models, the widespread use of ecological-systems thinking, and the pervasive structuring of assessment information into a biopsychosocial assessment document.

Prevention or Intervention Planning

Third, child assessment in social work is also defined as having as the central goal in gathering that information to inform the development of a social work prevention or intervention plan to help that child or group of children. Although systematic information about a child and his or her social environments may be gathered for other reasons—such as part of a research endeavor or eligibility evaluation—unless the ultimate goal is a formulation leading to the implementation of a social work service plan, the gathering of that information does not constitute an assessment as it is referred to in this chapter.

Thus, a social work assessment of a child includes (a) data collection, defined as a systematic gathering of information about the child, a struggle or challenge facing that child, and that child's multiple social environments; (b) data pursued from a contextual perspective oriented to how the child's social environments influence the child, the struggle or challenge, and efforts to resolve that struggle or challenge; and (c) development of an intervention plan to assist that child with that struggle or challenge as the primary goal of that data-collection effort.

The application of systemic and comprehensive assessment strategies has become more important given profession-wide efforts to build an evidence-based approach to social work services (Gambrill, 1999). Because service-delivery activities start with and are built on the assessment process, reliable and valid assessment strategies and tools are fundamental to identifying, developing, evaluating, and providing evidence-based interventions. For example, reliable and valid assessments provide a vehicle to evaluate interventions, thereby establishing evidence as to when and with whom such interventions can be effective. Further, the application of interventions with already established bodies of evidence as to their effectiveness should only be utilized after the application of systematic, comprehensive, reliable, and valid assessment strategies and tools to inform the selection of interventions appropriate for a specific child in a specific situation. Additionally, the results of a systematic assessment should influence the provision of the interventions chosen, thereby following long-established social work practice principles, such as starting where the client is, treating each client as an individual, and providing individualized services (Hepworth, Rooney, & Larsen, 2002; Pilsecker, 1994).

The wide variety of settings in which social workers serve children, the larger array of struggles and challenges faced by those children, and the wide range of what and who social workers are actually assessing—for example, the child, a potential home placement, the risk of a caregiver to abuse or neglect, the appropriateness of a classroom setting—all make a truly comprehensive discussion of assessment of children in social work seem daunting. Therefore, one goal of this chapter is to set the current state of assessment of children in social work in a historical context that encompasses our collective professional knowledge informing the assessment of children as a framework on which to add recent advancements.

Historical Background

Mary Richmond, in her seminal book *Social Diagnosis* (1917), presents the first comprehensive treatise on the assessment process in social work. Although she uses the term *diagnosis*, which, for most social workers today means something quite different than assessment, what she is referring to as a social diagnosis 90 years ago meets the three criteria for social work assessment offered here. In fact, for those who have not read all or even parts of her book, it is truly worth the time, and you may find it contains surprisingly still-relevant insights on assessment, social casework, and prescient glimpses of things to come. For example, Richmond describes her preparation to write *Social Diagnosis* as including systematically reviewing social work case records and recording interviews with caseworkers across five different sites over the course of a year "to bring to light the best social work practice that could be found" (p. 7). Is that not an effort to build a body of evidence about what works? Richmond further says of her efforts in the preparation of the book, "the most difficult of all my problems has been to make a presentation on the handling of evidence" (p. 9) in the assessment process. Richmond's book culminates in a series of structured interview protocols for the assessment of various clients and situations.

Assessment Informing Best and Evidence-Based Practices

The pursuit of providing clients with the best possible social work services available at a given point in time, basing assessment on gathering the best evidence possible, and collecting that evidence in a systematic manner are distinctly not new endeavors in the social work profession. In fact, social work has a rich history of professional knowledge development in the area of assessment.

Central to that accumulation of knowledge in the assessment of children has been the conceptual perspective of a child as embedded in a set of social contexts. Mary Richmond articulated that fundamental perspective 90 years ago. That perspective also guided Jane Addams and the Hull House staff. For example, in the area of juvenile delinquency, Hull House rejected dominant theories based on heredity and instead asserted that the most important factors leading to juvenile delinquency were environmental (Hart, 1990). With respect to assessment, that clearly means the gathering of information about, and analysis of, the social environment that a child inhabits in an effort to understand that child's development, struggles, and behavior.

The history of that perspective can be traced to today by examining social work textbooks over the decades detailing the state of the art and science of casework practices. For example, Hamilton (1951) states that assessment is an attempt to understand the client, the problem, and the situation; and such authors as Perlman (1957), Hollis (1964), and Pincus and Minahan (1973) iterate that triad of assessment. Hollis states this perspective succinctly when she points out that, in assessment, "strengths as well as weaknesses in both the person and the situation are important considerations" (p. 261). Hepworth et al. (2002) offer a similar triad. Assessment, they suggest, is a process "to gather information and formulation of that information into a coherent picture of the client and his or her circumstances," leading to "our inferences about the nature and causes of the client's difficulties" (p. 187). They do, however, describe a meaningful shift in one aspect of that triad in that they stress the assessment of the *needs* and the *strengths* of the client as much as the *difficulties* of the client. This strengths perspective continues to guide the development of structured assessment instruments for practice, such as a strength-based and culturally informed reliable and valid assessment tool for practice with Native American youth, their families, and communities (Gilgun, 2004). This sort of melding of the long-evolving social work ecological strengths and culturally informed orientation to helping clients with more recent and rigorous assessment methodology seems like a promising trajectory in social work assessment with children.

The focus on strengths has grown in part from the long-standing fundamental humanistic perspective in social work that all clients are doing their best and have resources and that, when clients struggle, it is because of a deficit in those available resources. Such resources can be both internal and environmental, and clients can call on those resources—social workers can likewise call on those resources in the assessment process—to help meet challenges and struggles clients face (McQuaide & Ehrenreich, 1997). Such a strengths perspective grows out of social work's values and ethical orientation to clients (a) as persons of worth, (b) as persons who have a fundamental right to choose their goals in the helping process and how they go about working on those goals, and (c) as persons who are capable of solving their own problems with appropriate support (Loewenberger & Dolgoff, 1985). The strengths perspective also stands in contrast to the still-pervasive medical model of diagnosing and labeling limitations, which is particularly prevalent in mental-health practice (Cox, 2006). The strengths perspective and the focus on the social environments of a client are reflected in the ubiquitous development of an ecological-systems orientation in social work practice.

Evolving Ecological-Systems Perspective

A seminal application of the ecological perspective in social work is the introduction of the life model of practice by Germain and Gitterman in 1980. As they put it, "the social purpose [of social work] calls for a practice method that is designed to engage people's strengths and the forces pushing them toward growth, and to influence organizational structures, other social systems, and physical settings so they will be more responsive to people's needs" (p. 2). In the 1980s, the ecological perspective was increasingly used to articulate the social work approach to assessment and service delivery. Further, some authors started adding concepts from the general systems theory to that ecological perspective to create what was termed the *ecosystems perspective* (Greif & Lynch, 1983).

The adaptation of systems theory to practice endeavors introduced several helpful theoretical concepts into social work thinking. Those concepts are especially helpful in assessment, as they offer insights into how social systems—the interactions between a client and his or her environment—work. For example, *equilibrium* is a concept that states that human systems (read families) tend toward establishing a balance that can be maintained, whether that balance is good or not so good for the members of the system. *Boundaries*, such as between members of the family or between the family and other systems, such as the school or neighborhood, are critical in the flow of information, resources, and support within and among systems. Social work has long asserted that assessing and attending to these dynamic processes are critical to effective assessment of a child and his or her social systems (Germain & Gitterman, 1980).

Another notable step in the evolution of the contextual orientation to assessment in social work is the person-in-environment (PIE) system, introduced by Karls and Wandrei (1992). The PIE system offers a common language and structure for social workers to use in formulating assessments from the unique orientation of social work. One goal in the development of the PIE system was to design an assessment structure that focuses on the "social well-being" of a client, which is identified as "different than physical or mental well-being" (p. 81), that assertion being supported by research about those three domains. The PIE assessment approach is systematic and comprehensive and includes information about the client, the problem, and the client's social environment, therefore possessing many of the characteristics described earlier for an effective assessment. It also introduces a coding system for client problems, with codes for duration, severity, and coping, as a way to quantify assessment information. The basic structure of the PIE system includes four factors: Factor 1–social role problems, Factor 2–environmental problems, Factor 3–mental disorders, and Factor 4–physical disorders. This system shares some structural characteristics with and foreshadows the multiaxial format of the *Diagnostic and Statistical Manual of Mental Disorders* (American Psychiatric Association, 2000) diagnostic format, and, although not widely used today, the PIE system represents an important development in social work's quest to build a professionally unique and uniform structure to assessment. Additionally, the PIE perspective continues to evolve; for example, the person-environment practice approach, as described by Kemp, Whittaker, and Tracy (1997), offers an ecological competence-oriented practice model that stresses the importance of ongoing assessment, social support, empowerment, and collective action.

Other developments in social assessment have also yielded systematic formats to gather and organize information. For example, there are two diagrammatic assessment tools that have seen widespread use in social work practice with children and families: the eco-map and the genogram (Hartman, 1995). Both tools grew out of the ecological-systems perspective and gained popularity in social work practice in the 1980s. Either or both can be drawn by a social worker in concert with a child and family during the assessment process and used as tools to elicit and synthesize information from the child and family as they help complete each diagram. Either can then be used to analyze family dynamics, gain a comprehensive picture of the family circumstances related to the struggle or challenge, or used to search for strengths, possible resources, and the ongoing collection of assessment information.

Hartman (1995), a social worker, first developed the eco-map for use in child welfare practice. An eco-map has, at its center, the child and family drawn as a circle (Figure 1.1). Then, surrounding the family and child is a system of circles representing other important people, resources, or activities, such as extended family; friends of the child and parents/guardians;

Figure 1.1

Example of an eco-map for Eddie, a 10-year-old boy with behavior problems

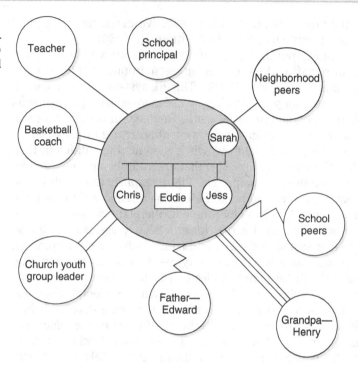

activities, such as recreation, sports, or hobbies; organizations, such as schools, churches, neighborhood groups, or workplaces; or other agencies, such as health-care providers, mental-health providers, or juvenile court. Care should be taken to include not just circles related to the presenting challenge or struggle but also those that represent strengths and resources to the child and family and other struggles or possible barriers to solving the presenting issue. Once all the needed circles have been drawn, various types of lines are drawn between the circles to represent the nature of the connection between the child and family and each particular circle. For example, a solid line depicts a strong relationship, and a dashed line represents a tenuous connection, whereas a line with hash marks across it suggests a stressful connection. Arrows are drawn along the connections to indicate the direction of flow of support, resources, and energy.

Murray Bowen (1978), a psychiatrist who was a pioneer in the field of family therapy, developed the genogram as an assessment tool. Carter and McGoldrick (1980), social workers who have been at the forefront of the evolution of family therapy over the past 25 years, particularly with respect to gender and ethnicity issues, introduced the use of genograms in social work. In drawing a genogram, three or even four generations of the family are depicted (Figure 1.2). Males are drawn as squares and females as circles, and a system of lines is utilized to connect family members and indicate the nature of their kinship. A genogram has levels for each generation, such that family members in the same generation are on the same level across the page. Once all the multigenerational members of

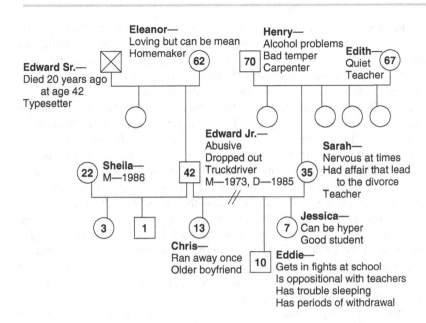

Figure 1.2

Example of a genogram for Eddie, a 10-year-old boy with behavior problems

the family are included and kinship lines are drawn, other aspects of the family dynamics and circumstances can be included, such as marriages and divorces, deaths and illnesses, alcohol or drug use, significant events in the family history, religion, occupation, education, mental-health problems, or any important events or family dynamics. Similar to the eco-map, various types of lines can also be added that characterize the nature of the relationships between family members. A genogram is used in practice not just as an assessment tool to identify family patterns, strengths and resources, and unresolved issues but also as an ongoing tool to identify strengths and resources in intervention planning and implementation. A comprehensive discussion of the use of genograms as an assessment and intervention tool is beyond this chapter; for more detail, see McGoldrick, Gerson, and Shellenberger (1999).

Another important step in the evolution of the ecological perspective in social work is the incorporation of a focus on risk and protective factors and the vulnerability or resilience to the impact of environmental stressors that such factors may offer (Fraser, Richman, & Galinsky, 1999). From this perspective, the characteristics of the physical environment and social relationships may act as risk or protective factors with respect to child and family functioning. Risk factors are environmental characteristics that predict undesirable developmental outcomes, whereas protective factors are promotive of positive developmental outcomes or may compensate for the negative impact of certain risk factors (Richman, Bowen, & Woolley, 2004). Central to this perspective is the concept of *resilience*, which has been defined as the dynamic interplay of environmental, social, and individual protective factors in the context of risk exposure, leading to positive adaptation and desirable developmental outcomes for youth (Luthar, Cicchetti, & Becker, 2000).

Related to the concept of resilience, it has become foundational in any assessment process in social work practice to assess client and client-system strengths (Saleebey, 2006). In the assessment of children, that means gathering information about the strengths of the child and the resources available to the child from his or her social environments. For example, Gleason (2007) details a strengths-based approach to completing a social developmental study in a school setting. That approach includes strategies for how to query children about strengths (for example, What are some things you have done that you are proud of?) and how to ask assessment interview questions from a strengths perspective (for example, When things are going well, what does that look like for you?). Then, the social worker frames intervention goals and objectives in positive ways and calls on assessed strengths and resources to achieve those objectives. Finally, a strengths perspective supports social workers striving to give children a voice in school meetings about their school service plans by preparing each child to speak and advocate for him- or herself in such meetings and making certain that time and space are made for the child to make those contributions to the process.

Bringing many of these concepts together in a manner that makes them applicable to assessment with children is the eco-interactional devel-opmental (EID) perspective, as described by Richman et al. (2004). This framework is informed by (a) the ecological-systems perspective in terms of the centrality of the social environment, and (b) the risk and resilience perspective in how that environment influences children, all within (c) a developmental orientation whereby child functioning can only be mean-ingfully interpreted in the context of that child's developmental trajectory and current developmental level, needs, and struggles. Within this eco-logical framework, there are three key environmental contexts that must be assessed in social work practice with children: family, neighborhood, and school. As described by Bronfenbrenner (2005), these *microsystems* are the environmental settings that directly influence a child, whereas *mezzosystems* represent the connections among those key microsystems. Examples of mezzosystems include the nature of the relationship between a child's family and a teacher or the relationships between the family and neighborhood residents and organizations. The larger social, cultural, and political environments that children and their families inhabit and the characteristics of those systems constitute the *macrosystem*.

Social work also has a rich history of stressing issues of cultural and ethnic diversity and historic and current forms of discrimination and oppression that emerge within a family's macrosystem and the various microsystems and mezzosystems surrounding a child and his or her fam-ily. Building on the ecological- and strengths-oriented PIE assessment system described earlier, Appleby, Colon, and Hamilton (2007) have com-prehensively approached the effects of race, culture, and social class in the dynamics of oppression and discrimination (including racism, sexism, homophobia, ableism, and religious bigotry) on healthy development and social functioning. Because a fundamental goal in social work assessment is to take a contextual perspective, it seems imperative to attend to the impact of such issues with respect to child clients and their families who may be members of currently or historically oppressed or discriminated groups. For example, the authors point out that culture is often seen as static, when, in fact, it is dynamic, changing as it develops, much like an individual develops and changes as the result of interactions with the environment and other cultures. Therefore, the culture in which the child client and his or her family are members is changing, as are the other cultures that child is surrounded by, and the dominant or majority culture, if that is different from the child's culture. Those multiple changing cultural contexts can at once serve as developmental settings for the child and family, sources of strengths and resources, mediators of struggles and challenges, or sources of oppression and discrimination, all potentially profoundly impacting child and family adaptation and functioning.

The pursuit of *social justice* has become an overarching framework in social work practice that refers to activities to reduce the causes and sequelae on clients, groups, and societies associated with oppression and discrimination. Finn and Jacobsen (2003) have offered a social work practice model that synthesizes well-established practice values, professional ethics, client engagement and professional relationship principles, and the PIE orientation to assessment while focusing on the impact of traditionally unjust structures and processes and the pursuit of socially just outcomes for clients. A comprehensive discussion of the impact on the child-assessment process of social justice issues associated with current or historical oppression and discrimination is beyond the scope of this chapter, so readers are encouraged to consult the literature starting with the references cited here. In fact, much research and intervention development and evaluation yet needs to be done related to the impact of issues of gender, race, ethnicity, culture, mental or physical ability, age, socioeconomic class, religion, family structure, sexual orientation, gender identity or expression, and citizenship status on clients and the social work helping process. However, a couple of examples may offer tangible reference points to illustrate that ambitious research and practice strategy development agenda.

In the context of working with Latino clients, Colon, Appleby, and Hamilton (2007) warn that traditional models of social work practice "ignore the interdependent, mutually supportive aspects of Latino group norms and individual values" (p. 302): for example, the centrality of familism (*familismo*) in the provision of social and economic support, and the importance of dignity (*dignidad*) and respect (*respeto*) in the dynamics of Latino families. Likewise, Colon et al. assert there are important practice implications to the historical racism experienced by African Americans, which today accounts for reduced access to socioeconomic resources, poor physical and mental-health outcomes, and limited access to social services, much of which is maintained by ongoing structural racism, particularly inequitable access to educational opportunity (Orfield, Losen, Wald, & Swanson, 2004). Finn and Jacobsen (2003) suggest that the application of the *empowerment* approach, an approach with a strong tradition in social work with respect to helping oppressed groups (Gutierrez & Lewis, 1999; Simon, 1994), presents a significant addition to an ecologically PIE-oriented framework to assessment in the pursuit of socially just outcomes for clients.

Identifying and building evidence to support the understanding of the practice assessment implications of such cultural and social justice dynamics that impact children and families require ongoing research efforts. For example, researchers (Ogbu, 1991, 1998; Oyserman, Bybee, & Terry, 2006; Oyserman, Terry, & Bybee, 2002; Woolley & Bowen, 2007; Woolley & Grogan-Kaylor, 2006) have empirically studied and furthered our knowledge (evidence) base about why and how children who are members of historically oppressed and discriminated groups struggle in school and how to reduce long-standing gaps in school achievement for such groups. However, such efforts must find the balance between making broad, or even stereotypical, assertions about members of certain cultural or ethnicity groups and identifying and explicating important cultural patterns impacting social functioning, assessment, and service delivery. The task for individual social work practitioners is to actively seek and synthesize knowledge about the client groups they are serving, from understanding cultural practices and norms to emerging research informing evidence-based assessment and intervention activities.

In sum, an effective assessment of a child in need of social work services requires data about not only the child's struggles, challenges, and functioning and the social microsystems—family, neighborhood, and school—in which that child is embedded but also the mezzosystem cultural dynamics of that child and his or her family along with the current and historical implications of that culture within the wider macrosystemic cultural context. Once such data have been gathered, the information must be organized into a coherent format for analysis and synthesis in order to inform intervention planning. A biopsychosocial assessment offers a format for such organization and synthesis.

Biopsychosocial Assessment Report

Organizing the data collected in a systematic and comprehensive social work assessment of a child involves bringing together these various elements that have evolved with the accumulation of social work practice knowledge. Reflecting the pervasive impact of the ecological perspective in social work, an assessment report of a child is most frequently termed a *biopsychosocial assessment* (Lukas, 1993), although some authors have referred to it as a *psychosocial study* (Cooper & Lesser, 2002) or a *multidimensional assessment* (Hepworth et al., 2002). The outline of a biopsychosocial assessment reflects the social work ecological orientation, including information about various aspects of the child, the presenting challenge, and the child's environment, that need to be attended to in the developing an effective service plan. Table 1.1 is a suggested

Table 1.1 Biopsychosocial Assessment Outline

Identifying Information

Child's name, age, race/ethnicity, physical appearance, religion
Child's place of residence, school, other important settings
Referral source and referral information

Presenting Struggle(s)

Child's definition
Parent/guardian's definition
Social worker's definition

History of the Struggle(s)

When did it start, how frequently, with whom, and where does it occur?
What social, emotional, psychological, learning, or medical/physical risk factors contribute to or are key
  factors in this struggle?
What are the consequences of the struggle to the child and family?
Results from assessment instruments: child reports, adult reports, and structured interviews
What attempts have been made to resolve this struggle:
—By the child or family?
—With the assistance of professional helpers?

Safety Concerns

Abuse or neglect concerns
Suicide or homicide risk

Developmental History

Current developmental challenges
Previous developmental challenges
Role of developmental issues in the presenting challenge

Family History

Multigeneration background of child's family setting
Ethnocultural issues: Acculturation stressors, language concerns, immigration/refugee status
Genogram

Strengths and Resilience Factors

Child's talents, resources, skills, and protective factors
Family strengths, resources, and protective factors
Extended family resources
Communal resources: Neighborhood, religious organization, ethnocultural organizations
Eco-map

Results, Interpretations, and Implications of Structured Assessment Instruments

Self-report instruments
Adult-report instruments
Structured interviews

Child and Family Needs

Economic: Income, housing, food, clothing, transportation
Social/emotional: Peer interaction, recreation
Educational: Appropriate school services
Medical: Health care, medication
Sociocultural: Translator, cultural specific support, community, advocacy
Legal: Guardian ad litem, current court involvement, advocacy

(continued overleaf)

Table 1.1 *(Continued)*

Mental Status Exam

Snapshot of child's social, psychological, cognitive, and behavioral functioning

Most often used in mental-health settings (see Cooper & Lesser, 2002)

Mental Health Diagnosis

DSM-V Axis Diagnosis—most often used in mental-health and other clinical settings; see the DSM-IV-TR
   (American Psychiatric Association)

Results from mental-health assessment instruments

Initial Contacts with Child and Family

Brief description of first meetings and actions taken

Child's and family's orientation to the social worker and helping process

Summary Statement

A paragraph or two summing up the key information

Initial Service Plan

Identify focus of initial service efforts

Goals and objectives for those efforts

Who will be involved, how, when, and for what purpose?

Note: This outline was adapted from Cooper and Lesser; Fraser, Richman, and Galinsky; Hepworth, Rooney, and Larson; and Lukas.

biopsychosocial assessment outline that reflects the evolution of social work thinking over the past 100 years as it relates to assessment. Some sections will not be called for, depending on the setting for practice, the child's developmental stage, the presenting struggle, and a child's particular circumstances. Further, additional sections may be needed in some situations to address specific issues that are relevant to a comprehensive assessment study of a specific child.

We have reviewed the evolution of the ecosystems perspective informing assessment in social work over the past 100 years: assessment tools that have grown out of that perspective, such as the PIE system, genograms, and eco-maps; the recognition of the critical role of issues in assessment, such as cultural diversity and oppression; and the organization of ecological assessment information into a systematic and comprehensive biopsychosocial assessment. These accumulated forms of social work assessment knowledge and strategies with children are still useful today across the very wide range of settings in which social workers serve children. However, there are setting- and situation-specific assessment tools that have more recently evolved since social work adopted the application of measurement theory in the 1970s and sought to develop more valid and reliable assessment tools for practice and research (Hudson, 1997). In the sections that follow, some of those assessment strategies for use in such categories as child welfare, schools, mental health, and health are detailed. This brings us into the 1990s and the emergence of the movement in social work toward evidence-based practice (Gambrill, 1999). This movement has been calling for increased practice evaluation and research efforts to build evidence supporting the effectiveness of social work practice. Fundamental tasks toward that end are the development and application of evidence-based assessment strategies.

Summary of Current Evidence-Based Assessment of Children

Since Mary Richmond reviewed case records and interviewed social workers more than 90 years ago, members of the social work profession have endeavored to identify, disseminate, and increase the widespread use of what we have evidence to believe works best for clients. Over those many decades, our methodological tools to measure (a) the struggles our clients face; (b) the functioning levels of children and families across social, emotional, and behavioral domains; and (c) the impact of our professional efforts to help have steadily advanced. Those advancements have increased the profession's ability to determine what works best for clients, and our expectations for the evidence in support of those determinations should, therefore, likewise progress. The pursuit of EBP is the latest effort toward that progression (Gambrill, 1999). However, efforts to move toward an evidence-based approach to the assessment of children are only just beginning; whereas there has been an increasing focus on evidence-based intervention approaches for use with children, less attention has been given to assessment (Mash & Hunsley, 2005). Although it does seem true that limited effort has gone into evaluating and synthesizing the assessment tools and strategies available for specific situations for children from an evidence-based perspective, there are many tools out there with supporting evidence that can be identified and applied. Next, a process to identify such tools and strategies is offered.

Defining what qualifies as *evidence* in support of child assessment tools and strategies evokes issues of epistemology, paradigmatic orientation, and research and practice methodologies, a comprehensive discussion of which is beyond the scope of this chapter. Social work has been historically epistemologically diverse, valuing different ways of knowing (Fraser, Taylor, Jackson, & O'Jack, 1991). Within that historical context, the paradigm of *pragmatism*, which supports the application of the research or practice methods that work best for a question or client, and a *mixed-methods* approach—combining quantitative and qualitative tools, which in the case of assessment means using both clinical interview techniques and empirically tested self-report instruments or structured interviews—provide the epistemological foundation for this chapter (Tashakkori & Teddlie, 2003).

Fitting within the definition of what can qualify as evidence, Gambrill (1999) has offered a hierarchy of possible evidence in support of interventions that can be adapted to assessment tools and strategies for use with children. Gambrill describes six levels; however, the last two are cases of the evidence indicating that an intervention would not be beneficial or even harmful. Therefore, the top four levels of evidence are adapted here:

1. Evidence level one, rigorously developed structured assessment instruments, which, attended to the developmental and cognitive characteristics of children, with resulting strong evidence of validity and reliability, demonstrated with multiple samples including in-practice settings substantially similar to the targeted population.

2. Evidence level two, well-developed assessment tools or strategies with some evidence of reliability and validity with at least one sample similar to the targeted population.

3. Evidence level three, child assessment tools or strategies with reliability and validity evidence from samples somewhat similar to the targeted population, or assessment tools with anecdotal or clinical evidence of utility with clients similar to the targeted population.

4. Evidence level four, tools or strategies that appear promising but for which no evidence exists about their utility with the targeted population.

However, locating the practice approach for any given situation with the best supporting evidence requires some effort. Applying EBP is more of a process or goal than a destination. A five-step process emerging from the medical field to locate the best evidence has been applied to child welfare practice (see Shlonsky & Wagner, 2005). Applying that five-step process to the various social work practice contexts in which assessment of children is needed can inform a systematic approach to deciding which assessment approaches would be best in a given setting with a specific population of children who are experiencing a certain range of struggles or challenges:

1. State the assessment needs in the situation of interest as a question that can be answered. For example, what is the best approach to assess depression in elementary-aged children in schools?

2. Search for the best evidence with which to answer that question. In the current example, that process might start with searching the literature for assessment tools and strategies that have been shown to be reliable and valid—see the following section for a discussion of the reliability and validity of assessment instruments—with latency-aged children, that are accessible to school social workers, and that would effectively and efficiently assess potentially large numbers of children.

3. Evaluate the tools and strategies found in light of the available evidence in support of their utility, in this case, comparing reliability and validity results and evaluating descriptions of their application in elementary school settings.

4. Relying on the clinical experience and judgment of the practitioners involved, integrate the results of the evaluation of the available tools and strategies with the specific characteristics and needs of the clients who will be assessed.

5. Appraise the performance of the previous four steps with the goal of making the next search for needed assessment tools and strategies more streamlined and effective.

With the state of our knowledge and evidence in support of our practices ever advancing, this process may need to be done with some regularity so current practices in an agency or utilized by a social worker do not fall significantly behind the current state of the evidence. That process points out that one of the advantages of EBP is the constant pursuit of providing the best services to clients, which is in sync with the ethical values of social work. Other advantages include encouragement of ongoing professional development and transparency of the effectiveness of social work services that maximize practitioners' providing clients with the opportunity to make informed consent about services (Gambrill & Shlonsky, 2001). Although such a process is needed to find the best currently available assessment tools for a specific situation, some general principles of an evidenced-based approach to the assessment of children can be gleaned from our accumulating knowledge. One is the use of multiple informants in the assessment of children.

Multiple Informants

As asserted earlier, the central goal in the assessment of a child is the formulation of an intervention plan. To effectively inform that intervention, an evidence-based assessment uses the best available tools and strategies to gather information about the child, the presenting struggle or challenge, and the critical microsystems that child inhabits, such as his or her family, school, and neighborhood. The accumulating evidence supports the conclusion that the most effective strategy is to collect that information from multiple informants who know and interact with that child (N. K. Bowen, Bowen, & Woolley, 2004; Pelham, Fabiano, & Massetti, 2005). Multiple informants (such as the child, parents/guardians, and teachers) typically do not agree on important aspects of the child's functioning, because those multiple informants will have different perspectives emerging from different settings, all of which may hold "truths" about the child (Bidaut-Russell, Valla, Thomas, Bergeron, & Lawson, 1998; Ivens & Rehm, 1988; March, Parker, Sullivan, Stallings, & Conners, 1997; Montgomery, 1994; Tinsley & Holtgrave, 1997; Wright-Strawdermann & Watson, 1992; Yugar & Shapiro, 2001). This is a very important point; no reporter providing assessment data about a child the child, parent, foster parent, sibling, teacher, police officer, probation officer, and so on—should be seen either as the gold standard or without merit. The type of data sought, the knowledge and experiences of the possible reporters pertaining to the child, the apparent veracity of those reporters, any complicating factors impacting the data provided by those reporters, and myriad other possible situational factors must be included in the evaluation and utilization of assessment data collected. Still, the most effective strategy is to gather assessment data about a child from multiple informants.

Child

Children have often been assessed by gathering information only from adults, such as parents/guardians and teachers. However, research has found that children often report higher rates or severity of social or emotional problems than adult informants—for example, depression—which is experienced internally and not easily observed (Breton, Bergeron, Valla, Berthiaume, & Gaudet, 1999; Wood, Kroll, Moore, & Harrington, 1995). Further, it has been found that children as young as 6 provide assessment data that can be more predictive of future functioning than adult-report assessment data (Ialongo, Edelsohn, & Kellam, 2001). These findings should lead clinicians and researchers to discontinue assessing children solely or even primarily by adult reports. Clearly, assessing a child should include gathering data directly from that child.

Parent/Guardian

There are many important aspects of the child's functioning for which the caregiving adults can provide vital information. It also seems self-evident that parents/guardians can provide important information about the family situation, information that is not appropriately gathered from the child, such as financial issues, parent/guardian health, mental health, substance abuse struggles, or marital conflicts negatively impacting parenting behaviors. Parents/guardians may also observe improvements, such as in behavior, mood, or other functioning, before the child does.

Other Family

Informed by the ecological-systems perspective, family therapists have long observed that other family members may provide valuable assessment information about a presenting challenge or struggle with a child (Haley, 1987). For example, a sibling may have a perspective on a child's problem or functioning that is not available to the child or parents/guardians. Similarly, cultures with strong extended families, such as extended family caregiving networks, may mean that grandparents, aunts, uncles, or even cousins may be vital participants in a child's life and provide important assessment data (Paniagua, 2005).

Teachers

How a child functions at school is an important question in any assessment of a child, because school performance is a vital developmental outcome for children (Woolley & Grogan-Kaylor, 2006). Teacher input is a valuable source of data about the child's school functioning, and that is why teachers are important reporters in several well-validated child assessment instruments for elementary school-aged children (e.g., N. K. Bowen et al., 2004; Essex et al., 2002).

Multiple Data Collection Strategies

Clinical Interviews

Assessment interviews are the traditional method of collecting assessment data in social work with children and their families. This is still a foundation strategy for assessing and intervening with children and likely always will be. A clinical interview is required as a starting point to determine what other assessment tools and strategies may be appropriate. Although the more structured assessment tools described next can collect reliable and valid data about children, the interpretation of those tools, their application to the presenting struggle or challenge, and the formulation of a plan for intervention are still tasks that can only be accomplished with the skills, experience, and judgment of a trained social worker. Additionally, once more structured assessment tools have been administered and scored, a social worker can use his or her clinical skills to gather more information from the child and family about what the scores may mean.

Structured Survey Instruments

Self-report instruments are completed by the child or other informant and mathematically represent the child's or informant's—parent/guardian, other family, teacher—perception about the extent or level of a struggle or challenge by assigning it a number. In the case of a child self-report instrument assessing depression for example, each question or item measures the presence and/or extent of a depression-related symptom. Therefore, a depression self-report measure relies on a child or other reporter to accurately answer questions about the child's behaviors, thoughts, beliefs, feelings, attitudes, and/or perceptions. Self-report assessment instruments typically consist of multiple questions or items with two or more response options. Most instruments include subgroups of items designed to measure different underlying symptoms impacting the child. Each such group of items constitutes a *scale*, and an assessment instrument may contain one or multiple scales (DeVellis, 2003). As discussed previously, the quality of such an instrument is a function of the evidence in support of its reliability and validity.

Reliability is the extent to which an assessment tool is consistent. When an instrument is consistent across time, it will result in similar depression scores at two different points in time with the same child (assuming the level of depression has not changed). That type of reliability is referred to as *test-retest* reliability. When an instrument is consistent across items in a scale, groups of items designed to measure the same underlying depression construct will show a pattern of similar answers within any given report. That type of reliability is known as *internal consistency reliability*, which is the most often reported form of instrument reliability and is usually estimated with Cronbach's formula for alpha (Cronbach, 1990).

Reliability coefficients range from 0.0 to 1.00. The closer to 1.00 the coefficient is, the more consistent the instrument is from administration to administration or among the items in the scale. A reliability coefficient can also be interpreted as revealing the percentage of an individual score that is attributable to the true score. In other words, if an instrument has an alpha of 0.80, 80% of the score is attributable to the child's level of depression, and 20% is attributable to something other than depression—in other words, sources of error. The reliabilities of child-report instruments are typically lower than for adult instruments. In general, reliabilities above 0.80 are considered good, with above 0.70 considered acceptable. However, given that an instrument with a reliability of 0.70 includes 30% error, then scores with such an instrument must be interpreted in that light. For example, if an intervention is anticipated to have a 30% effect on a struggle or challenge, and the assessment tool used to measure change in the client before and after that intervention has a 30% proportion of measurement error, then the assessment tool being used will be limited in its ability to consistently detect true change. Reliability is the most often reported characteristic of instrument quality, and although good reliability is a necessary characteristic of a quality instrument, it is not by itself sufficient to evaluate an instrument. For an instrument to be judged to have level one or two evidence as defined previously, evidence about its validity must also be available.

Validity is the extent to which an assessment tool measures what it is supposed to measure for a given individual at a given point in time. An instrument can be shown to be valid if it is shown to result in scores similar to a previously validated instrument or is predictive of outcomes or other variables with known relationships to the measured struggle or challenge. If an assessment tool is shown to result in similar scores to other tools that are known to be valid, it is said to have *criterion validity*. If an assessment tool is shown to be associated with related constructs in the predicted manner, the assessment tool is said to have *construct validity*. Assessing the validity of child-depression instruments can be difficult because there are often a limited number of quality instruments available for use with children for a given purpose. Developing reliable and valid assessment tools requires careful and rigorous research. When developing assessment tools for use with children, the combination of the developmental level and limited cognitive ability of children makes that process even more difficult.

In terms of the example of assessing depression in children, such an assessment tool would be the Mood and Feelings Questionnaire (MFQ), a 33-question self-report instrument designed for children ages 8 to 18. The child rates statements describing depressive symptoms within the past 2 weeks on a 3-point scale. In addition to the child form, there is also a parent form to collect multi-informant data. Studies have shown good reliability for both the child (alpha = 0.90 to 0.94) and parent (alpha = 0.90 to 0.92) forms of the MFQ (Angold et al., 1995; Wood et al., 1995). The correlation between the child and parent forms has been found to range from 0.51 to 0.65, which represents higher inter-reporter correlation than typically found (Kent, Vostanis, & Feehan, 1997; Wood et al., 1995). The child form has been shown to have significantly higher diagnostic validity (Wood et al., 1995). Efforts to merge child and parent data have failed, because no combination was more valid than the child data alone, which emphasizes the importance of gathering assessment information directly from children.

Structured Interview Instruments

Structured interview instruments consist of a set of scripted assessment questions that are asked of an informant by the social worker, with the responses to the questions indicated on the instrument form. The answers to the questions lead to a score, which will quantify specific struggles or symptoms that the child may be experiencing. Structured interview instruments are evaluated utilizing the same reliability and validity criteria used to evaluate the evidence in support of survey instruments. An example of such a tool is the Diagnostic Interview Schedule for Children (DISC), which is designed to assess for 30 different mental disorders in children. The DISC includes both a child and parent interview form and has been shown to have good reliability and validity in the assessment of mental disorders in children, from disruptive behavior disorders to anxiety and depressive disorders (Shaffer, Fisher, Lucas, Dulcan, & Schwab-Stone, 2000). However, few such structured interview instruments have been developed for social work practice settings, despite being a potentially reliable and valid strategy to collect assessment data while utilizing the interview skills of a social worker and interactions embedded within the social work relationship with a child and family.

Direct Observation

In many social work practice settings, such as schools, residential-treatment facilities, and inpatient psychiatric hospitals, social workers can directly observe children being assessed. Such observations can be made in various settings, structured and unstructured, and in interactions with various significant others, such as peers, teachers, parents/guardians, and other family. This allows the social worker to collect data about child functioning not filtered through the perceptual process of the child or other reporter. Such observation can be done in a systematic and structured manner utilizing observation protocols that can quantify the frequency and extent of targeted behaviors. For example, in the assessment of school behavioral struggles—referred to as a functional behavioral assessment—it is standard procedure for the social worker to observe the child in multiple circumstances at school, chosen in light of the behavioral struggles (Gresham, Watson, & Skinner, 2001). The data collected in those observations are vital to identifying the child and contextual factors that lead to and emerge from the behavior, informing strategies to create behavioral change.

Limitations of the Evidence

One limitation to the application of assessment tools with supporting evidence is the limited number of such tools for use with children. For example, in Corcoran and Fischer's (2000) widely used sourcebook of assessment tools for use in social work practice and research, there are 265 instruments listed for use with adults, whereas only 49 are listed for use with children. On closer examination of the instruments listed for children, 21 are for use exclusively with adolescents, 5 are completed by adults about youth, and 2 do not specify an age range or age information about the normative sample. This leaves only 21 child-report assessment tools presented as appropriate for use with children.

In terms of using the instruments that are available for use with children, significant limitations to the collection of reliable and valid assessment data can be seen as a function of three factors: first, children's cognitive ability is limited according to their age and developmental level to provide such assessment data, although they are still often the best, or only, source of assessment data about many childhood struggles and challenges; second, although adults can provide assessment data about many important targets of assessment, their reports are limited to their observations of the child and are filtered through their own perceptual processes, which are subject to distortion and bias; third, the quality of research methods applied to develop assessment tools to collect valid and reliable data directly from children varies. Next we discuss the limitations of children to provide assessment data followed by emerging and promising methods to develop better assessment tools for use with children.

Childhood can be separated into three phases: infancy, early childhood, and middle childhood (Ashford, LeCroy, & Lortie, 2001). Gathering assessment data about infants is limited to adult-report and observation of the infant. Children under the age of 6—early childhood—present cognitive limitations that severely constrain providing assessment information, and the reliability of such information can be difficult to determine. Therefore, for children in early childhood, assessment is largely limited to adult reports and observational data. However, as our methods improve and our understanding of child cognitive capacity continues to advance, we may yet develop tools to collect reliable and valid assessment data from children under 6.

In middle childhood (6–12 years), children develop their own culture, characterized by social rules, familiar games, interpersonal reciprocity, and attention to fairness (Ashford et al., 2001). This is a critical time in development when physical skills, social skills, and academic skills are acquired at a rapid rate. It is in this phase that children first have the cognitive ability to reliably and validly self-report perceptions, feelings, beliefs, and experiences. However, the cognitive ability of children in middle childhood is still much lower than adults, and careful attention to developmental issues is necessary in order to gather quality information (Chorpita, Albano, & Barlow, 1998; Garbarino, Stott, & Faculty of the

Erikson Institute, 1989). Still, recent research indicates that children have a mostly positive reaction to providing assessment data, such as filling out self-report assessment instruments, more positive than adolescents, and that girls are also more positive than boys (Saldana & DuBois, 2006).

However, the quality of evidence in support of assessment tools and strategies for use with children 6 to 12 is limited. The tools that are available typically have lower levels of reliability and validity evidence than seen for adult instruments. Childhood is a time of rapid growth, and children, as a function of their age and emerging cognitive ability, have limitations in their capacity to reliably and validly self-report perceptions, feelings, beliefs, experiences, and behaviors (N. K. Bowen et al., 2004; Chorpita et al., 1998; Woolley, Bowen, & Bowen, 2004).

Clearly, the cognitive demands of self-report instruments for children in middle childhood, including format and wording, are critical features in the development and selection of valid self-report instruments for children (N. K. Bowen et al., 2004). Instruments that meet these criteria are considered developmentally valid, which has been defined as the cognitive demands of an instrument—vocabulary, length and complexity of items, level of abstraction, nature of measured concepts—falling within the cognitive ability of children in the targeted age range (Woolley et al., 2004). These developmental issues impact the reliability and validity of child self-report instruments. However, the emerging use of *cognitive methods* to assess and advance the validity of assessment tools for use with children holds great promise to advance the validity of such instruments.

Emerging Trends in Child Assessment

Child struggles and challenges that are the attention of social work services can be measured with self-report assessment instruments. However, for the development of such instruments to lead to reliable and valid tools, that development process must follow consistent and rigorous methods. DeVellis (2003) has detailed a step-by-step procedure to construct reliable and valid assessment tools (Table 1.2).

Table 1.2 **Assessment Instrument Development Procedure**

Step	Task
1	Identify what struggle or challenge you want to assess.
2	Generate a pool of questions.
3	Determine the format for the assessment tool.
4	Seek review of question pool by experts in the specific area of practice.
5	Administer the assessment tool to a pilot sample.
6	Statistically evaluate questions and overall assessment-tool performance.
7	Optimize assessment-tool length.

Based on *Scale Development: Theory and Applications* (pp. 51–86), by R. F. DeVellis, 2003, Thousand Oaks, CA: Sage.

Such a procedure outlines the typical assessment-tool development process; however, such a procedure does not take into account the developmental level of children and the associated cognitive limitations of children to provide assessment data about themselves. *Cognitive methods* are a group of strategies used in the development of self-report questions used to assess the validity of assessment questions by collecting data directly from respondents about how they interpret and respond to such questions.

Cognitive methods emerged from a seminar held in 1983 that included cognitive psychologists and survey methodologists. The goal of that meeting was to develop a methodology to increase the validity of self-report questions through the application of theories of human cognition. Since that meeting, cognitive methods have been applied with adults (Jabine, Straf, Tanur, & Tourangeau, 1984; Jobe & Mingay, 1989), and only more recently with children (N. K. Bowen et al., 2004; Woolley et al., 2004). Cognitive interviewing is the cognitive method that is most applicable with children and involves interviewing a child while he or she reads and responds to an assessment question in order to collect data about four steps in the self-report process: (1) comprehension (reading and interpreting the item accurately), (2) retrieval (adopting the appropriate perspective for the item), (3) judgment (understanding the response continuum and the response options within the context of the item), and (4) response (providing an answer and demonstrating an ability to provide a rationale for the answer; DeMaio & Rothgeb, 1996; Jobe & Mingay, 1989; Tourangeau, Rips, & Rasinski, 2000). Table 1.3 details an example of an interview procedure to collect such data from children. Those data are used to evaluate the validity of the information gathered from children with respect to the intent of the self-report questions tested and to inform changes to the questions in order to increase the validity of child responses.

Once cognitive interview data have been collected about an assessment tool under development from children who are members of the

Table 1.3 Cognitive Interview Procedure

Step	Ask the Child
1	To read the assessment question out loud.
2	To describe what he or she thinks the question is trying to find out and/or what reading the question made the child think about.
3	To read the answer options out loud.
4	To pick the best answer option to the question for him or her.
5	To explain his or her answer.
6	If he or she can give an example of why he or she chose that answer.

Based on "Constructing and Validating Assessment Tools for School-Based Practitioners: The Elementary School Success Profile" (pp. 509–517), by N. K. Bowen, G. L. Bowen, and M. E. Woolley, in *Evidence-Based Practice Manual: Research and Outcome Measures in Health and Human Services*, A. R. Roberts and K. Y. Yeager (Eds.), 2004, New York: Oxford University Press; and "Cognitive Pretesting and the Developmental Validity of Child Self-Report Instruments: Theory and Applications," by M. E. Woolley, G. L. Bowen, and N. K. Bowen, 2004, *Research on Social Work Practice, 14*, pp. 191–200.

targeted population, that data can be analyzed to determine the validity of the interpretation of assessment-question meanings and chosen answers by that sample of children. That analysis is best guided by the construction of a validity codebook, which defines the acceptable ranges of question interpretations and rationale for chosen responses (Woolley, Bowen, & Bowen, 2006).

This approach has been used with promising results in the development of an assessment tool for use with children in school settings, the Elementary School Success Profile (N. K. Bowen et al., 2004; Woolley et al., 2006). N. K. Bowen and colleagues found that the methodology revealed significant validity problems in assessment questions for children that would not have otherwise been identified and that the methodology could be applied systematically and with reliable results (Woolley et al., 2006). This line of research suggests that the application of cognitive methods, specifically cognitive interviewing, in the development of assessment tools for use with children will result in more reliable and valid instruments and better evidence to support those qualities. More widespread application of this method will lead to better assessment tools available to social workers for practice purposes in the varied settings in which children are served.

Implications for Social Work on Micro-, Mezzo-, and Macrolevels

Child Protection

Few practice settings involve the level of potential consequences for the decisions made at the end of the assessment process than in child protection work. Although correct decisions can save children's lives, literally and metaphorically, wrong decisions can lead to death or long-term damage from traumatically removing children from their families when not necessary. Therefore, in the practice of child protection today, the primary goal is to assess *risk*. That risk comes from the behavior of the caretakers of that child, but, as in all areas of child assessment, assessment should include assessing the child, the caretakers, the social environment, and how those three interact. The risk being assessed can take on two forms: the child's being seriously mistreated in the immediate future or the cumulative negative impact on that child's developmental outcomes. However, much as in other areas of child assessment, there is tension between the two assessment strategies—clinical interview or structured instrument—in this context referred to as "actuarial and clinical" (Munro, 2002). Traditionally, assessment in child protection was clinical in nature and relied on the experience, judgment, and evolving practice wisdom of caseworkers. Over the past 20 years, that evolving practice wisdom has informed the development and empirical evaluation of risk-assessment actuarial instruments, which have consistently demonstrated higher predictive validity (Baird & Wagner, 2000). Table 1.4 lists factors often included in child-maltreatment risk-assessment instruments.

Table 1.4 Child-Protection Risk-Assessment Factors

Adult Factors

Number and severity of previous child-maltreatment events
Developmental history
  Instability
    Childhood—frequent moves, change in household members,
      parental absences
    Adolescence—substance abuse, mental illness, criminal behavior
    Inadequate parental nurturing or supervision
  Abuse history
    Victim of coercive, hostile, or neglectful parenting
    Was he or she a victim or witness of abuse as a child
    Nature, duration, frequency of that abuse
  Alcohol or drug abuse
    Currently using
    Failed attempts at treatment
  Mental-health or cognitive problems
    Mood disorder or personality disorder
    Insecure adult attachment style (ambivalent or avoidant)
    Low self-esteem
    Violent behavior toward others or suicide attempts
    Learning disability
    Low intellectual functioning
    Cognitive distortions in terms of the use of violence
    Noncompliance with treatment or medications
  Poor problem-solving skills
Age 20 or younger at birth of first child
    Gender—males at higher risk of reoccurrence
    Single parent
    Partner not biological parent of child
  Lack of social support
    Lack of knowledge about parenting or child development
    Lack of insight into or failure to anticipate child's needs
    Unrealistic expectations for child behavior
    Lack of or poor supervision of child
  Placing own needs above the needs of the child
  External locus of control
  Chronic illness
  Previous use and availability of weapons
  Previous service contacts

Family-Situation Factors

History of family violence
Attachment difficulties
  Lack of concern or warmth toward the child
  Negative attitude toward pregnancy
  Prolonged separation(s) of mother and child
Fewer than 18 months between births of children
High levels of family stress
Family feels isolated

(continued)

Table 1.4 *(Continued)*

Family-Situation Factors

Family targeted or exploited by local community
Family members emotionally supportive of each other
Is the house dirty, cluttered, or disorganized
Have other professional helpers felt intimidated or had needed services
 rejected
Any children under 18 not living at home
Previously found abuse or neglect
Economic struggles
　Unemployment
　Poor housing—unsafe, lack of privacy, residential instability
 Parental discipline
　Coercive parenting
　 Yelling, shouting, or criticizing
　 Hostile or threatening
　Random punishment
　Few positive strategies used to reinforce or change behavior

Child Factors

Unplanned child
History of attachment difficulties
Being younger (especially under age 5)
Adopted, foster child, or stepchild
Being premature, low birth weight, or currently underweight
Chronic illness, developmental delay, or birth defect
Difficult to comfort, cries frequently, or difficult temperament
Mental or physical disability
Gender
 Girls more likely to be sexually abused
 Boys more likely to be seriously physically abused
 Poor school attendance or frequent tardiness
Appearance
 Inappropriately dressed
 Looks tired, unkempt, or neglected
Child complaining about care or treatment at home

Note: This list of risk factors was adapted from Corby (2000); Fowler (2003); Munro (2002); and Righthand, Kerr, and Drach (2003).

The tension between clinical and actuarial risk assessment has spawned a debate in the literature that has been referred to as the "risk assessment wars" (Johnson, 2006). However, such an either/or debate about the relative merits of clinical versus actuarial assessment represents a false dichotomy leading to a pointless turf war—a false dichotomy because it implies the need to chose one or the other while ignoring the differential and complementary merits of each. It also ignores the fact that neither by itself has proven to be reliably effective in assessing risk for maltreatment so far, defined as both high rates of sensitivity and specificity (Munro, 2002). In fact, still-quite-limited research has examined the predictive validity of risk-assessment instruments for child protection, and some have shown marginal performance (Camasso & Jagannathan, 2000; Rittner, 2002). Such research has offered suggestions about how to improve the validity and utility of risk assessments, including making them shorter, easier to score and interpret, multilevel risk classification as opposed to binary in nature, better training of caseworkers in the science informing their development and use, and more input of clinical wisdom to their design (Baird & Wagner, 2000; Baumann, Law, Sheets, Grant, & Graham, 2005; Camasso & Jagannathan, 2000). Still, actuarial approaches have shown clear utility, and it is reasonable to anticipate that ongoing research will continue to advance their utility and predictive validity in the years to come. Alternatively, it seems illogical to remove the benefits of clinical information gathering and judgment informed by experience from the important work of protecting children while assessing and helping the huge diversity of families confronted by child-protection systems with respect and dignity.

In the general discussion of evidence-based assessment with children, the use of both multiple information sources and data-gathering strategies was advocated. Shlonsky and Wagner (2005) have called for just such an integrated approach in child-protection assessment. They assert that actuarial risk assessment has the best potential to predict future reoccurrence of child maltreatment, whereas clinical or contextual assessment of child and family functioning, as they call it, is the most effective way to identify treatment factors that need to be addressed and the services that would most benefit the family. The authors describe this *structured decision-making* process, which integrates actuarial risk assessment combined with clinical judgment. In this approach, an actuarial risk assessment determines the initial response, and clinical assessment of the child and family determines the case planning and services provided. That clinical assessment includes gathering information about family struggles as well as strengths in such areas as family relationships, social support, health, mental health, substance abuse, and housing. Other sections of this chapter and volume can be consulted for guidelines to assess these areas of child and family functioning and needs.

Forty states have adopted the use of structured risk-assessment instruments at various points in the child-protection service process, which may include many points from deciding to open a case, removing a child from the home, returning a child, or closing a case (Camasso & Jagannathan, 2000). Still, the process to gather the information and fill out the risk-assessment instrument, as well as to assess the current situation and functioning of the child and family, relies on the clinical skills, judgment, and experience of caseworkers. The future of assessment in child protection hopefully will bring the development of more predictive and utilitarian risk-assessment instruments and integration of those instruments with clinical skills and judgment, informing a more evidence-based approach to the vital work of child protection.

Schools

Schools are one of the few settings in which social workers can practice on micro-, mezzo-, and macrolevels. For example, a child who is being teased and bullied can be addressed on a microlevel to increase that child's ability to cope and respond when bullied, on a mezzolevel to reduce bullying in a classroom, or on a macrolevel to implement a program to change the social climate of a school system to reduce teasing and bullying throughout the district (Woolley, 2006). Because schools serve all children, including those in need of services from child protection, mental health, and health-care providers, school social workers provide assessment, referral, and intervention services literally to the whole population of children in a given area. Therefore, the assessment tools and strategies needed by school social workers bridge the needs of social workers from many other settings that serve children, and the trends discussed in other sections of this chapter may also be informative to school practice.

However, school social workers also have the unique task of completing an ecologically oriented systematic and comprehensive assessment of a child or groups of children, the findings of which can inform prevention or intervention planning to reduce the impact of specific struggles or challenges that negatively impact school success. To that end, there are assessment tools that have been rigorously developed and have level one or two evidence to support their use with children in schools. One such tool is the School Success Profile (SSP; G. L. Bowen, Woolley, Richman, & Bowen, 2001) for use with middle and high school students, and another is the Elementary School Success Profile (ESSP; N. K. Bowen et al., 2004) for use with children in third through fifth grades.

The SSP is an ecologically oriented self-report assessment instrument for use in school-based practice that includes 220 questions. Those questions gather assessment information about the risk and protective factors in a child's life across five domains affecting school outcomes, including school, family, peers, neighborhood, and health and well-being. The SSP has gone through multiple revisions over more than 10 years of research and practice use, and its reliability and validity have been demonstrated (G. L. Bowen, Rose, & Bowen, 2005). The SSP can be used to inform micro-, mezzo-, or macrolevel practice, because scoring the instrument can result in both individual student and group (classroom, grade, school) results that can then be used to inform prevention and intervention planning for students at risk of school failure.

Emerging from the development and use of the SSP, the ESSP includes three forms—child, parent/guardian, and teacher—and so fits within the use of multiple informants of information about children suggested earlier. Cognitive interviewing methods were applied in the rigorous development of the ESSP, and the child form is computerized and animated to appeal to younger children and hold their attention. For more information about the SSP or ESSP, please go to www.schoolsuccessprofile.org

Mental Health

The area of mental-health practice with children has the benefit of the most attention in terms of developing assessment tools. Partly as a benefit of the medical model, which is built on arriving at a diagnosis for the purpose of insurance and publicly funded health care, there are assessment instruments for many childhood mental-health problems. Such instruments have varied levels of evidence about their reliability and validity and include assessment tools to measure childhood depression (Angold et al., 1995), anxiety (Silverman & Ollenbeck, 2005), behavior problems (Macgowan, Nash, & Fraser, 2002), thought disorders (Kaufman et al., 1997), attention problems (Pelham et al., 2005), suicide risk (Reynolds & Mazza, 1999), trauma (Balaban, 2006), and multiple mental-health struggles (Shaffer et al., 2000). Social workers practicing in mental-health settings with children should have success in finding assessment tools with level one or two evidence for most mental-health issues with children by following the procedures outlined previously. However, professionals from other disciplines, such as psychology or psychiatry, have developed many of those instruments, with few being developed from the unique perspective of social work practice. That is also the case, although less so, in other areas of social work practice. In order for social work to develop its own assessment tools and strategies informed by a social work perspective that have supporting evidence, more social work researchers and practitioners need to engage in the work of developing assessment tools.

An example of a social work–constructed assessment tool is the Carolina Child Checklist, developed by Fraser et al. (2005) as part of an overall intervention research project to prevent aggression and behavior problems in children aged 8 to 12. This teacher-report instrument was developed utilizing rigorous methods, has demonstrated reliability and validity, identifies both male and female forms of aggression in children, and was developed not just as an assessment tool but also as a research tool to be sensitive enough to provide evidence about the effectiveness of a manualized preventive intervention for use with third-grade children and their families (Macgowan et al., 2002). Fraser and colleagues' work, from the construction of assessment tools to intervention development, implementation, and evaluation, presents a meritorious model for the pursuit of evidence-based practice in social work.

Child Struggles That Cross Settings

Research in social work across these various settings in which children are served has made it increasingly clear that assessment processes in one setting overlap with and should include the assessment of needs and struggles traditionally seen as the practice domain of other child-serving settings.

For example, Shannon and Tappan (2011) examine the practices of social workers in child protective services (CPS) with regard to the prevalence and implications of children served by CPS who have developmental disabilities. Their findings support a call for widespread systematic assessment of developmental disabilities among children served by CPS and the training of CPS workers in such assessment. Not only do a large percentage of children served by CPS have such disabilities, but such disabilities impact the capacity of such children to verbally report on their potential experiences of abuse or neglect. Further, CPS workers need training in understanding such disabilities and the treatment and service needs of such children, with the goal being CPS workers who no longer see a developmental disability as simply one more risk factor but as a parallel and interrelated issue needing specialized interventions and services.

Similarly, increasingly schools are seen as an ideal setting to provide mental-health services for children and screen children for mental-health struggles or needs. For example, Woolley and Curtis (2007), after discussing the natural fit of providing mental-health services in schools and the increasing frequency at which schools are becoming the site of mental-health delivery for children, then provide information for social workers on how to identify valid and reliable assessment tools, in particular for the assessment of depression in elementary-aged children. Similarly, Caselman and Self (2008) detail the importance in social work practice of early identification and intervention with young children with emerging educational or mental-health struggles. To that end, they review nine available adult—teacher and parent—report instruments to assess social, emotional, and behavioral development and struggles in children. They, too, point out how school social workers are uniquely positioned to complete such vital assessments.

Conclusion

To paraphrase Shakespeare, for something to go well, it must start well. Assessment is the starting point of all social work practice activities. Social workers provide services in a multitude of settings to children and their families who are facing a broad range of struggles and challenges. To serve children in the most ethical and effective manner, social workers must identify and apply the best assessment tools and strategies available. That goal is best accomplished by identifying the assessment tools and strategies with the best available evidence supporting their use and quality. This chapter reviews the history of the social work orientation to the assessment of children over the past 100 years. The wisdom accumulated over that century informs the current approach to such assessment offered here, including the format for organizing that assessment information into a biopsychosocial assessment report and the best available current tools and strategies to collect that information.

The approach to child assessment offered in this chapter includes an ecological-systems framework, which means (a) collecting data from the child, parents/guardians, and others, such as teachers; (b) using multiple data collection tools, such as clinical interviews, self-report instruments, and structured-interview instruments; and (c) direct observations of the child. The significant limitations—in number and quality—of the currently available assessment tools for use with children is described, and a process to identify what is available and how good the evidence for specific practice applications is offered. Emerging assessment-tool development methods are reviewed that promise to lead to more reliable and valid child-assessment tools in the future. Finally, social work practice setting-specific assessment issues in the arenas of child protection, school, and mental-health practice are reviewed.

In closing, social work has much work to do to develop more reliable and valid tools and strategies to assess children across all practice settings. If we are to move toward more EBP, then the need for assessment tools that start those services well and can effectively be used to measure the efficacy of prevention and intervention activities must be a primary focus of ongoing research and practice efforts.

Key Terms

Children	Biopsychosocial	Evidenced-based
Assessment	Ecological perspective	

Review Questions for Critical Thinking

1. What assessment information should be collected in social work practice in any assessment of a child and family across a wide range of social work service settings and child-presenting struggles?

2. Within the varying practice settings of school, mental health, child welfare, health, and juvenile justice, what are the advantages of taking a multi-informant and multiple data-collection methods approach?

3. Given that an ecologically informed comprehensive assessment of a child, family, and presenting struggle(s) should include clinical interviews, structured interviews, self-report instruments, direct obser-vations, and reviews of existing records, in what order would you complete those varying data-collection methods? What are the advan-tages or disadvantages, for example, of reading the prior records first or last? Would the setting or presenting struggle impact your decision on that order, and how would that be a factor?

4. Discuss social work values and practice ethics as they relate to the assessment of strengths and environmental resources and the use of genograms and eco-maps in direct practice with children and their families.

5. What are the importance and implications of the reliability and validity of self-report assessment instruments for use in both practice and research activities?

Online Resources

http://csmh.umaryland.edu/ *The Center for School Mental Health* at the University of Maryland. This site has information for school practitioners, school leaders, and families. Note that on the right under the "Practice" link, click "Tools for Clinicians," and you will find a link to a list of mental-health assessment tools and instruments for use in schools that are all free of charge.

http://www.cebc4cw.org/ *The California Evidenced-Based Clearing-house for Child Welfare* is funded by the California Department of Social Services. Note that in the links down the left side is "Assessment Tools," which brings you to a lengthy list of both child and family assessment instruments and tools, for which the quality of the validity and reliability of each instrument are listed along with how to access the instruments.

http://www.childwelfare.gov/famcentered/casework/assessment.cfm This is the *Family-Centered Assessment* page of the *Child Welfare Information Gateway* sponsored by the U.S. Department of Health and Human Services. Multiple assessment tools are listed and described for use with children and their families in child-welfare settings. See this page as an introduction to the organized and synthesized information available from the U.S. government on social work practice in general and assessment of children in particular. Try http://www.childwelfare .gov/systemwide/assessment/family_assess/childneeds/mental.cfm for information on assessment of child mental-health issues. Spend some time looking around this site and its links and see what useful assessment tools you may find for your practice.

http://www.modelsforchange.net/publications/328 This is a link to a report from the site *Models for Change: Systems Reform in Juvenile Justice* funded by the MacArthur Foundation. This report details assessments used in evidence-based juvenile justice practice, from assessing mental-health struggles of adjudicated children to assessing risk for reoffending. Also note, go to the "Home" of this site and plug "assessment" into the search function, and you will find many other links to assessment informations, tools, and strategies in juvenile justice practice.

http://smhp.psych.ucla.edu/pdfdocs/assessment/assessment.pdf This is a link to a report on assessment indicators and tools for mental-health practice in schools from the **Mental Health in Schools Center** at the University of California Los Angeles. Look at the whole website—home is http://smhp.psych.ucla.edu/—for a wide range of information about mental-health practice with children, and practice in school settings in particular.

References

American Psychiatric Association. (2000). *Diagnostic and statistical manual of mental disorders* (4th ed., text rev.). Washington, DC: Author.

Angold, A., Costello, E. J., Messer, S. C., Pickles, A., Winder, F., & Silver, D. (1995). Development of a short questionnaire for use in epidemiological studies of depression in children and adolescents. *International Journal of Methods in Psychiatric Research, 5*, 237–249.

Appleby, G. A., Colon, E., & Hamilton, J. (2007). *Diversity, oppression, and social functioning: Person-in-environment assessment and intervention* (2nd ed.). Boston, MA: Allyn & Bacon.

Ashford, J. B., LeCroy, C. W., & Lortie, K. L. (2001). *Human behavior in the social environment: A multidimensional perspective*. Belmont, CA: Wadsworth.

Baird, C., & Wagner, D. (2000). The relative validity of actuarial- and consensus-based risk assessment systems. *Children and Youth Services Review, 22*, 839–871.

Balaban, V. (2006). Psychological assessment of children in disasters and emergencies. *Disasters, 30*, 178–198.

Baumann, D. J., Law, J. R., Sheets, J., Grant, R., & Graham, C. (2005). Evaluating the effectiveness of actuarial risk assessment models. *Children and Youth Services Review, 27*, 465–490.

Bidaut-Russell, M., Valla, J.-P., Thomas, J. M., Bergeron, L., & Lawson, E. (1998). Reliability for the terry: A mental health cartoon-like screener for African American children. *Child Psychiatry and Human Development, 28*, 249–263.

Bowen, G. L., Rose, R. A., & Bowen, N. K. (2005). *The reliability and validity of the school success profile*. Philadelphia, PA: Xlibris Press.

Bowen, G. L., Woolley, M. E., Richman, J. M., & Bowen, N. K. (2001). Brief intervention in schools: The school success profile. *Brief Treatment and Crisis Intervention, 1*, 43–54.

Bowen, M. (1978). *Family therapy in clinical practice*. New York, NY: Aronson.

Bowen, N. K., Bowen, G. L., & Woolley, M. E. (2004). Constructing and validating assessment tools for school-based practitioners: The elementary school success profile. In A. R. Roberts & K. Y. Yeager (Eds.), *Evidence-based practice manual: Research and outcome measures in health and human services* (pp. 509–517). New York, NY: Oxford University Press.

Breton, J.-J., Bergeron, L., Valla, J.-P., Berthiaume, C., & Gaudet, N. (1999). Quebec Child Mental Health Survey: Prevalence of DSM-III-R mental health disorders. *Journal of Child Psychology and Psychiatry and Allied Disciplines, 40*, 375–384.

Bronfenbrenner, U. (Ed.). (2005). *Making human beings human: Bioecological perspectives on human development*. Thousand Oaks, CA: Sage.

Camasso, M. J., & Jagannathan, R. (2000). Modeling the reliability and predictive validity of risk assessment in child protection services. *Children and Youth Services Review, 22*, 873–896.

Carter, B., & McGoldrick, M. (1980). *The family life cycle.* New York, NY: Gardner Press.

Caselman, T. D., & Self, P. A. (2008). Assessment instruments for measuring young children's social-emotional behavioral development. *Children & Schools, 30*, 103–115.

Chorpita, B. F., Albano, A. M., & Barlow, D. H. (1998). The structure of negative emotions in a clinical sample of children and adolescents. *Journal of Abnormal Psychology, 107*, 74–85.

Clifford, D. (1998). *Social assessment theory and practice: A multidisciplinary framework.* Brookfield, VT: Ashgate.

Colon, E., Appleby, G. A., & Hamilton, J. (2007). Affirmative practice with people who are culturally diverse and oppressed. In G. A. Appleby, E. Colon, & J. Hamilton (Eds.), *Diversity, oppression, and social functioning: Person-in environment assessment and intervention* (pp. 294–311). Boston, MA: Allyn & Bacon.

Cooper, M. G., & Lesser, J. G. (2002). *Clinical social work practice.* Boston, MA: Allyn & Bacon.

Corby, B. (2000). *Child abuse: Towards a knowledge base* (2nd ed.). Philadelphia, PA: Open University Press.

Corcoran, K. J., & Fischer, J. (2000). *Measures for clinical practice: A sourcebook.* New York, NY: Free Press.

Cox, K. F. (2006). Investigating the impact of strength-based assessment on youth with emotional or behavioral disorders. *Journal of Child and Family Studies, 15*, 287–301.

Cronbach, L. J. (1990). *Essentials of psychological testing* (5th ed.). New York, NY: HarperCollins.

DeMaio, T. J., & Rothgeb, J. M. (1996). Cognitive interviewing techniques: In the lab and in the field. In N. Schwartz & S. Sudman (Eds.), *Answering questions: Methodology for cognitive and communicative processes in survey research* (pp. 177–196). San Francisco, CA: Jossey-Bass.

DeVellis, R. F. (2003). *Scale development: Theory and applications.* Thousand Oaks, CA: Sage.

Essex, M. J., Boyce, W. T., Goldstein, L. H., Armstrong, J. M., Kraemer, H. C., & Kupfer, D. J. (2002). The confluence of mental, physical, social, and academic difficulties in middle childhood: Developing the MacArthur Health and Behavior Questionnaire. *Journal of the Academy of Child and Adolescent Psychiatry, 41*, 588–603.

Finn, J. L., & Jacobsen, M. (2003). *Just practice.* Peosta, IA: Eddie Bowers.

Fowler, J. (2003). *A practitioners' tool for child protection and the assessment of parents.* Philadelphia, PA: Jessica Kingsley.

Fraser, M. W., Galinsky, M. J., Smokowski, P. R., Day, S. H., Terzian, M. A., Rose, R. A., & Guo, S. (2005). Social information-processing skills training to promote social competence and prevent aggressive behavior in third grade. *Journal of Consulting and Clinical Psychology, 73*, 1045–1055.

Fraser, M. W., Richman, J. M., & Galinsky, M. J. (1999). Risk, protection, and resilience: Toward a conceptual framework for social work practice. *Social Work Research, 23*(3), 131–143.

Fraser, M. W., Taylor, M. J., Jackson, R., & O'Jack, J. (1991). Social work and science: Many ways of knowing. *Social Work Research and Abstracts, 27*(4), 5–15.

Gambrill, E. (1999). Evidence-based practice: An alternative to authority based practice. *Families in Society: Journal of Contemporary Human Services, 80,* 341–350.

Gambrill, E., & Shlonsky, A. (2001). The need for comprehensive risk management systems in child welfare. *Children and Youth Services Review, 23,* 79–107.

Garbarino, J., Stott, F. M., & Faculty of the Erikson Institute. (1989). *What children can tell us: Eliciting, interpreting, and evaluating information from children.* San Francisco, CA: Jossey-Bass.

Germain, C. B., & Gitterman, A. (1980). *The life model of social work practice.* New York, NY: Columbia University Press.

Gilgun, J. F. (2004). The 4-d: Assessment instruments for youth, their families, and communities. *Journal of Human Behavior in the Social Environment, 10,* 51–73.

Gleason, E. T. (2007). A strengths-based approach to the social developmental study. *Children & Schools, 29,* 51–59.

Greif, G. L., & Lynch, A. A. (1983). The eco-systems perspective. In C. H. Meyer (Ed.), *Clinical social work in the eco-systems perspective* (pp. 35–71). New York, NY: Columbia University Press.

Gresham, F. M., Watson, T. S., & Skinner, C. H. (2001). Functional behavioral assessment: Principles, procedures, and future directions. *School Psychology Review, 30,* 156–172.

Gutierrez, L., & Lewis, E. (1999). Working with women of color: An empowerment perspective. *Social Work, 35,* 149–153.

Haley, J. (1987). *Problem-solving therapy* (2nd ed.). San Francisco, CA: Jossey-Bass.

Hamilton, G. (1951). *Theory and practice of social casework.* NY: Columbia University Press.

Hart, S. L. (1990). Working with the juvenile delinquent. In M. L. M. Bryan & A. F. Davis (Eds.), *100 years at Hull House* (pp. 145–150). Bloomington: Indiana University Press.

Hartman, A. (1995). Diagrammatic assessment of family relationships. *Families in Society, 76*(2), 111–122.

Hepworth, D. H., Rooney, R. H., & Larsen, J. A. (2002). *Direct social work practice: Theory and skills* (6th ed.). Pacific Grove, CA: Brooks/Cole.

Hollis, F. (1964). *Casework: A psychosocial therapy.* New York, NY: Random House.

Hudson, W. W. (1997). Assessment tools as outcome measures in social work. In E. J. Mullen & J. Magnabosco (Eds.), *Outcome measures in the human services: Cross-cutting issues and methods* (pp. 68–80). Washington, DC: National Association of Social Workers Press.

Ialongo, N. S., Edelsohn, G., & Kellam, S. G. (2001). A further look at the prognostic power of young children's reports of depressed mood and feelings. *Child Development, 72,* 736–747.

Ivens, C., & Rehm, L. P. (1988). Assessment of childhood depression: Correspondence between reports by child, mother, and father. *Journal of American Academy of Child and Adolescent Psychiatry, 27,* 738–741.

Jabine, T. B., Straf, M. L., Tanur, J. M., & Tourangeau, R. (1984). *Cognitive aspects of survey methodology: Building a bridge between disciplines.* Washington, DC: National Academy Press.

Jobe, J. B., & Mingay, D. J. (1989). Cognitive research improves questionnaires. *American Journal of Public Health, 79,* 1053–1055.

Johnson, W. (2006). The risk assessment wars: A commentary response to "evaluating the effectiveness of actuarial risk assessment models." *Children and Youth Services Review, 28,* 704–714.

Karls, J. M., & Wandrei, K. E. (1992). Pie: A new language for social work. *Social Work, 37,* 80–85.

Kaufman, J., Birmaher, B., Brent, D., Rao, U., Flynn, C., Moreci, P.,...Ryan, N. (1997). Schedule for affective disorders and schizophrenia for school-age children-present and lifetime (K-SADS-PL): Initial reliability and validity. *Journal of the American Academy of Child and Adolescent Psychiatry, 36,* 980–988.

Kemp, S. P., Whittaker, J. K., & Tracy, E. M. (1997). *Person-environment practice: The social ecology of interpersonal helping.* New York, NY: Aldine de Gruyter.

Kent, L., Vostanis, P., & Feehan, C. (1997). Detection of major and minor depression in children and adolescents: Evaluation of the Mood and Feelings Questionnaire. *Journal of Child Psychology and Psychiatry, 38,* 565–573.

Loewenberger, F., & Dolgoff, R. (1985). *Ethical decisions for social work practice.* Itasca, IL: Peacock.

Lukas, S. R. (1993). *Where to start and what to ask: An assessment handbook.* New York, NY: Norton.

Luthar, S. S., Cicchetti, D., & Becker, B. (2000). The construct of resilience: A critical evaluation and guidelines for future work. *Child Development, 71,* 543–562.

Macgowan, M. J., Nash, J. K., & Fraser, M. W. (2002). The Carolina Child Checklist of risk and protective factors for aggression. *Research on Social Work Practice, 12,* 253–276.

March, J. S., Parker, J. D. A., Sullivan, K., Stallings, P., & Conners, C. K. (1997). The Multidimensional Anxiety Scale for Children (MASC): Factor structure, reliability, and validity. *Journal of the Academy of Child and Adolescent Psychiatry, 36,* 554–565.

Mash, E. J., & Hunsley, J. (2005). Evidence-based assessment of child and adolescent disorders: Issues and challenges. *Journal of Clinical Child and Adolescent Psychology, 34,* 362–379.

McGoldrick, M., Gerson, R., & Shellenberger, S. (1999). *Genograms: Assessment and intervention.* New York, NY: Norton.

McQuaide, S., & Ehrenreich, J. H. (1997). Assessing client strengths. *Families in Society, 78,* 201–212.

Montgomery, M. S. (1994). Self-concept and children with learning disabilities: Observer-child concordance across six context-dependent domains. *Journal of Learning Disabilities, 27,* 254–262.

Munro, E. (2002). *Effective child protection.* Thousand Oaks, CA: Sage.

Ogbu, J. U. (1991). Low school performance as an adaptation: The case of Blacks in Stockton, California. In M. A. Gibson & J. U. Ogbu (Eds.), *Minority status and schooling: A comparative study of immigrant and involuntary minorities* (pp. 249–285). New York, NY: Garland Press.

Ogbu, J. U. (1998). Voluntary and involuntary minorities: A cultural-ecological theory of school performance with some implications for education. *Anthropology and Education Quarterly, 29,* 155–188.

Orfield, G., Losen, D., Wald, J., & Swanson, C. B. (2004). *Losing our future: How minority youth are being left behind by the graduation rate crisis.* Cambridge, MA: Civil Rights Project at Harvard University and the Urban Institute. Accessed at www.urban.org/url.cfm?ID=410936/

Oyserman, D., Bybee, D., & Terry, K. (2006). Possible selves and academic outcomes: How and when possible selves impel action. *Journal of Personality and Social Psychology, 91*, 188–204.

Oyserman, D., Terry, K., & Bybee, D. (2002). A possible selves intervention to enhance school involvement. *Journal of Adolescence, 25*, 313–326.

Paniagua, F. A. (2005). *Assessing and treating culturally diverse clients: A practical guide*. Thousand Oaks, CA: Sage.

Pelham, W. E., Fabiano, G. A., & Massetti, G. M. (2005). Evidence-based assessment of attention deficit hyperactivity disorder in children and adolescents. *Journal of Clinical Child and Adolescent Psychology, 34*, 449–476.

Perlman, H. H. (1957). *Social casework: A problem solving approach*. Chicago: University of Chicago Press.

Pilsecker, C. (1994). Starting where the client is. *Families in Society, 75*, 447–452.

Pincus, A., & Minahan, A. (1973). *Social work practice: Model and method*. Itasca, IL: Peacock.

Reynolds, W., & Mazza, J. (1999). Assessment of suicidal ideation in inner-city children and young adolescents: Reliability and validity of the Suicidal Ideation Questionnaire—JR. *School Psychology Review, 28*, 17–30.

Richman, J. M., Bowen, G. L., & Woolley, M. E. (2004). School failure: An eco-interactional developmental perspective. In M. W. Fraser (Ed.), *Risk and resilience in childhood: An ecological perspective* (2nd ed., pp. 133–160). Washington, DC: National Association of Social Workers Press.

Richmond, M. E. (1917). *Social diagnosis*. New York, NY: Sage.

Righthand, S., Kerr, B., & Drach, K. (2003). *Child maltreatment risk assessments*. Binghamton, NY: Haworth Press.

Rittner, B. (2002). The use of risk assessment instruments in child protection services case planning and closures. *Children and Youth Services Review, 24*, 189–207.

Saldana, L., & DuBois, D. L. (2006). Youth reactions to participation in psychological assessment procedures. *Journal of Clinical Child and Adolescent Psychology, 35*, 155–161.

Saleebey, D. (2006). *The stengths perspective in social work practice* (4th ed.). Boston, MA: Allyn & Bacon.

Shaffer, D., Fisher, P., Lucas, C. P., Dulcan, M. K., & Schwab-Stone, M. E. (2000). NIMH Diagnostic Interview Schedule for Children Version IV (NIMH DISC-IV): Description, differences from previous versions, and reliability of some common diagnoses. *Journal of the American Academy of Child and Adolescent Psychiatry, 39*, 28–38.

Shlonsky, A., & Wagner, D. (2005). The next step: Integrating actuarial risk assessment and clinical judgment into an evidence-based practice framework in CPS case management. *Children and Youth Services Review, 27*, 409–427.

Shannon, P., & Tappan, C. (2011). Identification and assessment of children with developmental disabilities in child welfare. *Social Work, 56*, 297–305.

Silverman, W. K., & Ollenbeck, T. H. (2005). Evidence-based assessment of anxiety and its disorders in children and adolescents. *Journal of Child and Adolescent Psychology, 34*, 380–411.

Simon, B. L. (1994). *The empowerment tradition in American social work: A history*. New York, NY: Columbia University Press.

Tashakkori, A., & Teddlie, C. (2003). Major issues and controversies in the use of mixed methods in the social and behavioral sciences. In A. Tashakkori &

C. Teddlie (Eds.), *Handbook of mixed methods in the social and behavioral sciences* (pp. 3–50). Thousand Oaks, CA: Sage.

Tinsley, B. J., & Holtgrave, D. R. (1997). A multimethod analysis of risk perceptions and health behaviors in children. *Educational and Psychological Measurement, 57,* 197–209.

Tourangeau, R., Rips, L. J., & Rasinski, K. (2000). *The psychology of survey response.* Cambridge, UK: Cambridge University Press.

Wood, A., Kroll, L., Moore, A., & Harrington, R. (1995). Proper ties of the Mood and Feelings Questionnaire in adolescent psychiatric outpatients: A research note. *Journal of Child Psychology and Psychiatry, 36,* 327–334.

Woolley, M. E. (2006). Advancing a positive school climate for students, families, and staff. In C. Franklin, M. B. Harris, & P. Allen-Meares (Eds.), *The school services sourcebook* (pp. 777–784). New York, NY: Oxford University Press.

Woolley, M. E., & Bowen, G. L. (2007). In the context of risk: Supportive adults and the school engagement of middle school students. *Family Relations, 56,* 92–104.

Woolley, M. E., Bowen, G. L., & Bowen, N. K. (2004). Cognitive pretesting and the developmental validity of child self-report instruments: Theory and applications. *Research on Social Work Practice, 14,* 191–200.

Woolley, M. E., Bowen, G. L., & Bowen, N. K. (2006). The development and evaluation of procedures to assess child self-report item validity. *Educational and Psychological Measurement, 66,* 687–700.

Woolley, M. E., & Curtis, H. W. (2007). Assessing depression in latency age children: A guide for school social workers. *Children & Schools, 29,* 209–218.

Woolley, M. E., & Grogan-Kaylor, A. (2006). Protective family factors in the context of neighborhood: Promoting positive school outcomes. *Family Relations, 55,* 95–106.

Wright-Strawdermann, C., & Watson, B. L. (1992). The prevalence of depressive symptoms in children with disabilities. *Journal of Learning Disabilities, 25,* 258–264.

Yugar, J. M., & Shapiro, E. S. (2001). Elementary children's school friendship: A comparison of peer assessment methodologies. *School Psychology Review, 30,* 568–587.

Chapter 2
Intervention With Children

Mary C. Ruffolo and Paula Allen-Meares

> **Purpose:** This chapter identifies key evidence-informed practices that are emerging for children with emotional and behavioral problems and their families across child-serving systems.
>
> **Rationale:** To educate readers about interventions that will help children who are at risk for emotional and behavioral problems in order to confront adversity and promote resiliency. This is a critical task facing social workers across the child-serving systems.
>
> **How evidence-informed practice is presented:** This chapter focuses on evidence-based practice (EBP) under two main categories: (1) evidence-informed individual child and family interventions and (2) schoolwide/community interventions.
>
> **Overarching questions:** How can students and practitioners identify interventions that work for children and families and critically analyze and evaluate these interventions? What common elements across these EBPs promote positive outcomes for a range of children and families experiencing emotional or behavioral challenges?

The purpose of this chapter is to identify key evidence-based practices (EBPs) that are emerging for children with emotional and behavioral problems and their families across child-serving systems. The chapter explores the challenges in developing and implementing EBPs. The EBPs reviewed are organized under two main categories: (1) evidence-based individual child and family interventions and (2) schoolwide/community interventions. For each intervention reviewed, the key components of the intervention are presented as well as the status of the empirical evidence to support this intervention with targeted child populations. Two key questions that emerge for practitioners and students are:

1. How to best capture the interventions that work for children and families and to critically analyze and evaluate these interventions?

2. What common elements across these EBPs can promote positive outcomes for a range of children and families experiencing emotional or behavioral challenges?

Intervening in the lives of children and their families is a challenging and dynamic process. Selecting evidence-based interventions that will help children who are at risk for emotional and behavioral problems to confront adversity and promote resiliency is a critical task facing social workers across the child-serving systems. Protecting children from harm and poor developmental outcomes involves targeting not only the child's behavior but also the family, school, and neighborhood environments that often contribute to challenges that the child faces. Interventions that evolve into EBPs can facilitate the process of promoting positive outcomes for children in need of treatment in real-world settings. Although children who are at risk for emotional or behavioral problems often experience impaired functioning at home, in school, or in their neighborhoods, EBP provides hope that these youth will experience better outcomes in many of these functioning areas.

Recent reports from the New Freedom Commission on Mental Health (2003), the U.S. Surgeon General (1999, 2001), and the National Research Council and Institute of Medicine (2009) highlight the need to improve mental-health services for children and their families by developing and using more evidence-based interventions and addressing prevention and early intervention for mental, emotional, and behavioral disorders among youth. Several federal and national organizations have developed lists of evidence-based or empirically supported interventions for work with children and their families in order to promote the use of those that have demonstrated success. For example, the Substance Abuse and Mental Health Services Administration (SAMHSA) compiled an expert consensus review of published and unpublished evaluations and a web-based listing of science-based prevention programs that may be replicated. It grouped these programs as models, effective, and promising practices (www.nrepp.samhsa.gov).

This chapter examines the development of EBPs with children at risk of emotional and behavioral problems, summarizes EBPs that are currently being used across child-serving systems, explores the limitations of implementing EBP interventions, and discusses the implications for social work intervention practice with children who are at risk for emotional and behavioral problems and who face adversity.

Development of EBPs for Children at Risk for Emotional or Behavioral Problems

The current child-serving systems have evolved from primarily institutional-based systems to community-based systems of care for children and their families. Although more children are served in community-based programs, the majority of expenditures on services for children are for institutional-based services (U.S. Surgeon General, 1999). Most children receiving intervention services in institutional-based settings are in residential treatment programs operated through the child-welfare or juvenile-justice systems (Lyons, 2004). Although little evidence exists to support residential treatment approaches in work with children, there is some evidence that indicates these approaches actually harm instead of helping children (Dishion, Bullock, & Granic, 2002).

The child-serving systems today are not comprehensive or integrated, resulting in many children in need of treatment getting inappropriate services, inadequate services, or no services. In addition, for those children who have access to intervention services, 40–60% may discontinue services before completing the treatment (Kazdin, 1997). Social work professionals who intervene with children often find themselves dealing with service systems that are unresponsive to emerging child and family needs. Furthermore, these professionals have limited access to EBPs that promote successful engagement and positive child outcomes. The need to address effective interventions for children at risk for emotional and behavioral problems across service system settings is urgent.

For an EBP to be effective in work with children at risk for emotional and behavioral problems, attention to developmental changes, age-related changes, the family context, and the service setting in which the intervention is being delivered (e.g., schools, mental-health organizations, juvenile-justice centers) is critical (Hoagwood, Burns, Kiser, Ringeisen, & Schoenwald, 2001; Mitchell, 2011). The social work profession, like other disciplines, has looked to the experiences in the health field to better understand ways to improve intervention outcomes for children and increase the use of EBPs across service settings.

The Institute of Medicine (IOM) defines EBP as "the integration of best research evidence with clinical expertise and patient values" (IOM, 2001). This definition involves three critical elements: best research evidence, clinical expertise, and patient values. Based on this definition, when intervening in the lives of children, social workers using the EBP model need to have access to the best intervention research evidence available, use clinical expertise to guide the intervention process, and partner with children and families in understanding their values and preferences in intervention work. EBP involves a collaborative process in which children and families are involved in defining the problem, determining what outcomes that the intervention will achieve, integrating and applying evidence to design the initial practice strategy, modifying the initial practice strategy based on child and family preferences and practice expertise, applying the tailored strategy, and evaluating the outcomes (Fraser, 2003). The challenge for social workers is to understand how the child and family values and preferences affect the decision-making process and to balance these factors with the best available clinical and empirically supported evidence.

The recent IOM report "Crossing the Quality Chasm: A New Health System in the 21st Century" (2001) highlights priority conditions for EBP in health care. These priority conditions include ongoing analysis and synthesis of the medical evidence, delineation of specific practice guidelines, the identification of best practices, the dissemination efforts to communicate evidence and guidelines, the development of decision support tools to assist clinicians and patients in applying the evidence, and the establishment of goals for improvement in care (IOM, 2001). In the new federal health reform law, Patient Protection and Affordable

Care Act of 2010, the legislation expands health and behavioral-health insurance coverage to include prevention-focused interventions as part of the essential benefits required of all insurance plans.

For social workers, using EBPs maximizes the likelihood of achieving child and family hoped-for outcomes and minimizes the potential for harm. Gambrill (2003) identifies 20 interrelated contributions of EBP to the social work profession. These include focusing on client concerns and hoped-for outcomes; encouraging a comprehensive, systemic approach to the provision of effective, efficient, and ethical services; describing a process for integrating evidentiary, ethical, and application concerns; promoting transparency and honesty; encouraging rigorous testing and appraisal of practice/policy-related claims; promoting the preparation and dissemination of critical appraisals of practice/policy-related research findings; highlighting applicability challenges; attending to individual differences; discouraging inflated claims; describing and taking proactive steps to minimize errors, accidents, and mistakes; welcoming criticism; recognizing our ignorance and consequent uncertainty; honoring a professional code of ethics; increasing available knowledge; considering both populations and individuals; minimizing harm in the name of helping; blowing the whistle on pseudoscience, propaganda, quackery, and fraud; creating educational programs that develop lifelong learners; and exploring how to decrease obstacles to EBP (Gambrill, 2003).

Efforts over the past 20 years to promote evidence-based social work practice, such as the evolution of program evaluation methods; encouraging social workers to read, synthesize, and apply intervention research in practice; and encouraging practitioners to use single subject designs to inform practice, have often resulted in significant resistance from social work professionals (Kirk, 1999). In the child-serving organizations, social work professionals have been strongly encouraged to use EBPs in their work with children, but organizations often do not have the resources to train and implement emerging EBPs. In addition, the readiness of many emerging evidence-based child interventions for large-scale dissemination is limited (Hoagwood et al., 2001).

Because evidence-based interventions often address the "average" child experiencing a problem condition, many social work practitioners do not find the information helpful, because the research does not necessarily address what intervention is best for the child at hand. In fact, child populations encountered in many social work service settings are often excluded from randomized controlled trials (RCT) because of the complexity of needs experienced by these youth. The development of practice guidelines for specific interventions and programs for children has been viewed as an important factor in helping social workers implement EBPs across various service settings. Practice guidelines are "systematically developed statements to assist practitioner and patient decisions about appropriate care for specific clinical circumstances" (IOM, 1990, p. 27). Use of practice guidelines increases "the predictability of practice around a set of standardized 'best practices' and [reduces] variability between social workers" in their work with children and families (Rosen & Proctor, 2003, p. 5). In addition to practice guidelines, evidence-based interventions develop treatment manuals that are more specific and provide guidelines for establishing the therapeutic relationships and suggestions for sequencing activities, monitoring outcomes, and addressing implementation issues in real-world settings (Fraser, 2003).

Current EBPs With Children

Although the state of EBPs in work with children and their families is expanding and new practices are being studied as they arise, this chapter focuses primarily on existing EBPs that have demonstrated positive outcomes for children at risk for emotional and behavioral problems and their families across child-serving systems. Some of the EBPs operate at a program level and others at the clinical level. These EBPs often involve child-, family-, and system-level changes in order to enhance positive outcomes for children.

The primary organizing framework for current evidence-based social work interventions with children who experience emotional or behavioral problems builds on an ecological, developmental, family-centered, resiliency-based, multisystem perspective (Fraser, 2004; Friesen & Stephens, 1998; Huang et al., 2005; Kazak et al., 2010).

The ecological-systems perspective encourages social workers to incorporate a transactional and dynamic approach to understanding children within their environmental contexts. Children are viewed within their social ecology that consists of interdependent and often nested systems (Bronfenbrenner, 1986). The developmental perspective highlights the need for social workers to assess a child's developmental level within his or her environmental contexts and use developmentally sensitive intervention techniques. The developmental course for children varies, and the youth's cognitive-developmental level may limit or enhance the degree to which a youth engages in change efforts (Holmbeck, Greenley, & Franks, 2003).

Social workers who use EBP interventions for children not only use empirically supported interventions but also integrate the child's and family's perspective into the design of the intervention strategy. A family-centered orientation encourages social workers to involve families as partners in all aspects of all interventions: planning, intervention strategies, outcome determination, and effectiveness evaluation (Duchnowski, Kutash, & Friedman, 2003).

A resiliency-based perspective requires that social workers understand children at risk within their environmental and cultural contexts. Resiliency is a dynamic process and is defined as "observing a normal or even exceptional positive developmental outcome in spite of exposure to major risk for the development of serious social and health problems" (Fraser, 2004, p. 22). Resilience has been defined as the dynamic interplay of individual, social, and environmental protective factors, in the context of risk exposure, resulting in positive developmental outcomes and adaptation

(Luthar, Cicchetti, & Becker, 2000). A resiliency-based framework requires that social workers who intervene with children look holistically at risk and protective factors present within the child, the family, the school, the neighborhood, and the child-serving delivery system and intervene to support child functioning and healthy development. A *risk factor* is any influence that increases the probability of harm, contributes to a more serious state, or maintains a problem condition (Coie et al., 1993; Fraser, 2004). Risk factors may frequently occur together, and as the number of risk factors increases, the chance for negative developmental outcomes for children increases (Dishion, Capaldi, & Yeager, 1999; Hawkins, Catalano, & Miller, 1992; Luthar, 1991). Protective factors can be defined as "both internal and external resources that modify risk" (Fraser, 2004, p. 28). Three main categories of protective factors have been identified by Garmezy (1985): (1) dispositional attributes, such as temperamental factors; (2) social orientation and responsiveness to change; and (3) cognitive abilities and coping skills.

Finally, social workers using a multisystem perspective when working with children with emotional and behavioral problems assess and intervene within family systems and across child-serving systems to improve outcomes. Essentially, child-serving systems have the overall goal of keeping children at home, in school, and in the community with improved functioning in critical life domains. Although social workers recognize that many of the children they serve are involved in more than one child-serving system, current funding streams for child services have resulted in fragmented, uncoordinated service-delivery systems with different traditions and often conflicting approaches to work with children and their families. The President's New Freedom Commission on Mental Health (2003) recommends that child-serving systems promote early screening for behavioral and emotional problems in children, improve access to quality care that is culturally competent, and develop individualized plans of care that involve families as partners. In addition, the Surgeon General's Conference on Children's Mental Health (U.S. Surgeon General, 2001) recommends four guiding principles for the development of responsive child-serving systems to meet the needs of children with behavioral and emotional problems: (1) promoting the recognition of mental health as an essential part of children's health; (2) integrating family, child, and youth-centered mental-health services into all systems that serve children and youth; (3) engaging families and incorporating the perspectives of children and youth in the development of all mental-health-care planning; and (4) developing and enhancing a public-private health infrastructure to support these efforts to the fullest extent possible. In addition, this report recommends that, in order to improve services for children at risk of emotional and behavioral problems, it is important to continue to develop, disseminate, and implement scientifically proven prevention and treatment services in the field of children's mental health and work to eliminate racial/ethnic and socioeconomic disparities in access to needed mental-health services across child-serving systems.

Table 2.1   Key Evidence-Based Practices Across Child-Serving Systems

Child- and Family-Based Interventions
Cognitive-behavioral therapy
Parent management training models and multidimensional therapeutic
    foster care
Multisystemic therapy
Brief strategic family therapy

Schoolwide/Community Interventions
Families and Schools Together
Strengthening Families Program
Project Achieve

The EBPs selected address the complex needs of children at risk for emotional and behavioral problems and their families, have been implemented by social workers, and have demonstrated success in the real-world child-service system settings. These evidence-based interventions have practice principles or intervention manuals that support replication and promote ways to assess fidelity to the intervention model. The EBPs reviewed are divided into emerging evidence-based individual child and family interventions and schoolwide/community interventions (see Table 2.1). For each intervention reviewed, the key components of the intervention are presented as well as the status of the empirical evidence to support this intervention with targeted child populations.

Child- and Family-Based Interventions

The child- and family-based intervention programs involve not only intervening with the child but also engaging the family in the work of promoting positive outcomes for the child. Although some of the interventions, such as cognitive-behavioral therapy, could be implemented without a family or parent component, in this chapter only the cognitive-behavioral interventions that involve the child and the parents or families are discussed.

Cognitive-Behavioral Therapy

Cognitive-behavioral therapy (CBT) approaches have been used successfully to address a range of internal and external emotional/behavioral disorders in children (Barrett, 1998; Beidas, Benjamin, Puleo, Edmunds, & Kendall, 2010; Cohen, Berliner, & Mannarino, 2010; Kendall et al., 1997; Shortt, Barrett, & Fox, 2001). These problems include living with anxiety, depression, or conduct disorders. Involving parents in the interventions enhances positive outcomes for the youth and family. CBT focuses on the relationship among cognitions, affect, and behavior. The process in CBT is to assist a child in moving from a dysfunctional cycle of thoughts (overly negative, self-critical), feelings (anxious, depressed, angry), and behavior (avoid, give up, act out inappropriately) to a functional system of thoughts (more positive, acknowledge success, recognize strengths), feelings (relaxed, happy, calm), and behavior (confront, try, appropriate; Stallard, 2002). Most CBT interventions involve at least eight sessions, focus on skills-based learning, and address current problems. Children learn how to monitor thoughts; identify cognitive distortions; develop alternative cognitive processes; learn new cognitive skills; learn affective monitoring and management; conduct behavioral experiments; use role-playing, modeling, exposure, and rehearsal skills; and engage in positive reinforcement and rewards (Stallard, 2002).

A Cochrane Collaboration Review of CBT for anxiety disorders in children found that CBT appears to be an effective treatment for children (over the age of 6 years) and adolescents (Soler & Weatherall, 2005). Thirteen studies of children and adolescents experiencing anxiety disorders met the criteria for inclusion in this review. The criteria included that the study had to be a randomized trial, conform to CBT principles through the use of a protocol, and comprise at least eight sessions (Soler & Weatherall, 2005). More than 50% of youth who received CBT for anxiety disorders showed improvement in their anxiety symptoms even 3 or more months after the intervention was completed (Soler & Weatherall, 2005).

One CBT family-based program called FRIENDS (Barrett, Lowry-Webster, & Turner, 2000) illustrates the steps involved in delivering CBT interventions. The acronym FRIENDS highlights the strategies taught in this intervention:

F: Feeling worried?

R: Relax and feel good.

I: Inner thoughts.

E: Explore plans.

N: Nice work, so reward yourself.

D: Don't forget to practice.

S: Stay calm, you know how to cope now.

FRIENDS focuses on working with children experiencing anxiety disorders and their parents and was part of the Cochrane Review of CBT for anxiety disorders in children and adolescents conducted by Soler and Weatherall (2005). This CBT family-based program could be delivered in community-based settings, schools, mental-health clinics, or family/social-service agencies.

In the FRIENDS program, cognitive distortions are seen as central to the maintenance of anxiety symptoms (Barrett & Shortt, 2003). Parents are involved in the intervention in order to facilitate new experiences for the child to test cognitive distortions and to assist the child in processing these new experiences on a daily basis (Barrett & Shortt, 2003).

According to Barrett and Shortt (2003, p. 103), the FRIENDS program encourages children to:

1. Think of their bodies as their friends, because it tells them when they are feeling worried or nervous by giving them clues.
2. Be their own friend and reward themselves when they try hard.
3. Make friends so that they can build their social support networks.
4. Talk to their friends when they are in difficult or worrying situations.

Parents are enlisted to help change the child's environment to reduce the child's anxiety and promote positive change.

This intervention is conducted in a group format and has two versions based on the developmental level of the child or adolescent. One group version is designed for children ages 7 to 11 years, and the other for adolescents ages 12 to 16 years. Both versions involve 10 sessions and 2 booster sessions (1 month and 3 months following completion of the sessions). Each session runs for approximately 1 hour and is conducted weekly. The family-skills or parenting component of the program usually runs 1 hour and 30 minutes for a total of 6 hours in a group format over four sessions. In the family-skills component, parents learn about the steps of FRIENDS; explore their own thoughts and ways to challenge thoughts; how to reinforce learning; and how to establish appropriate reward structures and strategies for promoting strengths in the youth, parent(s), and family.

The FRIENDS group format for youth involves teaching seven key skills. The skill taught in the F-Feeling Worried? segment of the intervention involves helping the child identify physiological and behavioral indicators of anxiety. In this skill area, a child might focus on the connection between how one feels (sick, faint) and what one does (avoid school or friend activities). The R-Relax and Feel Good skill teaches youth to engage in enjoyable activities when feeling worried or sad. The I-Inner Thoughts skill teaches youth how the way they talk to themselves influences how they feel and what they do. The E-Explore Plans skill teaches youth how to use the six-block problem-solving plan (what is the problem; list all possible solutions; list what might happen with each solution; select the best solution based on consequences; make a plan and do it; and evaluate the outcome). The N-Nice Work So Reward Yourself skill helps youth evaluate successes, set reasonable goals, and establish rewards for success. The D-Don't Forget to Practice skill encourages youth to role-play, rehearse, and practice new behaviors and ways to handle their anxieties or worries. The S-Stay Calm skill reminds youth that they have the skills to handle their worries and anxieties.

The CBT approaches used for youth with depressive symptoms or conduct disorders employs similar strategies but educates the youth about their specific problem area instead of anxiety disorders.

Parent Management Training Models and Multidimensional Therapeutic Foster Care

Parent management training models have evolved over several decades, and current models are based on successful findings from several clinical and prevention trials (Kazdin, 2005; Patterson, 2004). Parent management training (PMT) involves manualized interventions in which parents are taught social learning techniques to change the behavior of their children (Kazdin, 2005). In addition, PMT approaches do not assume that the solution to problem behaviors lies within the child but that it lies within the social environment (Patterson, 2005). Successful PMT approaches target working with parents of children experiencing antisocial behavior, oppositional or conduct disorders, delinquent behavior, or attention-deficit/hyperactivity disorders and who are at risk for substance use (Kazdin, 2005; Patterson, 2005). Kazdin reports that research studies of PMT approaches have demonstrated effectiveness in improving youth academic behavior and classroom performance, increasing prosocial behavior, preventing deviant behavior, and improving adherence to medication treatment.

Parent management training approaches are based primarily on operant-conditioning methods and social-learning techniques. These methods emphasize the control that environmental events exert on behavior. Kazdin (2005, p. 23) identifies four key principles of operant conditioning used in PMT approaches. These principles include:

1. *Reinforcement* (presenting or removing an event after a response that increases the likelihood or probability of that response).

2. *Punishment* (presenting or removing an event after a response that decreases the likelihood or probability of that response).

3. *Extinction* (no longer presenting a reinforcement event after a response that decreases the likelihood or probability of the previously reinforced response).

4. *Stimulus control and discrimination* (reinforcing the response in the presence of one stimulus but not in the presence of another).

In operant conditioning, the main focus is on examining the contingencies of reinforcement, and this involves describing antecedent events (A), behaviors (B), and consequences (C) and altering the sequence to promote desired outcomes. Parents learn how to track behavior using the A-B-C formula. For example, a parent might document that the antecedent event (A) was asking the child to clean the room, the behavior (B) of the child might be picking up toys, and the consequence (C) is that the parent gives the child verbal praise. The reinforcers used in PMT might include food or consumables, social reinforcers (e.g., attention, praise, and physical contact), privileges and activities, and tokens. The essential ingredients to make reinforcement programs successful involve the following factors: contingent application of consequences; immediacy of reinforcement;

continuous reinforcement, magnitude or amount of the reinforcer; quality or type of reinforcer; varied and combined reinforcers; or use of prompts, shaping, and practice trials (Kazdin, 2005).

Parent management training interventions involve working directly with the parent(s), who implement effective parenting skills at home using social learning techniques. According to Forgatch, Patterson, and DeGarmo (2005, p. 4), the core parenting skills taught in the PMT training work at the Oregon Learning Center involve:

1. *Skill encouragement*—Promotes prosocial development through scaffolding techniques (e.g., breaking behavior into small steps, prompting appropriate behavior) and contingent positive reinforcement (e.g., praise and incentives).

2. *Discipline* (i.e., limit setting)—Decreases deviant behavior through the appropriate and contingent use of mild sanctions (e.g., time-out, privilege removal).

3. *Monitoring* (i.e., supervision)—Involves tracking youngsters' activities, associates, whereabouts, and transportation.

4. *Problem solving*—Helps families negotiate disagreements, establish rules, and specify consequences for following or violating rules.

5. *Positive involvement*—Reflects the many ways that parents provide their youngsters with loving attention.

In general, PMT approaches involve several meetings with the parent(s). Parent management training approaches alter not only what the parent does in managing his or her child but also how the parent thinks and feels about parenting (Patterson, 2004). Kazdin (2005) in his review of PMT approaches identifies the following format for the core sessions: (a) a pretreatment introduction and orientation; (b) defining, observing, and recording behavior; (c) positive reinforcement; (d) time-out from reinforcement; (e) attending and planned ignoring; (f) shaping and school program; (g) review and problem solving; (h) family meeting; (i) low-rate behaviors; (j) reprimands; (k) compromising; and (l) skill review. Each core session involves a review of the previous week and how the behavior-change program is working or not, presentation of a principle or theme, practice in role-playing with the therapist and/or the youth, and the addition of some assignment or changes in the program that will be implemented at home for the next week.

The Oregon multidimensional treatment foster care (MTFC) model is a specialized community-based PMT program that has been used with children with antisocial problems involved in the juvenile-justice, mental-health, and child-welfare systems (Chamberlain & Smith, 2003). The MTFC model uses a comprehensive treatment approach that creates opportunities for youth to live successfully in their communities while providing them with intensive supervision, support, and skill development. Many of these youth would be placed in group homes or residential placement settings if they did not enter a MTFC program. The effectiveness of this model has been documented with a range of youth and in a variety of child-serving settings (Chamberlain & Reid, 1991; Fisher, Ellis, & Chamberlain, 1999).

Youth are placed in foster homes where the foster parents are trained to be the primary treatment agents, and the youth's biological/step/adoptive/relative families help shape the youth's treatment plan and participate in family therapy and home visits throughout placement to prepare for reunification with their youth at the program's end (Fisher & Chamberlain, 2000).

In order to deliver the MFTC program, a team consisting of the MTFC parent(s), program supervisor, family therapist for the biological/adoptive or relative family, individual therapist for the youth, behavioral support specialist, and consulting psychiatrist work together to conduct the treatment intervention (Chamberlain & Smith, 2003). Each team member has a separate role and specialized responsibilities.

The specific targets of treatment in MFTC include reinforcing normative and prosocial behavior of the youth, providing youth with close supervision, closely monitoring peer associations, specifying clear and consistent limits, following through on rule violations, encouraging youth to develop positive work habits and academic skills, supporting family members to increase the effectiveness of their parenting skills, decreasing conflict between family members, and teaching youth new skills for forming relationships with positive peers and for bonding with adult mentors and role models (Fisher & Chamberlain, 2000).

Multidimensional treatment foster-care parents participate in a 20-hour preservice training in which they are taught a four-step approach to analyzing behavior (knowing when a problem is a problem, developing a clear behavioral description of that problem, identifying what precedes the behavior, and identifying antecedents to the behavior; Chamberlain & Smith, 2003; Fisher & Chamberlain, 2000). Multidimensional treatment foster-care parents also learn how to implement an individualized daily program with the youth and how to work with the youth's biological family.

After training, the MFTC parents and youth are matched, and an individualized program is developed by the team. The individualized program is detailed and includes a behavior-management program within the foster home. The youth has opportunities to earn points for satisfactory performance and receive frequent positive feedback from the MFTC parents about his or her progress (Fisher & Chamberlain, 2000).

Multidimensional training foster-care parents receive daily telephone calls from program staff to monitor the interventions and provide support. In addition, program staff visit each MFTC home once a week and are available to foster parents 24 hours a day to provide back-up support.

The MTFC program is individually tailored to meet the needs of each youth and family and changes over time, based on the individual child's progress and family readiness to handle the challenges of their youth (Chamberlain, 2002).

Another specialized PMT program with a strong evidence base is the Incredible Years Training Series for parents of young children, ages 3 to 8 years, who have conduct problems. The Incredible Years Training Series is designed to promote social competence and prevent, reduce, and treat conduct problems by working with parents, teachers, and children using developmentally appropriate curricula (Webster-Stratton, 2001). The parent-training component of this training series teaches parents skills in how to play with children, how to give praise and rewards, effective limits setting, strategies to handle misbehavior, improving communication, anger management, problem solving, ways to get and give support, and how to promote children's academic skills. The training program uses video vignettes to help parents learn these new skills (Webster-Stratton, 1994). Children in this intervention develop skills in emotional literacy, empathy or perspective taking, friendship, anger management, interpersonal problem solving, school rules, and how to succeed in school. Teacher training helps teachers use effective classroom-management skills that involve positive attention; giving praise and encouragement; use of incentives for difficult behavior problems; how to manage inappropriate classroom behaviors; and how to teach empathy, social skills, and problem solving in the classroom.

Multisystemic Therapy

Multisystemic therapy (MST) is an ecologically based, short-term, intensive home- and community-based intervention program for families of youth with severe psychosocial and behavioral problems (Henggeler et al., 2009; Henggeler, Schoenwald, Borduin, Rowland, & Cunningham, 1998; Henggeler, Schoenwald, Rowland, & Cunningham, 2002; Ogden & Hagen, 2009; Swenson, Henggeler, Taylor, & Addison, 2005). MST provides an alternative to out-of-home placement of children and youth.

The MST program uses a family-preservation service-delivery model that provides time-limited, intensive services to the youth and their families over a period of 4 to 6 months (Henggeler et al., 1998). Therapists work with the youth and their families as a treatment team. The treatment team usually consists of three or four mental-health professionals with master's or doctoral degrees who share responsibility for the treatment and provide services to about 50 families a year. The MST program model involves being available to the youth and family 24 hours a day, 7 days a week. The treatment-team model allows for families to have more than one therapist to relate to over time to address the serious challenges that they face raising youth with severe psychosocial and behavioral problems. In addition, the treatment team has the opportunity to provide instrumental and affective support and coverage for one another during vacations or personal time off (Schoenwald & Rowland, 2002).

MST usually involves work not only with the child and the family but also with other social systems, including neighborhoods, schools, and peer groups (Swenson et al., 2005). In MST, the child and the family may receive a range of interventions that are individualized to address specific needs. The individual and family interventions may focus on cognitive and/or behavioral change, communication skills, parenting skills, family relations, peer relations, school performance, and/or social networks (Littell, Popa, & Forsythe, 2005).

The MST program is manualized and includes measures to ensure fidelity through supervision and organizational quality-improvement efforts. The MST program has nine principles that guide and organize the treatment team's work with the child and family. The nine principles that guide the assessment and intervention process include:

1. The primary purpose of assessment is to understand the fit between the identified problems and their broader systemic context.
2. Therapeutic contacts emphasize the positive and should use systemic strengths as levers for change.
3. Interventions are designed to promote responsible behavior and decrease irresponsible behavior among family members.
4. Interventions are present-focused and action-oriented, targeting specified and well-defined problems.
5. Interventions target sequences of behavior within and between multiple systems that maintain the identified problems.
6. Interventions are developmentally appropriate and fit the developmental needs of the youth.
7. Interventions are designed to require daily or weekly effort by family members.
8. Intervention effectiveness is evaluated continuously from multiple perspectives, with providers assuming accountability for overcoming barriers to successful outcomes.
9. Interventions are designed to promote treatment generalization and long-term maintenance of therapeutic change by empowering caregivers to address family members' needs across multiple systemic contexts (Henggeler et al., 1998, p. 23).

According to Schoenwald and Rowland (2002), the MST treatment team engages in an analytical process designed to:

- Gain a clear understanding for the reasons for referral.
- Assess and develop overarching treatment goals that build on the strengths of the child, the family, and other relevant social systems.
- Establish intermediary treatment goals that are linked to the overarching treatment goals.

- Engage in an ongoing assessment of advances and barriers to intervention effectiveness.

MST has a relatively robust evidence base, with several randomized controlled trials (RCTs). Eight MST RCTs met the selection criteria for inclusion in a rigorous Cochrane Collaborative Review conducted by Littell et al. (2005). Although many of the MST studies published in professional journals tend to show positive outcomes for children, Littell et al. (2005) conclude in their review that there may be no significant differences between the MST population and the usual services population. More studies are needed to assess the impact of MST. MST Services, Inc., was formed to standardize the dissemination of MST and to ensure fidelity to the model. MST has been replicated in several sites across the United States, Canada, and Norway.

Brief Strategic Family Therapy

Brief strategic family therapy (BSFT) is a culturally appropriate intervention that focuses on addressing substance abuse risks as it relates to Latino youth (ages 6–17 years) and their family members (Robbins et al., 2003; Szapocznik, Hervis, & Schwartz, 2003). This BSFT intervention uses a problem-focused and a family-systems-therapy approach. It usually involves 12 to 16 weekly sessions. The intervention was first developed for work with Latino youth involved with drugs and their families. BSFT is a manualized intervention and has been extensively evaluated for more than 25 years. The evaluation research supports BSFT's effectiveness in work with youth with substance abuse and conduct problems.

In BSFT, the family is viewed as the primary context for work. Three central themes guide the work in BSFT. These themes include *system, structures*, and *strategy* (Szapocznik & Kurtines, 1989). A family is a *system* comprising individuals whose behavior affects other family members; *structures* are repetitive patterns of interaction and involve content and process; and *strategy* is the interventions that are practical, problem-focused, and deliberate (Robbins et al., 2003). *Content* refers to what family members talk about, and *process* involves family-interaction behaviors (Szapocznik et al., 2003).

According to Robbins et al. (2003, p. 409), the key assumptions that guide BSFT include:

1. Changing the family is the most effective way of changing the individual.
2. Changing an individual and then returning him or her to a detrimental or negative environment does not allow the individual changes to remain in place.
3. Changes in one central or powerful individual can result in changes in the rest of his or her family.

BSFT involves the whole family in treatment. Family sessions typically take place once a week, and each session runs 1 hour to 90 minutes. The first step in BSFT is *joining* (building a therapeutic relationship with each family member and addressing barriers to engagement), followed by *diagnosing family strengths and weaknesses, developing a treatment plan,* and *restructuring* (implementing change strategies needed to transform family relations; Robbins et al., 2003). Change strategies include cognitive restructuring; directing, redirecting, or blocking communication; shifting family alliances; placing parents in charge; helping families develop conflict resolution skills; developing effective behavior-management skills; and fostering parenting and parental-leadership skills (Robbins et al., 2003). The restructuring techniques used are working in the present, reframing negativity, reversing, working with boundaries and alliances, detriangulating, and opening up closed systems and tasks (Szapocznik et al., 2003).

BSFT can be delivered in office- or community-based and in-home settings. The BSFT therapist works with 10 to 12 families.

Schoolwide/Community Interventions

There are numerous schoolwide prevention programs that have demonstrated initial success in early-evaluation studies across the country for children, especially relating to improving attendance and academic performance. In fact, many of the programs target behaviors that place students at risk for emotional and behavioral problems. Some of these programs focus on bullying behavior, anger management, and prevention of gang activity and substance misuse. Resilience research cites that positive school experiences for youth and having a parent who promotes the importance of education can serve as key protective factors (Luthar et al., 2000). Three specific prevention programs are discussed in this section that involve schools and communities in helping children and their families. The three programs include Families and Schools Together, Strengthening Families, and Project Achieve.

All three programs address the key principles of effective prevention programs. These program principles include (a) being comprehensive; (b) using varied teaching methods; (c) providing sufficient dosage to produce desired effects; (d) being theory driven; (e) providing exposure to adults and peers in a way that promotes strong, positive relationships; (f) being initiated early enough to have an impact; (g) being socioculturally relevant; (h) including evaluation of outcomes; and (i) training staff to implement the program with fidelity (Nation et al., 2003).

Families and Schools Together

The Families and Schools Together (FAST) program is a ";developmental, risk focused, early intervention/prevention program built on the knowledge that effective prevention programs must reduce cumulative risks and combinations of factors that increase risk for children, as well as enhance

protective factors in families that buffer children from such multiple risks"
(Coote, 2000, p. 2). The FAST program has been implemented in 45 U.S.
states, as well as in Australia, Canada, Germany, and Russia (Soydan, Nye,
Chacon-Moscosco, Sanchez-Meca, & Almeida, 2005).

In the FAST program, child well-being is viewed as linked to family
and community functioning. The FAST program model, through early intervention with at-risk children living in impoverished conditions, supports
families and integrates community development with family and individual
clinical approaches to reduce substance abuse, violence, delinquency, and
school failure (McDonald, Billingham, Conrad, Morgan, & Payton, 1997;
Knox, Guerra, Williams, & Toro, 2011).

The FAST program engages parents of at-risk elementary-school
youth in an 8-week, multifamily group that involves structured activities
aimed at enhancing family functioning, building social connections, and
reducing parent/family isolation (Coote, 2000; McDonald et al., 1997). The
FAST program integrates concepts from family-stress theory, community-
development theory, parent-mediated play therapy, and behavioral parent-
management strategies to help parents, families, and communities meet
the needs of at-risk children (McDonald et al., 1997). The FAST program
has the ultimate goal of "increasing the likelihood of the child being
successful in the home, in the school, and in the community" (Coote,
2000, p. 5). The specific outcome goals embedded in the program model
include (a) preventing school failure, (b) enhancing family functioning,
(c) reducing everyday stress by developing an ongoing support group for
parents, and (d) preventing substance abuse (Fischer, 2003).

The first phase of the FAST program involves teachers in the elementary school identifying children with behavioral, emotional, or learning
problems who are at risk of academic and social problems. The FAST
team, which includes FAST parent graduates, visits the homes of the identified children to invite the parent(s) and family to participate in the FAST
program. When 8 to 10 families have agreed to join the FAST program,
these families form an 8-week, multifamily group. The multifamily group
uses a structured, interactive format to empower parents to address the
behavioral, emotional, and learning needs of their children. The $2\frac{1}{2}$-hour
weekly meetings are led by a trained team that includes a parent, a school
professional (e.g., the school social worker), a clinical social worker from a
mental-health agency, and a substance-abuse counselor (McDonald et al.,
1997). Each session includes six basic elements: (1) a shared family meal,
(2) family games involving communication tactics, (3) a group discussion
for parents separate from a play session for the children, (4) play-focused
time involving parent and target child, (5) a family lottery in which each
family wins once to serve as the host for the next FAST session, and (6) a
closing ceremony with singing and recognition of family and individual
accomplishments (Fischer, 2003). Some of the specific strategies used in
the FAST sessions include the creation of a family flag; a FAST hello in
which each family is welcomed by another family; singing of the FAST
song; creation of individual pictures out of scribbles for positive family

communication; feelings charades in which children and parents act out their feelings and others guess; buddy time for adults during which couples and parents are paired up to share their day, their hassles, and what happened, without the other person giving advice; special play time during which the parent is coached by the FAST team to follow the child's lead; a door prize for one family each week; and special topic sessions to talk about hard-to-discuss issues, such as alcohol and drug use (Coote, 2000; McDonald et al., 1997). At the end of the 8-week, multifamily group, a graduation ceremony is held, with certificates presented to the parents from the school principal. Linkages to community services are also made for parents and families based on need. The parents then become a part of the next phase of the FAST program, called FASTWORKS. Families are invited to participate for 2 years in this phase of the program. FASTWORKS involves monthly meetings designed to provide continued family support and networking. These meetings are run by a parent-advisory council of graduates. Attendance at these meetings for parents is voluntary but encouraged by the FAST team.

Several evaluations and at least five randomized controlled studies have been conducted on the FAST program with promising results. In some of the studies, a significant positive overall effect of FAST on the child's academic performance after 2 years of school based on teacher's report was noted, and families sustained their positive changes for more than 6 months after completing the multifamily group.

Strengthening Families Program

The Strengthening Families Program (SFP) is designed for youth ages 6 to 14 years and their families. The program targets improving family relationships, parenting skills, and youth's social and life skills (Kumpfer & Alvarado, 2003). It was originally developed for children of parents who abuse drugs (Kumpfer, Alvarado, Tait, & Turner, 2002), but there are different versions of this program. The SFP uses a biopsychosocial vulnerability model (Kumpfer & Alvarado, 2003) and a resiliency-based framework to guide all program interventions.

The SFP for youth ages 6 to 12 years involves families in a 14-week training session using family systems and cognitive-behavioral approaches to increase protective factors and decrease risk factors in the youth and their families. These sessions are held at the school. This version of the SFP involves parents and youth attending 14 sessions that each run for 2 hours. The SFP sessions are structured and involve three components: family life-skills training, parent-skills training, and child problem-solving and social-skills training (Kumpfer et al., 2002). Parents meet separately from the youth for 1 hour, and this component is facilitated by two group leaders. The focus of the session is to help parents learn ways to increase positive behavior in their children, use discipline and limits setting effectively, improve parent-child communication, develop problem-solving skills, and address substance use. During this time, the youth meet with two children's trainers to learn about feelings and how to control anger, resist peer pressure, use problem solving, and develop social skills. In the second hour of each session, families meet together to engage in structured family activities and practice skills. After completing the sessions, families are invited to participate in a 6-month and a 12-month booster session to maintain intervention gains (Kumpfer et al., 2002).

The SFP for youth ages 10 to 14 years is video-based, addressing substance abuse and problem behavior in youth. This SFP is a universal prevention program, the objectives of which are to (a) build skills in youth to reduce risk and build protective factors, (b) improve parenting practices known to reduce risk in youth, and (c) build stronger family units to support and monitor youth (Molgaard & Spoth, 2001). This version of SFP consists of seven sessions plus four booster sessions for parents and youth. Similar to the SFP for youth ages 6 to 12 years, this version separates parents and youth for the first hour, and the second hour is spent in supervised family activities. Three group leaders are needed: one to lead the parent session and two to lead the youth session. The group leaders shift roles from teacher to facilitator for the second half of each session.

The SFP uses incentives, family meals, and other rituals to foster engagement and attendance at the sessions. Research on SFP has consistently found positive results for youth in reducing substance-use risk and increasing protective factors in the youth and families, even at 5-year follow-up measures (Kumpfer & Alvardo, 2003; Brook, McDonald, & Yan, 2012).

Project Achieve

Project Achieve is a school-based program that focuses on academic work, school safety, and positive climate and parent-involvement outcomes (Knoff & Batsche, 1995). According to Knoff, Finch, and Carlyon (2004, p. 6), Project Achieve's ultimate goal "is to help design and implement effective school and schooling processes to maximize the academic and social/emotional/behavioral progress and achievement of all students." It has a primary prevention focus, but it also will intervene with students in difficulty. The six primary goals of Project Achieve include (1) enhancing the problem-solving skills of teachers and other educators; (2) improving classroom- and behavior-management skills of school personnel; (3) intervening with students who are not performing at their expected levels; (4) increasing social and academic progress of students by increasing parent involvement and linking to community resources; (5) engaging in a comprehensive improvement process; and (6) creating a school climate in which every teacher, school staff member, and parent shares responsibility for building community (Knoff et al., 2004).

Project Achieve has seven major interdependent components that focus on building a schoolwide positive behavioral self-management system:

1. *Strategic planning and organizational analysis*: This component focuses on assessing the organizational climate, administrative style, and decision-making processes in the school.

2. *Referral questioning consultation (RQC)*: RQC is a problem-solving approach that links the problem assessment to intervention. All staff are trained in this technique.

3. *Classroom teacher/staff development*: This component assists teachers in securing the needed skills to implement various instructional styles to maximize student learning.

4. *Instructional consultation and curriculum-based assessment/intervention*: This component emphasizes direct instruction and a mastery model perspective in academic outcomes.

5. *Behavioral consultation and behavioral interventions*: This component focuses on establishing a schoolwide positive behavioral self-management system that addresses behavioral interventions designed to resolve students' behavioral problems or to improve teachers' classroom-management procedures. A major part of this component is implementing the Stop and Think Social Skills Program (Knoff, 2001). The Stop and Think Social Skills Program teaches students more than 60 behavioral skills (e.g., listening, problem solving, asking for help, responding to teasing). There are five steps in the Stop and Think Social Skills Program: (1) Stop and think. (2) Are you going to make a good choice or bad choice? (3) What are your choices or steps? (4) Do it! and (5) Good job! (Knoff et al., 2004).

6. *Parent training, tutoring, and support*: This component focuses on building an ongoing home-school collaboration and making parents an integral part of the school. Parent training sessions are conducted that help parents learn how to transfer the social skills and discipline/behavior management approaches used in the school into the home.

7. *Research and accountability*: This component addresses the evaluation of the program and ways to improve outcomes.

The implementation of Project Achieve components is sequenced over a 3-year period. Several schools have implemented this program, and initial evaluations of this schoolwide initiative indicate positive outcomes for youth in school engagement and prosocial skill development.

Limitations of the Evidence

Despite the availability of EBP for work with children and their families, many of these EBPs are not widely used in social work practice. The gap between research and practice continues to be a challenge for the social workers involved in delivering interventions in public child-serving systems. Although this chapter addresses a few of the EBPs that have a solid research base, there are many other emerging practices that also have promise for work with children and their families, such as motivational interviewing, parent-child interaction therapy, and wraparound services. All these EBPs require that social workers be trained to deliver the interventions with fidelity, and this requires ongoing supervision, monitoring the implementation process, and measuring relevant clinical outcomes.

The EBPs discussed in this chapter involve multiple strategies at different system levels to produce positive outcomes for children and their families. There are similar elements/strategies in each of the EBPs, especially relating to the use of behavioral and cognitive-behavioral techniques. In many of the interventions, parents are involved in learning new skills to facilitate management of child problem behaviors.

For some social workers, one of the limitations of EBPs is the use of prescriptive manuals that often do not allow for individualizing the intervention to better meet the needs of a child and family with multiple problems, and they may limit the opportunity to engage in collaborative work with families.

Although the EBPs presented in this chapter address multiple problem areas and are multicomponent, the social worker still needs to understand how and why the interventions work. In addition, more work is needed on how to tailor the interventions to include preferences of families based on, but not limited to, gender, ethnicity, culture, race, sexual orientation, gender identity, religion, and spirituality differences. The New Freedom Commission (2003) specifically identifies the need to tailor interventions for culturally diverse populations as one of the goals of transforming the mental-health system. The evaluation of the EBPs should include a range of child and family outcomes in order to assess the impact of the interventions over time.

Conclusion

For the greatest possibility of success, it is imperative that we use and continue to develop EBPs for children. Despite the many benefits of using these types of interventions, both practitioners and clients often are hesitant to employ them. Although practitioners prefer providers to use best evidence when they are clients, they feel that evidence-based interventions do not provide enough direction in their own practice. Pollio (2006) attributes this to the fact the EBP training and practice represent researchers and academics talking to practitioners rather than an open dialogue between the two groups. In addition, many practitioners feel that academics simply explain how EBP can be applied generically into practice rather than providing guidance on how to apply these interventions based on the specific circumstances of the case. Likewise, clinical practitioners report that their clients have often had negative experiences with evidence-based interventions that were ineffective and are uncomfortable implementing complicated data-collection methods. Their clients' preconceptions can make it difficult to utilize an evidence-based intervention during the treatment process.

Although these complaints and hesitations are certainly valid, it is important that practitioners are not discouraged but rather supported in analytically investigating the quality of the evidence undergirding the intervention. Furthermore, they need to determine for whom the intervention will be most effective and under what conditions, which in turn should be communicated clearly to the client. It is also important to remember that families and the various child-serving systems are a part of the solution. This keeps the family and child factors in the forefront of any EBP and allows for contextualization given the needs of the child and/or family.

Another aspect of the analytical process is understanding the psychometric properties and characteristics of the target population associated with the evidence (for example, ethnicity/race, culture, sexual orientation, and economic situation of the client). Attention should also be paid to the relevant theories that guide the various evidence-based interventions.

For EBP to be most effective, it must be integrated into the micro-, mezzo-, and macrolevels of social work. A *microsystem* is defined as the interpersonal interactions within an individual's immediate environment, such as the school or workplace. A *mezzosystem*, on the other hand, involves the way two or more microsystems interact with one another (for example, between one's school and home environments). Overarching both of these is the *macrosystem*, or the ideologies and values governing a society (Bronfenbrenner, 1986, as cited in Neville & Mobley, 2001).

On the microlevel, a comprehensive training and dissemination system, including manuals, guidelines, websites, and adequate consideration of treatment fidelity issues would provide a solid base for more fully integrating EBP into the social work profession. Continuing education and outreach is necessary for success on the mezzolevel. This will enable practitioners to remain up to date on interventions and relevant literature as well as to receive guidance from professionals trained in EBP to ensure they appropriately implement the interventions in the most effective and efficient manner. Agencies not only need to address ways to support the training and implementation of EBPs to ensure fidelity but also need to sustain these efforts over time. Finally, on the macrolevel, there are a variety of ways to inform the policy makers and funding agencies in order to heighten their awareness of the advantages of EBP so they can act accordingly. This can include informing local leaders who influence and assist in propagating information to practitioners, calling attention to effective practices/interventions before congressional groups, advocating quality improvement at the organizational level, or utilizing technology or mass-media campaigns to educate clients about their treatment options (Allen-Meares, 2006).

Replication of interventions in different contexts and with diverse children's groups is vital for advancing our practice knowledge. By adequately addressing needs at all levels, the result will be a broader understanding and more widespread use of EBP in a number of practice settings and organizational levels. The larger implications of reliance on EBP include a move toward recognition of professional standards, identification of common elements across EBPs, and a movement toward measurability in the results (Sexton, Chamberlin, Landsverk, Ortiz, & Schoenwald, 2010; Sexton & Kelley, 2010). Drawing on the examples prevalent in the health-care fields, EBP should be viewed as a way to increase effectiveness and quality of care by defining the best practices for the profession through wide dissemination of the subsequent findings (Sharts-Hopko, 2003).

Key Terms

Evidence-based practices and programs

Child- and family-based interventions

Schoolwide community interventions

Child emotional and behavioral problems

Ecological, multisystem perspective

Review Questions for Critical Thinking

1. How can we best assess how these emerging interventions will work with the population of children and families served by your organization/agency?
2. How do you bring a multisystems perspective in your assessment of the research and practice of what might work for children and families in your setting?
3. How do manuals, practice guidelines, and practice principles help replicate these interventions in diverse settings?
4. What might be some common elements that cross these EBPs presented in this chapter that can promote positive outcomes for a range of children and families experiencing emotional or behavioral challenges?
5. In what ways does understanding interventions that have worked in other settings guide your clinical decision-making and program-planning activities within your organization/agency?

Online Resources

www.bsft.org This is the main site for the *Brief Strategic Family Therapy Institute*. It contains information on this intervention, training, resource links, and evidence-informed data about its cost effectiveness.

www.familiesandschools.org This is the main website for *Families and Schools Together (FAST)*. This is an international program as well as one funded all over the United States. It presents evidence-informed practice as well as links about its values and efficacy.

www.mstservices.com *Multisystemic Therapy (MST)* is an intensive family- and community-based treatment program that focuses on the entire world of chronic and violent juvenile offenders—their homes and families, schools and teachers, neighborhoods, and friends. It provides information about evidence-informed practices using this method.

www.projectachieve.info *Project ACHIEVE* is an innovative, evidence-based school effectiveness and improvement program focusing on all students' academic, social, emotional, and behavioral progress and success. The program uses strategic planning, professional development, and on-site consultation and technical assistance to address student achievement, positive school and classroom climates, effective teaching and instruction, and parent and community outreach and involvement.

www.nrepp.samhsa.gov *NREPP* is a searchable online registry of more than 230 interventions supporting mental-health promotion, substance-abuse prevention, and mental-health and substance-abuse treatment. This is the SAMHSA National Registry of Evidence-Based and Promising Practices.

www.strengtheningfamiliesprogram.org *The Strengthening Families Program (SFP)* is a nationally and internationally recognized parenting and family-strengthening program for high-risk and regular families.

References

Allen-Meares, P. (2006). Where do we go from here? Mental health workers and the implementation of an evidence-based practice. In C. Franklin, M. B. Harris, & P. Allen-Meares (Eds.), *The school services sourcebook: A guide for school-based professionals* (pp. 1189–1194). New York, NY: Oxford University Press.

Barrett, P. M. (1998). Evaluation of cognitive-behavioral group treatments for childhood anxiety disorders. *Journal of Clinical Child Psychology*, *27*, 459–469.

Barrett, P. M., Lowry-Webster, H., & Turner, C. (2000). *FRIENDS program for children: Group leaders manual.* Brisbane, Australia: Australian Academic Press.

Barrett, P. M., & Shortt, A. L. (2003). Parental involvement in the treatment of anxious children. In A. E. Kazdin & J. R. Weisz (Eds.), *Evidence-based psychotherapies for children and adolescents* (pp. 101–119). New York, NY: Guilford Press.

Beidas, R., Benjamin, C. L., Puleo, C. M., Edmunds, J. M., & Kendall, P. C. (2010). Flexible applications of the Coping Cat Program for anxious youth. *Cognitive and Behavioral Practice*, *17*, 142–153.

Bronfenbrenner, U. (1986). Ecology of the family as a context to human development: Research perspectives. *Development Psychology*, *22*, 723–742.

Brook, J., McDonald, T. P., & Yan, Y. (2012). An analysis of the impact of the Strengthening Families program on family reunification in child welfare. *Child and Youth Services Review*, *34*, 691–695.

Chamberlain, P. (2002). Treatment foster care. In B. J. Burns & K. Hoagwood (Eds.), *Community treatment for youth: Evidence-based interventions for severe emotional and behavioral disorders* (pp. 117–138). New York, NY: Oxford University Press.

Chamberlain, P., & Reid, J. (1991). Using a specialized foster care treatment model for children and adolescents leaving the state mental hospital. *Journal of Community Psychology, 19,* 266–276.

Chamberlain, P., & Smith, D. K. (2003). Antisocial behavior in children and adolescents: The Oregon Multidimensional Treatment Foster Care Model. In A. E. Kazdin & J. R. Weisz (Eds.), *Evidence-based psychotherapies for children and adolescents* (pp. 282–300). New York, NY: Guilford Press.

Cohen, J., Berliner, L., & Mannarino, A. (2010). Trauma focused CBT for children with co-occurring trauma and behavior problems. *Child Abuse Neglect, 34*(4), 215–224.

Coie, J. D., Watt, N. F., West, S. G., Hawkins, J. D., Asarnow, J. R., Markman, H. J., & Long, B. (1993). The science of prevention: A conceptual framework and some directions for a national research program. *American Psychologist, 48,* 1013–1022.

Coote, S. (2000). *Families and Schools Together (FAST).* Paper presented at the conference reducing criminality: Partnerships and best practice, Australian Institute of Criminology, Perth, Australia.

Dishion, T. J., Bullock, B. M., & Granic, I. (2002). Pragmatism in modeling peer influence: Dynamics, outcomes, and change processes. *Development and Psychopathology, 14,* 969–981.

Dishion, T. J., Capaldi, D. M., & Yeager, K. (1999). Middle childhood antecedents to progressions in male adolescent substance use: An ecological analysis of risk and protection. *Journal of Adolescent Research, 14*(2), 175–205.

Duchnowski, A. J., Kutash, K., & Friedman, R. M. (2003). Community-based interventions in a system of care and outcomes framework. In B. J. Burns & K. Hoagwood (Eds.), *Community treatment for youth: Evidence-based interventions for severe emotional and behavioral disorders* (pp. 16–37). New York, NY: Oxford University Press.

Fischer, R. L. (2003). School-based family support: Evidence from an exploratory field study. *Families in Society, 84*(3), 339–347.

Fisher, P. A., & Chamberlain, P. (2000). Multidimensional treatment foster care: A program for intensive parenting, family support, and skill building. *Journal of Emotional and Behavioral Disorders, 8*(3), 155–164.

Fisher, P. A., Ellis, B. H., & Chamberlain, P. (1999). Early intervention foster care: A model for preventing risk in young children who have been maltreated. *Children Services: Social Policy, Research and Practice, 2*(3), 159–182.

Forgatch, M. S., Patterson, G. R., & DeGarmo, D. S. (2005). Evaluating fidelity: Predictive validity for a measure of competent adherence to the Oregon Model of Parent Management Training. *Behavior Therapy, 36,* 3–13.

Fraser, M. W. (2003). Intervention research in social work: A basis for evidence-based practice and practice guidelines. In A. Rosen & E. K. Proctor (Eds.), *Developing practice guidelines for social work intervention: Issues, methods and research agenda* (pp. 17–36). New York, NY: Columbia University Press.

Fraser, M. W. (2004). The ecology of childhood: A multisystems perspective. In M. W. Fraser (Ed.), *Risk and resilience in childhood: An ecological perspective* (2nd ed., pp. 1–12). Washington, DC: National Association of Social Workers Press.

Friesen, B. J., & Stephens, B. (1998). Expanded family roles in the system of care: Research and practice. In M. H. Epstein, K. Kutash, & A. J. Duchnowski (Eds.), *Outcomes for children and youth with behavioral and emotional disorders: Programs and evaluation best practices* (pp. 231–253). Austin, TX: ProEd.

Gambrill, E. (2003). Evidence-based practice: Implications for knowledge development and use in social work. In A. Rosen & E. K. Proctor (Eds.), *Developing practice guidelines for social work intervention: Issues, methods and research agenda* (pp. 37–58). New York, NY: Columbia University Press.

Garmezy, N. (1985). Stress-resistant children: The search for protective factors. In J. E. Stevenson (Ed.), *Recent research in developmental psychopathology* (pp. 213–233). Tarrytown, NY: Pergamon Press.

Hawkins, J. D., Catalano, R. F., & Miller, J. Y. (1992). Risk and protective factors for alcohol and other drug problems in adolescence and early adulthood: Implications for substance abuse prevention. *Psychological Bulletin, 112,* 64–105.

Henggeler, S., Letourneau, E., Chapman, J., Borduin, C., Schewe, P., & McCart, M. (2009). Mediators of change for multisystemic therapy with juvenile sexual offenders. *Journal of Consulting and Clinical Psychology, 77*(3), 451–462.

Henggeler, S. W., Schoenwald, S. K., Borduin, C. M., Rowland, M. D., & Cunningham, P. B. (1998). *Multisystemic treatment of antisocial behavior in children and adolescents.* New York, NY: Guilford Press.

Henggeler, S. W., Schoenwald, S. K., Rowland, M. D., & Cunningham, P. B. (2002). *Serious emotional disturbance in children and adolescents: Multisytemic therapy.* New York, NY: Guilford.

Hoagwood, K., Burns, B. J., Kiser, L., Ringeisen, H., & Schoenwald, S. K. (2001). Evidence-based practice in child and adolescent mental-health services. *Psychiatric Services, 52,* 1179–1189.

Holmbeck, G. N., Greenley, R. N., & Franks, E. A. (2003). Developmental issues and considerations in research and practice. In A. E. Kazdin & J. R. Weisz (Eds.), *Evidence-based psychotherapies for children and adolescents* (pp. 21–41). New York, NY: Guilford Press.

Huang, L., Stoul, B., Friedman, R., Mrazek, P., Frieson, B., Pires, S., & Mayberg, S. (2005). Transforming mental health care for children and families. *American Psychologist, 60*(6), 615–627.

Institute of Medicine (1990). *Guidelines for clinical practice: From development to use.* Washington, DC: National Academy Press.

Institute of Medicine, Committee on Quality of Health Care in America. (2001). *Crossing the quality chasm: A new health system for the 21st century.* Washington, DC: National Academy Press.

Kazak, A. E., Hoagwood, K., Weisz, J., Hood, K., Kratochwill, T., Vargas, L. A., & Banez, G. (2010). A meta-systems approach to evidence-based practice for children and adolescents. *American Psychologist, 65*(2), 85–97.

Kazdin, A. E. (1997). A model for developing effective treatments: Progression and interplay of theory, research, and practice. *Journal of Clinical Child Psychology, 26,* 114–129.

Kazdin, A. E. (2005). *Parent management training: Treatment for oppositional, aggressive and antisocial behavior in children and adolescents.* New York, NY: Oxford University Press.

Kendall, P. C., Flannery-Schroeder, E., Panichelli-Mindel, S. M., Southam-Gerwo, M., Henin, A., & Warman, M. (1997). Therapy for youths with anxiety disorders: A second randomized clinical trial. *Journal of Consulting and Clinical Psychology, 65,* 366–380.

Kirk, S. (1999). Good intentions are not enough: Practice guidelines for social work. *Research on Social Work Practice, 9,* 302–310.

Knoff, H. M. (2001). *The Stop and Think Social Skills Program (preschool, grade 1, grades 2/3, grades 4/5, middle school 6/8)*. Longmont, CO: Sopris West.

Knoff, H. M., & Batsche, G. M. (1995). Project ACHIEVE: Analyzing a school reform process for at-risk and underachieving students. *School Psychology Review, 24*(4), 579–603.

Knoff, H. M., Finch, C., & Carlyon, W. (2004). Project ACHIEVE and the development of school-wide positive behavioral self-management systems- prevention, intervention, and intensive needs approach. In K. E. Robinson (Ed.), *Advances in school-based mental health interventions: Vol. 19. Best practices and program models* (pp. 1–28). Kingston, NJ: Civic Research Institute.

Knox, L., Guerra, N., Williams, K. R., & Toro, R. (2011). Preventing children's aggression in immigrant latino families: A mixed methods evaluation of the Families and Schools Together program. *American Journal of Community Psychology, 48*, 65–76.

Kumpfer, K. L., & Alvardo, R. (2003). Family-strengthening approaches for the prevention of youth problem behaviors. *American Psychologist, 58*(6–7), 457–465.

Kumpfer, K. L., Alvardo, R., Tait, C., & Turner, C. (2002). Effectiveness of school-based family and children's skills training for substance abuse prevention among 6–8 year old rural children. *Psychology of Addictive Behaviors, 16*(4S), 565–571.

Littell, J. H., Popa, M., & Forsythe, B. (2005). Multisytemic therapy for social, emotional and behavioral problems in youth aged 10–17. *Cochrane Database of Systemic Reviews, 4*. Art. No: CD004797.pub4, DOI:10.1002/15671838.CD004797.pub4

Luthar, S. S. (1991). Vulnerability and resilience: A study of high-risk adolescents. *Child Development, 62*, 600–616.

Luthar, S. S., Cicchetti, D., & Becker, B. (2000). The construct of resilience: A critical evaluation and guidelines for future work. *Child Development, 71*(3), 543–562.

Lyons, J. S. (2004). *Redressing the emperor: Improving our children's public mental health system*. Westport, CT: Praeger.

McDonald, L., Billingham, S., Conrad, T., Morgan, A. O. N., & Payton, E. (1997). Families and Schools Together (FAST): Integrating community development with clinical strategies. *Families in Society, 78*(2), 140–155.

Mitchell, P. F. (2011) Evidence-based practice in real-world services for young people with complex needs: New opportunities suggested by recent implementation science. *Child and Youth Services Review, 33*, 207–216.

Molgaard, V., & Spoth, R. (2001). The Strengthening Families Program for Young Adolescents: Overview and outcomes. In S. I. Pfeiffer & L. A. Reddy (Eds.), *Innovative mental health interventions for children: Programs that work* (pp. 15–29). New York, NY: Haworth Press.

Nation, M., Crusto, C., Wandersman, A., Kumpfer, K. L., Seybolt, D., Morrissey-Kane, E., et al. (2003). What works in prevention: Principles of effective prevention programs. *American Psychologist, 58*(6–7), 449–456.

National Research Council and Institute of Medicine (2009). *Preventing mental, emotional and behavioral disorders among young people: Progress and possibilities*. Washington, DC: National Academies Press.

Neville, H. A., & Mobley, M. (2001). Social identities in contexts: An ecological model of multicultural counseling psychology processes. *Counseling Psychologist, 29*(4), 471–486.

New Freedom Commission on Mental Health (2003). *Achieving the promise: Transforming mental health care in America* (SMA 03–3832). Rockville, MD: Substance Abuse and Mental Health Administration.

Ogden, T., & Hagen, K. (2009). What works for whom? Gender differences in intake characteristics and treatment outcomes following multisystemic therapy. *Journal of Adolescence, 32*(6), 1425–1435.

Patient Protection and Affordable Care Act (2010). Public Law No. 11–148.

Patterson, G. R. (2004). Systematic changes in families following prevention trials. *Journal of Abnormal Child Psychology*. Retrieved from www.findarticles.com/p/articles/mi_m_0902/is_6_32/ai_n8590486/

Patterson, G. R. (2005). The next generation of PMTO models. *Behavior Therapist, 28*(2), 27–33.

Pollio, D. E. (2006). The art of evidence-based practice. *Research on Social Work Practice, 16*(2), 224–232.

Robbins, M. S., Szapocznik, J., Santisteban, D. A., Hervis, O. E., Mitrani, V. B., & Schwartz, S. J. (2003). Brief strategic family therapy for Hispanic youth. In A. E. Kazdin & J. R. Weisz (Eds.), *Evidence-based psychotherapies for children and adolescents* (pp. 407–424). New York, NY: Guilford Press.

Rosen, A., & Proctor, E. K. (2003). Practice guidelines and the challenge of effective practice. In A. Rosen & E. K. Proctor (Eds.), *Developing practice guidelines for social work intervention: Issues, methods and research agenda* (pp. 1–14). New York, NY: Columbia University Press.

Schoenwald, S. K., & Rowland, M. D. (2002). Multisystemic therapy. In B. J. Burns & K. Hoagwood (Eds.), *Community treatment for youth: Evidence-based interventions for severe emotional and behavioral disorders* (pp. 91–116). New York, NY: Oxford University Press.

Sexton, T., Chamberlin, P., Landsverk, J., Ortiz, A., & Schoenwald, S. (2010). Action brief: Future directions in the implementation of evidence based treatment and practices in child and adolescent mental health. *Administration and Policy in Mental Health and Mental Health Services Research, 37*(12), 132–134.

Sexton, T., & Kelley, S. (2010). Finding the common core: Evidence-based practices, clinically relevant evidence, and core mechanisms of change. *Administration and Policy in Mental Health and Mental Health Services Research, 37*(1–2), 81–88.

Sharts-Hopko, N. C. (2003). Evidence-based practice: What constitutes evidence? *Journal of the Association of Nurses in AIDS Care, 14*(3), 76.

Shortt, A. L., Barrett, P. M., & Fox, T. L. (2001). Evaluating the FRIENDS program: A cognitive-behavioral group treatment for anxious children and their parents. *Journal of Clinical Child Psychology, 30*, 525–535.

Soler, J. A., & Weatherall, R. (2005). Cognitive behavioural therapy for anxiety disorders in children and adolescents. *Cochrane Database of Systematic Reviews*, 4. Art. No: CD004690.pub2, DOI:10.1002/14651858.CD004690.pub2

Soydan, H., Nye, C., Chacon-Moscoso, S., Sanchez-Meca, J., & Almeida, C. (2005). Families and schools together (FAST) for improving outcomes of school-aged children and their families (Protocol). Cochrane Database of Systematic Reviews (Issue 2. Art. No CD005210).

Stallard, P. (2002). *Think good-feel good: A cognitive behaviour therapy workbook for children and young people.* Hoboken, NJ: Wiley.

Swenson, C. C., Henggeler, S. W., Taylor, I. S., & Addison, O. W. (2005). *Multisystemic therapy and neighborhood partnerships: Reducing adolescent violence and substance abuse.* New York, NY: Guilford Press.

Szapocznik, J., Hervis, O., & Schwartz, S. (2003). *Brief strategic family therapy for adolescent drug abuse.* (NIH Pub. No. 03–4751). Bethesda, MD: U.S. Department of Health and Human Services, National Institutes of Health, National Institute of Drug Abuse.

Szapocznik, J., & Kurtines, W. M. (1989). *Breakthroughs in family therapy with drug abusing and problem youth.* New York, NY: Springer.

U.S. Surgeon General. (1999). *Mental health: A report to the Surgeon General.* Washington, DC: Department of Health and Human Services.

U.S. Surgeon General. (2001). Report of the United States Surgeon General's Conference on children's mental health: A national action agenda. Washington, DC: Department of Health and Human Services.

Webster-Stratton, C. (1994). Advancing videotape parent training: A comparison study. *Journal of Consulting and Clinical Psychology, 62*(3), 583–593.

Webster-Stratton, C. (2001). The incredible years: Parents, teachers, and children training series. In S. I. Pfeiffer & L. A. Reddy (Eds.), *Innovative mental health interventions for children: Programs that work* (pp. 31–48). New York, NY: Haworth Press.

Chapter 3
Assessment of Adolescents

David W. Springer and Tara M. Powell

Purpose: This chapter provides an overview of assessment tools for adolescents, including methods of assessment, limitations of evidence-informed assessment tools, treatment goals, and implications for social work.

Rationale: To educate students and practitioners about appropriate assessment strategies and tools for adolescents.

How evidence-informed practice is presented: This chapter focuses on evidence used in assessments with adolescents, presenting options and strategies for choosing evidence-informed scales and assessment tools while considering such factors as a client's background, the clinical utility of the assessment tool, and treatment goals.

Overarching question: What is the acceptable protocol for choosing and implementing an assessment and treatment plan with adolescents?

"They love too much and hate too much, and the same with everything else. They think they know everything; and are always quite sure about it; this, in fact, is why they overdo everything." These words were written by Aristotle, the ancient Greek philosopher, more than 2,300 years ago (*Rhetoric, Book II*). Today's scientific study of adolescence can be traced back to the work of G. Stanley Hall (1904), who wrote a two-volume work on adolescence in which he proposes that adolescence is a separate stage of development. Now, fast-forward 100 years.

As recently as 2005, the *Journal of Clinical Child and Adolescent Psychology* devoted a special section on developing guidelines for the evidence-based assessment of child and adolescent disorders, where evidence-based assessment (EBA) is "intended to develop, elaborate, and identify the measurement strategies and procedures that have empirical support in their behalf" (Kazdin, 2005, p. 548). In this special issue on EBA, Mash and Hunsley (2005) emphasize the great importance of assessment as part of intervention but acknowledge that the development of EBA has not kept up with the increased emphasis on evidence-based treatment. In fact, there is a significant disconnect between EBA and evidence-based treatment. This is no small problem for those in the field. Several studies spanning different geographical locations (such as the United States, Puerto Rico, Canada, and New Zealand) have produced consistent results on the prevalence of disorders among children and adolescents, with estimates indicating that 17% to 22% suffer significant developmental, emotional, or behavioral problems (U.S. Congress, 1991; World Health Organization [WHO], 2004; as cited in Kazdin & Weisz, 2003).

The developmental tasks associated with adolescence only serve to complicate matters, because the practitioner must take into account many interrelated domains of the adolescent's life. Some behaviors may be considered quite normal at one age but later cross a threshold that suggests mental illness or impairment in functioning. In addition to the importance placed on recognizing the developmental tasks of adolescence during the assessment process, this chapter adopts the assumptions about assessment presented by Jordan and Franklin (1995): ''(1) assessment is empirically based, (2) assessment must be made from a systems perspective, (3) measurement is essential, (4) ethical practitioners evaluate their clinical work, and (5) well-qualified practitioners are knowledgeable about numerous assessment methods in developing assessments'' (p. 3). These assumptions serve as a guide for social workers when determining what type of assessment protocol to implement with adolescents (and their families).

Assessment is the first active phase of treatment (Springer, McNeece, & Arnold, 2003). Without a thorough and complete assessment, the social worker cannot develop a treatment plan that will serve the youth and his or her family. In this chapter, various methods of assessment, such as interviews and the use of standardized instruments that may be useful in assessment with adolescents, are reviewed. For a more comprehensive review of assessment methods and tools for youth, see other excellent sources, including a compilation of rapid-assessment instruments for children and families (K. Corcoran & Fischer, 2007), an overview of tools and methods for assessment with children and adolescents (Shaffer, Lucas, & Richters, 1999b), and a guide to empirically based measures of school behavior (Kelley, Reitman, & Noell, 2003; Roberts & Greene, 2009). The special section of *Journal of Clinical Child and Adolescent Psychology* referred to earlier is another excellent resource, as it examines the EBA of pediatric bipolar disorder (Youngstrom, Findling, Youngstrom, & Calabrese, 2005), anxiety disorders (Silverman & Ollendick, 2005), depression (Klein, Dougherty, & Olino, 2005), Attention-Deficit/Hyperactivity Disorder (ADHD; Pelham, Fabiano, & Massetti, 2005), conduct problems (McMahon & Frick, 2005), learning disabilities (Fletcher, Francis, Morris, & Lyon, 2005), and autism-spectrum disorders (Ozonoff, Goodlin-Jones, & Solomon, 2005).

After reviewing each of the articles in the special issue mentioned earlier, Kazdin (2005, p. 549) provided a commentary where he identifies common themes in child and adolescent clinical assessment:

1. There is no gold standard to validate assessment.
2. Multiple measures need to be used to capture diverse facets of the clinical problem.
3. Multiple disorders or symptoms from different disorders ought to be measured because of high rates of comorbidity.

4. Multiple informants are needed to obtain information from different perspectives and from different contexts.

5. Adaptive functioning, impairment, or, more generally, how individuals are doing in their everyday lives are important to assess and are separate from symptoms and disorders.

6. Influences (or moderators) of performance need to be considered for interpreting the measures, including sex, age, developmental level, culture, and ethnicity, among others.

These themes are certainly critical to the assessment of adolescents and will be revisited throughout the remainder of the chapter.

Evidence-Based Assessment With Adolescents

There are various methods of assessment available to social work practitioners that can be used with adolescents. These include, but are not limited to, interviews, self-observation, observation by others, family sculpting, individualized rating scales, rapid-assessment instruments, and standardized assessment tools. The focus of this chapter is primarily on the use of standardized assessment tools and interviews with adolescents.

Interviews

The assessment process typically starts with a face-to-face interview (e.g., psychosocial history) with the adolescent. The family should also be involved for at least part of this interview. The interview serves several purposes, such as an opportunity to establish rapport with the client and allow the client to tell his or her story. Recall that one key assumption of conducting a good assessment is to operate from a systems perspective. Involving the family during part of the interview may help meet this goal, because family members provide varying perspectives and are more often than not a key factor in an adolescent's life.

Morrison and Anders (1999) have written a useful book on interviewing children and adolescents in which they advocate for a blended interviewing style that uses both directive and nondirective techniques:

> In general, nondirective, open-ended style of questioning is important during the early stages of an initial interview, when you want to give the respondent greatest leeway to volunteer important observations concerning the child's or adolescent's behavior and emotional life. Later on, as you come to understand the scope of your respondent's concerns, use questions that require short answers to increase the depth of your knowledge.
>
> —(p. 20)

Consider the following case for illustration purposes. Ramon, a 16-year-old Hispanic male who has been diagnosed with ADHD and oppositional defiant disorder (ODD), is brought into an agency by his parents, because he is "failing 11th-grade Spanish and precalculus, and he won't listen." Ramon also has threatened to run away from home on more than one occasion. In addition to obtaining information from Ramon's parents that is typically covered in a psychosocial history (e.g., medical, developmental, social, and family history), some areas that the social worker may cover with Ramon's parents during an initial interview are as follows:

- Presenting problem and specific precipitating factor (e.g., Tell me in your own words what prompted you to bring Ramon in for help at this point in time?)
- Attempts to deal with the problem (e.g., What has your family done to try to deal with this problem(s)? What have you tried that has worked?)
- Hopes and expectations (e.g., What do you hope to get out of coming here for services? If you could change any one thing about how things are at home, what would it be?)

In addition to these areas (with variations of the corresponding sample questions), consider some topics that the social worker may ask Ramon about individually:

- Peer relationships (e.g., Tell me about your friends. What do you like to do together?)
- School (e.g., What are your favorite [and least favorite] classes at school? What about those classes do you like [not like]?)
- Suicide risk (e.g., When you feel down, do you ever have any thoughts of hurting/killing yourself? Do you ever wish you were dead? How would you end your life?)
- Substance use (e.g., What do you drink/use? When was the last time you had a drink/used? How much did you have? Have you ever unsuccessfully tried to reduce your substance use?)
- Targeted behavior/goal setting (e.g., If there was any thing that you could change about yourself/your life, what would it be? What do you like most about yourself?)

These questions are meant only to illustrate the range of questions that a social worker might ask during an interview. A complete psychosocial history would need to be conducted with Ramon.

J. Corcoran and Springer (2005) emphasize a strengths-and-skills-based approach to engage the adolescent client in the treatment process. This approach pulls primarily from solution-focused therapy, motivational interviewing, and cognitive-behavioral therapy. Youths, especially those with externalizing behavioral disorders, like Ramon, have often experienced a range of life stressors, such as poverty, overcrowded living conditions, parental divorce, incarceration of parents, community violence, and parental substance use. The practitioner's attempt to explore the adolescent's feelings and thoughts around such issues is often met with resistance. Rather than getting into a struggle with adolescents or trying to push them in a certain direction, the strengths-and-skills-based approach underscores building on strengths and past successes rather than correcting past failures and mistakes. Accordingly, the interviewer focuses on positives and solutions over negative histories and problems. Consider some of the following interviewing tips provided by J. Corcoran and Springer (2005, p. 136).

They propose the following options for dealing with the "I don't know" stance that adolescents take:

1. Allow silence (about 20–30 seconds).
2. Rephrase the question.
3. Ask a relationship question (adolescents sometimes feel put on the spot by having to answer questions about themselves but can take the perspective of others to view their behavior).
4. Say, "I know you don't know, so just make it up," which bypasses teens' resistance or fear that they don't know or don't have the right answer. Or, using presuppositional language, say, "Suppose you did know...."
5. Speak hypothetically about others: "What would (prosocial peers that teens respect) say they do to keep out of trouble (get passing grades or get along with their parents')?"

J. Corcoran and Springer (2005) go on to point out that asking evocative questions may help adolescent clients increase their readiness for change, and they provide a recommended line of questioning to explore the disadvantages of the status quo (e.g., "What difficulties or hassles have you had in relation to _____?" "What is there about _____ that you or other people might see as reasons for concern?") as well as the advantages of change (e.g., "What would you like your life to be like 5 years from now?" "If you could make this change immediately, by magic, how might things be better for you?" "What would be the advantages of making this change?").

Such social workers as Saleebey (1997), Clark (1998), and Lerner (2009) recommend that practitioners incorporate a strengths-based perspective into their assessment approach with adolescents. Cowger (1997, pp. 69–71) proposes specific exemplars for assessment of client strengths in five areas:

1. Cognition (e.g., is open to different ways of thinking about things).
2. Emotion (e.g., is positive about life).
3. Motivation (e.g., wants to improve current and future situations).

4. Coping (e.g., has dealt successfully with related problem in the past).
5. Interpersonal (e.g., makes sacrifices for friends, family members, and others).

For the complete list of exemplars, see Cowger (1997). Indeed, a thorough assessment includes a deliberate examination of the client's unique strengths that in turn can be amplified over the course of treatment.

In addition to these interviewing strategies, more structured and systematic interview protocols for use with adolescents are also available to practitioners. The Diagnostic Interview Schedule for Children (DISC) is one such interview.

The Voice Diagnostic Interview Schedule for Children

The Diagnostic Interview Schedule for Children (DISC) is a computerized respondent-based interview that assesses more than 30 common diagnoses found among children and adolescents, including anxiety disorders, eating disorders, mood disorders, attention-deficit and disruptive behavior disorders, and substance-use disorders (Shaffer, Fisher, & Lucas, 1999a; Shaffer, Fisher, Lucas, Dulcan, & Schwab-Stone, 2000). It was developed to be compatible with the *DSM-IV, DSM-III-R,* and the *International Classification of Diseases* (ICD-10) and is organized into six diagnostic modules that measure the major Axis I disorders and impairment. The DISC-IV includes assessment for three time frames—the present (past 4 weeks), the last year, and ever—with parallel versions existing for youth ages 9 to 17 (DISC-Y) and for parents or caretakers of youth ages 6 to 17 years (DISC-P). The present-state assessment is considered to be the most accurate, because it minimizes the risk of bias due to telescoping (Shaffer et al., 1999a). The DISC-IV is scored by algorithms that apply Boolean logic (i.e., "and" and "or") to combine answers to component questions and is "an ideal candidate for computerization, given the highly structured nature of the interview, the limited response options, the complicated branching and skipping instructions, and the need for the interviewer to keep close track of an informant's answers to numerous symptoms in order to ask onset and impairment questions correctly" (Shaffer et al., 1999a, p. 23). A recent voice adaptation allows youth to hear the interview over headphones (while also reading questions on the computer screen) and key in responses via computer.

The Center for the Promotion of Mental Health in Juvenile Justice at Columbia University is spearheading efforts to administer the voice version of the DISC-IV. It has already been tested in three states (Illinois, South Carolina, and New Jersey) with youth recently admitted to juvenile-correction institutions, with the primary aims to more accurately assess rates of mental-health disorders among incarcerated juveniles and to test the feasibility of using this type of structured, self-administered mental-health assessment with this population (Ko & Wasserman, 2002). The Voice DISC-IV provides a "provisional" diagnosis for youth assessed. Findings from initial feasibility studies indicate that the instrument is tolerated well by youth, parents, and agency staff and support its validity, revealing that information on psychiatric status matches existing justice-system information regarding current substance offenses (Wasserman, McReynolds, Lucas, Fisher, & Santos, 2002b). Adaptations for detention, correctional, and community juvenile-justice sites are ongoing in 10 other states. The DISC-IV has also been translated into a Spanish version (Bravo et al., 2001).

For sites that are willing and capable, the Center for the Promotion of Mental Health in Juvenile Justice will provide the Voice DISC-IV assessment software program, provide training for key personnel, offer ongoing technical support via phone and e-mail, assist with data interpretation and preparation of reports/presentations, and provide guidelines for appropriate mental-health referral. For more detailed information, see www.promotementalhealth.org/voicedisc.htm

Information gathered from the face-to-face interview can subsequently be used to inform a more in-depth assessment in targeted areas, which, in turn, guides treatment planning. Rapid assessment instruments and other standardized assessment protocols may prove useful for this purpose.

Rapid-Assessment Instruments and Standardized Assessment Tools

Rapid-assessment instruments (RAIs; Levitt & Reid, 1981) are short-form, pencil-and-paper assessment tools that are used to assess and measure change for a broad spectrum of client problems (Bloom, Fischer, & Orme, 2006; K. Corcoran & Fischer, 2007; Hudson, 1982). RAIs are used as a method of empirical assessment, are easy to administer and score, are typically completed by the client, and can help monitor client functioning over time. Given the proliferation of RAIs and standardized tools in recent years that measure various areas of adolescent functioning, it can be an overwhelming task to select a tool for use with an individual client. Thus, some guidelines are provided next.

The social worker practitioner needs to take several factors into consideration when choosing an RAI or standardized protocol for use with clients, such as the tool's reliability, validity, clinical utility, directness, availability, and so on (K. Corcoran & Fischer, 2007). To the extent that an RAI has sound psychometric properties, it helps practitioners measure a client's problem consistently (reliability) and accurately (validity). Using reliable and valid tools becomes increasingly critical as one considers the complexities surrounding assessment with adolescents who (potentially) have comorbid disorders. A brief overview of reliability and validity is provided next; however, the reader is referred to the following sources for a more detailed exposition on these topics: K. Corcoran & Fischer, 2007; Crocker & Algina, 1986; Hudson, 1982; Nunnally & Bernstein, 1994; Springer, Abell, & Hudson, 2002a; Springer, Abell, & Nugent, 2002b; Abell, Springer, & Kamata 2009.

Reliability

A measurement instrument is reliable to the extent that it consistently yields similar results over repeated and independent administrations. A tool's reliability is represented through reliability coefficients, which range from 0.0 to 1.0. What constitutes a satisfactory level of reliability depends on how a measure is to be used. For use in research studies and scientific work, a reliability coefficient of 0.60 or greater is typically considered acceptable (Hudson, 1982). However, for use in guiding decision making with individual clients, a higher coefficient is needed. Springer et al. (2002b) provide the following guidelines for acceptability of reliability coefficients for use with individual clients to aid in clinical decision making:

$$<0.70 = \text{Unacceptable}$$
$$0.70 \text{ to } 0.79 = \text{Undesirable}$$
$$0.80 \text{ to } 0.84 = \text{Minimally acceptable}$$
$$0.85 \text{ to } 0.89 = \text{Respectable}$$
$$0.90 \text{ to } 0.95 = \text{Very good}$$
$$>0.95 = \text{Excellent}$$

The greater the seriousness of the problem being measured (e.g., suicidal risk) and the graver the risk of making a wrong decision about a client's level of functioning, the higher the standard that should be adopted.

Validity

Where reliability represents an instrument's degree of consistency, validity represents how accurately an instrument measures what it is supposed to measure. There are various ways to determine an instrument's validity: content validity (which subsumes face validity), criterion-related validity (concurrent and predictive), and construct validity (convergent and discriminant).

The social worker must make decisions about a measure's validity in relationship to its intended use. In other words, the social worker must determine whether the measure is valid for that particular client in a particular setting at a given time. A measure may be valid for one client but not for another.

Additional Considerations in Selecting Scales

Age and Readability

Practitioners must take into consideration the client's age and reading ability when selecting a scale. Scales are developed, validated, and normed for an intended population and for specific uses. If a scale is developed for use with adult clients, and a practitioner administers the scale to a

13-year-old client with a fifth-grade reading level, then this scale is not being administered properly, and the results obtained from the scale are potentially meaningless and clinically irrelevant.

Ethnic and Cultural Diversity

A second consideration is to fully respect a client's ethnic and cultural background when using scales in practice. Ethnicity and culture affect all aspects of an adolescent's life, and acculturation experiences among minority youth can also have a significant impact on a youth's development and functioning (Jordan & Hickerson, 2003).

For example, consider the following challenges associated with assessing substance-abusing adolescents. An increasingly important issue in adolescent substance-abuse treatment is "amenability to treatment," which concerns the identification of subgroups of individuals in a target population who are likely to be the most amenable or responsive to a treatment (i.e., what interventions work for whom under what conditions; Kazdin, 1995). Family influences on substance use may be particularly profound for Latino and African American youth due to important ethnic variations in family rules and monitoring of children in relation to risk behaviors, such as substance use. In fact, some research suggests that these variations may decrease risk behaviors among Latino and African American youth (Catalano, Hawkins, & Krenz, 1993; Li, Fiegelman, & Stanton, 2000; Vega & Gil, 1998). The Latino preference for close family proximity may result in vulnerability when emigration from the country of origin causes family disruption (Vega, 1990). Moreover, there is evidence that traditional familial values can serve as a protective factor mitigating against adolescent maladjustment (Vega, Gil, Warheit, Zimmerman, & Apospori, 1993). Gil, Wagner, and Vega (2000) have shown that the loss of familism and parental respect that accompanies greater acculturation among Latino adolescents has negative impacts on predispositions toward deviant behaviors and alcohol use. So, although it seems clear that ethnicity and acculturation are likely to impact multiple aspects of the substance-abuse treatment process (Collins, 1993), there is a paucity of knowledge about the assessment (and subsequent treatment) of substance use among ethnic minorities (Cowan, 2009).

Additionally, standardized measurement instruments may be biased against certain ethnic and cultural groups. For example, Mercer (1979) has documented that African American children routinely scored 10 points lower than European American children on the Weschler Intelligence Scale for Children—Revised (WISC-R), indicating a cultural bias in the WISC-R when administering it to African-American children. Practitioners should exercise cultural sensitivity throughout the assessment and treatment process with clients.

Overall Clinical Utility

In addition to these factors, the overall clinical utility of a scale refers to several factors. Is the scale sensitive to changes in client functioning over time? Are the items direct and easy to understand? Is the length of the scale appropriate given its intended use by the practitioner? Lengthy scales may not be appropriate to administer in crisis situations, for example. Is the scale accessible at a reasonable cost? In addition to examining a scale's psychometric properties, these are all factors that must be considered when selecting a scale for use with a given population in a given setting.

The number of standardized tools developed specifically for use with adolescents has grown considerably in recent years, and it is impossible to review them all here. However, selected standardized tools that may be useful in assessing for comorbid disorders in adolescents are briefly reviewed next. Each tool reviewed has sound psychometric properties and can be used to help guide treatment planning and to monitor client progress over the course of treatment.

Problem Oriented Screening Instrument for Teenagers

The Problem Oriented Screening Instrument for Teenagers (POSIT) was developed by a panel of experts as part of the comprehensive Adolescent Assessment/Referral System (AARS) for use with 12- to 19-year-olds (Rahdert, 1991). The POSIT is a 139-item, self-administered tool. Items are measured on a dichotomous (yes/no) scale. The POSIT is intended to be used as a screening tool. It is not designed to measure treatment progress or outcomes. A more complete diagnostic evaluation requires that the practitioner implement another component of the AARS, called the Comprehensive Assessment Battery (CAB). The POSIT provides independent scores in 10 areas of functioning: substance use/abuse, physical health, mental health, family relations, peer relations, educational status, vocational status, social skills, leisure/recreation, and aggressive behavior and delinquency. The National Clearinghouse for Alcohol and Drug Information (NCADI) offers the AARS (National Institute on Drug Abuse [NIDA], 1991, DHHS Publication No. ADM 91-1735), which contains the POSIT, free of charge. (Contact NCADI, P.O. Box 2345, Rockville, MD 20847; 800-729-6686.)

Drug Use Screening Inventory–Revised

The Drug Use Screening Inventory—Revised (DUSI-R; Tarter & Hegedus, 1991) is a 159-item multidimensional pencil-and-paper instrument measured on a dichotomous (yes/no) scale that has recently been created to assess the severity of problems of adolescents and adults. Like the Addiction Severity Index (ASI; McLellan et al., 1985) and the POSIT (Rahdert, 1991), this instrument addresses areas in addition to substance abuse. The 10 domains of the DUSI-R are drug and alcohol use, behavior patterns, health status, psychiatric disorders, social competence, family system, school performance/adjustment, work adjustment, peer relationships, and leisure/recreation. A "lie scale" documents reporting validity. The information obtained from the completed DUSI-R can be used to develop an individualized treatment plan; however, scores do not indicate specific types of treatment needed. That decision is left to the clinical judgment of the practitioner. The instrument's developers report that it is able to identify adolescents (and adults) with *DSM-IV* substance-use disorders, including those with and without psychiatric disorders. In a sample of 191 adolescents with alcohol- and drug-abuse problems, internal reliability coefficients averaged 0.74 for males and 0.78 for females across the 10 life-problem areas. In a sample of polysubstance-abusing adolescents, the mean test-retest coefficients (1 week) were 0.95 for males and 0.88 for females (NIDA, 1994).

The DUSI-R is available from Ralph Tarter, Department of Pharmaceutical Sciences, University of Pittsburgh, School of Pharmacy, 711 Salk Hall, Pittsburgh, PA 15261. The instrument is copyrighted and is available in two formats: (1) paper questionnaire for manual scoring ($3 each) and (2) computer administration and scoring system ($495).

Child and Adolescent Functional Assessment Scale

The Child and Adolescent Functional Assessment Scale (CAFAS; Hodges, 2000) is a popular standardized multidimensional assessment tool that is used to measure the extent to which a youth's (ages 7–17) mental-health or substance-use disorder impairs functioning. It is completed by the practitioner and requires specialized training. Like the POSIT, a major benefit of the CAFAS in helping practitioners determine a youth's overall level of functioning is that it covers eight areas: school/work, home, community, behavior toward others, moods/emotions, self-harmful behavior, substance use, and thinking. The youth's level of functioning in each domain is then scored as severe, moderate, mild, or minimal. Additionally, an overall score can be computed. These scores can be graphically depicted on a one-page scoring sheet that provides a profile of the youth's functioning. This makes it easy to track progress over the course of treatment. The CAFAS also contains optional strengths-based and goal-oriented items (e.g., good behavior in classroom, obeys curfew) that are not used in scoring but are helpful in guiding treatment planning.

The psychometric properties of the CAFAS have been demonstrated in numerous studies (Hodges & Cheong-Seok, 2000; Hodges & Wong, 1996). One study on the predictive validity of the CAFAS indicates that this scale is able to predict recidivism in juvenile delinquents (Hodges & Cheong-Seok, 2000). Higher scores on the CAFAS are associated with previous psychiatric hospitalization, serious psychiatric diagnoses, below-average school performance and attendance, and contact with law enforcement (Hodges, Doucette-Gates, & Oinghong, 1999). The CAFAS is available for purchase online at http://www.fasoutcomes.com/Content.aspx?ContentID=19

The CAFAS would be a useful assessment tool to use with a client like Ramon, who presents with impaired functioning in multiple areas, to help monitor treatment progress.

Table 3.1   Ramon's CAFAS Scores: Intake and Termination

CAFAS Domain	Intake	Termination
School/work	30	10
Home	30	10
Community	30	0
Behavior toward others	30	10
Moods/emotions	20	10
Self-harmful behavior	0	0
Substance use	30	10
Thinking	10	0
Overall functioning	180	50

Based on the scores for each domain (see Table 3.1), Ramon's impairment in functioning could be interpreted as follows: severe (score of 30), moderate (score of 20), mild (score of 10), or minimal (score of 0). The overall scores can also be computed as severe (140 to 240), marked (100 to 130), moderate (50 to 90), mild (20 to 40), or minimal to no (0 to 10) impairment in functioning. Using these clinical cutting scores, the CAFAS results indicate that Ramon made clinically meaningful progress over the course of treatment, moving from "severe impairment in functioning" at intake to the low range of "moderate impairment in functioning" at termination.

The Substance Abuse Subtle Screening Inventory for Adolescents

The Substance Abuse Subtle Screening Inventory (SASSI; Miller, 1985; Miller, Miller, Roberts, Brooks, & Lazowski, 1997) is a 67-item pencil-and-paper instrument. There is also an updated adolescent version of the SASSI, referred to as the SASSI-A2, which is composed of 32 new items and 40 true/false items from the original adolescent version of the SASSI. The SASSI-A2 has been empirically validated as a screening tool for both substance dependence and substance abuse among adolescents, based on a sample of adolescents ($n = 2,326$) from treatment and criminal-justice programs. Like the SASSI, an appealing feature of the SASSI-A2 is that it contains both face-valid items that directly address alcohol and drug use and subtle true/false items that do not inquire directly about alcohol or drug use. Administering the subtle true/false items to an adolescent client before the more direct items related to alcohol and drug use may help minimize defensiveness and lead to more accurate responses. Research findings revealed that 95% of adolescents with a substance-use disorder were correctly identified with a "high probability" result in the SASSI-A2 decision rule, whereas 89% of adolescents without a substance-use disorder were correctly classified with a "low probability" decision rule. (All the SASSI instruments are available from the SASSI Institute at www.sassi.com or 800-726-0526.)

Adolescent Concerns Evaluation

The Adolescent Concerns Evaluation (ACE; Springer, 1998), a 40-item, multidimensional rapid-assessment instrument, measures the degree to which a youth may be at risk of running away (see Table 3.2). Items are scored on a 5-point Likert scale, and there are four separate yet interdependent domains: family, which addresses the youth's perception of relations and functioning of his or her family; school, which addresses the youth's self-esteem as it relates to school; peer, which addresses the youth's self-esteem as it relates to his or her peer relations; and individual, which addresses the youth's level of depression. The relevant literature on runaway youth, the ecological perspective (Germain & Gitterman, 1980), and the domain sampling model of measurement (Nunnally & Bernstein, 1994) provided the theoretical framework for the development of the ACE.

Participants in the validation study consisted of a clinical (youth at a runaway shelter; $n = 110$) and a nonclinical (students in grades 6 through 12, $n = 117$) sample. Each domain has excellent alpha and SEM values—Family (alpha = 0.9497, SEM = 0.206); School (alpha = 0.8884, SEM = 0.265); Peer (alpha = 0.9048, SEM = 0.222); and Individual (alpha = 0.9491, SEM = 0.214)—indicating excellent internal consistency and low error for each domain. The ACE has excellent known-groups validity, discriminating significantly ($a = 0.05$) between members of the clinical and nonclinical samples (Family Eta = 0.656, School Eta = 0.630, Peer Eta = 0.528, Individual Eta = 0.610). There is evidence of factorial validity using the Multiple Groups Method (Nunnally & Bernstein, 1994) as well as convergent and discriminant construct validity. The ACE performed very well in a discriminant-function analysis, often (87% of the time) classifying subjects correctly. The ACE is available for use from the chapter author at no cost from dwspringer@mail.utexas.edu

The ACE is scored by summing the item scores in each domain and collectively. After the client has completed the ACE, the practitioner reverse scores the items listed at the bottom of the ACE (2, 3, 5, 8, 11, 12, 13, 17, 18, 22, 24, 27, 28, 34, 36, 37). For example, if Ramon rated item 2 ("My mother and I get along well") with a score of 4 (agree), the practitioner would recode it as a 2 (disagree). Higher scores reflect a higher risk of running away. The possible range of scores for each domain on the ACE is listed in Table 3.3.

Ramon was potentially at risk of running away from home due to conflict with his parents and as indicated by his repeated verbal threats to run away. Accordingly, it would be appropriate for the social worker to administer the ACE to Ramon at the beginning of treatment to assess his risk of running away. Of course, the social worker would also want to administer the ACE to Ramon throughout the course of treatment to determine whether this risk increased, decreased, or stayed the same. Ramon's scores on the ACE (see Table 3.4) reveal that, over the course of treatment, his risk of running away decreased considerably.

Table 3.2   Adolescent Concerns Evaluation (ACE)

Name: _____   **Today's Date:** _____

This questionnaire is designed to measure how you see the world around you. Since these are your personal views, there are no right or wrong answers. Please answer as honestly as possible. Some items ask about relationships with parents. If you are not living with a parent, then for those items think about your primary adult caretaker(s).

Please rate how strongly you agree or disagree with each statement by placing a number beside each one as follows:

1 = strongly disagree
2 = disagree
3 = neither agree nor disagree
4 = agree
5 = strongly agree

First, think about your family life.

_____ I am not comfortable talking to my parents about my problems.
_____ My mother and I get along well.
_____ My father and I get along well.
_____ My parents do not understand me.
_____ I enjoy spending time with my family.
_____ I do not feel safe at home.
_____ I am not listened to in my family.
_____ My feelings are respected in my family.
_____ My parents demand too much from me.
_____ The rules in my family are not fair.
_____ I feel my parents trust me.
_____ All in all, I like my family.

Now, think about your experiences with school.

_____ I have good relationships with my teachers.
_____ My teachers are hard on me.
_____ I get into trouble at school.
_____ School is easier for other people than it is for me.
_____ Finishing high school is important to me.
_____ School is helping me prepare for my future.
_____ I am not usually happy with my grades.
_____ My friends generally do not go to school.
_____ I do not enjoy school.

Now, think about your experiences with your peers.

_____ I am well liked by my peers.
_____ I do not fit in with my peers.
_____ My peers seem to respect me.
_____ I do not feel like part of the group.
_____ My parents do not approve of my peers.
_____ My peers seem to care about me.
_____ I have a lot of fun with my peers.

(continued)

Table 3.2 (*Continued*)

Finally, think about your feelings about your life.

_____ I feel depressed a lot of the time.

_____ I feel hopeless about my situation.

_____ I think about suicide.

_____ I feel worthless.

_____ I can't do anything right.

_____ I handle my problems well.

_____ I feel trapped.

_____ I feel good about myself.

_____ I deal well with stress.

_____ I feel angry a lot of the time.

_____ I do not feel like I have control over my life.

_____ I feel that others would be glad if I wasn't around.

Table 3.3 Scoring the ACE

ACE Domain	Range of Scores
Family domain	12 to 60
School domain	9 to 45
Peer domain	7 to 35
Individual domain	12 to 60
Overall score	40 to 200

Table 3.4 Ramon's ACE Scores

ACE Domain	Intake	Termination
Family domain	55	20
School domain	35	15
Peer domain	30	12
Individual domain	45	15
Overall score	165	62

Additional Rapid-Assessment Instruments

In addition to the standardized tools reviewed, there are numerous RAIs that can be used with adolescents to measure functioning across various areas, such as suicidal tendencies (e.g., Multi-Attitude Suicide Tendency Scale), conduct-problem behaviors (e.g., Eyeberg Child Behavior Checklist), family functioning (e.g., Family Assessment Device, Index of Family Relations), and peer relations (Index of Peer Relations), to name just a few (K. Corcoran & Fischer, 2007). There are also standardized general-behavior rating scales (e.g., Louisville Behavior Checklist, Child Behavior

Checklist, and Conners Rating Scales) and tools that are useful for measuring the degree of functional impairment (e.g., Children's Global Assessment Scale; Shaffer et al., 1999b).

Having provided an overview of standardized assessment tools, a word of caution is in order. Recall Kazdin's (2005) common themes listed earlier in the chapter, where he underscores the notion that multiple measures need to be used to capture diverse facets of the clinical problem and that multiple informants are needed to obtain information from different perspectives and different contexts. It is ill-advised for a practitioner to rely solely on self-report measures when determining diagnostic impressions and a course of treatment for youth. Youth can easily present themselves as they wish to be perceived by others on such measures. Thus, clinical decisions should be supplemented by a thorough psychosocial history (which should include information gathered from external sources, such as parents, physicians, and teachers when at all possible), a mental status exam (when appropriate), and direct observation of the client. Indeed, there exists no gold standard of assessment with adolescents.

Limitations of Evidence-Based Assessment With Adolescents

Mash and Hunsley (2005) note that most practitioners routinely use traditional and accepted forms of assessment, even though very little evidence exists for the clinical utility of the measures. That is, although assessment measures are frequently evaluated for their psychometric criteria (reliable and valid), they are rarely examined for their applied value and accuracy in assessing the clinical populations they are intended to measure.

Understanding EBA for adolescents is especially daunting, given the multifaceted nature of assessment with youth, including developmental issues and the role of family and peer groups. Assessing adolescents with comorbid disorders only adds to these complexities, amplifying the conceptual soup surrounding systematic assessment of youth with multifaceted presenting problems. The terms *comorbid disorders* and *coexisting disorders* are frequently used interchangeably to describe adolescents who have two or more coexisting diagnoses on Axis I or Axis II of the *DSM-IV-TR* (American Psychiatric Association, 2000), whereas the term *dual diagnosis* is often reserved to refer to clients with at least one Axis I diagnosis and a substance-abuse problem. Approximately half of all adolescents who receive mental-health services have coexisting substance-abuse problems; common coexisting disorders are depression, conduct disorder, and ADHD (McBride, VanderWaal, Terry, & VanBuren, 1999).

Given the prevalence of coexisting disorders in clinical settings and the seriousness of making false-positive or false-negative diagnoses, it is critical that social work practitioners assess for the presence of comorbid disorders in a deliberate manner rather than making "on the spot" diagnoses. A social worker's assessment often helps guide treatment planning. Misdiagnosing an adolescent as not having (or having) a certain set of problems (e.g., mistaking acting-out behaviors related to poverty as conduct disorder, confusing symptoms of ADHD with pediatric bipolar disorder) can pose serious consequences for the course of treatment (e.g., the wrong medications may be prescribed, adolescents and their families may be turned off to treatment because of repeated treatment "failures"). Unfortunately, in many respects, our methods of assessment for youth with comorbid disorders are not as sophisticated as the adolescents that we're treating.

More generally speaking, standardized assessment measures have many strengths: They are quick and efficient to use, they are easy to score and interpret, and they provide other sources of data than can be gained in a client interview in that they measure or screen for specific client problems or characteristics. Yet, these measures do have some practical weaknesses other than possible limitations in their psychometric properties. Springer and Franklin (2003) identify the following limitations.

First, standardized assessment measures are subject to demand characteristics or social desirability. Clients may answer the questions on the measure to cast themselves in a favorable or unfavorable light.

Second, most rapid-assessment instruments present a narrow band of information and are not able to assess the whole client picture. Critics believe the measures have limited usefulness, because they treat characteristics of clients as if they are static instead of forever changing in response to environmental contingencies.

Third, standardized measures have been criticized for focusing on client problems instead of strengths. In this regard, standardized methods are believed to pathologize clients without pointing to their unique motivations and capacities. Some assessment measures, however, have begun to include scales on coping abilities or problem solving. For example, the *Behavioral and Emotional Rating Scale*, second edition (BERS-2; Epstein, 2004), is a strength-based battery of three instruments that measures functioning in youth across five different areas: interpersonal strength, family involvement, intrapersonal strength, school functioning, and affective strength. A key feature that distinguishes the BERS-2 from other standardized tools (e.g., Achenbach's widely used Child Behavior Checklist [CBCL]) is that it is truly based on a strengths perspective (in contrast to a deficit model), and the wording of the items reflects this perspective. The Teacher Rating Scale (TRS) has 52 items and is one of the three measures in the BERS-2 package. Some sample items from the TRS are:

- Maintains positive family relationships.
- Accepts responsibility for own actions.
- Pays attention in class.
- Identifies own feelings.

This makes the BERS-2 package popular among practitioners operating from a strength-based perspective, as well as with parents and teachers.

Finally, standardized assessment measures have been criticized for their inability to make direct linkages between client problems and interventions—that is, the measure does not prescribe a useful treatment plan, which is the main purpose of assessment.

Building on this last critique, there is also, too often, a disconnect between screening, assessment, and treatment planning. This is a truism across outpatient, inpatient, school-based, and juvenile-justice settings. In response to this challenge, a recent meeting of juvenile-justice assessment experts, dubbed the "Consensus Conference," produced recommendations for screening and assessing mental-health needs in the juvenile-justice system (Wasserman et al., 2002a). The Consensus Conference attendees suggest that screening mental-health problems and identifying needs with an eye to long-term service planning should occur for all youth prior to court disposition (Potter & Jenson, 2007; www.promotementalhealth.org/practices.htm). Developing a treatment plan involves practitioners' using information gathered from screening and assessment tools and, more importantly, from their own cognitive abilities to map out a set of tasks to undertake with the client. The section that follows addresses this task.

Treatment Goals

Treatment plans and treatment goals are established collaboratively between the social worker and the adolescent and help focus their work together. Goals specify what the adolescent wants to work on in treatment, and the treatment plan serves as a "game plan" for how these goals will be obtained. Treatment goals and treatment plans are critical components of effective social work practice, for without them, both social workers and clients run the risk of aimlessly "stumbling around in the dark" until they happen on a "problem" that needs to be addressed. As consumers of care, we expect our primary-care physicians to deliver services with some sense of purpose, direction, and expertise. We should expect no less from social workers and the care that they provide.

The first step in establishing treatment goals with any client is to conduct a thorough assessment, as has been discussed throughout this chapter. This entails allowing the client to tell his or her story, conducting a psychosocial history, and using standardized assessment tools and rapid-assessment instruments as needed. Clients may also need to be referred for medical and/or psychological testing. Following a thorough assessment, the social worker and client work together to establish goals for the client. In this sense, goals link the assessment and treatment process.

The following guidelines are helpful in establishing treatment goals. The goals should be (a) clearly defined and measurable; (b) feasible and realistic; (c) set collaboratively by the social worker and the client; (d) originated directly from the assessment process; and (e) stated in positive terms, focusing on client growth. Treatment goals "should specify *who, will do what, to what extent and under what conditions*" (Bloom et al., 2006, p. 104).

Treatment goals need to be defined clearly and stated in such a way that progress toward the goals can be measured. If goals are stated too ambiguously, clients may become discouraged or feel as if the goals are "out of reach." For example, compare the ambiguous goal of "Improve family communication" with the more concrete goal of "Ramon will have at least two 10-minute positive conversations per day with his parents over the next 2 weeks." The latter goal is more likely to be meaningful and obtainable to Ramon and his parents.

This leads to the second element of establishing treatment goals, which is that they must be feasible and realistic. "Improving family communication" is not only vague but may not be feasible or realistic, because it potentially covers so much ground. Additionally, little discussion between the social worker and the adolescent is needed to create vague goals. By contrast, concrete goals require a serious dialogue to take place between the worker and the client so that conceptual ideas about client functioning can be "wrestled to the ground" in clear day-to-day terms.

To the extent that adolescent clients participate in this discussion, the more likely it is that they will feel a sense of ownership over the established goals, which in turn means that they are more likely to follow through with the treatment plan. Clients (especially adolescents) will experience less "buy-in" to the treatment process if a social worker or parent imposes goals on them. Thus, goal setting needs to be a truly collaborative process among the social worker, adolescent, and his or her parents (when appropriate).

Treatment goals need to stem directly from the assessment process. The assessment should be thorough, empirically based, and grounded in a systems perspective. This minimizes the likelihood that the worker is creating treatment goals based solely on gut feeling or an on-the-spot diagnosis.

Finally, treatment goals need to be stated in positive terms. In other words, the goal should state what the client will do rather than what the client will not do. For example, a client will be more motivated and goal directed by a goal that states, "Attend the entire school day every day for the next 2 weeks," in comparison to a goal that states, "Stop skipping school."

Implications for Social Work

Adolescents present with multiple needs, and these needs must be adequately captured in the assessment process so that interventions are practical and relevant. Regardless of the method of assessment and intervention used, one truism rings loud and clear: *The assessment and intervention process with youths must be conducted in a therapeutic relationship that is driven by worker genuineness, warmth, empathy, and understanding.* In other words, youth need to connect with a caring adult. Wolkind's (1977) seminal study of 92 children in residential care supports this notion, where he finds that prolonged contact with the same houseparent was associated with lower rates of psychiatric disorders and acting-out behavior.

It is critical that researchers continue their efforts to sort out what methods of assessment are the most effective with adolescents and to subsequently relay any relevant findings to workers and policy makers in a meaningful and user-friendly manner. Mash and Hunsley (2005) propose that it might also be important for EBA to appraise therapeutic-relationship and client-satisfaction variables across specific disorders and assessment constructs. More systematic guidelines are needed to inform practitioners in their assessment with adolescents: "Ivory-tower pleas to use multiple perspectives from multiple contexts in the absence of specific guidelines for translating these recommendations into clinical practice are not close to the mark regarding what is needed or feasible based on the way current clinical practice is structured" (Kazdin, 2005, p. 556).

Conclusion

The field continues to make progress in developing user-friendly standardized assessment tools with sound psychometric properties that can be used in assessment with adolescents. Although these tools should not take the place of a face-to-face psychosocial history, they should be used to complement the assessment process and to track progress in client functioning over the course of treatment. It is important to emphasize that a standardized tool does not take the place of a solid therapeutic helping relationship. A limitation of RAIs is that a client may answer items in a way that presents him- or herself in a certain light to the social worker. This risk is minimized to the extent that rapport has been established between the social worker and the adolescent and to the extent that the adolescent understands the importance of the assessment process and how it will be used to help him or her make desired changes.

Social workers have an ethical obligation to utilize empirical assessment protocols and standardized tools whenever possible rather than relying solely on gut feeling when conducting assessments with adolescents. The potential consequences of misdiagnosing a client, such as Ramon, described earlier, can be severe. Thus, social work practitioners are encouraged to utilize available empirically based assessment tools within a systems framework to guide treatment planning, to monitor client functioning, and to evaluate the effectiveness of their interventions. In sum, although the practice of EBA with youth is itself in its adolescence, the field is maturing.

Key Terms

Evidence-based
  assessment

Standardized
  assessment tools

Treatment goals

Strengths-based
  approach

Rapid-assessment
  instruments

Review Questions for Critical Thinking

1. From the information provided on assessment tools in this chapter, how would you, as a practitioner, decide the most appropriate scale for your client to complete?

2. What are three important considerations to take into account when choosing an EBA instrument for your client?

3. What are the potential downsides to a practitioner's relying solely on self-report measures?

4. Name three limitations to standardized assessment tools?

5. What are some considerations a practitioner must take into account when creating treatment goals?

Online Resources

http://archives.drugabuse.gov/pdf/monographs/156.pdf This site is supported by the *National Institute on Drug Abuse* and provides detailed information on drug-abuse treatment and assessment instruments for adolescents.

http://humanservices.ucdavis.edu/Academy/pdf/104056-MentalHealthLR .pdf This website, which is supported by the *California Department of Social Services*, reviews 95 mental or social-emotional assessment tools available for children and adolescents.

http://www.aacap.org/cs/root/member_information/practice_information /practice_parameters/practice_parameters This website is supported by the *American Academy of Child and Adolescent Psychiatry* and provides a comprehensive set of clinical parameters for assessing and treating children and adolescents.

http://pubs.niaaa.nih.gov/publications/Assesing%20Alcohol/behaviors .htm This site is supported by the *National Institute on Alcohol Abuse and Alcoholism* and provides a comprehensive list of validated instruments that assess adolescent alcohol abuse.

http://www.nctsn.org/sites/default/files/assets/pdfs/satoolkit_4.pdf This website is supported by the *National Child Traumatic Stress Network*. It outlines a comprehensive list of validated assessment tools that target trauma and substance use.

References

Abell, N., Springer, D., & Kamata, A. (2009). *Developing and validating rapid assessment instruments*. New York, NY: Oxford University Press.

American Psychiatric Association (2000). *Diagnostic and statistical manual of mental disorders* (4th ed., text rev.). Washington, DC: Author.

Bloom, M., Fischer, J., & Orme, J. G. (2006). *Evaluating practice: Guidelines for the accountable professional* (5th ed.). Boston, MA: Allyn & Bacon.

Bravo, M., Ribera, J., Rubio-Stipec, M., Canino, G., Shrout, P., Ramírez, R., ... Taboas, A. (2001). Test-retest reliability of the Spanish version of the Diagnostic Interview Schedule for Children (DISC-IV). *Journal of Abnormal Child Psychology, 29*(5), 433–444.

Catalano, R. F., Hawkins, J. D., & Krenz, C. (1993). Using research to guide culturally appropriate drug abuse prevention. *Journal of Consulting and Clinical Psychology, 61*(5), 804–811.

Clark, M. D. (1998). Strength-based practice: The ABC's of working with adolescents who don't want to work with you. *Federal Probation Quarterly, 62*(1), 46–53.

Collins, L. R. (1993). Sociocultural aspects of alcohol use and abuse: Ethnicity and gender. *Drugs and Society, 8*, 89–116.

Corcoran, J., & Springer, D. W. (2005). Treatment of adolescents with disruptive behavior disorders. In J. Corcoran (Ed.), *Strengths and skills building: A collaborative approach to working with clients* (pp. 131–162). New York, NY: Oxford University Press.

Corcoran, K., & Fischer, J. (2007). *Measures for clinical practice: Vol. 1. A sourcebook* (4th ed.). New York, NY: Free Press.

Cowan, D. (2009). "Cultural competence: definition, delivery and evaluation." *Ethnicity & Inequalities in Health & Social Care, 2*(4), 27–38.

Cowger, C. (1997). Assessing client strengths: Assessment for client empowerment. In D. Saleebey (Ed.), *The strengths perspective in social work practice* (2nd ed., pp. 59–73). New York, NY: Longman.

Crocker, L., & Algina, J. (1986). *Introduction to classical and modern test theory*. Ft. Worth, TX: Harcourt Brace Jovanovich.

Epstein, M. H. (2004). *Behavioral and Emotional Rating Scale-2: A strength-based approach to assessment*. Austin, TX: ProEd.

Fletcher, J. M., Francis, D. J., Morris, R. D., & Lyon, G. R. (2005). Evidence-based assessment of learning disabilities in children and adolescents. *Journal of Clinical Child and Adolescent Psychology, 34*(3), 506–522.

Germain, C. B., & Gitterman, A. (1980). *The life model of social work practice*. New York, NY: Columbia University Press.

Gil, A. G., Wagner, E. F., & Vega, W. A. (2000). Acculturation, familism and alcohol use among Latino adolescent males: Longitudinal relations. *Journal of Community Psychology, 28*(4), 443–458.

Hall, G. S. (1904). *Adolescence*. New York, NY: Appleton.

Hodges, K. (2000). *The Child and Adolescent Functional Assessment Scale self-training manual*. Ypsilanti: Eastern Michigan University, Department of Psychology.

Hodges, K., & Cheong-Seok, K. (2000). Psychometric study of the Child and Adolescent Functional Assessment Scale: Prediction of contact with the law and poor school attendance. *Journal of Abnormal Child Psychology, 28*, 287–297.

Hodges, K., Doucette-Gates, A., & Oinghong, L. (1999). The relationship between the Child and Adolescent Functional Assessment Scale (CAFAS) and indicators of functioning. *Journal of Child and Family Studies, 8*, 109–122.

Hodges, K., & Wong, M. M. (1996). Psychometric characteristics of a multidimensional measure to assess impairment: The Child and Adolescent Functional Assessment Scale. *Journal of Child and Family Studies, 5*, 445–467.

Hudson, W. W. (1982). *The clinical measurement package: A field manual.* Homewood, IL: Dorsey Press.

Jordan, C., & Franklin, C. (1995). *Clinical assessment for social workers: Quantitative and qualitative methods.* Chicago, IL: Lyceum.

Jordan, C., & Hickerson, J. (2003). Children and adolescents. In C. Jordan & C. Franklin (Eds.), *Clinical assessment for social workers: Quantitative and qualitative methods* (2nd ed., pp. 179–213). Chicago, IL: Lyceum.

Kazdin, A. E. (1995). Scope of child and adolescent psychotherapy research: Limited sampling of dysfunctions, treatments, and client characteristics. *Journal of Clinical Child Psychology, 24*, 125–140.

Kazdin, A. E. (2005). Evidence-based assessment for children and adolescents: Issues in measurement development and clinical application. *Journal of Clinical Child and Adolescent Psychology, 34*(3), 548–558.

Kazdin, A. E., & Weisz, J. R. (2003). Context and background of evidence-based psychotherapies for children and adolescents. In A. E. Kazdin & J. R. Weisz (Eds.), *Evidence-based psychotherapies for children and adolescents* (pp. 3–20). New York: Guilford Press.

Kelley, M. L., Reitman, D., & Noell, G. R. (Eds.). (2003). *Practitioner's guide to empirically based measures of school behavior.* New York, NY: Kluwer Academic/Plenum Press.

Klein, D. N., Dougherty, L. R., & Olino, T. M. (2005). Toward guidelines for evidence-based assessment of depression in children and adolescents. *Journal of Clinical Child and Adolescent Psychology, 34*(3), 412–432.

Ko, S. J., & Wasserman, G. A. (2002). Seeking best practices for mental health assessment in juvenile justice settings. *Report on Emotional and Behavioral Disorders in Youth, 2*(4), 88–99.

Lerner, R. M. (2009). The positive youth development perspective: Theoretical and empirical bases of a strength-based approach to adolescent development. In C. R. Snyder & S.J. Lopez (Eds.), *Oxford handbook of positive psychology* (2nd ed., pp. 149–163). Oxford, UK: Oxford University Press.

Levitt, J., & Reid, W. (1981). Rapid-assessment instruments for practice. *Social Work Research and Abstracts, 17*(1), 13–19.

Li, X., Fiegelman, S., & Stanton, B. (2000). Perceived parental monitoring and health risk behaviors among urban low-income African-American children and adolescents. *Journal of Adolescent Health, 27*, 43–48.

Mash, E., & Hunsley, J. (2005). Evidence-based assessment of child and adolescent disorders: Issues and challenges. *Journal of Clinical Child and Adolescent Psychology, 34*(3), 362–379.

McBride, D. C., VanderWaal, C. J., Terry, Y. M., & VanBuren, H. (1999). *Breaking the cycle of drug use among juvenile offenders.* Washington, DC: National Institute of Justice. Retrieved from www.ncjrs.org

McLellan, A. T., Luborsky, L., Cacciola, J., Griffith, J., Evans, F., Barr, H. L., & O'Brien, C. (1985). New data from the addiction severity index: Reliability and validity in three centers. *Journal of Nervous and Mental Diseases, 173*, 412–423.

McMahon, R. J., & Frick, P. J. (2005). Evidence-based assessment of conduct problems in children and adolescents. *Journal of Clinical Child and Adolescent Psychology, 34*(3), 477–505.

Mercer, J. R. (1979). *System of multicultural pluralistic assessment technical manual.* San Antonio, TX: Psychological Corporation.

Miller, G. A. (1985). *The Substance Abuse Subtle Screening Inventory manual.* Bloomington, IN: Substance Abuse Subtle Screening Inventory Institute.

Miller, G. A., Miller, F. G., Roberts, J., Brooks, M. K., & Lazowski, L. G. (1997). *The SASSI-3.* Bloomington, IN: Baugh Enterprises.

Morrison, J., & Anders, T. F. (1999). *Interviewing children and adolescents: Skills and strategies for effective DSM-IV diagnosis.* New York, NY: Guilford Press.

National Institute on Drug Abuse (1991). *The adolescent assessment/referral system manual* (DHHS Publication No. ADM 91–1735). Rockville, MD: U.S. Department of Health and Human Services.

National Institute on Drug Abuse (1994). Mental health assessment and diagnosis of substance abusers: Clinical report series (NIH Publication No. 94–3846). Rockville, MD: U.S. Department of Health and Human Services.

Nunnally, J. C., & Bernstein, I. H. (1994). *Psychometric theory* (3rd ed.). New York, NY: McGraw-Hill.

Ozonoff, S., Goodlin-Jones, B. L., & Solomon, M. (2005). Evidence-based assessment of autism spectrum disorders in children and adolescents. *Journal of Clinical Child and Adolescent Psychology, 34*(3), 523–540.

Pelham, W. E., Jr., Fabiano, G. A., & Massetti, G. M. (2005). Evidence-based assessment of attention deficit hyperactivity disorder in children and adolescents. *Journal of Clinical Child and Adolescent Psychology, 34*(3), 449–476.

Potter, C. C., & Jenson, J. M. (2007). Assessment of mental health and substance abuse treatment needs in juvenile justice. In A. R. Roberts & D. W. Springer (Eds.), *Social work in juvenile and criminal justice settings* (3rd ed., pp. 133–150). Springfield, IL: Charles C. Thomas.

Rahdert, E. R. (1991). *The adolescent assessment/referral system manual* (DHHS Publication No. ADM 91–1735). Rockville, MD: U.S. Department of Health and Human Services, National Institute on Drug Abuse.

Roberts, A. R., & Greene, G. J. (Eds.). (2009). *Social workers' desk reference.* New York, NY: Oxford University Press.

Saleebey, D. (Ed.). (1997). *The strengths perspective in social work practice* (2nd ed.). New York, NY: Longman.

Shaffer, D., Fisher, P. W., & Lucas, C. P. (1999a). Respondent-based interviews. In D. Shaffer, C. P. Lucas, & J. E. Richters (Eds.), *Diagnostic assessment in child and adolescent psychopathology* (pp. 3–33). New York, NY: Guilford Press.

Shaffer, D., Fisher, P. W., Lucas, C. P., Dulcan, M., & Schwab-Stone, M. E. (2000). NIMH Diagnostic Interview Schedule for Children, Version IV (NIMH DISC-IV): Description, differences from previous versions, and reliability of some common diagnoses. *Journal of the American Academy of Child and Adolescent Psychiatry, 39*, 28–38.

Shaffer, D., Lucas, C. P., & Richters, J. E. (Eds.). (1999b). *Diagnostic assessment in child and adolescent psychopathology.* New York, NY: Guilford Press.

Silverman, W. K., & Ollendick, T. H. (2005). Evidence-based assessment of anxiety and its disorders in children and adolescents. *Journal of Clinical Child and Adolescent Psychology, 34*(3), 380–411.

Chapter 4
Intervention With Adolescents

Craig Winston LeCroy
and Lela Rankin Williams

Purpose: This chapter presents an overview of current evidence-informed practices for social work interventions with adolescents.

Rationale: The developmental period of adolescence accompanies a certain amount of risk, but today's adolescents begin exposure to risky behaviors at a much earlier age than adolescents of the past. Social workers are increasingly needed who understand the unique developmental capacities of adolescents and how to intervene when normative developmental issues become a concern. This includes understanding effective strategies for working with youth and how to engage youth in treatment.

How evidence-informed practice is presented: We provide a developmental framework from which we can interpret common adolescent issues, concerns, and problems. We appraise empirical literature to help guide us in selecting best evidence-informed practice interventions specific to the problems adolescents typically face. We include practical information that social workers can use when deciding how to best intervene with adolescent clients and/or populations in various settings across the social ecology.

Overarching question: What have we learned from evidence-informed practice that helps social workers effectively intervene with adolescents?

Adolescents in today's society face significant risks that can compromise their health and well-being. The developmental period of adolescence is recognized as one in which a certain amount of risk taking is considered normative and developmentally appropriate (e.g., coping with anxiety, gaining peer acceptance, creating a sense of identity), but many risk-taking behaviors place youth at risk for long-term adverse health outcomes (e.g., using substances, engaging in unprotected sex; Burrus et al., 2012). Of concern is that modern adolescents begin exposure to risky behavior at a much earlier age than adolescents of the past. Globally, adolescents today consume more alcohol, use more illicit drugs, have earlier ages of first sexual intercourse, and have more sexual partners compared to adolescents of the 1990s (Geels et al., 2012; Johnston, O'Malley, Bachman, & Schulenberg, 2012; Sweeting, Jackson, & Haw, 2011). The Internet and the media have been held at least partly responsible for the increase in risk-taking behaviors in adolescence (e.g., the use of synthetic marijuana) and has sparked debate regarding their impact on adolescent sexual behaviors (Brown,

2011; Steinberg & Monahan, 2011). According to a recent nationally representative survey across the United States, 20% of adolescents will experience a mental disorder in their lifetime that will impact their ability to function (Merikangas et al., 2010). This prevalence rate supersedes even the most frequent major physical conditions in adolescence, including asthma or diabetes. Even those adolescents who are not considered to be at risk must navigate through adolescence—a period easily characterized as a playing field of obstacles and barriers to healthy development.

Those interested in interventions for adolescents have become increasingly focused on programs that can promote positive youth development, reduce risk factors, and remediate adolescent problem behaviors and disorders. Better assessment tools and better interventions have paved the way for improving the quality of the mental health and well-being of adolescents. An increasing emphasis on best practices, research-based practice, and evidence-based practice (EBP) is being supported and promoted by varying groups of professionals (see, e.g., Carr, 2000, 2002; Evans et al., 2005; Hibbs & Jensen, 2005; Kazdin, 2000; Rutter & Taylor, 2002; U.S. Public Health Service, Office of the Surgeon General, 2004). Furthermore, advocacy groups, parents, and local government are also putting a renewed emphasis on effective interventions for adolescents (Hoagwood, 2005).

This chapter reviews current issues and problems facing adolescents and examines prevention and intervention strategies and programs designed to improve adolescent mental health and well-being. The central concern is which interventions are effective with adolescents. This chapter also examines treatment-delivery factors that influence outcomes.

Overview of Issues and Problems Facing Adolescents

Developmental characteristics of adolescents are important considerations in the design and implementation of effective interventions. During early adolescence, physical changes occur more rapidly than at any other time in the life span except infancy (Ashford & LeCroy, 2010). The production of sex hormones, puberty, and appearance of secondary sex characteristics are significant changes that take place in adolescence. During adolescence, the shift from concrete to formal operational thinking takes place, and adolescents begin to think more abstractly. This has significance for the design of interventions, because young adolescents or troubled adolescents often have difficulty linking thoughts, feelings, and behaviors. Identity formation and self-development come to the forefront of the adolescent's attention and can lead to positive or negative behaviors. Peers are an important source of support and stress. Pressure by peers for approval and conformity are directly related to engagement in risky behaviors. Last, emotional development is maturing, and adolescents often experience a wide fluctuation of emotional reactions. Learning how to cope with negative emotions is important in developing a positive sense of well-being.

Table 4.1 **Developmental Considerations in Conducting an Assessment With Adolescents**

Routine Observation	Developmental Concerns	Developmental Observations Requiring Attention
Brain development and abstract thought	Egocentrism	Anxiety
Increased caloric intact	Focus on physical appearance Heightened concern with body image	Eating disorders
Menstruation (girls) and nocturnal emission (boys)	Early maturing girls	Early pregnancy Sex abuse and rape
Romantic involvement	Sexual identity exploration Sexual behavior	Sexually transmitted infections Teen dating violence
Decreased interest in school	Academic difficulties	School dropout
Heightened emotions	Moodiness	Depression
Independence	Spending more time alone Spending less time with family	Violent behaviors and exposure to violence
Autonomy	Increased parent-child conflict	Risk behaviors (e.g., automobile safety, substance use)
Transition to middle school	Increased peer influence	Conduct disorder and delinquency Firearm exposure/use

An important skill in working with adolescents is being able to identify common developmental concerns, issues needing closer observation, and developmental observations requiring attention (Table 4.1).

In addition to the risks associated with adolescence, young people bring strengths to this developmental period. Adolescents have increased resilience, a more complex sense of morality, and greater peer support and look to their parents for guidance on personal values and career-making decisions. Although adolescence is a time for significant rapid development, it is also the time that many of the major mental disorders begin. Furthermore, after onset, many of these disorders persist into adulthood, leading to significant impairment in adulthood. Beyond mental disorders, many adolescents engage in at-risk behavior or are exposed to social conditions that impact their development. These high-risk behaviors often pave the way for dysfunctional adult behavior, such as substance abuse and unprotected sex.

It is now understood that many problem behaviors and mental disorders are common in adolescence (Table 4.2). Epidemiological studies of adolescents have obtained a better understanding of the likelihood of occurrence of such behaviors and disorders.

Of particular concern is the rising prevalence of mental disorders in children and adolescents over the years. Perhaps better assessment and detection can account for some of this, but the stressful and difficult environments that many adolescents experience are also likely to contribute. Another important factor is that adolescence is a longer time period than in the past. Indeed, many believe a new phase of "emerging adulthood" is needed to address the lengthening time period many

Table 4.2 **Prevalence Rates for Selected Behavior Problems and Disorders**

Behavior Problems and Disorders	Prevalence Rates

Drug use[1]	Reported drinking in the past 30 days:
	  13% of 8th graders.
	  27% of 10th graders.
	  40% of 12th graders.
	By high school graduation:
	  50% have used illicit drugs.

Substance-use disorders[2]	11% of youth meet the criteria for a substance-use disorder (10% of adolescent females and 12% of adolescent males). Rates of drug abuse/dependence are 9% and for alcohol abuse/dependence are 6%.
Sexual behavior[3]	Birth rates for 15- to 19-year-old females: 34 per 1,000 (56 per 1,000 for Hispanic adolescents). In 2010, there were 740,000 adolescent pregnancies per year. About half of adolescents are sexually active before they graduate from high school.
School dropout[4]	*Status dropout rate*: the percentage of an age group that is not enrolled in school and has not earned a high school diploma. Approximately 8% of 16- to 24-year-olds (who were out of school without a high school diploma).
Suicide[5]	Overall suicide rate of 7% for 15- to 19-year olds (2% of adolescent females and 11% of adolescent males).
Depression[2]	Depression rates range from 3% for bipolar disorder to 12% for major depressive disorder or dysthymia. When any kind of mood disorder is included, the rate is about 14% (18% of adolescent females and 10% of adolescent males). Rates among 17- to 18-year-olds are double that of 13- to 14-year-olds.
Anxiety disorders[2]	Overall rate for any kind of anxiety disorder is 32% (38% of adolescent females and 26% of adolescent males). Rates of social phobia are 9% and specific phobia is 19%.
Eating disorders[2]	About 4% of the adolescent female population (2% of the adolescent male population) suffer from eating disorders.
Behavioral disorders[2]	Overall rate for any kind of behavioral disorder is 20% (16% of adolescent females and 24% of adolescent males). Rates of oppositional defiant disorder are 13% and conduct disorder are 7%.
Autism-spectrum disorder[6]	Rates have shown increases in the past 30 years. Recent estimates are 1 in 88 (1 in 252 girls and 1 in 54 boys).

Data drawn from [1]Johnston et al. (2012); [2]Merikangas et al. (2010); [3]Centers for Disease Control and Prevention (2012a); [4]Chapman, Laird, & Kewal Ramani (2010); [5]Centers for Disease Control and Prevention (2011); [6]Centers for Disease Control and Prevention (2012b).

adolescents find themselves in (Arnett, 2004). However, the critical consideration is the availability of potentially harmful environments (exposure to drugs, poverty, and homelessness) that can take their toll on young people (Evans & Seligman, 2005).

Adolescent interventions can be categorized according to two main types. The first refers to the "absence of dysfunction in psychological,

emotional, behavioral, and social spheres" (Kazdin, 1993, p. 128). Dysfunction is defined as impairment in everyday life. Mental-health disorders,
such as anxiety disorder, depression, and autism, are examples of dysfunctions. Adolescents who suffer from disorders such as these are impaired in
their everyday functional abilities (e.g., social relationships, school performance), and their dysfunction is likely to influence their well-being (e.g.,
suicide attempts, substance abuse). As Kazdin (1993, p. 128) notes, it is
important to recognize that

> a variety of behaviors in which adolescents engage (e.g., substance use, antisocial
> acts, school dysfunction) and conditions to which they are exposed (e.g., poverty,
> homelessness, physical abuse) are dysfunctional because they impede the quality
> of current functioning and often portend deleterious physical and psychological
> consequences.

The second main type of adolescent intervention focuses on optimal
functioning or well-being in psychological or social domains (Kazdin,
1993). *Well-being* is the presence of strengths that promote optimal
functioning—it is not just the absence of impairment. The strengths perspective and positive psychology promote social competence, coping skills,
and positive attachments to significant others—all of which are a part of
optimal functioning. Social competence is considered a key concept that
directs attention to adolescents' ability to cope with the demands of
the environment by using cognitive and social skills to achieve positive
outcomes.

These two approaches are part of a continuum of interventions with
adolescents but suggest different conceptualizations, models of treatment,
and intended outcomes. Promoting optimal functioning or positive mental
health is fundamentally based on promoting certain competencies (Kazdin,
1993; LeCroy, 2006). The goal of these interventions is to build strengths,
teach coping skills, and learn new social skills to enhance everyday
functioning. In addition to being more socially competent, adolescents

Table 4.3   **Some Common Adolescent At-Risk Problems and Diagnoses**

Anxiety disorders
Conduct disorder and delinquency
Depression
Eating disorders
Substance use and abuse
Sexual abuse
Sexual behavior
Running away from home
Oppositional defiant disorder
School problems and dropping out
Cutting behavior
Suicide risk

may benefit from these approaches, because they limit clinical dysfunction (Kazdin, 1993). In contrast, interventions designed to address dysfunction are based on the diagnosis of disorders and the administration of certain interventions to reduce impairment. More intensive interventions are often needed, such as long-term therapy, residential treatment, hospitalization, and medication. Table 4.3 lists some of the major at-risk problems and clinical disorders evident in adolescence.

To address the problem behaviors and clinical disorders so many adolescents confront, adolescent interventions are based on promoting competencies and positive functioning in prevention or the clinical treatment of specific disorders in treatment.

Promising Programs of Prevention and Intervention

For this chapter, *promising programs* are defined as research-based programs that have some demonstrated positive outcomes. Programs have been identified through multiple sources, including literature reviews, recent books on EBP (e.g., Nathan & Gorman, 1998, *A Guide to Treatments That Work;* Carr, 2000, *What Works With Children and Adolescents?;* Evans et al., 2005, *Treating and Preventing Adolescent Mental Health Disorders: What We Know and What We Don't Know;* Fonagy, Target, Cottrell, Phillips, & Kurtz, 2002, *What Works for Whom? A Critical Review of Treatments for Children and Adolescents*), and federal and nonprofit institutional websites (e.g., www.promisingpractices.net, operated by the RAND Corporation). Programs identified as effective or promising are by no means inclusive of all effective programs. Also, in this chapter there is not a distinction between well-established treatments and probably efficacious treatments, as discussed by the Task Force Report on Promoting and Dissemination of Psychological Procedures (1995). Since this report, a groundswell of new data have entered the field, and additional reviews have contributed to what constitutes "evidence-based," "promising," or "empirically supported" treatments. As a result, there is no clear agreement on criteria and standards, and different judgments are made in regard to studies that can be classified under the empirical rubric.

Promoting the Development of Competencies and the Prevention of Disorders

Prevention programs are described according to the Institute of Medicine (IOM, 1994) definitions. In this report, *prevention* refers to interventions that occur before the initial onset of a disorder. *Universal prevention* is defined as efforts that are beneficial to a whole population or group. As such, they target the whole population or group that has not been identified as being at risk for the disorder being prevented. *Selective prevention* is defined as efforts that target individuals or groups of the population whose

Table 4.6 Skills and Content in the Coping With Depression Course

Skill	Content
Mood monitoring	Examining feelings and understanding how to assess your mood.
Social skills	Learning conversation skills, social-planning skills, and how to make friends.
Pleasant activities	Learning self-change strategies, such as setting goals.
Relaxation	Learning how to decrease anxiety using relaxation.
Constructive thinking	Learning how to reduce negative cognitions related to depression, replacing self-defeating thoughts with self-enhancing thoughts.
Communication	Learning how to resolve conflict, how to communicate clearly, and how to use active listening.
Negotiation and problem solving	Learning how to negotiate, applying problem-solving skills to situations.
Maintenance of gain	Integrating the skills, developing a life plan, setting goals, and developing a relapse plan for what to do.

Adapted from "The Adolescent Coping with Depression Course: A Cognitive-Behavioral Approach to the Treatment of Depression," by P. Rohde, P. M. Lewinsohn, G. N. Clarke, H. Hops, and J. R. Seeley. In E. D. Hibbs and P. S. Jensen (Eds.), *Psychosocial Treatments for Child and Adolescent Disorders: Empirically Based Strategies for Clinical Practice* (pp. 219–238), Washington DC: American Psychological Association, 2005.

Multisystemic Therapy

Multisystemic therapy (MST) is a broad-based therapy that has been used for adolescents who engage in "willful misconduct" (Henggeler & Lee, 2003). The most frequent applications of this treatment have been with youth who suffer from conduct disorder, are classified as juvenile offenders, have substance-abuse problems, or have experienced psychiatric crises. The overarching goals of multisystemic therapy are to decrease antisocial behavior, improve psychosocial functioning, and reduce out-of-home placements. This multifaceted intervention is based on ecological theory and attempts to influence factors within adolescent, family, school, peer-group, and community spheres that can have a positive impact on the youth. A typical application of MST would target an adolescent's social and academic skills. Family work might include improving family communication, parental supervision, and parent-management skills. Peer interventions may address limiting contact with deviant peers and substituting new nondeviant peer groups. School-focused interventions might examine educational placement and enhance parent-school communication.

Henggeler and Lee (2003) discuss some critical aspects of the design and implementation of MST, noting the following: multidetermined nature of serious clinical problems (behavior is multidetermined, and individual, family, peer, school, and community factors need to be considered);

Table 4.7 The MST Treatment Principles

Treatment Principle	Description
Finding the fit	Using ecological notions to deliver treatment across appropriate social domains
Positive and strength focused	Emphasizing the positive and focusing on family strengths, building hope, and enhancing confidence
Increasing responsibility	Using interventions to promote responsible behavior
Present focused, action oriented, and well defined	Setting clear goals and determining measurable outcomes
Targeting sequences	Using interventions that target sequences of behavior within and between multiple systems that help maintain the problems
Developmentally appropriate	Using interventions that fit the developmental needs of youth
Continuous effort	Using ongoing interventions that require daily or weekly effort by family members to maximize the change process
Evaluation and accountability	Evaluating interventions continuously from multiple perspectives
Generalization	Using interventions that promote treatment generalizations and maintenance of change

Adapted from *Multisystemic Therapy for Antisocial Behavior in Children and Adolescents* (2nd ed.), by S. W. Henggeler, S. K. Schoenwald, C. M. Borduin, M. D. Rowland, and P. B. Cunningham, New York, NY: Guilford Press, 2009.

caregivers are key to long-term outcomes (the focus is on developing the caregiver's ability to parent effectively and facilitating support systems for the family); integration of EBPs (MST is based on incorporating evidence-based treatments, such as family therapy, parent-management training, and use of medications); intensive services that overcome barriers to service access (intense services are provided to overcome barriers using a home-based treatment model and low caseloads); and rigorous-quality assurance system (systems are in place to promote treatment fidelity, such as protocols, workshops on the treatment model, weekly consultation, and off-site consultants). However, generally nine treatment principles are often presented as the foundation of MST (Table 4.7). Research studies from eight published articles (Henggeler & Lee, 2003) have found positive outcomes when compared to control-group subjects on criminal behavior, substance abuse, and emotional disturbance. Short-term gains include improved school/work, home, community, and mood/emotional functioning. Long-term gains include a threefold reduction in rearrest, and, if rearrested, arraignment for fewer new offenses 18 months posttreatment (Timmons-Mitchell, Bender, Kishna, & Mitchel, 2006).

Functional Family Therapy

This intervention model evolved from an early effort to use a family system's conceptual framework with delinquent adolescents (Alexander & Parsons, 1982). Functional family therapy (FFT) has a strong social learning focus but uses systems theory and behavioral and cognitive strategies to influence functioning. The functional part of FFT is that problems are examined in terms of the function they serve for the individual adolescent and the family system. In general, family members are helped to change their communication patterns, increase parental supervision, and use new parenting skills to alter behavior. The fundamental approach is based on earlier studies that showed delinquents have more defensive communication, less supportive communication, and less supervision when compared with nondelinquents. The intervention involves conjoint family treatment. Initial treatment focuses on teaching communication skills, problem-solving skills, and negotiation skills. Reframing is used extensively to reduce blaming and help parents perceive problem behavior as maintained by environmental contingencies rather than intrinsic factors. As treatment progresses, the emphasis is on contingency contracts, whereby parents and adolescents exchange behaviors that they each would like to see more of. Several studies (see reviews by Carr, 2000; Fonagy & Kurtz, 2002) have found that FFT was effective in improving communication, reducing conduct problems and out-of-home placement, and reducing recidivism rates in delinquent adolescents as well as their siblings.

Problem-Solving and Social-Skills Training

Research has documented that the capacity to use problem solving for social and interpersonal problems is an important aspect of adaptive functioning. Indeed, deficits in problem-solving abilities are related to both dysfunctional difficulties and clinical disorders. For example, problem-solving deficits are related to delinquent behaviors (Kazdin, 2003), depression (Lewinsohn & Gotlib, 1995), and coping with stress (Compas, Benson, Boyer, Hicks, & Konik, 2002; Compas, Connor-Smith, Saltzman, Thomsen, & Wadsworth, 2001). Without social skills, adolescents are more likely to experience friendship difficulties, inappropriately expressed emotions, and an inability to resist peer pressure (LeCroy & Wooton, 2002). Problem-solving and social-skills training are widely used interventions that focus on either learning how to generate and use more effective solutions to situational conflicts or learning the skills needed to respond effectively to situational conflicts. Sometimes these interventions are used separately and sometimes they are combined, such as when problem solving is conceived of as an accessory social skill. *Problem solving* is a cognitive-behavioral strategy that teaches thought processes to help adolescents confront difficult interactions. *Social-skills training* is a behavioral strategy that teaches new behaviors or skills for addressing difficult situations. Implementing problem-solving interventions typically follows the primary components of problem-solving skills (D'Zurilla & Nezu, 1990):

- Problem definition and formulation.
- Generation of alternative solutions.
- Decision making and selection of a solution.
- Implementation and evaluation of a solution.

Application of problem-solving interventions was spearheaded by the classic work of Spivack and Shure (1976) using the interpersonal cognitive problem-solving (ICPS) model that includes three basic skills: *alternative thinking*, which is generating alternative solutions to a problem; *consequential thinking*, which is the ability to examine the short- and long-term consequences of a decision; and *means-ends thinking*, which is the ability to plan a sequence of goal-directed actions in order to avoid obstacles and solve problems in a timely manner. The intervention process is described by Kazdin's (2005) program of problem-solving therapy for aggressive and antisocial youth, as presented in Table 4.8.

Social-skills training is typically presented in a small-group format using behavior group-therapy principles and strategies for teaching specific skills. The group format provides support and a reinforcing context for learning new responses and appropriate behaviors in a variety of social situations. The group allows for extensive use of modeling and feedback that are successful components of group treatment. Table 4.9 presents a summary of the steps used in social-skills training.

Research studies support the use of problem-solving therapy. Kazdin (2005) reviews 10 studies that document a variety of outcomes in comparison with control groups. In particular, the studies find significant reductions in antisocial behavior and increases in prosocial behavior. Combining problem-solving therapy with parent-management treatment tends to increase the effectiveness. Many studies add to the evidence of problem

Table 4.8 Strategies for Implementing Problem-Solving Therapy

Problem solving is taught in a systematic step-by-step process.

Adolescents learn how to approach situations that can use problem-solving skills.

Adolescents learn to make self-statements that focus attention on the process.

Solutions are selected that are deemed important to the youth and significant others.

Modeling and reinforcement are used to promote prosocial behaviors.

Structured tasks like games, activities, and stories are used to teach the skills.

Applications of problem solving move from canned versions to real-life applications.

Problem-solving abilities are modeled by applying statements to particular problems.

Cues are used to prompt the use of the problem-solving skills.

Feedback, re-rehearsal, and praise are used to train adolescents in the use of the skills.

Essential ingredients include modeling, practice, role-plays, feedback, and praise.

Adapted from "Child, Parent, and Family-Based Treatment of Aggressive and Antisocial Child Behavior", by A. E. Kazdin, in *Psychosocial Treatments for Child and Adolescent Disorders: Empirically Based Strategies for Clinical Practice* (pp. 445–476), E. D. Hibbs and P. S. Jensen (Eds.), 2005, Washington, DC: American Psychological Association.

Table 4.9 **Steps for Teaching Social Skills**

Step	Description
Present the social skill taught.	Solicit an explanation of the skill and get group members to provide rationales for the skill.
Discuss the social skill.	List the skill steps and get group members to give examples of using the skill.
Present a problem situation and model the skill.	Evaluate the performance and get group members to discuss the model.
Set the stage for role-playing the skill.	Select members for role-playing and get group members to observe the role-play.
Group members rehearse the skill.	Provide coaching if needed and get members to provide feedback on verbal and nonverbal elements.
Practice using complex skill situations.	Teach accessory skills (e.g., problem solving) and get members to discuss situations and provide feedback.
Train for generalization and maintenance.	Encourage practicing skills outside the group and get members to bring in their own problem situations.

Adapted from "Social Skills Training," by C .W. LeCroy, in *Handbook of Evidence-Based Child and Adolescent Treatment Manuals* (pp. 99–136), C. W. LeCroy (Ed.), 2008, New York: Oxford University Press; and "Designing and Facilitating Groups With Children," by C. W. LeCroy, in *The School Services Sourcebook: A Guide for School-Based Professionals* (pp. 595–602), C. Franklin, M. B. Harris, and P. Allen-Meares (Eds.), 2006, New York, NY: Oxford University Press.

solving if you consider studies that include elements of problem-solving therapy in their overall model.

Research on social-skills training is more varied and has been examined in prevention and with specific clinical disorders. In the prevention field, social-skills training is often the key component (for example, resistance-skills training in substance-abuse and pregnancy-prevention programs). There are many evidence-based prevention programs that emphasize social-skills training. With clinical disorders, social-skills training is much more of a component of the treatment. For example, with delinquent adolescents, social-skills training may be one part of a comprehensive treatment package. In general, studies have supported the use of social-skills training as an effective component (Carr, 2000; Kazdin, 2005; LeCroy, 2008).

Ongoing Treatment and Case Management

As noted earlier, interventions for adolescents form a continuum from brief structured treatments to longer, ongoing treatment strategies. These longer ongoing interventions are designed for adolescents with persistent and long-term conditions. Typically, multimodel interventions will be directed at youth, such as residential treatment, special education, ongoing family treatment, medication management, and special education. An important aspect of intervention at this level is the awareness and understanding that the problems being confronted are serious and chronic. In many respects, the mental-health system has not adapted an approach to intervention that acknowledges and responds to these chronic conditions.

Multidimensional Foster Care

This model of care was designed as an alternative to placement in group-care settings and uses a series of multicomponent, multilevel interventions that occur in family, school, and community settings (Chamberlain, 1994; Chamberlain & Smith, 2005). This model assumes that problems are determined by multiple causes and effects, and, therefore, the intervention focuses on multiple settings. This program has been used with a variety of adolescents, including adolescents leaving mental hospitals (Chamberlain & Reid, 1991), adolescents with low cognitive functioning and inappropriate sexual behavior (Chamberlain, 2003), and adolescents with behavioral and emotional problems (Smith, Stormshak, Chamberlain, & Bridges Whaley, 2001). This program recruits foster families and trains and supervises them to provide daily care of the adolescents placed with them. A major aspect of the intervention is training foster parents in the social-learning, parent-training model. It integrates six service elements, including individual therapy and skill training, family therapy with biological relatives, school consultations and school-based interventions, consultation with parole or probation officers, psychiatric consultation, and case-management services, to coordinate all aspects of the program. Regular home visits are conducted throughout the youth's placement, where the goal is to return the adolescent to his or her family of origin following placement in the Multidimensional Treatment Foster Care (MTFC) program. The placement usually lasts 6 to 9 months. Research results from three studies (see Chamberlain & Smith, 2005, for a review) of MTFC using comparison or control groups have found promising outcomes. For example, one study (Chamberlain, Ray, & Moore, 1996) reports outcome data favoring the intervention over the control group, noting significantly fewer arrests, self-reported delinquent behavior, fewer days incarcerated, and fewer instances of running away. Cost-benefit data also suggest the program is cost effective. A similar program is multiple family group (MFG) treatment, although it is not long term. MFG interventions have been increasingly offered as treatments for clinically diagnosed youth (Fristad, Goldberg-Arnold, & Gavazzi, 2003; McKay, Harrison, Gonzales, Kim, & Quintana, 2002). The program offers family meetings and addresses multiple goals, such as psychoeducation, information exchange, parent support, parent management, family communication, supervision, and household rules. Studies have found that MFG leads to better outcomes than treatment as usual and engages more families in treatment.

This chapter presents a limited number of evidence-based interventions with adolescents. Table 4.10 presents some of the more commonly used treatment manuals and resources for prevention and intervention.

Table 4.10 **Commonly Used Treatment Manuals and Resources for Prevention and Intervention**

Alexander, J., & Parsons, B. (1982). *Functional family therapy*. Monterey, CA: Brooks/Cole.

Botvin, G. (2001). *Life skills training manual*. New York, NY: Cornell University Medical Center.

Chamberlain, P. (1994). *Family connections: A treatment foster care model for adolescents with delinquency*. Eugene, OR: Castalia Press.

Clarke, G., & Lewinsohn, P. (1984). *The Coping with Depression Course—Adolescent Version: A psychoeducational intervention for unipolar depression in high school students*. Eugene, OR: Castalia Press.

Dishion, T. J., & Kavahagh, K. (2001). *Intervening in adolescent problem behavior*. New York, NY: Guilford Press.

Fairburn, C., & Wilson, G. (1993). *Binge eating: Assessment and treatment*. New York, NY: Guilford Press.

Feindler, E., & Ecton, R. (1985). *Adolescent anger control: Cognitive-behavioral techniques*. New York, NY: Pergamon.

Forgatch, M., & Patterson, G. (1989). *Parents and adolescents living together: Part 2. Family problem solving*. Eugene, OR: Castalia Press.

Henggeler, S., & Bordvin, S. (1990). *Family therapy and beyond: A multisystemic approach to treatment the behavior problems of children and adolescents*. Pacific Grove, CA: Brooks/Cole.

Kendall, P., Chansky, T. E., Kane, M. T., Kim, R. S., Kortander, E., Ronan, K. R., . . . Siqueland, L. (1992). *Anxiety disorder in youth: Cognitive behavioral interventions*. Needham Heights, MA: Allyn & Bacon.

LeCroy, C. W., & Daley, J. (2001). *Empowering adolescent girls: Building skills for the future with the Go Grrrls program*. New York, NY: Norton.

Mufson, L., Moreau, D., Weissman, M., & Klerman, G. (1993). *Interpersonal psychotherapy with depressed adolescents*. New York, NY: Guilford Press.

Robin, A., & Foster, S. (1989). *Negotiating parent-adolescent conflict*. New York, NY: Guilford Press.

Robin, A. (1998). *ADHD in adolescents: Diagnosis and treatment*. New York, NY: Guilford Press.

Szapocznik, J., & Kurtines, W. (1989). *Breakthroughs in family therapy with drug abusing youth*. New York, NY: Springer.

Considerations in Service Delivery

A critical issue in service delivery with adolescents is their ability to find and accept help when they deem it necessary. Although adolescence is a time when some serious problems can emerge, it unfortunately is also a time when adolescents face acute barriers to accessing the help they need. Adolescents all too often do not know where to go for help or who they can trust to get help. Consider the following scenarios: the adolescent girl who is raped but too ashamed to tell her friends or parents, an adolescent trapped in a sexually intimate relationship with no birth control or STD protection, the adolescent who has depressed moods and feels hopeless, or an adolescent who feels trapped by a gang into illegal behavior.

Given their level of need, adolescents vastly underutilize systems of care. Research studies have found that adolescents seek care less than any other age group (Cypress, 1984). The key factors in this underutilization of services are cost, poor organization of services, lack of availability, and concerns regarding confidentiality (Millstein & Litt, 1990). Furthermore, many of the serious problems confronted by adolescents, such as mental disorders, sexually transmitted diseases, and abuse, are not covered by many health-insurance plans, or the coverage is so restrictive and complex that access to help is impeded (Ashford & LeCroy, 2010; National Research Council, 1993).

Interventions or systems of care must become more sensitive to adolescents' concerns about their privacy and confidentiality (LeCroy & Daley, 2001). Survey results reveal that under conditions in which medical treatment would be confidential, adolescents would be significantly more likely to seek care for depression, birth control, STDs, and drug use (Council on Scientific Affairs, 1993). One study (Kobocow, McGuire, & Blau, 1983) administered personal interviews requiring substantial self-disclosure to a group of 195 seventh- and eighth-grade students and found that "56.8% of females and 38.6% of males listed assurance of confidentiality as the most important statement made to the interviewer prior to the interview" (p. 422). These results illustrate the high value that adolescents place on confidentiality as well as the need for increased sensitivity to adolescents' strong concerns about their privacy. If we want to help young people in trouble or at risk, we need to pave a road for them that is easy to follow and will lead to a successful outcome. Access to professionals who are specifically trained with adolescents is only one component of successful intervention for youth in trouble. Youth who need help must feel cared for and respected by a network of people.

Motivation for Treatment

A distinguishing feature of interventions with adolescents, as compared with adults, is that often the client has not sought help of his or her own accord. Many adolescents end up in treatment because they were arrested, a parent found drugs in their room, or a teacher reported behavior problems. Although we have stressed promising or evidence-based interventions with adolescents, all are dependent on engagement in the treatment. Engagement is a significant issue for both adolescents and their families, if doing family therapy.

Increasingly, engagement is being addressed as a significant aspect of delivering effective services. The popularity of motivational interviewing (Miller & Rollnick, 2002) is related to awareness of the need for proper engagement in treatment. The stages-of-change model (Prochaska & DiClemente, 1986) also helps focus intervention efforts on motivation. For example, the majority of people who quit smoking do so on their own—once they are in the proper stage of change and motivated to take action toward the problem. Dishion and Kavanagh (2003) discuss initial strategies for engaging adolescents in treatment. Table 4.11 presents a summary of those ideas.

Table 4.11 **Strategies for Engaging Adolescents in Treatment**

Strategy	Description
Respect privacy and space.	Adolescents often begin treatment with a sense of mistrust. Empathize with their reluctance to participate in the treatment.
Normalize experiences.	Try to normalize the adolescent's need for help—for example, "This can be a difficult time, and a lot of young people have found talking with someone helpful."
Advocate the adolescent's interest.	Be clear about your relationship with the adolescent. Communicate about how you perceive his or her situation and describe what the benefit is for his or her involvement.
Link interests and services.	Adolescents are more engaged if they see the connection between their concerns, the assessment, and the intervention.
Create optimistic reframes.	The extent of an adolescent's engagement in treatment is related to the use of positive reframes.
Keep it brief, start slowly.	Don't make the mistake of being too friendly or too confrontational, or both, too early in treatment. Adolescents may be better helped in a brief time period, such as 30 minutes, rather than the standard 50-minute session.

Adapted from *Intervening in Adolescent Problem Behavior: A Family-Centered Approach*, by T. J. Dishion and K. Kavanagh, New York: Guilford Press, 2003.

Context and Focus of Treatment

Typically when an adolescent is identified as needing help, the most common provision of treatment is the individual adolescent. Although this may be appropriate for many situations, focusing only on the adolescent ignores the context—the various systems that can influence one's functioning. Environmental factors play an important role in understanding and intervening in adolescent problem behaviors. The adolescent's individual and cognitive functioning are important, interpersonal relationships and peer relationships are considered critical in adolescence, the school system provides an important context for understanding difficulties, and the community and neighborhood can have a direct influence of functioning. Many adverse contextual features have been shown to have direct implications for adolescent functioning and clinical disorders. For example, such factors as sexual abuse or participation in a peer drug culture are going to directly impact an adolescent's functioning. As a contextual factor, poverty limits access to, participation in, and effectiveness of interventions. These multiple influences raise the question, "To whom should the treatment be directed?" (Kazdin, 2000). Interventions can occur at the individual, family, peer, school, and neighborhood level. A common error is to limit the intervention to just the individual level (LeCroy, 1992). Family and peer interventions are sometimes needed to produce desired outcomes. Many of the evidence-based programs reviewed in this chapter stress a multidimensional approach to treatment. At the prevention level, neighborhoods and communities are reasonable targets for change. Increasingly, researchers and practitioners are embracing the value of an ecological perspective for intervention.

Conclusion

Progress in developing and implementing interventions for adolescents that achieve measurable benefit has been substantial (Carr, 2000; Kazdin & Weisz, 2003). This limited review has presented a variety of programs that represent different strategies for intervention. The strategies vary from prevention to intervention and suggest a continuum of intervention. Figure 4.1 depicts the ecological context, showing at the center the

Figure 4.1

Ecological framework for adolescent intervention

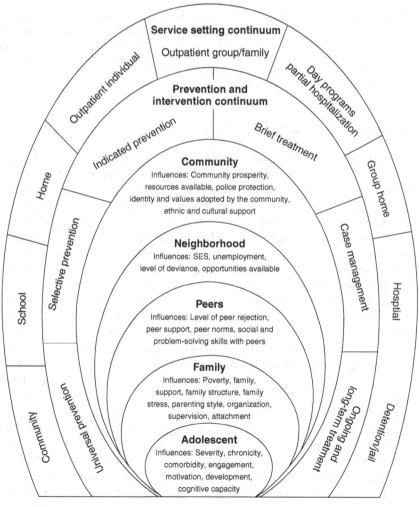

Adapted from Mrazek and Haggarty (1994); Stroul and Friedman (1986); and Weisz, Sandler, Durlak, and Anton (2005).

adolescent, family, peer, neighborhood, and community context. Factors that can have impending influences are identified at each level. Interventions can range from universal prevention to ongoing and long-term treatment, as suggested by Figure 4.1. The figure also depicts the multiple intervention settings where interventions occur, such as school or community settings.

Adolescents face critical issues in today's complex society. Too often, adolescents face risks that they are not prepared to cope with. However, interventions for adolescents suggest promising new developments, and there is new evidence for the effectiveness of these interventions. Implementation issues, such as access to services and motivation for treatment, are also being acknowledged, and ongoing knowledge of these factors can enhance the interventions being used with young people.

Key Terms

Intervention strategies   Developmental   Evidence based

Engaging adolescents   considerations   Help seeking

Review Questions for Critical Thinking

1. What unique developmental capacities are important to consider in creating and implementing effective interventions for adolescents?

2. List common adolescent problem behaviors and mental disorders. Why are they of particular concern?

3. When working with adolescents, why is it important to implement treatment or intervention programs that are promising or evidence based?

4. Compare and contrast universal, selective, and indicated prevention. What implications do these have for working with youth with diverse needs (i.e., from normative populations to youth with developmental concerns to adolescents requiring treatment)?

5. What are effective intervention strategies for working with adolescents? How do these vary by the type of treatment being offered (e.g., substance abuse, early pregnancy/HIV prevention, etc.)? What universal strategies do we know to be effective with youth?

6. List relevant skill sets that can be taught to adolescents to enhance their resiliency and promote healthy transitions into adulthood. Which ones do you think would be the easiest/hardest to change?

7. What factors help us understand why adolescents are reluctant to seek help? How can we reduce the barriers to help-seeking?

8. Describe effective strategies for engaging youth in treatment. Give an example of how you could use one of these strategies in your own practice.

9. Identify the ecological contexts of adolescents' behavior. Give an example of how interventions can occur at multiple intervention settings and the impact on adolescent behavior and well-being.

Online Resources

http://www.socialworkers.org/practice/adolescent_health/default.asp
   This website contains resources and recommendations for practitioners for improving the health and well-being of adolescents.

http://www.promisingpractices.net/ This website provides a list of promising and evidence-based interventions for youth.

http://www.cdc.gov/ This website belongs to the Centers for Disease Control and Prevention and is linked to many health-related studies that used evidence-informed approaches and evidence-based practices.

http://nih.gov/ These national websites provide information on the health of adolescents as well as funding initiatives and opportunities.

References

Alexander, J. F., & Parsons, B. V. (1982). *Functional family therapy*. Monterey, CA: Brooks/Cole.

Arnett, J. J. (2004). *Emerging adulthood: The winding road from the late teens through the twenties*. New York, NY: Oxford University Press.

Ashford, J. & LeCroy, C. (2010). *Human behavior in the social environment: A multidimensional perspective* (4th ed.). Pacific Grove, CA: Wadsworth.

Barth, R. P., Fetro, J., Leland, N., & Volkan, K. (1992). Preventing adolescent pregnancy with social and cognitive skills. *Journal of Adolescent Research, 7*, 208–232.

Botvin, G. (2001). *Life skills training manual*. New York, NY: Cornell University Medical Center.

Botvin, G., Baker, E., Busenbury, L., Tortu, S., & Botvin, E. (1990). Preventing adolescent drug abuse through a multimodal cognitive behavioural approach: Results of a three year study. *Journal of Consulting and Clinical Psychology, 58*, 437–446.

Botvin, G., Schinke, S., Epstein, J., & Diaz, T. (1994). Effectiveness of culturally focused and generic skills training approaches to alcohol and drug abuse prevention among minority youths. *Psychology of Addictive Behaviours, 8*, 116–127.

Brown, J. D. (2011). The media do matter: Comment on Steinberg and Monahan (2011). *Developmental Psychology, 47*, 580–581. doi:10.1037/a0022553

Burrus, B., Leeks, K. D., Sipe, T. A., Dolina, S., Soler, R., Elder, R.,...Dittus, P. (2012). Person-to-person interventions targeted to parents and other caregivers to improve adolescent health: A community guide systematic review. *American Journal of Preventive Medicine, 42*, 316–326.

Carr, A. (2000). *What works with children and adolescents? A critical review of psychological interventions with children, adolescents and their families*. New York, NY: Routledge.

Carr, A. (2002). *Prevention: What works with children and adolescents? A critical review of psychological prevention programmes for children, adolescents and their families*. New York, NY: Taylor & Francis.

Catania, J., Kegeles, S., & Coates, T. (1990). Towards an understanding of risk behaviour: An AIDS Risk Reduction Model (ARRM). *Health Education Quarterly, 17*, 53–72.

Centers for Disease Control and Prevention (2011). CDC health disparities and inequalities report – United States, 2011. *MMWR, 60*(Suppl), 56–59.

Centers for Disease Control and Prevention (2012). Birth rates for US Teenagers reach historic lows for all age and ethnic groups. *NCHS Data Brief, 89.*

Centers for Disease Control and Prevention (2012). Prevalence of autism spectrum disorders—autism and developmental disabilities monitoring network, 14 sites, United States, 2009. *MMWR, 61*(3), 1–19.

Chamberlain, P. (1994). *Family connections: A treatment foster care model for adolescents with delinquency*. Eugene, OR: Castalia.

Chamberlain, P. (2003). *Treating chronic juvenile offenders*. Washington, DC: American Psychological Association.

Chamberlain, P., Ray, J., & Moore, K. J. (1996). Characteristics of residential care of adolescent offenders: A comparison of assumptions and practices in two models. *Journal of Child and Family Studies, 5*, 259–271.

Chamberlain, P., & Reid, J. B. (1991). Using a specialized foster care treatment model for children and adolescents leaving the state mental hospital. *Journal of Community Psychology, 19*, 266–276.

Chamberlain, P., & Smith, D. K. (2005). Antisocial behavior in children and adolescents: The Oregon Multidimensional Treatment Foster Care Model. In A. E. Kazdin & J. R. Weisz (Eds.), *Evidence-based psychotherapies for children and adolescents* (pp. 557–574). New York, NY: Oxford University Press.

Chapman, C., Laird, J., & Kewal Ramani, A. (2010). *Trends in high school dropout and completion rates in the United States: 1972–2009* (NCES 2011–012). National Center for Education Statistics, Institute of Education Sciences, U.S. Department of Education. Washington, DC.

Chou, C., Montgomery, S., Pentz, M., Rohrback, L., Johnson, C., Flay, B., et al. (1998). Effects of a community based prevention program on decreasing drug use in high risk adolescents. *American Journal of Public Health, 88*, 944–948.

Chou, C., Yang, D., Pentz, M., & Hser, Y.-I. (2004). Piecewise growth curve modeling approach for longitudinal prevention study. *Computational Statistics & Data Analysis, 46*, 213–225.

Clarke, G., & Lewinsohn, P. (1984). *The coping with depression course—Adolescent version: A psychoeducational intervention for unipolar depression in high school students*. Eugene, OR: Castalia Press.

Clarke, G., Rohde, P., Lewinsohn, P. M., Hops, H., & Seeley, J. R. (1999). Cognitive-behavioral treatment of adolescent depression: Efficacy of acute group treatment and booster sessions. *Journal of American Academy of Child and Adolescent Psychiatry, 38*, 272–279.

Compas, B. E., Benson, M., Boyer, M., Hicks, T. V., & Konik, B. (2002). Problem-solving and problem-solving therapies. In M. Rutter & E. Taylor (Eds.), *Child and adolescent psychiatry* (4th ed., pp. 938–948). Malden, MA: Blackwell.

Compas, B. E., Connor-Smith, J. K., Saltzman, H., Thomsen, A. H., & Wadsworth, M. E. (2001). Coping with stress during childhood and adolescence: Progress, problems and potential. *Psychological Bulletin, 127*, 87–127.

Council on Scientific Affairs, American Medical Association. (1993). Confidential health services for adolescents. *Journal of the American Medical Association*, *269*, 1420–1424.

Cypress, B. K. (1984). *Health care of adolescents by office-based physicians: National Ambulatory Care Survey, 1980–1981* (DHHS, NCHS Publication, No. 99). Washington, DC: U.S. Government Printing Office.

Dishion, T. J., & Kavanagh, K. (2003). *Intervening in adolescent problem behavior: A family centered approach*. New York, NY: Guilford Press.

D'Zurilla, T. J., & Nezu, A. M. (1990). Development and preliminary evaluation of the social problem-solving inventory. *Psychological Assessment: A Journal of Consulting and Clinical Psychology*, *2*, 156–163.

Evans, D. L., Foa, E. B., Gur, R. E., Hendin, H., O'Brien, C. P., Seligman, M. E. P., et al. (2005). *Treating and preventing adolescent mental health disorders: What we know and what we don't know*. New York, NY: Oxford University Press.

Evans, D. L., & Seligman, M. E. P. (2005). Introduction. In D. L. Evans, E. B. Foa, R. E. Gur, H. Hendin, C. P. O'Brien, M. E. P. Seligman, & B. T. Walsh (Eds.), *Treating and preventing adolescent mental health disorders: What we know and don't know* (pp. xxv–xi). New York, NY: Oxford University Press.

Fairburn, C., & Wilson, G. (1993). *Binge eating: Assessment and treatment*. New York, NY: Guilford Press.

Feindler, E., & Ecton, R. (1985). *Adolescent anger control: Cognitive-behavioral techniques*. New York, NY: Pergamon Press.

Fonagy, P., & Kurtz, A. (2002). Disturbance of conduct. In P. Fonagy, M. Target, D. Cottrell, J. Phillips, & Z. Kurtz (Eds.), *What works for whom? A critical review of treatments for children and adolescents* (pp. 106–192). New York, NY: GuilfordPress.

Fonagy, P., Target, M., Cottrell, D., Phillips, J., & Kurtz, Z. (2002). *What works for whom? A critical review of treatments for children and adolescents*. New York, NY: GuilfordPress.

Forgatch, M., & Patterson, G. (1989). *Parents and adolescents living together: Pt. 2. Family problem solving*. Eugene, OR: Castalia Press.

Fristad, M. A., Goldberg-Arnold, J. S., & Gavazzi, S. M. (2003). Multi-family psychoeducation groups in the treatment of children with mood disorders. *Journal of Marital and Family Therapy*, *29*, 491–504.

Geels, L. M., Bartels, M., van Beijsterveldt, T. C. E. M., Willemsen, G., van der Aa, N., Boomsma, D. I., & Vink, J. M. (2012). Trends in adolescent alcohol use: Effects of age, sex, and cohort on prevalence and heritability. *Addiction*, *107*, 518–527.

Hansen, W., Graham, J., Wolkenstein, B., & Rohrback, L. (1991). Program integrity as a moderator of prevention program effectiveness: Results for fifth-grade students in the adolescent alcohol prevention trial. *Journal of Studies on Alcohol*, *52*, 568–579.

Henggeler, S. W., & Bordvin, S. (1990). *Family therapy and beyond: A multisystemic approach to the treating the behavior problems of children and adolescents*. Pacific Grove, CA: Brooks/Cole.

Henggeler, S. W., & Lee, T. (2003). Multisystemic treatment of serious clinical problems. In A. E. Kazdin & J. R. Weisz (Eds.), *Evidence-based psychotherapies for children and adolescents* (pp. 301–322). New York, NY: Guilford Press.

Henggeler, S. W., Schoenwald, S. K., Borduin, C. M., Rowland, M. D., & Cunningham, P. B. (1998). *Multisystemic treatment of antisocial behavior in children and adolescents*. New York, NY: Guilford Press.

Hibbs, E. D., & Jensen, P. S. (2005). *Psychosocial treatments for child and adolescent disorders: Empirically based strategies for clinical practice* (2nd ed.). Washington, DC: American Psychological Association.

Hoagwood, K. (2005). Family-based services in children's mental health: A research review and synthesis. *Journal of Child Psychology and Psychiatry: Annual Research Review, 46,* 690–713.

Institute of Medicine (1994). *Reducing risk for mental disorders: Frontiers for prevention intervention research*. Washington, DC: National Academy Press.

Jemmott, J., Jemmott, L., & Fong, G. (1992). Reductions in HIV risk-associated sexual behaviours among Black male adolescents: Effects of an AIDS prevention intervention. *American Journal of Public Health, 82,* 372–377.

Johnson, C., Pentz, M., Weber, M., Dwyer, J., Bear, N., MacKinnon, D., . . . Flay, B. (1990). Relative effectiveness of comprehensive community programming for drug abuse prevention with high risk and low risk adolescents. *Journal of Consulting and Clinical Psychology, 58,* 447–456.

Johnston, L. D., O'Malley, P. M., Bachman, J. G., & Schulenberg, J. E. (2012). *Monitoring the Future national results on adolescent drug use: Overview of key findings, 2011*. Ann Arbor: Insitute for Social Research, University of Michigan.

Kazdin, A. E. (1993). Psychotherapy for children and adolescents: Current progress and future research directions. *American Psychologist, 48,* 644–657.

Kazdin, A. E. (2000). *Psychotherapy for children and adolescents: Directions for research and practice*. Oxford, UK: Oxford University Press.

Kazdin, A. E. (2003). Problem solving skill training and parent management training for conduct disorder. In A. E. Kazdin & J. R. Weisz (Eds.), *Evidence-based psychotherapy for children and adolescents* (pp. 241–262). New York, NY: Guilford Press.

Kazdin, A. E. (2005). Child, parent, and family-based treatment of aggressive and antisocial child behavior. In E. D. Hibbs & P. S. Jensen (Eds.), *Psychosocial treatments for child and adolescent disorders: Empirically based strategies for clinical practice* (pp. 44–476). Washington, DC: American Psychological Association.

Kazdin, A. E., & Weisz, J. R. (2003). *Evidence-based psychotherapy for children and adolescents*. New York, NY: Guilford Press.

Kendall, P. T. E., Chansky, M. T., Kane, R. S., Kim, E., Kortander, K. R., Ronan, F. M., et al. (1992). *Anxiety disorder in youth: Cognitive behavioral interventions*. Needham Heights, MA: Allyn & Bacon.

Kobocow, B., McGuire, J. M., & Blau, B. I. (1983). The influence of confidentiality conditions on self-disclosure of early adolescents. *Professional Psychology: Research and Practice, 14,* 435–475.

LeCroy, C. W. (1992). Enhancing the delivery of effective mental health services to children. *Social Work, 37,* 225–233.

LeCroy, C. W. (2006). Designing and facilitating groups with children. In C. Franklin, M. B. Harris, & P. Allen-Meares (Eds.), *The school services sourcebook: A guide for school based professionals* (pp. 595–602). New York, NY: Oxford University Press.

LeCroy, C. W. (2008). Social skills training. In C. W. LeCroy (Ed.), *Handbook of evidence-based child and adolescent treatment manuals* (pp. 99–138). New York, NY: Oxford University Press.

LeCroy, C. W., & Daley, J. (2001). *Empowering adolescent girls: Building skills for the future with the Go Grrrls Program*. New York, NY: Norton.

LeCroy, C. W., & Wooton, L. (2002). Social skills groups in the schools. In R. Constable, S. McDonald, & J. P. Flynn (Eds.), *School social work: Practice, policy, and research* (pp. 441–457). Chicago, IL: Lyceum.

Lewinsohn, P. M., Clarke, G. N., Hops, H., & Andrews, J. (1990). Cognitive-behavioral group treatment of depression in adolescents. *Behavior Therapy, 21*, 385–401.

Lewinsohn, P. M., & Gotlib, I. H. (1995). Behavioral theory and treatment of depression. In E. E. Beckam & W. R. Leber (Eds.), *Handbook of depression* (pp. 352–375). New York, NY: Guilford Press.

McKay, M., Harrison, M., Gonzales, J., Kim, L., & Quintana, E. (2002). Multiple family groups for urban children with conduct difficulties and their families. *Psychiatric Services, 53*, 1467–1469.

Merikangas, K. R., He, J., Burstein, M., Swanson, S. A., Avenevoli, S., Cui, L.,...Swendsen, J. (2010). Lifetime prevalence of mental disorders in U.S. adolescents: Results from the National Comorbidity Study-Adolescent Supplement (NCS-A). *Journal of the American Academy of Child and Adolescent Psychiatry, 49*, 980–989.

Miller, W. R., & Rollnick, S. (2002). *Motivational interviewing: Preparing people for change* (2nd ed.). New York, NY: Guilford Press.

Millstein, S. G., & Litt, I. F. (1990). Adolescent health. In S. Feldman & G. R. Elliott (Eds.), *At the threshold: The developing adolescent* (pp. 213–223). Cambridge, MA: Harvard University Press.

Mrazek, P. J., & Haggerty, R. J. (1994). *Reducing risks for mental disorders: Frontiers for preventive intervention*. Washington, DC: National Academies Press.

Mufson, L., Moreau, D., Weissman, M. W., & Klerman, G. L. (1993). *Interpersonal psychotherapy with depressed adolescents*. New York, NY: Guilford Press.

Nathan, P., & Gorman, J. (1998). *A guide to treatments that work*. New York, NY: Oxford University Press.

National Research Council (1993). *Losing generations: Adolescents in high-risk settings*. Washington, DC: National Academy Press.

Pentz, M., Trebow, E., Hansen, W., MacKinnon, D., Dwyer, J., Johnson, C.,...Cormack, C. (1990). Effects of program implementation on adolescent drug use behaviour: The Midwestern Prevention Project (MPP). *Evaluation Review, 14*, 264–289.

Perry, C. L., Williams, C. L., Komro, K. A., Veblen-Mortenson, S., Forster, J. L., Bernstein-Lachter, R,...McGovern, P. (2000, February). Project Northland High School Interventions: Community action to reduce adolescent alcohol use. *Health Education and Behavior, 27*, 29–49.

Perry, C. L., Williams, C. L., Veblen-Mortenson, S., Toomey, T., Komro, K., Anstine, P.,...Wolfson, M. (1996). Project Northland: Outcomes of a community wide alcohol use prevention programme during early adolescence. *American Journal of Public Health, 86*, 956–965.

Prochaska, J. O., & DiClemente, C. C. (1986). Toward a comprehensive model of change. In W. Miller & N. Heather (Eds.), *Treating addictive behaviors: Processes of change* (pp. 3–27). New York, NY: Plenum Press.

Robin, A. (1998). *ADHD in adolescents: Diagnosis and treatment*. New York, NY: Guilford Press.

Robin, A., & Foster, S. (1989). *Negotiating parent-adolescent conflict*. New York, NY: Guilford Press.

Rohde, P., Clarke, G. N., Mace, D. E., Jorgensen, J. S., & Seeley, J. R. (2004) An efficacy/effectiveness study of cognitive-behavioral treatment for adolescents with comorbid major depression and conduct disorder. *Journal of the American Academy of Child and Adolescent Psychiatry, 43*, 660–668.

Rohde, P., Lewinsohn, P. M., Clarke, G. N., Hops, H., & Seeley, J. R. (2005). The adolescent coping with depression course: A cognitive-behavioral approach to the treatment of depression. In E. D. Hibbs & P. S. Jensen (Eds.), *Psychosocial treatments for child and adolescent disorders: Empirically based strategies for clinical practice* (pp. 219–238). Washington, DC: American Psychological Association.

Rutter, M., & Taylor, E. (2002). Clinical assessment and diagnostic formulation. In M. Rutter & E. Taylor (Eds.), *Child and adolescent psychiatry* (pp. 247–272). Malden, MA: Blackwell.

Schinke, S., & Gilchrist, L. (1983). Coping with contraception: Cognitive with behavioral methods with adolescents. *Cognitive Therapy and Research, 7*, 379–388.

Schinke, S., Gordon, A. N., & Weston, R. E. (1990). Self-instruction to prevent HIV infection among African-American and Hispanic-American adolescents. *Journal of Consulting and Clinical Psychology, 58*, 432–436.

Sheeran, P., Abraham, C., & Orbell, S. (1999). Psychosocial correlates of condom use: A meta-analysis. *Psychological Bulletin, 125*, 90–132.

Smith, D. K., Stormshak, E., Chamberlain, P., & Bridges Whaley, R. (2001). Placement disruptions in treatment foster care. *Journal of Emotional and Behavioral Disorders, 9*, 200–205.

Spivack, G., & Shure, M. B. (1976). *Social adjustment of young children*. San Francisco, CA: Jossey-Bass.

Spoth, R. L., Randall, G. K., Trudeau, L., Shin, C., & Cleve, R. (2008). Substance use outcomes 5-1/2 years past baseline for partnership-based, family-school preventive interventions. *Drug and Alcohol Dependence, 96*, 57–68.

St. Lawrence. J. S., Jefferson, K. W., Alleyne, E., & Brasfield, T. L. (1995). Comparison of education versus behavioral skills training interventions in lowering sexual HIV-risk behaviour of substance-dependent adolescents. *Journal of Consulting and Clinical Psychology, 63*, 154–157.

Steinberg, L., & Monahan, K. C. (2011). Adolescents' exposure to sexy media does not hasten the initiation of sexual intercourse. *Developmental Psychology, 47*, 562–576. doi:10.1037/a0020613

Stroul, B., & Friedman, R. (1986). A system of care for severely emotionally disturbed children and youth. Washington, DC: Georgetown University, CASSP Technical Assistance Center.

Sweeting, H., Jackson, C., & Haw, S. (2011). Changes in the socio-demographic patterning of late adolescent health risk behaviours during the 1990s: Analysis of two West of Scotland cohort studies. *BMC Public Health, 11*, 829–843.

Szapocznik, J., & Kurtines, W. (1989). *Breakthroughs in family therapy with drug abusing youth*. New York, NY: Springer.

Task Force on Promotion and Dissemination of Psychological Procedures (1995). Training in and dissemination of empirically validated psychological treatments: Report and recommendations. *Clinical Psychologist, 48*, 3–23.

Timmons-Mitchell, J., Bender, M. N., Kishna, M. A., & Mitchel, C. C. (2006). An independent effectiveness trial of multisystemic therapy with juvenile justice youth. *Journal of Clinical Child and Adolescent Psychology, 35,* 226–236.

U.S. Public Health Service, Office of the Surgeon General (2004). *Report of the Surgeon General's conference on children's mental health: A national action agenda.* Rockville, MD: Author.

Weisz, J. R., Sandler, I. N., Durlak, J. A., & Anton, B. S. (2005). Promoting and protecting youth mental health through evidence-based prevention and treatment. *American Psychologist, 60,* 628–648.

Chapter 5
Assessment of Adults

Elaine Congress

> **Purpose:** This chapter presents challenges and different evidence-informed assessments used with adult clients in a variety of practice settings.
> **Rationale:** Clients present with a range of different problems that require different assessment protocols and approaches.
> **How evidence-informed practice is presented:** A variety of assessment theories and tools used with clients who present with a variety of psychosocial problems is presented in this chapter.
> **Overarching question:** What are five essential ingredients one must consider to make an effective assessment of an adult client?

In order to provide effective evidence-based interventions with adult clients, a thorough assessment is essential. Although fundamental in planning and providing effective treatment for adult clients, assessment is a challenging endeavor. Although there are a variety of definitions of social work assessment, this chapter is based on the following definition from the *Social Work Desk Reference*:

> *Assessment is the process of systematically collecting data about a client's functioning and monitoring progress in client functioning on an ongoing basis. Assessment is defined as a process of problem selection and specification that is guided in social work by a person in environment systems orientation. Assessment is used to identify and measure specific problem behaviors as well as protective and resilience factors, and to determine if treatment is necessary. Information is usually gathered from a variety of sources (e.g., individual, family member, case records, observation, rapid assessment tools and genograms). Types of assessment include bio-psycho-social history taking, multiple dimensional crisis assessment, symptom checklists, functional analysis, and mental status exams.*
>
> —*(Roberts & Greene, 2002, p. 830)*

Using the social work framework of person in environment, a successful assessment involves understanding the individual not only as a physical and psychological entity but also as one engaged in a relationship with both micro- and macro-environments. In looking at the intersection of this person in an environmental matrix, the social worker is in the best position to complete a comprehensive client assessment. Although many regard social work assessment as focusing on problems and diagnosis, the assessment of strengths and resilience is as important in completing a comprehensive assessment of the client. Other common features of current social work assessment models outlined by Jordan and Franklin (2003) include the following:

- Social work assessment models are eclectic and integrative and are not based on one underlying theory.

- Long history taking is deemphasized, and there is a focus on seeking only relevant history that is related to the function of service. For example, a social worker in a medical setting might be most interested in past and present physical health, whereas a social worker in a family-therapy agency might focus on past and present history of family relationships.

- Social work assessment involves a collaborative process between client and worker. Using an evidence-based practice (EBP) approach, the client is actively involved in sharing information with the goal of deciding on the best possible treatment. Involving the client in a short-term active participatory approach to diagnosis is the best way to ensure that the client continues to participate in treatment.

- Assessment and treatment are seen as a unified whole. There is no longer a lengthy assessment period during which clients' needs and problems are held in abeyance. Having a short-term focused assessment enables the client to see the relevance of assessment and helps ensure that the client will remain in treatment. A corollary of this is that assessment does not end before intervention begins. Assessment continues throughout the treatment process. With an ongoing assessment process, the social worker can modify treatment based on new information that emerges from the ongoing assessment process.

A comprehensive client assessment includes many factors, both in terms of the individual (appearance, developmental history, past and current physical health, cognitive ability and style, intellectual capacity, mental status, psychiatric diagnosis, and cultural/racial identity) as well as the individual relationship to environment (role within family, family history, physical environment of home and neighborhood, and relationship to the outside community). An important part of the assessment process involves focusing not only on the deficits that a client presents but also on the client's strengths and resilience.

There are many challenges to completing a comprehensive assessment of a client. First, with the current focus on short-term treatment models, a thorough assessment is often not possible. Clinicians frequently focus only on information needed to complete forms or to select an intervention. In fact, many EBP models look primarily at the client's participation in the choice of intervention and minimize the assessment process. Yet a thorough assessment is most helpful in making the best intervention decision.

Another challenge has been that assessment is often accomplished with a singular focus. Some assessment models favor an individual psychological assessment, whereas others look more at environmental factors influencing the client. The best assessment involves an integrative approach that uses a broad lens for assessing clients from both bio-psychosocial and person-in-environment perspectives. Often, a rating scale, such as the one developed by Pomeroy, Holleran, and Franklin (2003), is helpful in providing a comprehensive individual assessment.

Another frequent criticism of assessment is that it often relies on a deficit model. The assessment of a client often involves diagnosis using *DSM-IV*. Applying only a *DSM-IV* diagnosis to a client focuses on a psychiatric problem and pathology and neglects strengths that should be viewed as important aspects of assessment and intervention with clients.

There is much current emphasis on accurate assessment following a traumatic event. The usual belief that having the individual relive the traumatic event has been challenged by recent evidence (Dyregrov & Regel, 2012) that suggests that rapid assessment followed by early intervention is the most effective treatment.

Historical Background

Psychosocial Diagnostic Assessment

From the birth of the social work profession, many different assessment models have been used. Perhaps the most well known is the psychosocial or diagnosis approach first developed by Hollis. This model relies heavily on family and developmental history to reach a psychodiagnostic assessment of the client. An ego-psychology framework (Goldstein, 2002) is fundamental to this approach. Although this approach initially focused to a large extent on a client's developmental history, now the person/client in relationship to the current environment is stressed. According to a psychosocial-ego-psychology perspective, the assessment process has the following steps: (a) assessing the client's interactions with his or her environment in the here and now and how successfully he or she is coping effectively with major life roles and tasks; (b) assessing the client's adaptive, autonomous, and conflict-free areas of ego functioning as well as ego deficits and maladaptive functioning; (c) evaluating the impact of a client's past on current functioning; and (d) examining environmental obstacles that impede a client's functioning (Goldstein, 2002; Hollis & Wood, 1981). According to a psychosocial diagnostic approach, information for client assessment was collected in a variety of ways, including (a) psychiatric interviews to determine a diagnosis, (b) the use of standardized and projective testing to support diagnostic assessment, (c) current psychosocial assessment and study of prior development and adjustment to identify problem areas, (d) use of standardized interviewing to assess problem areas and current functioning, and (e) study of the client-social work relationship to ascertain client's patterns of interactions (Jordan & Franklin, 2003).

The psychosocial assessment model is well suited to today's medical model that involves the study, diagnosis, and treatment format. Many medically based behavioral-health settings use this approach. Furthermore, the focus of many behavioral-health centers on clients' return to more adaptive functioning is also compatible with a psychosocial-diagnostic-ego-psychology model. A *DSM-IV* diagnosis is usually a requirement for beginning treatment, and thus the detailed study using a psychosocial approach is often helpful in arriving at a diagnosis. Structured assessment tools, such as the eco-map (Hartman & Laird, 1983) and the genogram (McGoldrick, Gerson, & Schallenberg, 1999), are also helpful for practitioners in completing assessments. There is a need for more outcome-focused research, however, on the effectiveness of using these instruments. Finally, the development of standardized semistructured interviews using a psychosocial approach is most helpful in promoting current evidence-based assessment.

Problem-Solving Assessment

Another major assessment model was the problem-solving assessment originally developed by Helen Harris Perlman in 1957. This model is based on the psychosocial diagnosis model described earlier and the functional model that focuses on growth and potential as well as agency function. Perlman saw assessment as an eclectic model with four Ps—person, problem, place, and process—as a way to organize information about the client. In terms of person, the social worker should think of the client's personality characteristics and which interactions with the environment are significant. A second area involves a focus on problem: How can the problem be defined? Is it a crisis, a repetitive issue? What other ways has the client sought to resolve the problem? The third category is place or agency. What concerns does the client have about contact within the agency? What is most helpful and what is most harmful about the agency in the process of client assessment? The fourth relates to process. Which intervention will be most successful? What will be the consequences of a particular choice of treatment?

Current assessment still relies a great deal on the problem-solving approach to assessment. First, a very quick assessment tool, such as that outlined by Perlman, is most helpful in the current social-service environment, with its focus on short-term assessment and intervention. Another advantage, especially for culturally diverse clients who may be fearful of interaction with the agency, is the inclusion of Perlman's third P—place—in the assessment process. This approach encourages the social worker to look at how the fears and feelings that clients may have about the agency affect the assessment process. This may be especially true for undocumented clients who are apprehensive that social workers will use their power and authority to report their immigration status.

There are two major concerns about the problem-solving approach as used in current assessment practice. First, there is limited attention to the person's strengths and resilience in resolving the problem. Modern assessment models seek to focus specifically on the strengths a client brings to the situation. The client's definition of the "problem" and what strengths he or she can use and has used in the past to address the problem are considered key. Another major concern about the problem-solving approach is that it is based primarily on practice wisdom, with limited empirical research to support its use. With the emphasis on EBP, research is needed to ascertain the effectiveness of this assessment model as a foundation for treatment interventions with diverse clients.

Cognitive-Behavior Assessment

Cognitive-behavior assessment models have made a major contribution to current practice and research about assessment. Meichenbaum (1993) outlines three metaphors that have guided this complex model—conditioning, information processing, and constructive narrative. Early cognitive behaviorists focused primarily on conditioning as the way certain behaviors were learned. Then the focus shifted to a greater emphasis on cognitions, social learning, and the development of belief systems. Most recently, the focus has been on the use of client narratives and life stories as part of the assessment process.

Jordan and Franklin (2003) identify four attributes of cognitive behavior assessment that are particularly useful in today's practice:

1. Because much of today's practice focuses on short-term intervention, the focus on rapid assessment and treatment is particularly useful. Assessment includes history only as it is related to the client's current functioning, but the main focus is on identifying the faulty learning and cognitive patterns that have contributed to current maladaptive behavior.

2. Much research has been conducted on outcomes of cognitive behavior approaches. This is particularly useful with today's emphasis on evidence-based assessment and treatment.

3. Many assessment and treatment manuals for use with assessing a number of identified client problems, such as depression, substance abuse, personality disorders, and posttraumatic stress disorder, have been developed using the cognitive-behavioral approach.

4. Ongoing assessment has been stressed as essential in evaluating the effectiveness of treatment. The integration of assessment with treatment is very much part of current beliefs about assessment.

Life-Model Assessment

The life-model assessment (Germain & Gitterman, 1996) uses an ecological framework that focuses on the client's interactions with the environment in three main areas—life transitions, environmental pressures, and maladaptive interpersonal processes. Major aims of this theory are to closely link person and environment, stress the client's perspective, and provide linkages among direct service, administration, and policy planning.

There has been some concern that the life-model assessment does not guide current practice interventions very well (Wakefield, 1996). With the need for short-term evidence-based assessment and intervention, the weakness of this link is problematic. The ecological model, however, has served as a foundation for developing multisystematic therapy, an evidence-based therapy that has proven to be useful with youth and families (Henggeler, Schoenwald, Borduin, Rowland, & Cunningham, 1998). An assessment tool, such as the eco-map (Hartman & Laird, 1983) that is based on the life-model ecological approach, has been useful, although research on this has been limited. Computer software programs may help practitioners use this assessment tool more effectively, standardize its use, and provide more opportunities for research about its effectiveness.

Task-Centered Assessment

The task-centered assessment model developed by Reid (1988) focuses on specific target problems and their desired outcomes. Major steps in this model include task planning, implementation, and review. Task planning builds on initial problem formulation. The client's perception of the problem is considered most important, and the practitioner helps the client in exploring, clarifying, and specifying the problem. Task-centered assessment focuses on a thorough understanding of the client's problems and goals, prioritizing problems and developing a specific contract to achieve the defined goals. This approach is most useful in practice today with a focus on time-limited and evidence-based outcomes.

Solution-Focused Assessment

A major new assessment model is the brief solution-focused therapy assessment developed by De Jong and Berg (2001) for work with mandated clients. With this model, assessment is part of the intervention process. Franklin and Moore (1999) have identified the following methods for conducting a solution-focused assessment:

- Tracking solution behaviors or exceptions to the problem.
- Scaling the problem.
- Using coping and motivation questions.
- Asking the miracle question.

This approach is very client centered and focuses on client's strengths—what clients can do and want to do, not on their deficits and failures. Franklin (2002) identifies positive features of this model with mandated clients:

- Using a nonjudgmental approach in understanding client problems.
- Making the congruence between what the client wants and what services can be provided as close as possible.

- Emphasizing clients' choices as much as possible.
- Providing education to clients about what treatment will involve.
- Developing specific goals with clients.
- Discussing what is nonnegotiable from the agency's standpoint.

Although research on the use of this model has been positive, more work in this area is necessary to evaluate its effectiveness.

Strengths-Perspective Assessment

A final perspective that has had a major influence on current assessment practice is the strengths perspective developed by Saleeby (1997). This perspective is fundamental to the values-based perspective of social work in that all people are seen as having dignity and worth as individuals as well as the right to self-determination. Using this approach, the practitioner looks for knowledge, competencies, hidden resources, and resilience in each and every client who comes for treatment. The practitioner moves away from identifying only deficits or diagnosing pathology with *DSM-IV* toward a broader understanding of person-in-environment client functioning. The strengths perspective has had a significant impact on mental-health services. Yet the strengths perspective is often seen as only one aspect of a comprehensive assessment, with a diagnostic *DSM-IV* approach having more importance in a behavioral-health service-delivery system. There have been various attempts to develop standardized measures to assess strengths and competencies (Jordan & Franklin, 2003) and also to incorporate a strengths approach into a more traditional psychosocial assessment. Incorporating a strengths-based assessment process has been used in work with battered women (Lee, 2007). With the current emphasis on evidence-based assessment and practice, much more empirical research is needed on outcomes with strengths-based assessment.

Summary of Current Evidence-Based Assessment for Individuals

There are a number of sources of information that a social worker can use in completing assessments on individual clients. These sources include:

- Background information on clients from case records.
- Verbal reports from clients about their feelings, history, and problems.
- Direct observation of nonverbal behavior.
- Observation of interaction with family members and others in clients' environment.
- Collateral information from families, relatives, physicians, teachers, employers, and other professionals.
- Tests or other assessment instruments.

Social workers often begin to work with clients after reading lengthy case records. Although there are advantages to having a preliminary understanding of a client before contact is made, the major disadvantage is that case records may unduly influence the social worker's perception of the client. Case records are often written from a deficit perspective. Frequently, a *DSM-IV* diagnosis is included that may not be current. This may be especially true in mental-health settings when the client has had a long history of mental-health treatment. Research on whether the assessment process is helped or hindered by the social worker's prior perusal of a case record is needed.

The primary source of information for assessment should come directly from the client. The practitioner needs to be a skilled interviewer to elicit information that is particularly relevant to the client's problem. Previously, client assessment was a very lengthy process, often spanning several interviews. The current trend is brief assessment to learn information that is particularly pertinent to the client problem and what will be most helpful in future work. A thorough assessment usually includes the following categories (Cooper & Lesser, 2002):

- Identifying information.
- Referral source.
- Presenting problem.
- History of the problem.
- Previous counseling experiences.
- Family background.
- Developmental history.
- Educational history.
- Employment history.
- History of trauma.
- Medical history.
- Cultural history.
- Spirituality/religion.
- Mental status and current functioning.
- Mental status exam.
- Multiaxial *DSM-IV* diagnosis.
- Recommendations and goals for treatment.
- Plans to evaluate.

Including an evaluation plan provides an empirical foundation for the assessment process.

A major source of information for assessment comes from the social worker's observation of nonverbal behavior. What demographic information do we learn nonverbally—sex, age, race? How is the client dressed? How does the client answer questions? How does the client relate to the worker?

Often, the social worker has an opportunity to observe the individual client in interaction with others—family members, friends, group members, or other professionals. This can be an important source of information about the client's challenges in personal relationships with others.

The social worker can learn important information about the client from collateral contact with others, including family and other professionals. It is important, however, that the social worker not rely too much on negative reports of family members. Family members may present distorted views of clients based on their own interests. Reports from others should only be a *secondary* method for receiving information to use in a client assessment.

The final method of gathering information for assessment is through tests or assessment instruments. Because many of these instruments have been standardized, assessment through these measures is considered important in promoting EBP.

Assessment Scales and Tools

The next section explores some of the scales and assessment tools that have been used in assessment of individual clients.

One of the earliest and most well-known scales is the Wechsler Adult Intelligence Scale (WAIS), first published in 1955 and now in its fourth edition (2007). The current version, which is used to measure adult intelligence of people between 16 and 90 years of age, consists of 10 core subtests and 5 supplemental subtests. The 10 core subtests include under the area of verbal comprehension, similarities, vocabulary, information; under the area of perceptual reasoning, block design, matrix reasoning, and visual puzzles; under the area of working memory, digit span and arithmetic; and under the area of processing speed, symbol search and coding. The median full-scale IQ is 100, and 68% of adults fall within one standard deviation, or within 85 to 115. It has been suggested that there may be age differences that are not sufficiently taken into account in WAIS IV (Benson, Hulac, & Kranzler, 2010).

The person-in-environment (PIE) testing scale developed by Pomeroy et al. (2003) is helpful in that each area is considered either as a problem or strength. The categories are appearance, biomedical/organic, use of substances, developmental issues/transitions, coping abilities, stressors, capacity for relationships, social functioning, behavioral function, sexual functioning, problem-solving/coping skills, creativity, cognitive functioning, emotional functioning, self-concept, motivation, cultural and ethnic identification, role functioning, spirituality/religion, and other strengths. Not only is the individual client assessed on these different areas, but each area is also studied in relationship to family, friends, school/work, community, and social work intervention. The value of the PIE rating scale is that it provides an organized, systematic way to acquire important information about the client.

Cultural Assessment

One area of much importance in today's practice is that of cultural and ethnic identification. An increasing number of urban, suburban, and rural clients are either first- or second-generation Americans (U.S. Census, 2000). Understanding a client's cultural background is very important in completing an assessment. The culturagram (Congress, 1994, 2002; Congress & Kung, 2005) has been useful in assessing people of color (Lum, 2004), victims of domestic violence (Congress & Brownell, 2007), older people (Brownell, 1997), children (Webb, 1996), and clients with health problems (Congress, 2004). Making use of a paper-and-pen diagram, the culturagram (see Figure 5.1) looks at reasons for immigration, length of time in the United States, legal status, language spoken at home and in the community, health beliefs, crisis events, holidays, contact with religious and cultural institutions, beliefs about education and work, and beliefs about family structure and roles. As the United States becomes increasingly

Figure 5.1

Culturagram—2007

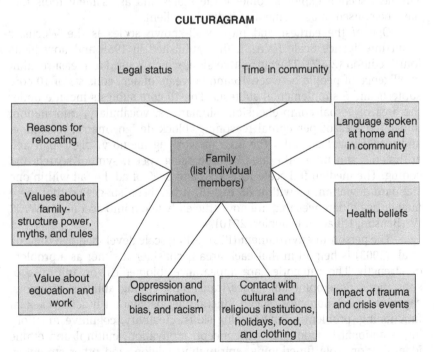

CULTURAGRAM

From "The Culturagram," by E. Congress (Figure 144.1, p. 971; Figure 144.2, p. 974), in A. R. Roberts (Ed.), *Social Workers' Desk Reference*, 2008, New York, NY: Oxford University Press. Reprinted with permission.

diverse, it will be even more important to develop and use assessment tools to better understand clients from different cultural backgrounds.

Suicide Assessment

Suicide assessment and prevention is an important part of any comprehensive assessment process. The number of suicide attempts is on the rise, especially among adolescents. The following factors have been cited as associated with high risk of suicide (Hepworth, Rooney, Rooney, Larsen, & Strom-Gottfried, 2005):

- Feelings of despair and hopelessness.
- History of previous suicide attempts.
- Concrete, available, and lethal plans to commit suicide.
- Family history of suicide.
- Ruminations about suicide.
- Lack of support systems.
- Feelings of worthlessness.
- Belief that others would be better off if one were dead.
- Age—very old or adolescent.
- Substance.

In completing a comprehensive assessment in which the client speaks of feelings of hopelessness, the social worker should not avoid introducing the discussion of suicide, because it is a misconception that talking about suicide will give a client the idea.

There have been a number of scales developed to ascertain suicide risk for adults, such as the Hopelessness Scale (Beck, Resnik, & Lettieri, 1974); the Scale for Suicide Ideation (Beck, Kovacs, & Weissman, 1979), and the Suicide Probability Scale (Cull & Gill, 1991). The Children's Depression Scale (Kovacs, 1992) and the John Hopkins Depression Scale (Joshi, Capozzoli, & Coyle, 1990) are helpful instruments in assessing children's and adolescents' risk of suicide.

DSM-IV **Assessment**

In behavioral-health settings, social workers are frequently expected to understand and make a *DSM-IV-TR* diagnosis. The following categories are included in *DSM-IV* (American Psychiatric Association, 1994):

- Disorders usually first diagnosed in infancy, childhood, or adolescence.
- Delirium, dementia, and amnestic and other cognitive disorders.
- Mental disorders due to a general medical condition.

- Substance-related disorders.
- Schizophrenia and other psychotic disorders.
- Mood disorders.
- Anxiety disorders.
- Somatoform disorders.
- Factitious disorders.
- Dissociative disorders.
- Sexual and gender-identity disorders.
- Eating disorders.
- Sleep disorders.
- Impulse-control disorders not otherwise classified.
- Adjustment disorders.
- Personality disorders.

These diagnoses are descriptive in nature and not tied to any theoretical framework. A *DSM-IV* diagnosis has five axes:

Axis I: Primary clinical disorder.

Axis II: Personality disorder or mental retardation.

Axis III: Medical problems.

Axis IV: Psychosocial issues.

Axis V: Global Assessment of Functioning.

Many settings only made use of Axis I. Although reliability and validity are seen as important in the use of any scale, there is a question about whether *DSM-IV* has satisfied this criterion. Kutchins and Kirk (1997) are particularly concerned about the lack of reliability, whereas Neimeyer and Raskin (2002) see *DSM-IV* as based on social-political processes rather than evidence-based research. Social workers, however, are most concerned that *DSM-IV* is based on a deficit model with no focus on the context or environment in diagnostic assessment. To increase understanding of diagnosis as related to person and environment, the National Association of Social Workers (NASW) has published the PIE system developed by Karls and Wandrei (1994), which looks at roles and conflicts in roles as crucial in assessment.

Use of the multiaxis approach in *DSM-IV* is most compatible with social work's focus on PIE. Whereas Axes I, II, and III are psychiatric or medical classifications, Axis IV and Axis V consider context and social environment. There is some concern, however, that Axis I receives the most attention. Another positive factor about *DSM-IV* is the inclusion of the Appendix I Outline for Cultural Formulation and Glossary of Culture Bound Syndromes. This demonstrates recognition that there are psychiatric disorders other than the ones most frequently known in American culture.

A very useful diagnostic tool in evaluating mental functioning is the mental-status exam. The Mini-Mental State Examination (MMSE) that has been published by Paveza, Cohen, and Blaser (1990) addresses the following issues:

- Orientation to time and place.
- Registration (how much repetition is needed to understand a concept).
- Attention and calculation.
- Recall and memory.
- Language.

The practitioner asks the client certain structured questions with a cut-off score of 23 that is considered acceptable for both cognitive and mental-health functioning, although those tested with less education, who are older, or who are from different ethnicities may show different results (Fillenbaum, Heyman, Williams, Prosnitz, & Burchett, 1990).

Depression and Anxiety Tests

There have been a number of tests developed to measure mental-health disorders in adults. In practice, social workers frequently encounter clients with depressive disorders, including Major Depressive Disorder and Dysthmic Disorder. The most widely used measurement for assessing depressive symptoms in adults is the Beck Depression Inventory (Beck, Steer, & Brown, 1996). This test consists of 21 items rated on a 4-point scale ranging from 0 to 3 that measures the intensity of depressive symptoms. A score of 0 to 13 indicates normal level of depression; 14 to 19, mild to moderate level; 20 to 28, moderate to severe level; and 29 to 63, extremely severe level of depression. The client fills out this depression inventory in a short period of time. Since the Beck Depression Inventory was first developed in 1951, numerous research studies have shown it to have excellent reliability, with a test-retest coefficient of 0.90 as well as concurrent and criterion validity.

Clients self-administer the Beck Depression Inventory, but the Hamilton Rating Scale for Depression (Hamilton, 1967) is completed by the interviewer. It consists of 18 items measured on a 5-point Likert scale and contains items on depressed mood, suicide, anxiety, general somatic symptoms, and loss of interest in work and social activities. The Hamilton Rating Scale has been widely used with the elderly, people with HIV/AIDS, and adults with minor depressive disorders.

A number of instruments have been developed to measure anxiety disorders, especially trauma and phobia. The State Trait Anxiety Inventory (STAI) is a standardized self-report instrument with 20 questions in the state section and 20 questions in the trait section. The scale has been validated and reported to have alpha reliability coefficients ranging from 0.86 to 0.95 (Spielberger, 1983).

A challenge with self-report anxiety and depression scales is that often there is not good differentiation among them. Stulz (2010) has developed versions of the Beck Anxiety Inventory and Beck Depression Inventory-II that strive to differentiate these two psychological symptoms. The result of purified scales, however, has been limited, as these two sets of symptoms seem to be linked and difficult to differentiate. The use of purified scales, however, may help clarify the effects of interventions on anxiety and depressive symptoms.

To evaluate posttraumatic stress disorder (PTSD), the Trauma Symptom Checklist (TSC-33) is useful. A client rates 33 items, such as insomnia and feeling isolated from others from 0 (never) to 3 (very often). The scale has been shown to have internal consistency, with an alpha of 0.89 (Briere & Ruentz, 1989).

The Fear Questionnaire (FQ) developed by Fisher and Corcoran (1994) is a 24-item instrument designed to assess target phobias as well as general fears. The instrument has an alpha of 0.82 for the three subscales and 0.92 for target phobias.

Personality disorders (Axis II on *DSM-IV*) have long been difficult to assess in only one interview. Often the client with a personality disorder does not have any other mental disorder and may be of above-average intelligence. In contrast to other psychiatric disorders, those people with personality disorders may not experience much discomfort and often do not seek mental-health treatment except in crisis. When a client has repeated difficulties in work and personal relationships, the possibility of a personality disorder should be considered. Personality disorders include Borderline Personality Disorder, Antisocial Personality Disorder, Paranoid Personality Disorder, Narcissistic Personality Disorder, and Obsessive-Compulsive Personality Disorder. Because personality disorders may be difficult to recognize in clients, social workers can help ensure the accuracy of the diagnosis by the use of standardized, structured interviews, such as the Structured Clinical Interview for Diagnosis (SCID-II; Garb, 1998). Because clinicians tend to overdiagnose or underdiagnose clients, the use of a structured interview often yields more reliable results (Wood, Garb, Lilienfeld, & Nezworski, 2002).

The Minnesota Multiphasic Personality Inventories (MMPI and MMPI-II) developed by psychologists in the 1940s are well-established standardized tests for assessing personality disorders (Jordan & Franklin, 2003). Other standardized personality-assessment tests, including the Millon Clinical Multiaxial Inventory-III (Millon, 1997) and the California Psychological Inventory (McAllister, 1996), are also useful standardized personality-assessment measures. It is important for social workers who want to make the assessment process more evidence based to learn more about these standardized psychological tests that measure personality disorders.

Substance-Abuse Assessment

A social worker who is asked to assess adults often misses a diagnosis of alcohol abuse and dependence. Part of the challenge is that alcohol is a legal substance and also a very accepted part of social interactions. *DSM-IV* has very specific diagnoses for alcoholism, but often social workers think primarily of another diagnosis. Frequent alcohol use may result in the development of symptoms (anxiety, depression, medical conditions, cognitive difficulties) that may suggest diagnoses other than alcohol abuse. Furthermore, many adults with other psychiatric disorders attempt to self-medicate with drugs or alcohol, with the result of a dual diagnosis of alcohol abuse and another psychiatric disorder. A contributing factor is that few clients directly state that they have a problem with alcohol, as denial is frequently used in an attempt to cover up a substance-abuse problem. The social worker must often act as a detective in looking for signs that may indicate an alcohol problem. During the assessment process, often a client who indicates work difficulties because of frequent absences or encounters with the law because of domestic violence or driving violations may be signaling a problem with substance abuse.

There are a number of assessment instruments that have been developed to measure the presence, extent, and severity of substance-abuse problems. Two widely used assessment tools are CAGEii, developed by Ewing (Mayfield, McLeod, & Hall, 1994), and the Michigan Alcohol Screening Test (MAST; Selzer, 1971). CAGEii makes use of four questions related to desire to cut down on drinking, response of others to drinking, guilty feelings about drinking, and time of drinking. A positive response to two or more questions signifies a possible substance-abuse problem and need for further investigation. The MAST makes use of 25 items to ascertain alcohol use or abuse. More comprehensive than the CAGEii, the MAST is often used to find out more information about the extent or severity of a client's substance abuse. A version of this test, Drug Abuse Screening Test (DAST), has also been used to detect drug abuse.

Assessment of Older People

Because social workers often encounter older people in their practice, assessment issues for older people need special attention. Depression is frequently an emotional disorder experienced by older people, yet it is commonly underdiagnosed. The Geriatric Depression Scale (GDS) is most helpful in assessing depression in older people (Brink et al., 1982). There are a number of versions of this test ranging from 1 to 30 items. This test is very helpful as an initial screening tool to assess depressive symptoms among the elderly.

Another frequently used assessment tool with older adults is one that assesses functional status. There are numerous assessment tools that evaluate functional status. Some of the issues covered in functional-assessment instruments include the following areas: ability to use the telephone, shopping, food preparation, housekeeping, laundry, medication responsibility, and financial management.

In summary, the social worker should probably best begin with a general psychosocial-assessment report, including the diagnosis that was outlined previously. As part of the assessment report, the social worker can use or consult with other professionals about standardized assessment instruments for depression, anxiety, substance abuse, and functional ability.

Evidence-Based Assessment

There have been some attempts to provide evidence about the use and effectiveness of different evidence-based assessments. For example Moon (2002) looks at the diagnosis of separation-anxiety disorder and reviews evidence-based methods of assessment, including clinical interviews, self-report scales, parent-teacher reports, behavioral observations, and self-monitoring, whereas O'Hare (2002) looks at three major functions of evidence-based social work practice, including assessment. The assessment protocol is based on the use of valid scales to complement the qualitative interview. Key factors are seen as domain-specific research on relevant psychosocial risk factors, especially those that are amenable to change.

Much of the evidence on the effectiveness of various assessment tools are specific to various assessment tools, such as Shek and Ma's 2010 article that examines a specific family-assessment instrument (namely, the Chinese Family Assessment Instrument [C-FAI]: Hierarchical confirmatory factor analyses and factorial invariance).

Efforts to gather general assessment information through specific computer-software programs or semistructured interviews, however, represent an attempt to standardize information taken for assessment. Although standardized general-assessment tools are in their infancy, in contrast, there are a number of well-researched inventories for specific disorders, such as depression and anxiety. Reliability and validity have been well established for many of these diagnostic instruments. One challenge, however, is that these diagnoses must be identified before a client can be given a specific test. Another challenge is that these tests focus on a specific disorder, and there is no provision for strengths that a client may have in coping with the psychiatric disorder or for social-support systems that can help mitigate the negative effects of the mental disorder.

Implications for Social Work on Micro-, Mezzo-, and Macrolevels

The importance of a comprehensive assessment for individual clients is evident. No treatment intervention can begin before there is assessment

Paveza, G., Cohen, D., & Blaser, C. (1990). A brief form of Mini-Mental State Exam for use in community care settings. *Behavior, Health, and Aging, 1*(2), 133–139.

Perlman, H. (1957). *Social casework: A problem-solving process.* Chicago, IL: University of Chicago Press.

Pomeroy, E., Holleran, L., & Franklin, C. (2003). Adults. In C. Jordan & C. Franklin (Eds.), *Clinical assessment for social workers* (pp. 155–197). Chicago, IL: Lyceum.

Reid, W. (1988). Brief task-centered treatment. In R. Dorfman (Ed.), *Paradigms of clinical social work* (pp. 96–219). New York, NY: Brunner/Mazel.

Roberts, A., & Greene, G. (Eds.). (2002). *Social workers desk reference.* New York, NY: Oxford University Press

Saleeby, D. (1997). *The strengths perspective in social work practice* (2nd ed.). New York, NY: Longman.

Selzer, M. (1971). The Michigan Alcoholism Screening Test: The quest for a new diagnostic instrument. *American Journal of Psychiatry, 127,* 89–94.

Shek, D., & Ma, C. (2010). The Chinese Family Assessment Instrument (C-FAI). *Research on Social Work Practice, 20*(1), 112–123.

Spielberger, V. (1983). *Manual for the State-Trait Anxiety Inventory.* Palo Alto, CA: Consulting Psychologists Press.

Stulz, N. (2010). Distinguishing anxiety and depression in self-report: Purification of the Beck Anxiety Inventory and Beck Depression Inventory: II. *Journal of Clinical Psychology, 66*(9), 927–940.

U.S. Census (2000). *Mapping census 2000: The geography of U.S. diversity.* Retrieved from www.census.gov/population/www/cen2000/atlas.html

Wakefield, J. (1996). Does social work need the ecosystems perspective? Is the perspective clinically useful? *Social Service Review, 70*(1), 1–32.

Webb, N. (1996). *Social work practice with children.* New York, NY: Guilford Press.

Wood, J., Garb, H., Lilienfeld, S., & Nezworski, T. (2002). Clinical assessment. *Annual Review of Psychology, 53,* 519–543.

Table 6.2   What Is a Systematic Review?

A systematic review uses transparent procedures to identify, assess, and synthesize results of research on a particular topic. These procedures are explicit, so that others can replicate the review, and are defined in advance of the review:

Clear inclusion/exclusion criteria specify the study designs, populations, interventions, and outcomes that will be covered in the review.

An explicit search strategy is developed and implemented to identify all published and unpublished studies that meet the inclusion criteria. The search strategy specifies keyword strings and sources (i.e., electronic databases, websites, experts, and journals) that will be included in the search.

Systematic coding and analysis are provided for included studies' methods, intervention and comparison conditions, sample characteristics, outcome measures, and results.

Meta-analysis (when possible) estimates pooled effect sizes (ES) and moderators of ES.

How Are C2 Systematic Reviews Different From Other Systematic Reviews?

C2 reviews must include a systematic search for unpublished reports (to avoid publication bias).

C2 reviews are usually international in scope.

A protocol (proposal) for the review is developed in advance and undergoes careful peer review by international experts in the substantive area, experts in systematic review methods, and a trial search coordinator.

Study inclusion decisions and coding decisions are accomplished by at least two reviewers who work independently and compare results.

C2 reviews undergo peer review and editorial review.

Completed C2 reviews are published in C2-RIPE and may be published elsewhere.

From "What Is a Systematic Review?" by Social Welfare Group, Campbell Collaboration. Retrieved March 16, 2007, from www.campbellcollaboration.org/SWCG/reviews.asp

Health-care professionals from a variety of disciplines (including social work) located around the world volunteer to serve on Cochrane Review Groups (CRGs), of which there are dozens, such as the Childhood Cancer Group; Depression, Anxiety, and Neurosis Group; Drug and Alcohol Group; HIV/AIDS Group; Pain, Palliative, and Supportive Care Group; Pregnancy and Childbirth Group; and the Schizophrenia Group, to list a few of particular relevance to social work. There are also various methods groups and many brick-and-mortar Cochrane Centers located around the world. The CC hosts an annual international conference and many regional or national meetings.

On its website, you can also locate the *Cochrane Manual*, a detailed guide to designing and evaluating systematic reviews (SRs) of high-quality research on health-care interventions and methods of assessment, roughly categorized by the subject matter of the various review groups (see Table 16.2). There are free summaries of these SRs available on the website, and your local university library most likely subscribes to the CC library, allowing you free access to these invaluable resources. In terms of timely, comprehensive, and minimally biased appraisals of the effects of various treatments, the CC reviews represent the state of the art. The CC does admittedly focus on physical-health conditions, which includes mental illnesses; the majority of the reviews deal with medical interventions, not psychosocial ones, but categorizing issues as either medical and psychoso-cial problems or as medical treatments versus psychosocial treatments is not always easy. An example is a report appearing in the *British Medical Journal* describing a randomized controlled trial of the effects of providing insulation in homes on the health and well-being of residents (Howden-Chapman et al., 2007). The 4,407 low-income participants lived in 1,350 households, half of which were randomly selected to receive upgraded insulation (to keep the homes warmer). The provision of more insulation produced improved health, fewer days absent from work or school, and fewer visits to the doctor. Is this a medical intervention? Regardless, the implications for social work clinical and community practice seem clear, and studies such as this, which will eventually be incorporated in CC reviews, make it worthwhile for social workers to become familiar with this database of information and reports on treatments for disorders that afflict adult social work clients.

The Campbell Collaboration (C2; see www.campbellcollaboration .org), named after psychologist Donald Campbell, is closely modeled after the work, operation, and products of the Cochrane Collaboration. Unlike CC, the C2, founded in 1999, focuses on preparing SRs in the fields of education, criminal justice, and social welfare. It, too, hosts an annual conference, supports a variety of centers around the world, devises methodological standards, and encourages international social work schol-ars to propose topics for SRs, develop research protocols related to those titles, and then actually carry out these protocols and publish the SRs. At present, there are more proposed titles and protocols (representing SRs in development) than there are completed SRs (about 70 are available), but the list of published SRs will expand greatly over the next few years. The approach taken by the C2 with respect to systematic reviews is outlined in Table 6.1. Strenuous efforts are made to control for or minimize bias when completing these reviews, and they can be said to represent the most methodologically rigorous and comprehensive evaluations of the literature dealing with EBP-style answerable questions that are available to contem-porary social workers. Both the Cochrane and Campbell Collaborations are inclusive organizations, and they are always looking for competent social workers to volunteer to serve on their various review groups or even to undertake SRs in various areas of social welfare. Do not be bashful about contacting them to see if you can help.

The two initiatives covered in this section—EST and EBP—seem to have much in common, although EBP is a more sophisticated and fully developed model. Within psychology, the language of EST and EBP is slowly moving in the direction of the latter, to the detriment of EBP. The reason is that lists of treatments perhaps inevitably take on an aspect of imperativeness—that is, the sense that one *must* use one of these approved therapies and to not do so is somehow ethically and professionally suspect. This is a problem with lists of ESTs. Now, EBP on the other hand, does not endorse particular interventions and clearly leaves open the option to make conscientious decisions to *not* make use of the most scientifically

Table 6.4 **Treatment Manuals for Adult Disorders Available in Van Hasselt and Hersen (1996)**

Panic Disorder and Agoraphobia
Obsessive-Compulsive Disorder
Cognitive-Behavioral Treatment of Social Phobia
Social-Skills Training for Depression
Cognitive-Behavior Therapy for Treatment of Depressed Inpatients
Biobehavioral Treatment and Rehabilitation for Persons With Schizophrenia*
Community Reinforcement Training With Concerned Others
Cognitive-Behavioral Treatment of Sex Offenders
Treatment of Sexual Dysfunctions
A Comprehensive Treatment Manual for the Management of Obesity
Lifestyle Change: A Program for Long-Term Weight Management
Managing Marital Therapy: Helping Partners Change
Insomnia
Cognitive-Behavioral Treatment of Body-Image Disturbances
Cognitive-Behavioral Treatment of Postconcussion Syndrome
Trichotillomania Treatment Manual
Anger Management Training With Essential Hypertensive Patients

*This manual was co-authored by a social worker, Stephen E. Wong, PhD.
Source: Sourcebook of Psychological Treatment Manuals for Adult Disorders, by V. B. Van Hasselt and M. Hersen (Eds.), 1996, New York, NY: Plenum Press.

provide another listing of treatment manuals and how to obtain them, but not copies of the actual manuals themselves.

The Campbell and Cochrane Collaborations are another exceedingly useful resource for learning about the evidentiary status of various interventions potentially useful to social workers serving adult clients. If you visit the websites of these two organizations, you will find a long list of proposed topics (to be the subject of future SRs), a shorter list of protocols proposed by various research teams that have been approved by the respective collaborations, and an even shorter list of actual SRs. However, although limited in number, these SRs probably represent the most scientifically credible and up-to-date summaries of the research literature regarding the usefulness of various interventions and assessment methods. Table 6.5 lists a selection of completed SRs that you can locate on these collaborations' websites. The last one listed, *Work Programs for Welfare Recipients*, was completed in August 2006 and is an analysis of randomized controlled studies, quasi-experimental outcome studies, and cluster-randomized controlled trials of welfare-to-work programs for persons receiving public assistance, such as Temporary Assistance for Needy Families (TANF). The analysis of the research literature involved 46 programs encompassing more than 412,000 participants, with outcomes reported for up to 6 years. The free document is 122 pages long. You can see how an SR of this nature is potentially far more informative than reading a single study appearing in a journal; and if you are a social worker

Table 6.5 **Examples of Completed Systematic Reviews Addressing Psychosocial Interventions for Adults**

From the Cochrane Collaboration (www.cochrane.org)

- Screening and Case Finding Instruments for Depression
- Marital Therapy for Depression
- Short-Term Psychodynamic Psychotherapies for Common Mental Disorders
- Interventions for Helping People Recognize Early Signs of the Recurrence of Bipolar Disorder
- Psychological Debriefing for Prevention of Posttraumatic Stress Disorder (PTSD)
- Psychological Treatment of Posttraumatic Stress Disorder (PTSD)
- Individual Psychotherapy in the Outpatient Treatment of Adults With Anorexia Nervosa
- Interventions for Vaginismus
- Alcoholics Anonymous and Other 12-Step Programs for Alcohol Dependence
- Psychotherapeutic Interventions for Cannabis Abuse and/or Dependence in Outpatient Settings
- Family Intervention for Schizophrenia
- Token Economy for Schizophrenia
- Cognitive-Behavior Therapy for Schizophrenia
- Hypnosis for Schizophrenia
- Life-Skills Programmes for Chronic Mental Illnesses
- Art Therapy for Schizophrenia or Schizophrenia-Like Illnesses
- Supportive Therapy for Schizophrenia
- Individual Behavioural Counseling for Smoking Cessation
- Group-Behaviour-Therapy Programmes for Smoking Cessation
- Strategies for Increasing the Participation of Women in Community Breast-Cancer Screenings
- Reminiscence Therapy for Dementia
- Psychological Treatments for Epilepsy

From the Campbell Collaboration (www.campbellcollaboration.org)

- Cognitive Behavioral Programs for Juvenile and Adult Offenders: A Meta-Analysis of Controlled Intervention Studies
- The Effectiveness of Incarceration-Based Drug Treatment on Criminal Behavior
- Interventions for Learning Disabled Sex Offenders
- Work Programmes for Welfare Recipients
- Advocacy Interventions to Reduce or Eliminate Violence and Promote the Physical and Psychosocial Well-Being of Women Who Experience Intimate Partner Abuse
- Cognitive Behavioural Therapy for Men Who Physically Abuse Their Female Partners
- Court-Mandated Interventions for Individuals Convicted of Domestic Violence
- Cross-Border Trafficking in Human Beings: Prevention and Intervention Strategies for Reducing Sexual Exploitation
- Effects of Drug-Substitution Programs on Offending Among Drug Addicts
- Effects of Second-Responder Programs on Repeat Incidents of Family Abuse
- Mindfulness-Based Stress Reduction (MBSR) for Improving Health, Quality of Life, and Social Functioning in Adults
- Motivational Interviewing for Substance Abuse
- Personal Assistance for Adults (19–64) With Physical Impairments

Online Resources

http://www.cochrane.org/ The website of the *Cochrane Collaboration* (CC). Founded in 1993, the Cochrane Collaboration is an international network of more than 28,000 dedicated people from more than 100 countries. We work together to help health-care providers, policy makers, patients, their advocates, and caretakers make well-informed decisions about health care, based on the best available research evidence, by preparing, updating, and promoting systematic reviews in the area of health care.

http://campbellcollaboration.org/ The *Campbell Collaboration* (C2) helps people make well-informed decisions by preparing, maintaining, and disseminating systematic reviews in education, crime and justice, and social welfare.

http://www.psychology.sunysb.edu/eklonsky-/division12/ The website supported by *Division 12, Section III of the American Psychological Association* is devoted to providing information on psychosocial treatments that meet certain minimal standards of research support.

http://www.nrepp.samhsa.gov/ The *National Registry of Evidence-Based Practices and Policies* is supported by the federal Substance Abuse and Mental Health Services Administration.

http://www.psych.org/psych_pract/treatg/pg/prac_guide.cfm The website is maintained by the *American Psychiatric Association*, which provides access to the practice guidelines developed by this professional organization. Most guidelines are centered around the assessment and treatment of mental illnesses.

References

Barker, R. L. (Ed.). (2003). *The social work dictionary* (5th ed.). Washington, DC: National Association of Social Workers Press.

Bledsoe, S. E., Weissman, M. M., Mullen, E. J., Ponniah, K., Gameroff, M. J., Verdeli, H.,...Wickramartne, P. (2007). Empirically supported psychotherapy in social work training programs: Does the definition of evidence matter? *Research on Social Work Practice, 17,* 449–455.

Chambless, D. L., Baker, M. J., Baucom, D. H., Beutler, L. E., Calhoun, K. S., Crits-Critsoph, P.,...Woody, S. R. (1998). Update on empirically validated therapies (Pt. 2). *Clinical Psychologist, 51*(1), 3–16.

Chambless, D. L., & Ollendick, T. H. (2001). Empirically supported psychological interventions: Controversies and evidence. *Annual Review of Psychology, 52,* 685–716.

Chambless, D. L., Sanderson, W. C., Shoham, V., Bennet Johnson, S., Pope, K. S., Crits-Cristoph, P.,...McCurry, S. (1996). An update on empirically validated therapies. *Clinical Psychologist, 49*(2), 5–18.

Corcoran, J. (2000). *Evidence-based social work with families.* New York, NY: Springer.

Corcoran, K. (1998). Clients without a cause: Is there a legal right to effective treatment? *Research on Social Work Practice, 8,* 589–596.

Cournoyer, B. R. (2004). *The evidence-based social work skills book.* New York, NY: Allyn & Bacon.

Gibbs, L. E. (2003). *Evidence-based practice for the helping professions.* Pacific Grove, CA: Brooks/Cole.

Gray, M., Plath, D., & Webb, S. (Eds.). (2009). *Evidence-based social work: A critical stance.* New York, NY: Routledge.

Guyatt, G., & Rennie, D. (Eds.). (2002). *Users' guides to the medical literature: Essentials of evidence-based clinical practice.* Chicago, IL: American Medical Association.

Guyatt, G., & Rennie, D. (Eds.). (2006). *Users' guides to the medical literature: Essentials of evidence-based clinical practice* (2nd ed.). Chicago, IL: American Medical Association.

Hollis, F. (1964). *Casework: A psychosocial therapy.* New York, NY: Columbia University Press.

Howard, M. O., & Jensen, J. M. (1999a). Clinical practice guidelines: Should social work develop them? *Research on Social Work Practice, 9,* 283–301.

Howard, M. O., & Jensen, J. (Eds.). (1999b). Practice guidelines and clinical social work [Special issue]. *Research on Social Work Practice, 9*(3).

Howden-Chapman, P., Matheson, A., Crane, J., Vigers, H., Cunningham, M., Blakely, T., ... Davie, G. (2007, February 27). Effective of insulating existing houses on health inequality: Cluster randomised study in the community. *British Medical Journal.* doi:10.1136/bmj.39070.573032.80

Hunsley, J., & Mash, E. J. (Eds.). (2008). *A guide to assessments that work.* New York, NY: Oxford University Press.

Institute of Medicine (1990). *Clinical practice guidelines: Directions for a new program.* Washington, DC: National Academy Press.

Kazdin, A. E. (2008). Evidence-based treatment and practice: New opportunities to bridge clinical research and practice, enhance the knowledge base, and improve patient care. *American Psychologist, 63,* 146–159.

Moore, A., & McQuay, H. (2006). *Bandolier's little book of making sense of the medical evidence.* New York, NY: Oxford University Press.

Myers, L. L., & Thyer, B. A. (1997). Should social work clients have the right to effective treatment? *Social Work, 42,* 127–145.

Nathan, P. E., & Gorman, J. M. (Eds.). (1998). *A guide to treatments that work.* New York, NY: Oxford University Press.

Nathan, P. E., & Gorman, J. M. (Eds.). (2002). *A guide to treatments that work* (2nd ed.). New York, NY: Oxford University Press.

Nathan, P. E., & Gorman, J. M. (Eds.). (2007). *A guide to treatments that work* (3rd ed.). New York, NY: Oxford University Press.

National Committee on Lesbian and Gay Issues (1992). *Position statement on reparative therapies.* Washington, DC: National Association of Social Workers Press.

Norcross, J. C., Beutler, L. E., & Levant, R. F. (Eds.). (2006). *Evidence-based practices in mental health: Debate and dialogue on the fundamental questions.* Washington, DC: American Psychological Association.

O'Hare, T. (2005). *Evidence-based practices for social workers: An interdisciplinary approach.* Chicago, IL: Lyceum.

Perry, R. E. (2006a). Do social workers make better child welfare workers than non-social workers? *Research on Social Work Practice, 16,* 392–405.

Perry, R. E. (2006b). Education and child welfare supervisor performance: Does a social work degree matter? *Research on Social Work Practice, 16,* 591–604.

Persons, J. B., Thase, M. E., & Crits-Christoph, P. (1996). The role of psychotherapy in the treatment of depression. *Archives of General Psychiatry, 53,* 283–290.

Roberts, A. R., & Yeager, K. R. (Eds.). (2006). *Foundations of evidence-based social work practice.* New York, NY: Oxford University Press.

Rosen, A., & Proctor, E. (Eds.). (2003). *Developing practice guidelines for social work interventions: Issues, methods, and research agenda.* New York, NY: Columbia University Press.

Rubin, A., & Parrish, D. (2007). Views of evidence-based practice among faculty in MSW programs: A national survey. *Research on Social Work Practice, 17,* 110–122.

Sanderson, W. C., & Woody, S. (1995). Manuals for empirically validated treatments: A project of the Task Force on Psychological Interventions, Division of Clinical Psychology, American Psychological Association. Retrieved from www.apa.org/divisions/div12/est/MANUALSforevt.html

Seligman, M. E. (1998). Foreword: A purpose. In P. Nathan & J. Gorman (Eds.), *A guide to treatments that work* (pp. v–vii). New York, NY: Oxford University Press.

Social Welfare Group, Campbell Collaboration. (n.d.). *What is a systematic review?* Retrieved from www.campbellcollaboration.org/SWCG/reviews/asp

Steering Committee on Practice Guidelines (2006, May). *Practice guideline development process.* Washington, DC: American Psychiatric Association. Retrieved from www.psych.org/psych_pract/treatg/pg/prac_guide.cfm/

Strauss, S. E., Glasziou, P., Richardson, W. S., & Haynes, R. B. (2011). *Evidence-based medicine: How to practice and teach EBM* (4th ed.). New York, NY: Elsevier.

Task Force on Promotion and Dissemination of Psychological Procedures (1995). Training in and dissemination of empirically-validated psychological treatments. *Clinical Psychologist, 48*(1), 3–23.

Thyer, B. A. (1994). Are theories for practice necessary? *Journal of Social Work Education, 30,* 147–151.

Thyer, B. A. (1995). Promoting an empiricist agenda within the human services: An ethical and humanistic imperative. *Journal of Behavior Therapy and Experimental Psychiatry, 26,* 93–98.

Thyer, B. A. (2001). What is the role of theory in research on social work practice? *Journal of Social Work Education, 37,* 9–25.

Thyer, B. A. (2002). Developing discipline-specific knowledge for social work: Is it possible? *Journal of Social Work Education, 38,* 101–113.

Thyer, B. A. (2003). Social work should help develop interdisciplinary evidence-based practice guidelines, not discipline-specific ones. In A. Rosen & E. Proctor (Eds.), *Developing practice guidelines for social work interventions: Issues, methods, and research agenda* (pp. 128–139). New York, NY: Columbia University Press.

Thyer, B. A. (2007). Social work education and clinical learning: Towards evidence-based practice. *Clinical Social Work Journal 35,* 25–32.

Thyer, B. A., & Kazi, M. A. F. (Eds.). (2004). *International perspectives on evidence-based practice in social work.* Birmingham, UK: Venture.

Thyer, B. A., & Myers, L. L. (2011). The quest for evidence-based practice: A view from the United States. *Journal of Social Work, 11,* 8–25.

Thyer, B. A., & Pignotti, M. (2011). Evidence-based practices do not exist. *Clinical Social Work Journal, 39*, 328–333.

Thyer, B. A., & Wodarski, J. S. (Eds.). (2007). *Social work in mental health: An evidence-based approach*. Hoboken, NJ: Wiley.

Van Hasselt, V. B., & Hersen, M. (Eds.). (1996). *Sourcebook of psychological treatment manuals for adult disorders*. New York, NY: Plenum Press.

Weissman, M. M., Verdeli, H., Gameroff, M. J., Bledsoe, S. E., Betts, K., Mufson, L., . . . Wickramaratne, P. (2006). National survey of psychotherapy training in psychiatry, psychology, and social work. *Archives of General Psychiatry, 63*, 925–934.

Weisz, J. R. (2004). *Psychotherapy for children and adolescents: Evidence-based treatments and case examples*. Cambridge, UK: Cambridge University Press.

Woody, S. R., & Sanderson, W. C. (1998). Manuals for empirically supported treatments: 1998 update. Retrieved from www.apa.org/divisions/div12/est/manual60.pdf

Woody, S. R., Weisz, J., & McLean, C. (2005). Empirically supported treatments: Ten years later. *Clinical Psychologist, 58*(4), 5–11.

Chapter 7
Assessment of the Elderly

Gregory J. Paveza

> **Purpose:** The purpose of this chapter is to provide the reader with an understanding of comprehensive geriatric assessment and its various aspects.
>
> **Rationale:** As more social workers are confronted with older adult clients, it is critical that they understand how to initially assess older adults who come in to receive care.
>
> **How evidence-informed practice is presented:** Information is presented on Mental Status exams and the usefulness of those instruments in assessing for initial signs of dementia; data are presented on various instruments for assessing functional status and their importance in determining need for services.
>
> **Overarching question:** When working with older adults, how could I best include elements of an assessment into my interview, and which elements should I include?

Comprehensive geriatric assessment (CGA) has emerged as an important method for helping social workers address the needs of older adults, particularly as the number of older adults and their need for services continues to grow within the United States.

CGA is a process of engaging in a total evaluation of older adults. It requires that the practitioner gather information in multiple areas of client functioning, including medical history, cognitive status, emotional well-being, the ability to perform activities of daily living (ADLs) and instrumental activities of daily living (IADLs), the person's social-support system, the physical environment in which the person lives, and many other areas of the older person's life. Such a process requires that the social work practitioner have a broad command of all areas of aging practice. One must understand how to effectively gather medical information; assess current cognitive status, the emotional well-being of the client, ADLs and IADLs, and the person's social-support system; and conduct an effective and thorough assessment of the older adult's physical environment (Gallo & Bogner, 2006). Finally, the social work practitioner must be able to comprehensively link the findings from the assessment to an intervention plan for the individual client (Gallo, Fulmer, Paveza, & Reichel, 2000).

Because the process of CGA is not a single subject but rather an amalgamation of several areas, this chapter of necessity addresses both the broad subject as well as the specific elements that comprise a CGA.

This chapter details a process for gathering and organizing information rather than a specific intervention or method of engaging in practice. As such, this chapter is organized differently than other chapters in this book. This chapter reviews each of the elements that comprise a CGA, discusses some of the instruments that may be of assistance for obtaining information in that area of the assessment, summarizes some of the unique issues encompassed in that area of the assessment process, and looks at the import of the area for arriving at a care plan. The chapter concludes with a discussion concerning the integration of the elements of the assessment into a whole that informs a recommended care plan for the client and a review of the literature on effectiveness of the process.

The elements that are recommended for inclusion in a CGA have broadened over the past several years. This is evident when one reviews any text on geriatric assessment with multiple editions. A perfect example is the *Handbook of Geriatric Assessment*. The first edition, published in 1988, consists of 10 chapters totaling 231 pages of text and index, with a single contributed chapter (Gallo, Reichel, & Andersen, 1988). By the second edition, published in 1995, the book still has 10 chapters, but it has expanded to 257 pages of text and index, with 2 contributed chapters (Gallo, Reichel, & Andersen, 1995). The third edition of the *Handbook* consists of 13 chapters with 361 pages of text and index, with 5 contributed chapters (Gallo et al., 2000). The latest edition of the *Handbook*, the fourth edition, has expanded to 20 chapters with 473 pages of text and index, and 18 of the chapters include authors other than the editors of the book (Gallo, Bogner, Fulmer, & Paveza, 2006). These changes in the *Handbook* suggest that both the amount and complexity of information has so expanded that no single group of authors can adequately address the topic.

As stated at the beginning of this chapter, CGA is not an intervention technique but rather a process for gathering comprehensive information on older adults within the context of the older person's environment. Given the breadth and depth of this biopsychosocial environmentally cognizant approach to gathering information on older adults, one might suspect that the approach was developed by social workers to address their work with older adults. Unfortunately, there is no substantive evidence to support this contention. Rather, this approach seems to be built on the experiences of early geriatric physicians. They discovered that, when working with older adults in in-patient settings, information beyond that of the medical history and presenting medical problems was required in order to effectively create a treatment plan for their older patients (Gallo et al., 1988).

Historical Background

CGA is a direct outgrowth of the earlier movement within geriatric medicine to develop comprehensive geriatric assessment units (GAUs).

GAUs identified the need for a comprehensive assessment process, usually beginning with a physical exam and medical history and then adding information on functional status—that is, the ability to perform basic activities of daily living, mental health, size of the social-support network, and interactions that support network, economic needs, and environmental considerations (L. A. Rubenstein, 1995). These domains with some modifications continue to remain the focus of CGA (Mouton & Esparza, 2006; Chang & Mamun, 2008). A comprehensive assessment should consist of assessment in at least six areas: mental status, functional assessment, social and environmental assessment, nutritional- and health-practices review, medical history and treatments, and assessment of emotional well-being (Paveza, 1993). The consistency across authors and across disciplines in identifying the areas essential to the assessment process suggests that there is a generally accepted concept of the information that needs to be gathered to adequately address the care needs of the older adult patient, whether that person is in the hospital or residing in the community.

Moving from this historical perspective, let us begin a more in-depth discussion of the elements comprising the assessment process. Each of these elements is discussed from the perspective of how the element helps us understand the current biopsychosocial status of the older adult, techniques and instruments the practitioner can use to assess an element of the comprehensive assessment, potential problems with using some of the discussed instruments, and the relationship of that element of the assessment to care planning for the older adult.

Elements of the Comprehensive Assessment

I have already suggested that the comprehensive-assessment process should address some common areas, including current medical problems and medical history, assessment of the person's ability to perform the basic activities of daily living, assessment of emotional problems, and social and economic issues (Gallo et al., 1995; Mouton & Esparza, 2006; Paveza, 1993; L. A. Rubenstein, 1995). Beyond these basic elements, authors differ on the other elements to be included in the assessment. When discussing the assessment of functional status, several authors also suggest that, in addition to basic activities of daily living, the assessment of functional status must include the instrumental or independent activities of daily living (Older Americans Resources and Services [OARS] Methodology, 1978). The addition of assessment for elder mistreatment has also recently been suggested as important to a thorough and complete assessment (Fulmer & O'Malley, 1987; Gallo et al., 2000; VanderWeerd, Firpo, Fulmer, & Paveza, 2006). The need to assess values and the impact of those values on do-not-resuscitate directives and durable power of attorney for health care have also been added to the growing list of items to be covered in the assessment process (Doukas, McCullough, & Crane, 2006). Additional areas suggested for incorporation into the process include older adults' ability to continue to drive, their use of alcohol and drugs, and pain assessment (Carr & Rebok, 2006; Richardson, 2006; Zanjani & Oslin, 2006). Some of these special areas of concern were originally considered to be part of one of the broader categories, such as medical history, social history, or environmental assessment, the assessment for elder mistreatment being a perfect example. In an earlier edition of the *Handbook of Geriatric Assessment*, the discussion of elder mistreatment is included in the chapter on social assessment, but in the latest edition, it merits a chapter of its own (Gallo et al., 2000; VanderWeerd et al., 2006). Although these special areas are addressed in this chapter, most are included under broader headings to more appropriately place them in the context of the assessment process. This chapter also discusses the elements of CGA using a modification of my previously mentioned framework. The elements of the assessment are discussed under six broad areas: mental status, functional assessment, medical history, and treatments including nutrition- and health-practices review, emotional/psychological well-being, and social and environmental assessment (Paveza, 1993).

Mental Status

The assessment of mental status should be one of the initial components, if not *the* initial component, of the comprehensive assessment. Although the social work practitioner needs to be cognizant that clients may be somewhat taken aback by the introduction of this item as the first element of the interview, I have argued consistently that, after establishing initial rapport, starting the remainder of the assessment process with the mental-status review is essential to avoid engaging in an information-gathering process that could yield little or no useful information while taking up a significant amount of both the client's and practitioner's time and money (Paveza, Cohen, Blaser, & Hagopian, 1990a; Paveza, Prohaska, Hagopian, & Cohen, 1989).

Gathering information on a client's mental status has generally been described as requiring the practitioner to assess at a minimum the client's level of consciousness, her or his orientation to time and place, and his or her attention and memory (Gallo & Wittink, 2006a). Additional areas that may be covered include information concerning language, the ability to engage in abstract thinking, and constructional ability (Chodosh, 2001; Gallo & Wittink, 2006a; Scalmati & Smyth, 2001). Each of the domains covered in a mental-status exam can provide important information concerning the client's ability to provide historically accurate information, engage in conversations that require abstract thinking, and consent to or reject care plans or elements of care plans (Paveza, 1993; Paveza et al., 1990b; Paveza et al., 1989).

Gathering mental-status information has become relatively standardized. This means that a social work practitioner can quickly ask the questions needed to obtain information in this area. Included among the instruments commonly used are the Folstein Mini-Mental Status Exam (MMSE; Folstein, Folstein, & McHugh, 1975), Pheiffer's Short Portable Mental Status Questionnaire (SPMSQ; Pheiffer, 1975), and the six-item Orientation-Memory-Concentration Test (Katzman et al., 1983). Other tests that can provide additional information are category-fluency sets and the clock-drawing test. These two instruments provide some additional benefits over those more typically used for screening, with the set test generally being seen as less offensive to older adults than the more traditional screens (Gallo & Wittink, 2006a). Moreover, the clock-drawing test can provide useful information about the ability of the older adult to transition between abstract and concrete thinking and his or her use of judgment as he or she draws the clock and puts in the required elements (Gallo & Wittink, 2006a). Mental-status screening has been well researched, and a general description of some of the problematic issues with these screens can be found in the *Handbook of Geriatric Assessment*, fourth edition (Gallo & Wittink, 2006a); the *Geropsychology Assessment Resource Guide* (National Center for Cost Containment, 1993); and *Measuring Health: A Guide to Rating Scales and Questionnaires* (McDowell & Newell, 1996).

In general, issues of importance when interpreting a mental-status screen focus on the level of formal education of the older adult, with those having less formal education often scoring lower than their actual level of cognitive functioning and those with higher levels of education often appearing to do better than their actual level of cognitive functioning (Gallo & Wittink, 2006a). For this reason, as well as others discussed in the literature, the clinician should never use the results of any single mental-status assessment to arrive at a diagnosis of dementia, nor should a client accept this diagnosis based solely on a mental-status screen. The diagnosis of dementia must be arrived at in a manner that addresses all criteria established either in the *Diagnostic and Statistical Manual of Mental Disorders*, fourth edition (American Psychiatric Association, 1994), or in the NINCDS-ADRDA Consensus Criteria (McKhann et al., 1984). The purpose of the mental-status exam is to assist the clinician in determining whether the client can provide useful information for consenting to treatment and for planning care, and whether the client needs referral for a complete neuropsychological exam.

Functional Assessment

Probably the most critical element of the assessment is determining the client's functional ability. Functional ability is the capacity of the individual to perform certain personal-care behaviors that are seen as essential to being able to care for him- or herself independently in a community-living environment. The original seven behaviors seen as essential to being able to function in the community, and usually referred to as activities of daily living, are feeding, bathing, grooming, dressing, continence, toileting, and transfer (Gallo & Paveza, 2006; Katz, Ford, Moskowitz, Jackson, & Jaffe, 1963). Eventually, to these six behaviors was added an additional set of behaviors usually referred to as the instrumental activities of daily living. These behaviors were seen as more complex and demanding than the ADLs but still important for a person who wanted to reside independently in the community (OARS Methodology, 1978). The behaviors initially included in the IADLs were telephone usage and the ability to travel around town, go shopping, prepare his or her own meals, do housework, take needed medications, and manage his or her own money. Although, over time, this initial set of IADLs has been modified for various reasons (Fillenbaum, 1995; Paveza et al., 1990a; Paveza et al., 1989), in general the behaviors included in the IADLs have remained relatively stable.

As with the other areas of the comprehensive-assessment process, a number of different standardized instruments have been developed to measure either separately or in combination ADLs and IADLs. These assessment instruments use different metrics to arrive at the determination of functional ability, but all offer a quick and easy method to obtain this information (Fillenbaum, 1995; Katz et al., 1963; Paveza et al., 1989). Some, such as the direct assessment of functioning (DAF), which was developed for use with dementia patients (Lowenstein et al., 1989), were designed for use with specific types of clients.

The importance of a well-conducted functional assessment cannot be overstated. The measure of functional ability has been shown to be the best single predictor of cost of community-based services (Paveza, Mensah, Cohen, Williams, & Jankowski, 1998) and is the essential component for developing a care plan that identifies those client behaviors most likely requiring intervention (Gallo & Paveza, 2006; Paveza et al., 1989).

The assessment of mental status and functional status sets the first two elements of the assessment process. With these two elements completed, the next most logical step is to gather medical history and information on nutritional and health practices.

Medical History and Nutritional and Health-Behaviors Assessment

The next elements of the comprehensive assessment focus on obtaining an accurate medical history and gathering information about the person's nutritional well-being and other health practices that may impact the client's well-being or quality of life. The medical history needs to gather information about both current and past medical conditions. One of the easiest ways to obtain information on medical conditions is to use a body-systems approach. Information concerning both past and current medical conditions for each of the body's systems serves as a reference point for a set of questions about various medical conditions that might occur in that bodily system. One seeks information on the circulatory system, for example, by asking questions that address likely medical conditions a client may have or have had, such as hypertension, angina, heart attack, and other diseases of the circulatory system. By taking this structured approach to obtaining medical history, it is less likely that the clinician will forget to ask questions about likely medical conditions or that a client will forget to provide information on a specific illness (Paveza et al., 1989). Included as part of gathering information about medical conditions is obtaining information about the medications that are being taken. This includes both physician-prescribed medications as well as all over-the-counter medications and includes vitamin and mineral supplements, herbal and other homeopathic remedies, aspirin and other nonsteroidal anti-inflammatory agents (NSAIDS), cold and flu medications, and anything else that the client may use on a regular basis. It is important to recognize, however, that many clients may be unsure about which medication is for which medical condition. To assist the client in providing and the social work practitioner in obtaining accurate information in this area, it is often helpful to work with the client to complete a drug inventory.

The drug inventory is conducted by asking the client to bring all prescribed medications, over-the-counter medications, herbal medicines, and vitamin and mineral supplements to a common area. When assembled, the clinician first reviews all the prescribed medications and writes down the name of the medication, the date that it was prescribed, and the doctor who prescribed it. Then, all other medications and supplements are recorded. After the completion of the interview, the clinician should work with a knowledgeable pharmacist to ensure that there are no potential interactions either between the prescribed medications or between any of the prescribed medications and the other medications and supplements taken. Should potential interactions be discovered, the clinician should contact the client or caregiver and raise the concern with him or her as well as include this information in the care plan.

Having completed the medical history and drug inventory, it is also important that the clinician gather information concerning nutritional status and health practices. A simple procedure for obtaining information on nutritional status is to use the Nutritional Screening Initiative Checklist. This simple 14-item questionnaire gathers information about issues that impact older adults' ability to stay nutritionally healthy, including financial, emotional, and logistic ability to identify, purchase, and prepare appropriate foods as well as identifying the potential impact of medications and psychological illness on food intake (Wallace, Shea, & Guttman, 2006). In addition to the nutrition screening, it is important for the clinician to seek information from the client concerning the use of alcohol, smoking behavior, the amount of exercise engaged in, whether he or she is experiencing any problems with sleep, and whether the older adult has been able to obtain various recommended immunizations. Each of these areas has the potential to impact both the older adult's risk of mortality as well as his or her quality of life. An area that is often overlooked but needs to be included in this portion of the assessment is the current sexual activity and practices of the older adult. This area is often overlooked because of the clinician's discomfort in seeking this type of information from the older adult. Yet unless some time is spent talking about this important area of functioning, an area of potential emotional distress and risk-taking behavior in some older adults will be missed (Nicklin, 2006).

The clinician should also include in this section an assessment of pain. Many older adults experience pain from the same causes as younger adults, to which can be added the pain impact of many chronic illnesses. Although it was once believed that older adults did not experience pain with the same intensity as younger adults, recent literature suggests this is not true. Moreover, older adults are often given the impression that they should be able to tolerate the pain they are experiencing based on this mistaken notion that their qualitative perception of pain is diminished. Simple assessments of pain include the Numeric Rating Scale, in which a client is asked to rate his or her pain on a scale from 0 to 10, with 0 equaling "no pain" and 10 equaling "the worst pain the person can imagine." A Visual Analog Scale—in which a 10-cm line is shown to the client, with one end being labeled "no pain" and the other end labeled as "worst imaginable pain" on which the client then indicates where his or her pain falls—is another alternative for quickly assessing the current level of pain experienced by the client. Although both of these measures are useful for monitoring pain, because they can be used to detect small changes in the client's experience of pain, it is important to remember that these scales do not provide information on changes in psychological distress or physical function that may be caused by pain (Richardson, 2006).

To assess pain in areas other than intensity, one must consider the use of a multidimensional pain scale, such as the McGill Pain Questionnaire (MPQ). This instrument assesses pain in sensory, affective, and evaluative areas. Although the MPQ has been used in a variety of settings, it can take up to 20 minutes to complete and may not be appropriate for use during the initial assessment of the client. Rather, the clinician may wish to indicate that, as part of the care plan, a more comprehensive assessment of the client's pain be conducted with a referral to a pain clinic.

Having completed this portion of the medical history and assessment of health behaviors and practices, it is important for the clinician to include recommendations in the care plan that will help mitigate or remove the impact of any deficiencies (Wallace et al., 2006).

The final area to cover as part of the medical history and assessment of health behaviors and practices is an assessment of emotional well-being.

Assessment of Emotional Well-Being

The assessment of emotional well-being as part of the comprehensive assessment should focus at a minimum on the presence of depression and/or anxiety. However, if at all possible, the clinician should explore a range of psychiatric symptoms and the psychiatric illnesses associated with those symptoms.

The assessment for depression in older adults is probably the most easily accomplished because of the amount of clinical anecdotal information on the frequency of depression in older adults, the research suggesting that rates of depression in older adults are higher than for younger populations, or the belief that depression is considered to be among the more treatable of emotional conditions experienced by older adults (Gallo & Wittnik, 2006b). Regardless of the reason for this focus on depression, it is important that it be assessed. Because of the amount of attention paid to depression, the availability of aids to assist in determining the presence of depression is extensive. A discussion of those aids occurs in almost any book addressing the care of older adults as well as those that specifically address mental-health issues with this population (Blazer, 1995, 1998; Chiu & Ames, 1994; Gallo et al., 2006; Kurlowicz, 2001; Schneider, Reynolds, Lebowitz, & Friedhoff, 1994). What the clinician must remember is that whichever aid he or she chooses, the focus should be on ease and simplicity of administration during an extended information gathering process.

Assessment of anxiety is also important with older adults, and Blazer (1998) probably provides one of the more cogent discussions of the need for assessing this area of emotional well-being in older adults. One particular reason for assessing anxiety is the fact that, in older adults, depression and anxiety can present with similar symptom pictures. Thus, an appropriate differential diagnosis assessment of both becomes important (Blazer, 1998; Diffenbach, 2001).

Additionally, should the older adult present with symptoms or describe symptoms to the social work practitioner that suggest the presence of other psychiatric illnesses, the clinician should assess for that emotional problem as well or, at the very least, refer the older adult for a complete psychiatric evaluation.

Once the clinician has completed gathering information on medical history, nutritional status, health practice and behaviors, and emotional well-being, the focus of the interview should turn to obtaining information on the social, economic, and environmental well-being of the older adult.

Assessment of Social, Economic, and Environmental Well-Being

The assessment of the social, environmental, and economic well-being of the older adult client as part of a CGA encompasses a wide range of topics. It is also during this part of the interview that the clinician will interview those providing care to the older adult to determine the stability of the caregiving relationships and the stress that those providing care may be experiencing (Morano & Morano, 2006). This is the area of assessment in which the social work practitioner is likely to be most comfortable, because it mirrors those areas of assessment in which the social worker has received extensive training and has had the most practice experience.

Social Assessment

The focus of the social assessment should be on both the extent of the social system or social network that surrounds the older adult and on the quality of that system. The clinician needs to determine the number of persons who make up the support system; the number of persons in the support system whom the client identifies as significant; the relationship to the older adult of each person who is identified as significant; and the amount, intensity, and quality of contact that the older adult has with those as identified as significant. Some sense of the amount and quality of contact with those identified as less significant should also be determined. The clinician needs to particularly identify those serving as caregivers to the older adult and determine the amount of care that each is providing. Once this information has been obtained from the client, the clinician should seek permission from the client to, at a minimum, meet and talk with those providing care.

Interaction with the caregivers should focus on the medical conditions, ADLs, IADLs, and other areas in which care is provided; the amount of care required by the client in terms of hours per day; how the caregiving load is distributed among the various caregivers; the extent to which each caregiver experiences providing care as a burden; and the degree to which each of the caregivers derives satisfaction from the caregiving experience. Morano and Morano (2006) provide an excellent discussion of these elements of social assessment.

Unique areas included with the social assessment of older adults include specific assessment for the presence of elder mistreatment, assessment of spiritual well-being, and values clarification to assist with advanced directives. The assessment for elder mistreatment should focus on determining whether the older adult has been or is the victim of physical abuse, caregiver or self-neglect, psychological abuse, and financial exploitation (VanderWeerd et al., 2006). Assessing for the possibility of elder mistreatment is particularly important when conducting an assessment in which the older adult has a dementing illness, because the research suggests that the presence of elder mistreatment in these families is significantly higher than in the general population (Paveza et al., 1992).

In addition to assessing for elder mistreatment, the clinician should spend some time assessing the spiritual well-being of the older adult. This is a time in the older adult's life when he or she may rekindle his or her spirituality. Other older adults, who may have always been spiritually active, find themselves cut off from those activities that have been part of their spiritual life (Morano & Morano, 2006). For this reason, it is important to determine previous level of spiritual activity, current level of activity, and desired level of activity as well as some understanding of the general importance of spiritual beliefs and activity in the older adult's life. Building on this, the clinician should determine whether there has been a change in the level of activity, information concerning the older adult's perception of the importance of such activity in his or her life, and any impact that a change in participation may be having on the older adult's quality of life (Morano & Morano, 2006).

The exploration of the importance of spirituality in the older adult's life can also serve as a good starting point for a discussion of values and a clarification of values related to the older adult's wishes concerning end-of-life care. What are the older adult's beliefs concerning the use of heroic measures to being kept alive? Are there circumstances in which the older adult would not wish to be resuscitated? What are they specifically? It is also important to explore whether the older adult has designated health-care surrogates and whether the appropriate documents are in place to permit his or her wishes concerning end-of-life health care to be acted on. It is important to determine whether the older adult has shared with the health-care surrogates his or her wishes about health-care choices so that, if the older adult is no longer able to make those decisions, the health-care surrogate can effectively act for the older adult.

If this discussion has not occurred, then the information obtained during this part of the assessment can be used as part of the care-planning process to engage family members around these wishes and have everyone who might have an interest in the well-being of the older adult clearly aware of what the person's wishes are concerning end-of-life care. In far too many instances, the older adult may have in place a do-not-resuscitate document, a durable power of attorney for health care and possibly for finances, and a living will; however, the older adult has never had a conversation with family members about these things. With a lack of clear direction from the older adult, family members often end up disagreeing about the type and level of care to be provided. Significant animosity can and does develop in families around such decisions, often resulting in lifelong disruptions in family relationships. With a little planning and preparation, the older adult can be assisted by the clinician to engage with other members of the family about the specific type and level of care he or she desires under various circumstances. This information can then be reduced to a written document that is provided to all relevant members of the family. Although not a perfect solution, it is likely to reduce the frustration that family members experience when having to make health-care decisions for their parents or siblings (Doukas et al., 2006).

With the completion of the assessment of the social network and related elements, the clinician can turn his or her focus to the final two areas of the assessment process: economic well-being and environmental assessment.

Economic Well-Being

Assessment of economic well-being involves determining not only how much income the older adult has but also the number of persons dependent either completely or in part on that income. However, economic well-being goes beyond a simple accounting of income and those dependent on it. The assessment needs to determine what demands are placed on that income in terms of expenditures and whether the older adult perceives that income to be sufficient to meet his or her needs and those of the persons dependent on that income (Fillenbaum, 1988; Morano & Morano, 2006). A thorough review of the older adult's economic well-being permits the clinician to have a clear sense of what types of economic assistance the older adult might need and how willing the person is to accept help.

Environmental Assessment

The final area for review in the comprehensive assessment is the assessment of the older adult's physical-living environment. This requires the clinician to visit the place where the older adult lives, whether this is an independent-living situation, an assisted-living facility, or a long-term-care facility. If the clinician is conducting an assessment prior to a hospital discharge, it will be important for the clinician to consider making a visit to the place to which the older adult will be initially discharged and also to the place where the client will permanently live, if it is different.

Environmental assessment should include a complete tour of the residence, with the clinician paying particular attention to elements in the environment that may affect the quality of life for the older adult or pose a physical impediment or hazard. Elements that the clinician needs to observe, for instance, are the presence of handrails and grab-bars in bathing and toileting areas, presence of stairways, and how often they must be used by the older adult. Additionally, the clinician should note the presence of throw rugs and/or electrical extensions that may pose a hazard to the older adult with mobility problems. Attention should be paid to whether heating, cooling, and ventilation are adequate for both summer and winter, whether lighting is adequate to permit objects to be seen and recognized, whether knobs on faucets can be turned easily and water temperature adjusted without the older adult being scalded or burned, and whether door knobs can be easily opened and closed as well as some general sense of the atmosphere of the living environment. Morano and Morano provide an excellent checklist in the *Handbook of Geriatric Assessment*, fourth edition (2006). A consideration during this review should be determining the number of persons who occupy the physical environment. The clinician needs to determine whether there is ample room for all to live adequately and for all to have some privacy when needed.

Once the clinician has completed the review of the older adult's actual living quarters, attention needs to be directed to the surrounding environment. Things to be considered include the safety of the neighbor-hood; ease and access to transportation, including a through review of whether the older adult is still driving; and whether this is still in the older adult's best interest (Carr & Rebok, 2006; Morano & Morano, 2006). Other items of interest should include the availability of sidewalks and their state of repair in relation to the impact this might have on the older adult's mobility. Depending on the information obtained during the review of the client's total environment, important recommendations may need to be included in the care plan concerning modifications to the living environment and its surroundings, the older adult's ability to continue driving, and transportation alternatives that can help ensure that the older adult can obtain food, pay bills, and keep doctor's appointments (Carr & Rebok, 2006).

The Care Plan

On conclusion of the assessment process, the clinician needs to compile a complete report that summarizes all the relevant findings from the assessment. What specifically should be included in the report depends on what the clinician uncovers during the assessment process. At a minimum, information from all the areas explored should be included in the care plan, including findings on mental status, functional ability, medical history, nutrition and health practices, social network, economic well-being, and the living environment. The plan should report on the older adult's ability to function in the community and on the older adult's quality of life as well as provide information that supports the recommendations for services or assistance. A person reading the report should be able to connect any intervention recommended as part of the care plan to a clearly stated finding from the assessment process by referencing specific links to elements of the assessment (Gallo et al., 2000). The format of the report should be such that both a layperson—most likely the older adult, the caregiver, or some other family member—as well as paraprofessionals working in the health-care and social-service fields and professionals working in a variety of medical-care and social-service settings can all easily understand the recommendations and the information that brought the clinician to those recommendations. Such a report will make it easier for the clinician to negotiate and advocate for the older adult as the clinician seeks appropriate services for him or her.

In making recommendations, the clinician needs to be prepared to draw from a wide range of potential interventions, particularly when working with community-dwelling older adults. Recommendations might include education for family caregivers to assist them with improving their skills in caring for the older adult, family counseling to help the family cope with the stress of their situation, and community-based health and social services, including home health care, adult day care, and other services. Also included in the services to be considered is placement in either an assisted-living facility or other more intense long-term-care living arrangement. The clinician needs to be prepared to support and assist the older adult and the family members as they review the recommendations and make their choices. The clinician must always remember that the ultimate choice in selecting interventions belongs to the older adult and those providing care to that older adult, not to the person doing the assessment and making recommendations.

Conclusion

In concluding this chapter, I wish to briefly discuss the literature that provides some insight into the effectiveness of CGA. Findings concerning the effectiveness of CGA have been mixed. Several studies have raised questions about the effectiveness of CGA, with Ruben et al. (1995) clearly showing that such assessments did not improve the health or survival of hospitalized geriatric patients, and Siu et al. showing that assessments carried out prior to hospital discharge did not improve outcomes for frail elderly (1996). On the other hand, Rubenstein et al., Struck et al., Alessi et al., Naylor et al., Buurman et al., Ellis et al., and Pilotto et al. all provide evidence for the effectiveness of comprehensive assessment in improving outcomes and delaying disability in older adults, helping identify new problems when assessment is repeated annually and in fewer recurring hospitalizations (Alessi et al., 1997; Buurman, Parlevliet, van Deelen, de Haan, & de Rooij, 2004; Ellis, Whitehead, Robinson, O'Neill, & Langhorne, 2011; Naylor et al., 1999; Pilotto, Addante, D'Onofrio, Sancarl, & Ferrucci, 2009; Pilotto et al., 2011; L. Z. Rubenstein, Stuck, Siu, & Wieland, 1991; Stuck et al., 1995b). The meta-analysis of several studies clearly suggests that although the evidence might be divided, the majority of the studies included in the meta-analysis and the meta-analysis itself conclude that CGA enhances implementation of care recommendations and client adherence to those recommendations (Stuck, Wieland, Rubenstein, Siu, & Adams, 1995a).

Conducting a CGA as described here is likely to improve the care provided to older adult clients and result in delaying more negative outcomes.

Key Terms

Geriatric assessment	Mental status	Effectiveness of
Functional status	Care planning	geriatric assessment

Review Questions for Critical Thinking

1. Why do I need to have an understanding of CGA for my practice?
2. What are the critical elements for me to include in my work with older adults, and what is my rationale for including those elements?

3. How can I effectively include such elements in my interview and practice that allow me to gather this information while maintaining my relationship with my clients?

Online Resources

http://hometownhealthonline.coursehost.com/engine/Academic/Tools/ CoursePublicize.asp?pk=76426&LID=1&ky=d_BPDiQVRgHzDiPRUmf _DgHzKrvOMqjz HomeTown Health University offers an online course to learn how to conduct comprehensive assessment in geriatrics. This course is designed to instruct health-care personnel on how to provide a CGA.

http://www.medscape.com/viewarticle/465308_4 General information about the components of a CGA as well as various screening tests that are offered (brief description of each). The site also gives information regarding who would benefit from this screening.

http://www.uptodate.com/contents/comprehensive-geriatric-assessment This website outlines components of CGAs, its efficacy, and its indications. Sections are outlined that review the assessment team, how to conduct the assessment, assessment tools, and so on.

References

Alessi, C. A., Stuck, A. E., Aronow, H. U., Yuhas, K. E., Bula, C. J., Madison, R.,...Beck, J. C. (1997). The process of care in preventive in-home comprehensive geriatric assessment. *Journal of the American Geriatrics Society, 45*(9), 1044–1050.

American Psychiatric Association. (1994). *Diagnostic and statistical manual of mental disorders* (4th ed.). Washington, DC: Author.

Blazer, D. (1995). *Depression*. In G. L. Maddox (Ed.), *The encyclopedia of aging: A comprehensive resource in gerontology and geriatrics* (2nd ed., pp. 265–266). New York, NY: Springer.

Blazer, D. (1998). *Emotional problems in later life: Intervention strategies for professional caregivers* (2nd ed.). New York, NY: Springer.

Buurman, B. M., Parlevliet, J. L., van Deelen, B. A. J., de Haan, R. J., & de Rooij, S. E. (2004). A randomised clinical trial on a comprehensive geriatric assessment and intensive home follow-up after hospital discharge: The transitional care bridge. *Journal of the American Geriatrics Society, 52*, 1417–1423.

Carr, D., & Rebok, G. W. (2006). The older adult driver. In J. J. Gallo, H. R. Bogner, T. Fulmer, & G. J. Paveza (Eds.), *Handbook of geriatric assessment* (4th ed., pp. 45–58). Sudbury, MA: Jones & Bartlett.

Chang, L. S., & Mamun, K. (2008). Comprehensive geriatric assessment. *Hospital Wide Clinical Meeting: Geriatric Medicine, 17*(3).

Chiu, E., & Ames, D. (Eds.). (1994). *Functional psychiatric disorders of the elderly*. Cambridge, UK: Cambridge University Press.

Chodosh, J. (2001). Cognitive screening tests: The mini-mental status exam. In M. D. Mezey (Ed.), *The encyclopedia of elder care: The comprehensive resource on geriatric and social care* (pp. 142–144). New York, NY: Springer.

Diffenbach, G. (2001). Anxiety and panic disorders. In M. D. Mezey (Ed.), *The encyclopedia of elder care: The comprehensive resource on geriatric and social care* (pp. 61–63). New York, NY: Springer.

Doukas, D. J., McCullough, L. B., & Crane, M. K. (2006). Enhancing advanced directive discussions using the values history. In J. J. Gallo, H. R. Bogner, T. Fulmer, & G. J. Paveza (Eds.), *Handbook of geriatric assessment* (4th ed., pp. 59–75). Sudbury, MA: Jones & Bartlett.

Ellis, G., Whitehead, M. A., Robinson, D., O'Neill, D., & Langhorne, P. (2011). Comprehensive geriatric assessment for older adults admitted to hospital: Meta-analysis of randomized controlled trials. *British Medical Journal, 343,* 6553–6563.

Fillenbaum, G. G. (1988). *Multidimensional functional assessment of older adults: The duke older Americans resources and services procedures.* Hillsdale, NJ: Erlbaum.

Fillenbaum, G. G. (1995). Multidimensional functional assessment. In G. L. Maddox (Ed.), *The encyclopedia of aging: A comprehensive resource in gerontology and geriatrics* (2nd ed., pp. 653–654). New York, NY: Springer.

Folstein, M., Folstein, S., & McHugh, P. (1975). Mini-mental state: A practical method for grading the cognitive state of patients for the clinician. *Journal of Psychiatric Research, 12,* 189–198.

Fulmer, T. T., & O'Malley, T. A. (1987). *Inadequate care of the elderly: A health care perspective on abuse and neglect.* New York, NY: Springer.

Gallo, J. J., & Bogner, H. R. (2006). The context of geriatric care. In J. J. Gallo, H. R. Bogner, T. Fullmer, & G. J. Paveza (Eds.), *The handbook of geriatric assessment* (4th ed., pp. 3–13). Sudbury, MA: Jones & Bartlett.

Gallo, J. J., Bogner, H. R., Fulmer, T., & Paveza, G. J. (Eds.). (2006). *Handbook of geriatric assessment* (4th ed.). Sudbury, MA: Jones & Bartlett.

Gallo, J. J., Fulmer, T., Paveza, G. J., & Reichel, W. (Eds.). (2000). *Handbook of geriatric assessment* (3rd ed.). Gaithersburg, MD: Aspen.

Gallo, J. J., & Paveza, G. J. (2006). Activities of daily living and instrumental activities of daily living assessment. In J. J. Gallo, H. R. Bogner, T. Fulmer, & G. J. Paveza (Eds.), *Handbook of geriatric assessment* (4th ed., pp. 193–240). Sudbury, MA: Jones & Bartlett.

Gallo, J. J., Reichel, W., & Andersen, L. M. (Eds.). (1988). *Handbook of geriatric assessment.* Rockville, MD: Aspen.

Gallo, J. J., Reichel, W., & Andersen, L. M. (Eds.). (1995). *Handbook of geriatric assessment* (2nd ed.). Rockville, MD: Aspen.

Gallo, J. J., & Wittink, M. N. (2006a). Cognitive assessment. In J. J. Gallo, H. R. Bogner, T. Fulmer, & G. J. Paveza (Eds.), *Handbook of geriatric assessment* (4th ed., pp. 105–151). Sudbury, MA: Jones & Bartlett.

Gallo, J. J., & Wittnik, M. N. (2006b). Depression assessment. In J. J. Gallo, H. R. Bogner, T. Fulmer, & G. J. Paveza (Eds.), *Handbook of geriatric assessment* (4th ed., pp. 153–173). Sudbury, MA: Jones & Bartlett.

Katz, S., Ford, A. B., Moskowitz, R. W., Jackson, B. A., & Jaffe, M. W. (1963, September 21). Studies of illness in the aged. The index of ADL: A standardized measure of biological and psychosocial function. *Journal of the American Medical Association, 185,* 914–919.

Katzman, R., Brown, T., Fuld, P., Peck, A., Schechter, R., & Schimmel, H. (1983). Validation of a short orientation-memory-concentration test of cognitive impairment. *American Journal of Psychiatry, 140,* 734–739.

Kurlowicz, L. H. (2001). Depression measurement instruments. In M. D. Mezey (Ed.), *The encyclopedia of elder care: The comprehensive resource on geriatric and social care* (pp. 210–212). New York, NY: Springer.

Lowenstein, D. A., Amigo, E., Duara, R., Guterman, A., Hurwitz, D., Berkowitz, N.,...Eisdorfer, C (1989). A new scale for the assessment of functional status in Alzheimer's disease and related disorders. *Journal of Gerontology: Psychological Sciences, 44*(4), P114–P121.

McDowell, I., & Newell, C. (1996). *Measuring health: A guide to rating scales and questionnaires* (2nd ed.). New York, NY: Oxford University Press.

McKhann, G., Drachman, D., Folstein, M., Katzman, R., Price, D., & Stadlan, E. M. (1984). Clinical diagnosis of Alzheimer's disease: Report of the NINCDS-ADRDA work group under the auspices of department of health and human services task force on Alzheimer's disease. *Neurology, 34,* 939–944.

Morano, C., & Morano, B. (2006). Social assessment. In J. J. Gallo, H. R. Bogner, T. Fulmer, & G. J. Paveza (Eds.), *Handbook of geriatric assessment* (4th ed., pp. 241–271). Sudbury, MA: Jones & Bartlett.

Mouton, C. P., & Esparza, Y. B. (2006). Ethnicity and geriatric assessment. In J. J. Gallo, H. R. Bogner, T. Fulmer, & G. J. Paveza (Eds.), *Handbook of geriatric assessment* (4th ed., pp. 29–44). Sudbury, MA: Jones & Bartlett.

National Center for Cost Containment (1993). *Geropsychology assessment resource guide.* Milwaukee, WI: Department of Commerce, National Technical Information Service.

Naylor, M. D., Brooten, D., Campbell, R., Jacobsen, B. S., Mezey, M. D., Pauly, M. V., & Schwartz, J. S. (1999). Comprehensive discharge planning and home follow-up of hospitalized elders: A randomized clinical trial. *Journal of the American Medical Association, 281*(7), 613–620.

Nicklin, D. (2006). Physical assessment. In J. J. Gallo, H. R. Bogner, T. Fulmer, & G. J. Paveza (Eds.), *Handbook of geriatric assessment* (4th ed., pp. 273–317). Sudbury, MA: Jones & Bartlett.

Older Americans Resources and Services (OARS) Methodology. (1978). *Multidimensional Functional Assessment Questionnaire* (2nd ed.). Durham, NC: Duke University Center for the Study of Aging and Human Development.

Paveza, G. J. (1993). Social services and the Alzheimer's disease patient: An overview. *Neurology, 43*(8, Suppl. 4), 11–15.

Paveza, G. J., Cohen, D., Blaser, C. J., & Hagopian, M. (1990a). A brief form of the mini-mental state examination for use in community care settings. *Behavior, Health and Aging, 1*(2), 133–139.

Paveza, G. J., Cohen, D., Eisdorfer, C., Freels, S., Semla, T., Ashford, J. W.,...Levy, P. (1992). Severe family violence and Alzheimer's disease: Prevalence and risk factors. *Gerontologist, 32*(4), 493–497.

Paveza, G. J., Cohen, D., Hagopian, M., Prohaska, T., Blaser, C. J., & Brauner, D. (1990b). A brief assessment tool for determining eligibility and need for community-based long-term care services. *Behavior, Health and Aging, 1*(2), 121–132.

Paveza, G. J., Mensah, E., Cohen, D., Williams, S., & Jankowski, L. (1998). Costs of home and community-based long-term care services to the cognitively impaired aged. *Journal of Mental Health and Aging, 4*(1), 69–82.

Paveza, G. J., Prohaska, T., Hagopian, M., & Cohen, D. (1989). *Determination of need revision: Final report* (Vol. 1). Chicago: University of Illinois, Gerontology Center.

Pheiffer, E. (1975). A short portable mental status questionnaire for the assessment of organic brain deficit in elderly patients. *Journal of the American Geriatrics Society, 23,* 433–441.

Pilotto, A., Addante, F., D'Onofrio, G., Sancarl, D., & Ferrucci, L. (2009). The Comprehensive Geriatric Assessment and the multidimensional approach. A new look at the older patient with gastroenterological disorders. *Best Practices and Research in Clinical Gastroenterology, 23,* 829–837.

Pilotto, A., Sancarlo, D., Panza, F., Paris, F., D'Onofrio, Cascavilla, L.,... Ferrucci, L. (2011). The multidimensional prognostic index (MPI), based on a comphrehensive geriatric assessment, predicts short- and long-term mortality in hospitalized older patients with dementia. *Journal of Alzheimer's Disease, 18,* 191–199.

Richardson, J. P. (2006). Pain assessment. In J. J. Gallo, H. R. Bogner, T. Fulmer, & G. J. Paveza (Eds.), *Handbook of geriatric assessment* (4th ed., pp. 319–329). Sudbury, MA: Jones & Bartlett.

Ruben, D. B., Borok, G. M., Wolde-Tsadik, G., Ershoff, D. H., Fishman, L. K., Ambrosini, V. L.,... Beck, J. C. (1995). A randomized trial of comprehensive geriatric assessment in the care of hospitalized patients. *New England Journal of Medicine, 332*(20), 1345–1350.

Rubenstein, L. A. (1995). Geriatric assessment units: Their rationale, history, process and effectiveness. In G. L. Maddox (Ed.), *The encyclopedia of aging: A comprehensive resource in gerontology and geriatrics* (2nd ed., pp. 403–406). New York, NY: Springer.

Rubenstein, L. Z., Stuck, A. E., Siu, A. L., & Wieland, D. (1991). Impacts of geriatric evaluation and management programs on defined outcomes: Overview of the evidence. *Journal of the American Geriatrics Society, 39,* 8–16.

Scalmati, A., & Smyth, C. (2001). Cognition instruments. In M. D. Mezey (Ed.), *The encyclopedia of elder care: The comprehensive resource on geriatric and social care* (pp. 137–139). New York, NY: Springer.

Schneider, L. S., Reynolds, C. F., III, Lebowitz, B. D., & Friedhoff, A. J. (Eds.). (1994). *Diagnosis and treatment of depression in late life: Results of the NIH consensus development conference.* Washington, DC: American Psychiatric Press.

Siu, A. L., Kravitz, R. L., Keeler, E., Hemmerling, K., Kington, R., Davis, J. W.,... Reuben, D. B. (1996). Postdischarge geriatric assessment of hospitalized frail elderly patients. *Archives of Internal Medicine, 156*(1), 76–81.

Stuck, A. E., Wieland, D., Rubenstein, L. Z., Siu, A. L., & Adams, J. (1995a). Comprehensive geriatric assessment: Meta-analysis of main effects and elements enhancing effectiveness. In L. Z. Rubenstein, D. Wieland, & R. Bernabei (Eds.), *Geriatric assessment technology: The state of the art* (pp. 11–26). Milano, Italy: Editrice Kurtis-Milano.

Stuck, A. E., Zwahlen, H. G., Neuenschwander, B. E., Meyer Schweizer, R. A., Bauen, G., & Beck, J. C. (1995b). Methodologic challenges of randomized controlled studies on in-home comprehensive geriatric assessment: The EIGER project—Evaluation of in-home geriatric health visits in elderly residents. *Aging, Clinical and Experimental Research, 7*(3), 218–223.

VanderWeerd, C., Firpo, A., Fulmer, T., & Paveza, G. J. (2006). Recognizing mistreatment in older adults. In J. J. Gallo, H. R. Bogner, T. Fulmer, & G.

J. Paveza (Eds.), *Handbook of geriatric assessment* (4th ed., pp. 78–101). Sudbury, MA: Jones & Bartlett.

Wallace, M., Shea, J., & Guttman, C. (2006). Health promotion. In J. J. Gallo, H. R. Bogner, T. Fulmer, & G. J. Paveza (Eds.), *Handbook of geriatric assessment* (4th ed., pp. 331–368). Sudbury, MA: Jones & Bartlett.

Zanjani, F., & Oslin, D. (2006). Substance use and abuse assessment. In J. J. Gallo, H. R. Bogner, T. Fulmer, & G. J. Paveza (Eds.), *Handbook of geriatric assessment* (4th ed., pp. 175–192). Sudbury, MA: Jones & Bartlett.

Chapter 8
Intervention With the Elderly

Michael J. Holosko, Jeffrey F. Skinner, Catherine A. Patterson, and Kimberly Brisebois

Purpose: This chapter offers an overview of current and practical issues related to social work interventions with the elderly.

Rationale: With our aging population rapidly increasing, gerontological social workers will be needed more than ever. They require basic knowledge of the required intervention skills necessary for both entry and advanced levels of practice with the elderly.

How evidence-informed practice is presented: We present a summary of current evidence-informed practice interventions and analyze this literature in terms of: conceptual/theoretical frameworks for treatment, effectiveness studies, and specified intervention and outcome studies. Implications for education are then discussed from this framework.

Overarching question: How does evidence-informed practice inform social work interventions with the elderly?

This chapter presents an overview of issues related to interventions with the elderly. Gerontological social work is predicted to be one of the high-demand future job markets for our profession, as we in the United States are rapidly becoming an aging society (U.S. Bureau of Labor Statistics, 2004). Thus, it seems both relevant and timely to include a chapter about this area of social work practice. Prior to presenting the materials that assess the efficacy of evidence-based interventions with the elderly, a brief historical background provides the context and rationale for understanding this information.

Historical Background

The Demographic Reality

In most industrialized countries of the world, a demographic population explosion has occurred among those aged 65 and older. This is primarily attributed to improved medical treatment, earlier changes in lifestyle, reduced mortality rates, increased financial independence, old age pensions, governmental assistance, advances in technology, greater mobility and access to health and social services, and formal and informal support networks (Holosko & Feit, 2004).

For the past 40 or 50 years, U.S. policy makers at federal, state, and/or local levels have both witnessed and acknowledged this exponential growth, but they don't quite know how to deal with it. For example, in an article written by A. Otten in the *Wall Street Journal*, on Monday, July 10, 1984, a three-part series was titled: "The Oldest-Old: Ever More Americans Live into Their 80's and 90's and Cause Big Problems" [Part I]; "The Strain on Social Services and Relatives Will Rise: Should Care Be Rationed?" [II]; and, "A Five-Generation Family" [III]. Concerns about how to reconcile or address this reality are a long-standing and ubiquitous feature of our society. Breaking these data down a bit further provides additional insights into some interesting and challenging policy and practice realities for social workers practicing in this area.

Although there is some disagreement in the literature about what constitutes an elderly person, policy makers deem 65 as the present age benchmark (Holosko & Leslie, 2004). From a formative or Level I life-span perspective, persons over 65 represent the fastest growing age group in the United States. Projections are that by the year 2030, over 70 million Americans will be at least 65 years of age (Administration on Aging, 2003). At a Level II perspective, this subgroup is further broken down by current health, aging, and lifecycle markers as: young-old, or 65–75; moderately old, or 75–90; and old-old, being 90 + years. Indeed, since about 1988, the fastest growing cohort on our lifecycle continuum is the 85 + year-old category (Feit & Cueuves-Feit, 1991, 2004).

From a Level III demographic perspective, (a) there are and will continue to be more women than men who live beyond age 65 in the United States; (b) more of the 65 + age group will come from ethnically diverse groups; (c) more elderly will be actively employed in the future; (d) more elderly will be residing in urban centers rather than rural settings; and (e) more elderly will become meaningfully involved in our day-to-day lives, for example, in arts, literature, movies, athletics, politics, educational and economic institutions, and so on. Indeed, as indicated by Holosko and Holosko (2004), as a society, we can no longer take an out-of-sight, out-of-mind mentality with the elderly because they are and will continue to be in plain sight and clearly in our minds. Just where and when these three growth trends will subside or even plateau is nowhere to be seen on our current society's horizon.

Practice Implications

In attempting to discern how these trends may impact on social work practice with the elderly, the first author conducted a literature search on emerging practice issues about the elderly from 1975 to 2006. Tables of contents for main teaching texts written by social workers, as well as training institute workshops offered by the Council on Social Work Education (CSWE) and the National Association of Social Workers (NASW), served as the database for this cursory review. One rather interesting finding emerged. The so-called emerging-practice issues cited early on in documents by Lowry (1979); Schneider, Decker, Freeman, Messerschmidt, and Syran (1984); and Greene (1988) were the same emerging practice topics listed by the Hartford Foundation's Gero-Education Group at a recent CSWE Conference (www.Gero-EdCenter.org), almost verbatim circa 1988.

To the nascent reader of these admittedly rather spurious comparative data, it would appear that practice issues that were deemed on the forefront some 20 years ago by our profession are still on the forefront today. However, what has changed is not the issues themselves but (a) the sheer numbers of elderly; (b) their various subgroups; (c) their health and psychosocial problems, and the context in which they present; (d) the variety of interventions we offer to deal with these issues; and (e) our ability to assess the efficacy of our interventions. Sadly, what else has not changed (in this brief chronological snapshot) is the dire shortage of social workers educated and trained to practice in this area (Hooyman & Kayak, 2002; Lowry, 1979). A recently released NASW National Workforce Study of licensed social workers reported the number of new social workers providing services to older adults is decreasing, despite the projected increases in the number of older adults who will need social work services (NASW, 2006).

Defining and Assessing the Evidence-Based Practice Interventions

Social workers' decade-long affair with evidence-based practice (EBP) has been significantly tempered (Gambrill, 2006). This is due in large part to the profession's inability to realistically define the concept and practitioners' inability to implement it in practice (Thyer & Kazi, 2004). An evolving and much more realistic definition of EBP is "the conscientious and judicious use of current best practice in making decisions for individual treatment" (Howard, McMillan, & Pollio, 2003; Pollio, 2002, 2006; Sackett, Richardson, Rosenberg, & Haynes, 1997). This less stringent definition is used in this chapter.

As a result, the information reviewed herein included both quantitative and qualitative research as well as evaluation research studies. In short, as long as empirical data were systematically collected to either inform or direct practice, they were retained for subsequent analyses. Figure 8.1 presents a three-cohort conceptualization of these data-driven studies.

Figure 8.1 shifts the perceptual lens of more traditionally delimiting definitions of EBP to a looser definition of "social work practice [in this case with the elderly] based on empirical data" or the actual evidence per se. Thus, published articles, studies, chapters, texts, or monographs not grounded in this way were not retained for analyses for this chapter.

Nonempirically based studies, historical reviews, frameworks (conceptual, theoretical, treatment) not based on empirical data, studies about gerontological workers themselves, policy analyses, critiques of practice, opinion pieces, and trend analyses were consequently excluded. Ironically, this latter literature accounted for approximately 35% of the published

Figure 8.1

Three cohorts of evidence-based studies used in a review of interventions for the elderly

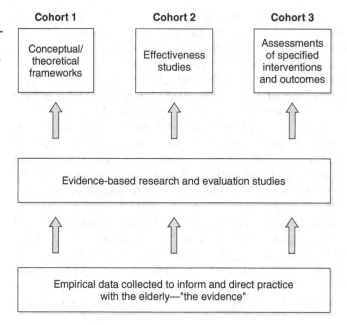

Too often in overviews of the literature of this nature, published accounts are summarily dismissed if they do not include a readily identifiable method section or empirical data, for example, tables of statistics. This nascent approach unfortunately delimits a host of important literature that, on further investigation, has an empirical basis to it. Figure 8.1 conceptualized literature in Cohort 1 as having an empirical basis to it. That is, empirical data were used to develop these conceptual and/or theoretical frameworks that guided gerontological social work practice.

critical mass captured by the initial search parameters. Further, in order to keep this chapter relatively current, only literature from 1995 onward was reviewed. Key words used in searching these literature sources were: *gerontology, interventions, outcomes, social work practice, effectiveness, assessing practice,* and *evidence-based practice.*

In addition, we attempted to seek out EBP literature and present it in ways that emphasized the practice → evidence linkage. After a presentation of the summarized evidence-based intervention studies, as indicated in the three cohorts in Figure 8.1, a model for integrating such evidence into practice is then presented.

Summary of Current Evidence-Based Interventions With the Elderly

Cohort 1—Conceptual/Theoretical Frameworks

Too often in overviews of the literature of this nature, published accounts are summarily dismissed if they do not include a readily identifiable method section or empirical data, for example, tables of statistics. This nascent approach unfortunately delimits a host of important literature that, on further investigation, has an empirical basis to it. Figure 8.1 conceptualized literature in Cohort 1 as having an empirical basis to it. That is, empirical data were used to develop these conceptual and/or theoretical frameworks that guided gerontological social work practice.

Three criteria were used to determine literature suitable for inclusion here. First, all these published accounts clearly had to be empirically linked to practice interventions with the elderly. This was operationalized in one of two ways: (1) greater than 50% of the references cited at the end of the chapter/article had to have analyzed/cited primary or secondary data, and/or (2) case examples were used in the document as the basis for the proposed conceptual/theoretical framework. For the most part, such chapters/articles grounded the rationale for the proposed framework in empirical studies that, in turn, presented the basis for their subsequent development.

As previously mentioned in this chapter, elders are living longer, proliferating in number, and incurring escalating costs of care. Ironically, many of these potential clients did not expect to live as long as they presently are, and their resources have significantly diminished as their lives are extended. As such, residential long-term care and end-of-life planning were prevalent topics among many studies considered for inclusion in Cohort 1 (Table 8.1).

Thus, the quality of life in long-term care facilities is becoming a more salient issue. Solomon (2004) explored providing for quality of life in long-term residential homes for elderly clients by suggesting nine criteria that have a positive contributive influence. These were good physical care, pleasant environment, autonomy/choice, attentive staff, respectful treatment, personal meaning, engaging activities, opportunities for significant relationships, and interdisciplinary collaboration. Revisiting a common intervention for clinical practice with elderly populations (group work) with a unique taxonomy, Solomon presented four group types: self-government, support, educational, and resident volunteer. By using case examples, this study showed how providing for quality of life in residential homes can improve overall health status, increase self-determination within the residents, foster interprofessional collaboration, and decrease misunderstandings that may occur among providers and recipients of this care modality.

Similarly, Pinquart, Sörensen and Peak (2004), recognized the familial imperative to develop a realistic care plan for later life relatives. They provided a strategic eight-step process model designed to support older adults through the preparatory development of their future care needs. Additionally, they suggested three contextual opportunities for intervention (i.e., educational settings, direct referrals, and discharge planning). This framework assists a social worker in enhancing a client's right to self-determination, sense of wellness, and affects some alleviation of stress for the client's extended family. It was shown that being knowledgeable about phenomena and tendencies common to older adults and their families related to the approaching need for care enables practitioners to better assist these clients.

Another study in this cohort addressed a social worker's role in issues of death and dying. Hobart (2001) explored the ever-expanding role of the social worker in advance-care planning and end-of-life decision making.

Table 8.1 Conceptual/Theoretical Frameworks: Interventions for the Elderly

Reference	Title of Citation	Target Group	Main Variables	Other Comments
Haight and Gibson (2005)	A Social Work Perspective	Nursing home elderly, cognitive and sensory alert and impaired elderly	Multidisciplinary misunderstandings, conflict, and interactions Elderly group work dynamics Special issues	Role-play exercises for interprofessional collaboration. Case example: self-determination and relevant participation in group work.
socialworkers.org (2004)	End-of-Life Care	Older adults	Efforts to increase research and translate findings A list of end-of-life references	Series of all studies empirical studying showing effectiveness for these protocols
Pinquart, Sörenson, and Peak (2004)	Helping Older Adults and Their Families Develop and Implement Case Plans	Older adults who have no care plan, those with unrealistic plans, families in conflict about care plans	Response styles regarding approaching need for care or help Influences on preparation Positive effects of preparing in advance	Section on intervention strategies Three contexts for intervention, eight-step process model of strategies. Case example for process model application.
Solomon (2004)	The Role of the Social Worker in Long-Term Care	Residents of homes for the aged and other long-term facilities	Nine primary qualities for a good life in a nursing home (e.g., having autonomy and choice, new relationships inside and outside the institution)	30 days (following hospital discharge)
Naleppa and Reid (2003)	Case Management	Elderly in need of multiple services	Three components of the task-centered case management practice model Research conducted to evaluate and develop the model	Includes a small-scale, hospital study
Bisman (2003)	Rural Aging: Social Work Practice Models and Intervention Dynamics	Rural elderly	Three central social work components: assessment and case theory, biopsychosocial perspective, and self-awareness/use of self Four theoretical models and ideas to guide intervention	Five theoretical models Social support, family systems, group work, case management, and community practice; many authors cited in section on intervention ideas
Graziano (2003)	Trauma and Aging	Older adults who have experienced trauma at any point in the life cycle	Trauma response manifestation Partial list of those at risk for re-emergence of traumatic stress symptoms Suggestions for incorporating a trauma framework into practice	Three case examples representing different trauma experiences across the life cycle and differences in trauma responses

Author (Year)	Title	Population	Content	Notes
Li and Blaser (2003)	Rural Program Planning and Development for Older Adults	Rural elderly	Description of social care systems model; Description of the nature and use of informal support networks and formal services; Strategies for rural service and program development	Websites are listed at the end
McInnis-Dittrich (2002)	Alternative Interventions in the Socioemotional Problems of Elders	Older adults, those with Alzheimer's disease	Music therapies; Art therapies; Drama therapies; Animal-assisted therapies	
Peck (2001)	Looking Back at Life and Its Influence on Subjective Well-Being	Older adults	Model of subjective well-being and explanations of key concepts. Psychosocial development influences. Social work interventions	Interventions; Life review therapy, environment-focused interventions
Hobart (2001)	Death and Dying and the Social Work Role	Older adults	Death and dying laws (e.g., Patient Self-Determination Act) and implication; 2001 Ethnographic Study; Solutions for problems in advance-care planning and end-of-life medical decision making (e.g., combining advance directive forms into one document)	6 months (included seven 1-hour sessions and weekly SSS support from psychiatric nurse)
Leon, Altholz, and Dziegielewski (1999)	Compassion Fatigue: Considerations for Working with the Elderly	Older adults	Compassion fatigue definition; Contributing factors (e.g., the labor-intensive yet short-term nature of the work); Effects on the worker (e.g., feelings of incompetence); Preventive measure (e.g., learning to identify signs)	A case example is used to illustrate variables contributing to compassion fatigue (e.g., worker's age, personal dynamics, agency factors)

The complexity of this advocacy role is highlighted as well as the obligatory responsibility of the social worker to be well versed on issues, legislation, policy, providers, and patient's rights. Additionally, being able to navigate through the quagmire of psychosocial currents is crucial for the efficacy of the social worker's praxis. Hobart discussed Advance Directive Education (ADE), right-to-die legislation, the Patient Self-Determination Act of 1991 (PSDA), and argued for ethnographic sensitivity in one's approach to issues of death and dying. The conceptual framework provided here reminds us of the multiplicity of skills and working knowledge one must bring to the person in their environment. Among these studies, is a NASW end-of-life care protocol. This helpful study compiles, summarizes, and delimits a multitude of critical studies on end-of-life care that will prove advantageous to a clinician in his or her professional endeavors. More than 20 articles were presented in this review covering the broad gamut of issues relating to caring for this population as they prepare for the end of life.

Cohort 1 studies also included interventional theoretical frameworks for working with the elderly within a particular sociocultural situatedness, namely rural settings (Bisman, 2003; Li & Blaser, 2003). These studies highlight the unique challenges that social workers face when intervening with rural elderly populations. The lower-than-average general health, the narrow range of available services, the economic stratification of the clientele, the limited access to formal and diverse service providers, and the concomitant geographic isolation often exacerbate the presenting problems of this treatment group. Bisman (2003) suggested four theoretical models for intervention with rural elderly clients: social support, family systems, group work, and case management/community practice, thus reinforcing the ubiquitous modality for practice with the elderly. This article is efficacious to a practitioner and contains helpful information for further reading and research.

The Li and Blaser (2003) study moves beyond the micro- and mezzolevels of social praxis and into macrolevel social work. These authors suggest an integrative social-care systems model for rural program planning with older adults that amalgamates both formal and informal sources of care, community leaders and residents, and culture and creativity. This model seeks to provide for both the client as well as the community. Through the use of case studies, Li and Blaser (2003) illustrate the essential strategies that are fundamental to success in rural program planning and development for older adults.

The last intervention area of these studies relates to the uniqueness of working with this population. Here, numerous conceptual/theoretical frameworks are provided that address issues of compassion fatigue (Leon, Altholz, & Dziegielewski, 1999), trauma as it relates to aging (Graziano, 2003), elder morbidity and subjective well-being (Peck, 2001), alternative socioemotional interventions for depression (McInnis-Dittrich, 2002; Motohashi, Kaneko & Sasaki, 2004), and task-centered case management (Naleppa & Reid, 2003). The task-centered case-management practice model is for work with the elderly in need of multiple services. The model

Study	Intervention/Methods	Population	N	Duration	Outcome	Conclusion
Kochevar, Smith, & Bernard (2001)	NT with exercise program	Native-American CDS in urban area	22	6 weeks	Significant decrease in blood pressure and respirations	Physical and emotional health can improve among Native-American seniors as a result of exercise and nutritional training.
Kuhn and Mendes de Leon (2001)	ED intervention	Alzheimer's caregivers	58	6 months	Modest benefits in knowledge of disease and coping	Study data suggests that knowledge of Alzheimer's can assist caregiver coping.
Camberg et al. (1999)	Personalized simulated presence, MMSE	Nursing home residents with ADRD	54	Ongoing	No significant change as a result of intervention	Simulated presence may prove to be effective in enhancing well-being and decreasing problem behaviors in nursing home settings.
Inouye et al. (1993)	CCT, PCS, NCEP	General medicine wards at teaching geriatric hospital—frail elders	216	Ongoing	Beneficial effects (e.g., reduction of delirium, functional impairment, incontinence, and pressure sores, were achieved without increasing per-day hospital costs)	NCEP appears effective to decrease functional decline in targeted elderly hospitalized medical patients.
Campbell et al. (1997)	RCT, PT, home exercise program of strength and balance retraining exercises, ECG	Female general practice patients in New Zealand who are at risk for falling	233	12 months	Rate of falls was lower in the exercise than in the control group and balance improved	An individual program of strength and balance retraining exercises improved physical function and was effective in reducing falls and injuries in women 80 years and older.
Banerjee, Shamash, Macdonald, and Mann (1996)	RCT, PGT, AGECAT, pharmaco-logical	Depressed disabled people receiving home care	69	6 months	Outcome, significant recovery within the treatment group	Depression is treatable in elderly people receiving home care.

[1] ADRD = Alzheimer's disease and related dementia; AGECAT = Automatic geriatric examination for computer assisted taxonomy; CBT = Cognitive behavioral therapy; CCT = Controlled clinical trial; CDS = Community-dwelling seniors; CIHBT = Community-integrated home-based treatment; ECG = Educational control group; ED = Education; EKI = Elderly Korean immigrants; MMSE = Mini mental-state examination; NCEP = Nursing-centered educational program; NT = Nutritional training; PCS = Prospective cohort study; PEARLS = Program to encourage active rewarding lives for seniors; PGT = Psychogeriatric team; PST = Problem solving therapy; PT = Physiotherapy; RCSG = Random controlled support group; RCT = Random clinical trial; SRT = Structured reminiscence therapy; SSS = Social service support; SSW = Session with social worker; STEP = Start talking early program; VA = Veterans Administration.

because of the absence of targeted outcomes specified prior to the study. Their methodological criteria allowed these studies to be dichotomized into two practice effectiveness categories, namely, those interventions that worked and those that did not.

At first glance, you might think that the needs of the elderly have remained quite consistent over the past 20 years. However, the studies in Cohort 2 (and the subsequent Cohort 3) reveal that the presenting problems of the elderly have become more complicated than before. The cost of adequate care has escalated far beyond the economic viability of the client group. Even though technology has created the possibility of instantaneous digital interactivity, it appears that social groups and communities have become more polarized and collectivities have become ever more stratified (Dunlop & Holosko, 2006). With these societal changes anonymously thrust on the variegated collectivities that make up our culture, we witness the exacerbation of the numerous presenting problems of the elderly. Thus, interventional strategies have become more strategic, multidimensional, and time framed as needs arise.

These studies sought to ascertain the efficacy of various interventions ranging from education to structured reminiscence therapy, from physical therapy to supervised eating in social settings, from Eastern Chinese meditative/movement oriented practices to pharmacological interventions for depression. The wide array in Cohort 2 exemplified the clinician's creativity and willingness to experiment in order to address the presenting problems within the elderly community. Some tested educational curricula, whereas others investigated the utility of technology and physiotherapy. These studies were selected, in part, because they satisfied the criteria of our search, and also because they represented a considerable range in interventional approaches in a variety of settings both locally and internationally. Some were clinically based, whereas others were community- or home-based interventions.

Among the clinically based interventions, Abrahamson and Khan (2006) found that osteoporosis education among elderly patients with low trauma fractures significantly improved the functional independence and psychological well-being of the patients. This educational intervention did not reduce levels of actual pain experienced by the subjects. However, the interrelated connection between cognitively understanding the disease and cultivating strategies to manage the pain of the disease resulted in both greater physical confidence and decreased depressive symptoms. This study demonstrated the direct corollary between the experience of pain and declining ambulatory function to depressive symptomology.

Tsang, Mok, Yeung, and Chan (2003) also recognized the correlation between pain and depression in their study of the efficacy of *Quigong*. From the Chinese words *Qi* [chi], which means energy and *gong* [kung] which means skill, this ancient practice merges meditation and deliberate movement. *Quigong* is famous in China for reducing stress, lowering blood pressure, and fostering a better attitude about life. Tsang et al. (2003) found that elderly patients with chronic subacute physical illnesses and pain also experienced depressive symptoms. The control group that received the

Quigong intervention for 12 weeks showed significant improvement in physical, psychological, and general health well-being. The results of this study suggested that alternatives to pharmacological interventions for pain and depression exist.

The relationship among acute illness, pain, recovery, and the propensity to socially isolate oneself was addressed in the Wright, Hickson, and Frost (2006) study. They evaluated a nurse-aided supervised dining intervention. Generally, acutely ill nursing-home patients have a tendency to eat alone in their rooms. This self-imposed social isolation has a corroborative negative effect on recovery, weight-loss, and general health. Their intervention involved encouraging these elderly residents to go to the formal dining hall during lunchtime rather than eating alone in their rooms. The simple act of communal dining, rather than social isolation, resulted in increased food intake, healthy weight gain, and corresponding improvements in nutritional status and rehabilitation. The effect of communal interactivity on the general health status of the geriatric client cannot be overstated.

Community-based interventions were also quite common among the studies reviewed (Ciechanowski et al., 2004; Kochevar, Smith, & Bernard, 2001). Both studies sought to explore the correlation between physical and general health and the biopsychosocial wellness of the subjects. Kochevar et al. (2001) utilized nutritional training and a physical exercise program among Native-American urban elders for 6 weeks. As a result of this intervention, the physical and emotional health of the subjects significantly increased. Ciechanowski et al. (2004) evaluated an educational program, Program to Encourage Active Rewarding Lives for Seniors (PEARLS), among 138 elderly patients with minor depression and/or dysthymia. PEARLS proved to be an efficacious community-integrated, home-based treatment for depression by significantly reducing depressive symptoms and improving the general health status of the participants.

Several studies employed technology, for example, telephones, computers, Internet, and recording devices, as an integral part of their interventional strategy (Bradley & Poppen, 2003; Camberg et al., 1999; De Leo, Buono, & Dwyer, 2002; White et al., 2002). These interventions ranged in duration from 6 months to 10 years. Cohort 2 studies also included professional and semiprofessional practitioners in the administering of their interventions.

Other studies integrated physiotherapy and education (Campbell et al., 1997; Kapasi, Ouslander, Schnelle, Kutner, & Fahey, 2003; Kochevar et al., 2001; Mo-Kyung, Belza, LoGerfo, & Cunningham, 2005; Tsang et al., 2003). The duration of these interventions ranged from 12 to 32 weeks. Some addressed specific ethnic groups, that is, elderly Korean immigrants (Mo-Kyung et al., 2005), whereas others focused on specific impairments and risks, that is, elderly frail women who are at risk of falling (Campbell et al., 1997). Regardless of the population, merging physiotherapy and education proved to be efficacious among geriatric clients, in general.

One final trend to highlight within gerontological work and these studies was the aging-in-place model. The ubiquitous modality of care in the past was the institutionalization of the elderly in personal care/residential homes. For the past two decades, however, the devolution of health care has challenged the federal role in domestic health and human-services policy. Consequently, in light of the contextual verities of the managed-care movement, the sociodemographics of aging, and the preferential biases of the elderly to die at home, a new paradigm for elder care is emerging.

In North America, much of the decision making in health-related issues has been devolved to local authorities. The raison d'être behind such a new model of care emerges from three areas of concern: (1) the governmental expectation for equitable care; (2) the providers' economic, social, and health-related interests; and (3) the clients' health care-related preferences and needs (Lomas, Woods, & Veenstra, 1997). The aging-in-place model has transpired as a new model for care, particularly among aging populations, as a response to the escalating costs of care (Mollica & Morris, 2005), the scarcity of adequate space for an ever-increasing population of elderly, and in response to the expressed desires of the elderly to die at home (Formiga, Chivite, Ortega, Cassas, Ramon & Pujol, 2004; Groth-Juncker & McCusker, 1983).

Two of the studies in Cohort 2 addressed the aging-in-place model (Banerjee, Shamash, Macdonald, & Mann, 1996; Leff et al., 2005). The fact that these two studies were conducted nearly a decade apart demonstrates that the aging-in-place model of health care continues to be prototypical of present and future modalities of treatment. Banerjee et al. (1996) involved 69 disabled patients suffering from depression. For a period of 6 months, the subjects received a multifaceted intervention combining pharmacological aides and automatic geriatric examination for computer-assisted taxonomy assessment (AGECAT) from a psychogeriatric team in the clients' home settings. The treatment group experienced significant alleviation of depressive symptoms and an overall increase in their general health status.

In the Leff et al. (2005) study, 455 acutely ill community-dwelling seniors received the hospital-at-home model of care for 22 months. As a result, the subjects had a shorter length of stay and lower mean costs of treatment compared to acute hospital care. This study demonstrated the efficacy of the hospital-at-home model as feasible, safe, and cost effective for certain older patients with selected acute medical illnesses. The aging-in-place paradigm underlying this study will continue to be an important impetus in future interventional strategies, particularly among aging populations.

Cohort 3—Specified Intervention and Outcome Studies

Cohort 3 represents a summarized collection of studies retained from the hundreds reviewed that satisfied certain criteria.

Namely, these studies (Table 8.3) contained clearly identified interventions, specified populations, particular time frames within which the interventions were conducted, and targeted and/or specified outcomes.

Table 8.3 Specified Interventions and Outcomes With Elderly Populations Between 2006 and 1995

References	Interventions Provided	Presenting Problems	Specified Populations	Duration of Interventions	Targeted Outcomes	Effectiveness of Interventions
Engelhardt, Toseland, Gao, and Banks (2006)	RCT, GEM	Males who were above-average users of outpatient VA services	160	48 months	Although no increase in survival of patient indicated, intervention achieved outcome (e.g., costs of services decreased at the 24- to 48-month period)	The GEM program can reduce the costs to senior citizen veterans who are proven to be above-average users of outpatient VA services.
Hunkeler et al. (2006)	RCT, CCM (IMPACT–CBT, PST, ED, pharma-cological)	Patients with major depression, dysthymia, or both in primary care clinics	1801	36 months	Outcomes achieved (e.g., depressive symptoms, physical functioning, quality of life, self-efficacy, and satisfaction of care)	The IMPACT model may show the way to less depression and greater, overall health in older adults.
Thomas et al. (2005)	Random CCT, Tai Chi exercise, resistance training	Chinese subjects	180	12-month longitudinal study	Outcomes not achieved (e.g., no cardiovascular risk from Tai Chi)	Tai Chi as an intervention is no more or less beneficial to cardiovascular risk in the elderly.
Poon, Hui, Dai, Kwok, and Woo (2005)	RCT, CBT, MDT, telemedicine, CBP, FTFG, video-conferencing, SSS	CDS with mild dementia and mild cognitive impairments in China	22	12 weeks	MMSE, RBMT, HDS showed higher scores (e.g., attention, memory, spatial construction, and language)	Telemedicine is a feasible and acceptable means in providing cognitive assessments and interventions to elder persons with mild cognitive deficits.
Enguidanos, Davis, and Katz (2005)	RCT, PCCBT, PST, and pharmaco-logic aids	Moderately/severely depressed patients referred to geriatric care management service	153	19 months	PCCBT efficacious (e.g., significantly reduced depressive symptoms)	Education, PST, and PCCBT can help moderately/severely depressed seniors to reduce depressive symptoms—case study approach used.

(continued overleaf)

Table 8.3 *Continued*

References	Interventions Provided	Presenting Problems	Specified Populations	Duration of Interventions	Targeted Outcomes	Effectiveness of Interventions
Tse, Pun, and Benzie (2005)	Affective images during PT	Patients suffering from chronic pain	15	6 weeks	Outcomes achieved (e.g., subjects reported increase in health-related quality of life)	Affective images may provide moderate, nonpharmacological intervention for elderly persons with chronic pain.
Ryan-Woolley and Rees (2005)	RCT, concordance, use of medicine organizer, ED	Sheltered housing residents in United Kingdom	62	12 months	Outcomes achieved (e.g., more prescription change, decrease in the number of prescriptions, less waste of medicine)	Pharmacists using concordance and medicine organizers can reduce medicine waste and misuse.
Caplan, Williams, Daly, and Abraham (2004)	RCT, MDT, CGA, DEED II program	Patients discharged home from emergency department in urban area, Australia	739	30 days (following hospital discharge) and 18 month follow-up	Outcomes achieved (e.g., lower rate of emergency admissions, greater degree of mental and physical function, lower costs of care for patients)	DEED II, a multidisciplinary intervention, can improve health outcomes for the elderly and lower rates of readmission to hospitals.
Cummings (2003)	GT (remotivation and supportive therapy techniques)	Depressed assisted-living residents	17	10 sessions, 5 weeks	Outcomes achieved (e.g., participants experienced significant decrease in depressive symptoms and reported higher degree of life satisfaction)	GT can increase life satisfaction and decrease depressive symptoms in assisted-living elderly with depressive symptoms.
Dipko, Xavier, and Kohlwes (2003)	ECG, ADE, SSW, DPAHC, LW	Outpatients in primary care clinic	203 (ECG) and 13,913 (comparison group)	33 months	Outcomes achieved (e.g., ECG was twice as effective as SSW, patients were more likely to complete advance directives independent of education strategy)	Group education is an effective and time- and cost-effective social work tool for completion of advance medical directives for elderly patients.

Study	Method	Population	Sample	Duration	Outcomes	Conclusion
Ball et al. (2002)	RCT, CBT, ECG	Independently living residents in six metropolitan areas	2,832	46 months	Outcomes achieved (e.g., significant improvement in speed of processing, in reasoning, and of memory, cognitive improvement)	Results support the effectiveness and durability of cognitive training interventions in improving targeted-cognitive abilities in the elderly.
Gill, Baker, and Gottschalk (2002)	RCT, ECG, and competency-based exercise program to increase balance	Physically frail patients of primary care practices who live at home	176	12 months	Outcomes achieved (e.g., treatment participants demonstrated improvement in physical functioning)	In physically frail older people, a home-based intervention reduced the functional decline in subjects.
Dougherty et al. (2002)	RCT, CBT, biofeedback, and pelvic muscle exercise	Rural women with urinary incontinence	178	24 months	Outcomes achieved (e.g., participants reported less urine loss and greater quality of life)	In older rural women with urinary incontinence, a behavioral management approach for continence intervention reduced urine loss.
Schonfeld et al. (2000)	CBT, psychoeducation (GET SMART)	Outpatient veterans with substance abuse problems	110	16 weeks	Outcomes achieved (e.g., increase in abstinence among patients 6 months later and longer time between relapses reported by patients)	GET SMART can be an effective intervention with elderly subjects with substance abuse problems.
Mazzuca, Brandt, Katz, Hanna, and Melfi (1999)	CCT, self-care, ED	Rheumatoid arthritis and osteoarthritis	211	48 months	Outcomes achieved (e.g., education reduced frequency and cost of primary care visits)	Education can benefit seniors in management of pain from arthritic conditions and reduce health costs.
Proctor et al. (1999)	RCT, CBT, SSS	Residents in nursing homes in United Kingdom who displayed depression and organic symptoms	120	6 months (included seven 1-hour sessions and weekly SSS support from psychiatric nurse)	Outcomes (e.g., organic and depressive symptoms improved but behavioral and physical disability did not)	Behavioral outreach (CBT) teams can assist elderly with depressive and organic symptoms but are not efficacious to the improvement of behavioral or physical symptoms.

(continued overleaf)

Table 8.3 *Continued*

References	Interventions Provided	Presenting Problems	Specified Populations	Duration of Interventions	Targeted Outcomes	Effectiveness of Interventions
Keefe, Caldwell, Baucom, Salley, and Robinson (1999)	RCT, spouse-assisted CBT	Osteoarthritis knee pain	88	12 months	Outcomes achieved (e.g., overall higher self-efficacy, lower levels of psychological and physical disability, and improved pain levels)	Spouse-assisted CBT is effective in increasing self-efficacy and managing pain in seniors with osteoarthritis-related knee pain.
Tennstedt et al. (1998)	RCT, CBP, ED	Adults from 40 senior housing sites in urban area who reported fear of falling	434	12 months (6-week, 6-month, and 12-month follow-ups)	Outcomes (e.g., immediate but not statistically significant improvement in mobility, social functionality, and mobility control)	Community-based education to reduce fear of falling in older adults has modest beneficial effects.
Glasgow et al. (1997)	RCT, ED with emphasis on goal setting and PST	CDS with type 2 diabetes	206	12 months	Outcomes achieved (e.g., significant improvements in food habits, caloric consumption, serum cholesterol levels, and percentage of fat)	Educational health programs with emphasis on goal setting and problem solving can work with elderly patients with type 2 diabetes.
Fries, Carey, and McShane (1997)	RCT, mail-delivered ASMP	Rheumatoid arthritis and osteoarthritis	375	6 months	Outcomes achieved (e.g., decreased pain, global vitality increased, joint count improved, and clinical visits decreased)	Self-management courses can improve the health of the elderly and decrease costs of clinical care for pain.

Study	Intervention	Population	Sample	Duration	Outcomes achieved (e.g., ...)	Conclusion
Sharpe et al. (1997)	ED and physical activity program with emphasis on strength, balance, motor-coordination, and mobility	Adults in rural congregate nutrition sites	110—treatment group (61) and comparison group (49)	12 months (twice-weekly sessions)	Outcomes achieved (e.g., greater improvements in physical functioning over the previous year than the comparison group)	Low-intensity exercise can benefit the overall health and physical functionality of elderly subjects.
Slaets, Kauffmann, Duivenvoor-den, Pelemans, and Schudel (1997)	MDT, PSYG team, CBT, and SSS	Medical inpatients with poor physical functioning	237—treatment group (140) and control group (97)	12 months (following discharge)	Outcomes achieved (e.g., improvement in the physical functioning of the treatment group participants)	Combining elements from psychiatric, social service, and geriatric consultation with elements of unit-driven service improves physical functioning among the elderly.
Rich, Gray, Beckham, Wittenberg, and Luther (1996)	RCT, MDT, NT, ED, and SSS	CHF patients with poor behavioral medication compliance	156—intervention group (80) and conventional care group (76)	30 days (following hospital discharge)	Outcomes achieved (e.g., medication compliance in patients increased)	A MDT can improve medication compliance during first 30 days following discharge from the hospital in elderly patients with CHF.
Maisiak, Austin, and Heck (1996)	RCT, telephone monitoring and counseling	Rheumatoid arthritis and osteoarthritis	405	9 months	Outcomes achieved (e.g., better health status scores, number of medical visits decreased)	Elderly patients with rheumatoid arthritis and osteoarthritis are responsive to telephone counseling and support for pain.

(continued overleaf)

Table 8.3 *Continued*

References	Interventions Provided	Presenting Problems	Specified Populations	Duration of Interventions	Targeted Outcomes	Effectiveness of Interventions
Rich et al. (1995)	PRT, Nurse-directed MDT, NT, ED, and SSS	CHF patients with poor behavioral compliance to treatment who were at risk for re-admittance to hospital following discharge	282—treatment group (142) and control group (140)	90 days (following hospital discharge)	Outcomes achieved (e.g., hospital readmission was significantly reduced)	Nurse-directed MDT can improve the quality of life and reduce both hospital use and medical costs for elderly patients with CHF.
Bailly and DePoy (1995)	ADE, ECG	Clients at a family medical care practice in rural area	10	2 weeks	Statistically significant increase in knowledge of ADE was not reported	Authors suggest that ADE may be a family issue rather than solely an individual issue.

ADE = Advance directive education; ASMP = Arthritis self-management program; CBP = Community-based group; CBT = Cognitive behavioral therapy; CCM = Collaborative care management; CCT = Controlled clinical trial; CDS = Community-dwelling seniors; CGA = Comprehensive geriatric assessment; CHF = Congestive heart failure; DEED II = Discharge of elderly from the emergency department program; DPAHC = Durable power of attorney for health care; ECG = Educational control group; ED = Education; FTFG = Face to face group; GEM = Geriatric evaluation and management program; GET SMART = Geriatric evaluation team: substance misuse/abuse recognition and treatment program; GT = Group therapy; HDS = Hierarchical dementia scale; LW = Living will; MDT = Multidisciplinary team; MMSE = Mini-mental-state examination; NT = Nutritional training; PCCBT = Patient-centered cognitive behavioral therapy; PRT = Prospective randomized trial; PST = Problem solving therapy; PSYG = Psychogeriatric; PT = Physiotherapy; RBMT = Rivermead behavioral memory test; RCT = Random clinical trial; SSS = Social service support; SSW = Session with social worker; VA = Veterans Administration.

They employed a range of practitioners including professionals, semiprofessionals, health-care agents, and family members of the subjects examined. Additionally, interventions were offered in clinical and nonclinical locations and in an array of social settings, including urban, suburban, and rural, both in the United States and abroad.

The collective interventional framework of the studies in Cohort 3 can be generalized into two overlapping spheres, mental health and physical health. This may be due to the fact, in part, that the presenting problems of many elderly patients/clients are diametrically related to the unique transitions of later life, for example, declining health, chronic and acute pain, increased limitations in physical performance, loss of social connections and relationships, sociocultural isolation, cognitive changes, the escalating cost of health care, and anxiety and depressive disorders. And many of these are interrelated. As the unprecedented increase in the number of elderly continues to proliferate and the life expectancy of older adults extends, empirical evidence-based research on efficacious interventions will continue to be an essential tool to the social work practitioner (Cummings & Kropf, 2009). Curiously, of the hundreds of studies reviewed here, most of the discipline-specific social work publications failed to meet the stringent intervention-outcome identified criteria in Table 8.3.

Many of these study designs included interdisciplinary, and/or multi-interventional strategies to address presenting problems (Caplan, Williams, Daly & Abraham, 2004; Poon, Hui, Dai, Kwok, & Woo, 2005; Rich, Gray, Beckham, Wittenberg, & Luther, 1996; Slaets, Kauffmann, Duivenvoorden, Pelemans, & Schudel, 1997). Multidisciplinary teamwork in treating the elderly is the norm and appears to be the most effective interventional stratagem. Perhaps this is due in part to the complexities that are concurrent to later-life experiences and its respective host of challenges. Among the uniqueness of gerontological practice is the biopsychosocial holistic approach to using interventions with the client. Using a multidisciplinary approach is one way of addressing the whole person in his or her environment.

Cohort 3 studies clearly reveal an eclectic methodological range in their interventions. These interventions range in duration from 2 weeks to 48 months and every possibility in between. Some synthesized pharmacological and therapeutic stratagems to address presenting problems of severe depression in the elderly subjects (Enguidanos, Davis, & Katz, 2005; Hunkeler et al., 2006). Others utilized a collaborative approach of technology and therapy to address presenting problems ranging from cognitive impairment to chronic pain, from depression to arthritis, and from urinary incontinence to dementia (Dougherty et al., 2002; Poon et al., 2005; Tse et al., 2005).

Since the 1950s, the ubiquitous modality for treating the elderly is group work (Husaini et al., 2004). This approach continues to be apparent, having success in both achieving desired outcomes (Ball et al., 2002) and nonsuccess in accomplishing specified outcomes (Bailly & DePoy, 1995; Gill et al., 2002). Thus, from these data, group work/therapy remains an efficacious interventional stratagem within the elderly population. Many of such interventions included problem solving, remotivational, and/or cognitive-behavioral therapy (Ball et al., 2002; Cummings, 2003; Dougherty et al., 2002; Enguidanos et al., 2005; Glasgow et al., 1997; Hunkeler et al., 2006; Keefe et al., 1999; Proctor et al., 1999; Schonfeld et al., 2000). This finding was recently corroborated in another review of evidence and outcome literature with this population (Kolomer, 2008).

The eclecticism of these interventions demonstrates the expediency of taking more than one approach to a presenting problem. In short, they suggest that multifaceted presenting problems require multimethodological interventions. Rich et al.'s (1996) study on congestive heart failure patients who demonstrated poor behavioral compliance to their treatment were at risk of readmission to the hospital, thus increasing the cost of care and potentially exacerbating their physical ailment. By utilizing a nurse-led multidisciplinary team that provided nutritional training, education, and social service support, hospital readmission was significantly reduced among those in the treatment group, thus reducing the costs of care and increasing the general health of these subjects.

Further, when examining the overall cohort, we recognize that the variegated interventions are quite similar in their recognition of the inextricable connection between pain and depressive symptoms. Acute and chronic pain have the potential to lower health-status scores, quality of life, self-efficacy, and social functioning of elderly clients/patients. These studies show that many of the targeted outcomes of the interventions were consistently related to the symptomatic experiences that are concomitant to chronic and acute pain. For example, Maisiak et al. (1996) conducted a study on elderly patients suffering from rheumatoid arthritis and osteoarthritis. The chronic and acute pain of these conditions lowered the health-status scores of the study group and increased the number of medical visits, thus increasing the cost and inconvenience of health care for these 405 subjects. The 9-month intervention of telephone monitoring and counseling bettered the health-status scores, decreased the number of medical visits, and decreased the concomitant costs of care for these subjects. This study showed that elderly patients with rheumatoid arthritis and osteoarthritis are responsive to telephone counseling and support for pain.

Overall, the studies in Cohort 3 suggest that the greater the specificity of the target group, the more precise the interventional strategy, the more defined the desired/targeted outcomes, the greater likelihood of success. Additionally, they reveal that the complexities of experiences in later life necessitate interdisciplinary multi-interventional strategies that synthesize several methods toward specific and desired outcomes. The implication for the social work practitioner is that he or she must become more adept at reviewing, conducting, and using evidence-based empirical research and become acquainted with a variety of disciplines in order to navigate the quagmire of the biopsychosocial experiences of elderly clients (Cummings & Kropf, 2009).

In these studies, the specified targeted outcomes ranged from the very broad; for example, reduction of depressive symptoms, increase in degree of life satisfaction, improvement in physical functioning, and/or increase of knowledge about end-of-life planning, to the very specific; for example, reducing the loss of urine, lowering serum cholesterol levels, completion of advance directives, and/or lowering costs for outpatient services over a 48-month period. These studies also reflect the well-known bias of published literature, that is, treatments that work. Nevertheless, the contributive importance of these studies along the continuum of practice presented in this chapter help social workers understand the inimitable synergistic value of using EBP for their intervention strategies.

Limitations of the Evidence

As with any overview chapter of this nature, the search process used to collect the articles/chapters/published accounts of EBP interventions may not have captured all of the available published literature. For this we apologize. Second, the processes used to define evidence-based practice and the subsequent conceptualization of it depart somewhat from more traditional notions of its use in reviews of this nature (e.g., Cummings & Kropf, 2009).

Despite these limitations and based on Figure 8.1, we collected and analyzed literature according to three cohorts: (1) conceptual/theoretical frameworks for treatment, (2) effectiveness studies, and (3) specified intervention and outcome studies. Prior to a discussion of these subsections, the limitations and conceptualization of how the residual published accounts were retained is discussed.

What became apparent in this overall review is the need for the social work profession to develop a more relevant definition of EBP. This has been noted before (Gambrill, 2006; Holosko, 2004; Pollio, 2002, 2006; Sackett et al., 1997; Thyer & Kazi, 2004). Such a definition should embrace the practice reality of professionals working in our field, have an empirical basis to it, and should inform and direct practice in meaningful ways. All of the submissions offered in this chapter meet these minimal criteria.

Implications for Social Work at Micro-, Mezzo-, and Macrolevels

If we were to look at various practice trends in the field of gerontology, four main trends prevail. First, there are and will continue to be a shortage of trained personnel to work in this area. Second, education and training needs far exceed the ability for practitioners working in this area to provide

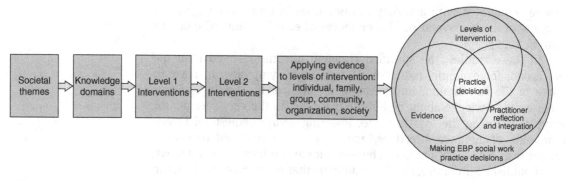

Figure 8.2

Minimal knowledge and skills necessary to use evidence-based practice with the elderly

adequate, timely, and much needed care. Third, practitioners are required to integrate specialized knowledge, skills, and interventions in order to be effective in working with the elderly. Fourth, social work practitioners must embrace the principles of advanced generalist practice and move fluidly and seamlessly in providing competent interventions to their clients. The latter implies that the micro/mezzo/macro distinction delimits our ability to be effective with such clients (Holosko, White, & Feit, 2004).

In an effort to illustrate how EBP underpins practice in this field, Figure 8.2 illustrates how a cumulative progression of societal issues, levels of intervention, and the application of such evidence to practice results for better-informed practice decisions. Rather than illustrating *what* evidence should be used to affect practice, this figure shows *how* evidence directs and informs our practice. In each step of Figure 8.2, a series of current and minimal knowledge requirements are identified. Then, the assumptions underpinning each will be identified followed by a brief discussion.

Societal Themes Issues

Social workers require a formative contextual knowledge of what's going on in society and in my community with the elderly. Having such awareness allows us to understand how broader issues truly impact day-to-day practice realities in working with the elderly. These current themes are presented in Table 8.4.

The main assumptions around these cornerstone societal issues or themes are (a) as society evolves, these themes will inevitably change, (b) they systemically interrelate with each other, and (c) all gerontological practice in any "community of care" is shaped by broader societal issues that frame such practice.

In regard to the latter, workers need to (a) understand how to work creatively in limited resources; (b) demystify stereotypes typically

Table 8.4 Current Societal Issues/Themes

The escalating number of elderly and their unique and specialized health, mental health, and social issues

"Aging-in-place" or supporting individuals to reside in their homes and communities for as long as possible

Not enough resources to adequately serve and treat the demands of this subpopulation

The impact of new technologies that can be used to better serve and treat this subpopulation

The systematic devolution of federal and state monies and supports to local community-based initiatives

Out-migration of elderly person from rural to urban centers to avail themselves of services

Long-standing and prevailing ageism challenges our ability to practice in this field

---

presented about elderly persons; (c) understand policies, procedures, and best practices that shape how and what they do; and (d) not practice in a contextual vacuum. Indeed, gerontological social work has been a forerunner in recognizing and responding to the political, societal, and practice realities of the elderly today. Our long-standing work with the marginal and vulnerable populations of society has perhaps made us more prepared and clearer about how to effectively approach practice in a time of limited and rationed health and social services (Holosko & Holosko, 2004).

Basic Knowledge Areas

The minimal knowledge areas in quadrant 2 (Figure 8.2) for social work practitioners working with the elderly are presented in Table 8.5.

The main assumptions underpinning Table 8.5 are (a) each involves core knowledge, values, and skills that are differentially applied to each

Table 8.5 Basic Knowledge Areas for Working With the Elderly

Biopsychosocial holistic approach
Formal and informal support systems
Grief and loss
Death and dying
Sexuality
Medical conditions unique to the elderly
Mental health conditions unique to the elderly
Social and family situations and conditions unique to the elderly
Spirituality
Diversity and culture
Unique family situations

client or client situation; and (b) there are minimal knowledge requirements in each area that practitioners need in order to offer responsible and ethical practice (Vourlekis, Zlotnick, & Simons, 2005).

As a precursor to the application of interventions with the elderly, these then are deemed as the basic knowledge domains of any geronto-logical social work practitioner. Indeed, there is much to learn here, and a healthier reframe might be to look at these as a process of career pro-fessional learning and systematically developing and accruing knowledge about each area on a case-by-case basis. Seeking and finding relevant empirical evidence to understand such knowledge and integrating it into day-to-day practice are challenges that every worker faces in his or her unique way.

Level 1—Intervention Skills

As indicated in the numerous studies previously reviewed in this chapter, a variety of interventions often multiplied and differentially applied are the norm, not the exception, for practitioners who work in this field (see Tables 8.1, 8.2, and 8.3). These are referred to as "Level 1—Skills" because they are the basic or minimal ones necessary to work at the entry levels of practice with the elderly. As Figure 8.2 also illustrates, they are cumulative in nature or build on a practitioner's ability to integrate both the previously described societal themes and formative knowledge domains. These are presented in Table 8.6.

In today's practice reality, these Level 1 skills are typically provided in any accredited BSW program in North America. It is *how* they are used with the elderly, however, that characterizes their uniqueness for practitioners working in this field. There are two underlying assumptions about their current use with the elderly: (1) all need to be grounded in a strengths-based perspective, and (2) they require an overt client-centered focus in their application.

From a strengths-based framework, the notion is to apply such interventions to promote factors of successful aging. These include the avoidance of disease and disability, involvement in society, continued

Table 8.6   Level 1 Intervention Skills

Assessment
Counseling
Discharge planning
Treatment planning and monitoring treatment
Case management
Group work
Advocacy and brokering
Community outreach coordination
Education

high cognitive and physical impairment, and maintained or acquired sense of purpose and autonomy (Rowe & Kahn, 1998). As society gives responsibility for care back to individuals, families, and communities, clearly there is renewed support for a client-centered focus with the elderly. The elderly person, then, despite capacity, physical abilities, and financial resources is to be considered *as the person with the resources to make changes in his or her situation to be more functional* (Holosko & Holosko, 2004, p. 37).

Level II Intervention Skills

Building on the previous areas, Table 8.7 presents a list of minimal Level II intervention skills that gerontological practitioners require. Again, many of these were mentioned in the numerous evidence-based studies previously reviewed in Tables 8.1 and 8.2, which assessed practice efficacy.

Table 8.7 presents a set of skills that clearly delineate specialization criteria for social workers working with the elderly. Although such skills are more likely to be offered in our MSW, rather than BSW curricula (Holosko, 1995), they require more knowledge, specialized training, and education than these curricula currently offer. The two assumptions on which they stand are (1) you must be an advanced generalist practitioner in order to be effective in this field, and (2) instilling hope with each client and client situation and needs to become integrated into each intervention offered.

Gerontological social worker practitioners epitomize the essence of advanced generalist practice. Staying current with new developments in the field, working simultaneously and fluidly with all levels—micro/mezzo/macro—and evaluating their practice are the norm, not the exception, for such practitioners (Holosko & Feit, 2004; Vourlekis et al., 2005). It is at this level that one begins to see how judiciously using empirical data, seeking and using current literature and case material and the best available evidence, and judiciously using these data to direct and inform practice are part-and-parcel of everyday gerontological practice. Thus, there is no option for not integrating empirical data into practice, whether

Table 8.7   Level II Intervention Skills

Defining what is unique about social work practice with the elderly
Complex ethical decision making
Capacity assessment
Caregiving dynamics
End-of-life protocols and caring
Working in multisystem levels
Working effectively and creatively with minimal resources
Anchoring all interventions in the best available evidence
Routinely evaluating one's own practice effectiveness

it is secondary or primary data collected by the practitioners themselves or learned from the literature (Rosen, 2003).

The issue of the instillation of hope into each client, client situation, intervention, and so on becomes a formidable challenge for practitioners working in this field. We cannot rely solely on the outcomes of our interventions, for example, "most clients should do better after the 12 weeks of treatment," to be the only indicator of our intervention successes or failures. Neither can we "buy in" to self-pitying clients or colleagues who have given up hope on themselves or their situations. These challenges are consistently confronted in areas such as advanced stages of dementia, chronic physical disease, and/or end-of- life transitions.

Applying Evidence to Render Better Practice Decisions

The final grid and circle synthesizing the integration of these areas in this cumulative process implies applying evidence to impact a better practice decision. Whether such evidence results in a better set of practice questions (Gibbs, 2005), it is the synergy of the application of the available evidence through an intervention that results in better-informed practice decisions. This then becomes the culmination (in this model) of the evidence-informing practice process.

One of the three intersecting circles in Figure 8.2 involves practice reflection and integration. Thus, having the evidence and knowing how to apply it requires some practice wisdom, as we used to say. This is truly where the art side of practice meets the empirical side, and both are necessary to render better-informed practice decisions. The perennial false dichotomy that has polarized these two areas of social work (for a number years) is, therefore, rooted in this synthesis model.

For instance, if social work practitioners use the best available evidence to render a practice decision as such, they cannot be accused of dismissing either side of the science-art continuum. It is the precise synthesis of their interaction that is the trigger for the eventual practice decision. However, if a practice decision is made without this synthesis, it would be deemed unethical and irresponsible by default (Gambrill, 2006).

This critical intersect is the very place where (a) a looser definition of EBP can be rationalized (as is argued in this chapter); (b) statistical and clinical significance can be deemed as equally relevant; and, most importantly, (c) practitioners working in this field can render an empirically based practice decision in a reflective, individualized, and integrative knowledge-based fashion—EBP defined in gerontological social work practice.

Conclusion

This chapter presented an overview of EBP interventions with the elderly. At the onset, it was suggested that understanding the context in which these interventions occurred may help social work practitioners to better understand the literature and data presented herein. These broader contexts included: the demographic reality of a rapidly growing aging society, social policies or so-called best practices that shape current gerontological practice and practice implications.

A model (Figure 8.1) based on a less stringent definition of EBP categorized these literature/studies into three related cohorts. Cohort 1 was called conceptual/theoretical frameworks, Cohort 2 was called effectiveness studies, and Cohort 3 was intervention and outcome studies. The parameters of each of these and their conceptual rationales were presented prior to a discussion of the data within them.

After a discussion of these data, a second figure (Figure 8.2) configured a relationship about not *what* this evidence was, but *how* it could be used in a practice model. Thus, the integration of evidence into gerontological practice was then discussed.

Based on this chapter, the question becomes—*What do social work practitioners need to know about evidence-based interventions with the elderly?* There are a few things that seem important.

First, despite the fact that more social workers are practicing with the elderly than ever before and considerable progress has been made in the profession's ability to conduct more research and evaluation (Padgett, 2005), we must strive to continue to evaluate our practice interventions with the elderly. Morrow-Howell and Burnette (2001) indicated that the top priority identified by gerontological social workers and researchers was the development and tending of psychosocial interventions with the elderly.

In a recent review of literature about evidence-based practice with the elderly, Cummings and Kropf (2009) concluded their insights review by stating:

> *Researchers acknowledge that greater understanding about how different intervention approaches promote beneficial outcomes within the diversity of the older population is required. Since limited evidence exists in many areas of practice with older adults, researchers have abundant opportunities to conduct research that will add to the knowledge base about effective intervention approaches. Indeed, continuing to build a social work research agenda about practice interventions is seen as being essential to developing timely knowledge about our practice efforts.*

Second, as is argued in this chapter, the social work profession has acknowledged that it requires a more relevant definition of evidence-based practice (Gambrill, 2006). This definition should guide and inform practice and be able to be easily operationalized in the practice worlds of our practitioners (Pollio, 2006). The integrative model (Figure 8.2) presented a case supporting this contention. The cohort definitions on which this model was based (Figure 8.1) further argued for a new definition of EBP. Indeed, as is presented throughout this chapter, the nexus for understanding the relationship between research/evaluation and practice is first how research/evaluation data guides/directs/informs practice. Second, how it becomes integrated into day-to-day practice activities is where the real proof is in the pudding—to quote an old English proverb.

Overall, Tables 8.1, 8.2, and 8.3 taken together revealed that:

- Social work is not the only profession taking a leadership role in assessing practice efficacy with the elderly.
- Inherent internal and external validity threats, for example, history, maturation, subject and experimenter expectancy, and generalizability are part and parcel of conducting research/evaluations of practice interventions with this population.
- Multidisciplinary team interventions are the norm for practitioners working in this field.
- Group-work intervention is still the prevailing practice modality for providing intervention to the elderly.
- Multiple intervention strategies targeting specific multifaceted problems are the current practice in this field.
- Empowerment and strengths-based approaches have significantly influenced social work practice with the elderly.
- Issues, problems, and concerns of the elderly are slowly being reframed as normalized, not pathological.
- Describing and measuring our practice outcomes in more precise ways has resulted in ameliorating specific problems of clients, better time framed treatment protocols, sharper interventions, and better-informed practice decisions.

Finally, gerontological social work practice holds a promising future for our profession. It is a field rife with both challenges and opportunities in which social work can take an active leadership role. Basing our practice and interventions on empirical evidence that directs and informs judicious practice decisions is an important way for us to impart such leadership. Social work has the necessary knowledge, values, and skills to affect such responsible and ethical practice.

Key Terms

Elderly	Outcomes	Data
Interventions	Evidence	

Review Questions for Critical Thinking

1. What is the contributive importance of evidence-based practice for gerontological social work intervention strategies?

2. Why is worker self-awareness and self-care especially important when working with the elderly?

3. Explain why client autonomy and sense of control may be especially important when working with an aging population. What barriers do you foresee that may impede self-determination for the elderly client?

4. According to the NASW, social workers involved in palliative care must be prepared to deal with ethical dilemmas inherent in this type of work. Discuss the potential value conflicts that could arise for social workers dealing with end of life issues.

5. Describe those activities that will promote specialization for social workers working with the elderly.

Online Resources

http://seniors.lovetoknow.com/Social_Work_Skills_for_Working_With_the_Elderly This website highlights necessary social work skills for working with the elderly.

http://www.naswdc.org/practice/bereavement/standards/default.asp This link directs the reader to the NASW standards for social work practice in palliative and end-of-life care.

http://www.state.gov/m/dghr/flo/c23141.htm This website provides practical information on caring for elderly parents. Some highlights include communicating with the aging parent, elder care options, and deterioration warning signs.

http://www.longtermcarelink.net/ This website contains resources and information on long-term care planning and elder-care services.

http://www.ahrq.gov/research/olderam/oldam1.htm This website provides information on the ways to improve the health of older Americans.

References

Abrahamson, S. J., & Khan, F. (2006). Brief osteoporosis education in an inpatient rehabilitation setting improves knowledge of osteoporosis in elderly patients with low-trauma fractures. *International Journal of Rehabilitation Research*, *29*(1), 61–64.

Administration on Aging (2003). A profile of older Americans. Retrieved from www.aoa.gov/prof/Statistics/profile/2003/profiles2003.asp

Bailly, D., & DePoy, E. (1995). Older people's responses to education about advance directives. *Health and Social Work*, *20*(3), 223–229.

Ball, K., Berch, D. B., Helmers, K. F., Jobe, J. B., Leveck, M. D., Marsiske, M., . . . Willis, S. L. (2002). Effects of cognitive training interventions with older adults: A randomized controlled trial. *Journal of the American Medical Association*, *288*(18), 2271–2281.

Banerjee, S., Shamash, K., Macdonald, A. J. D., & Mann, A. H. (1996). Randomized controlled trial of effect of intervention by psychogeriatric team on depression in frail elderly people at home. *British Medical Journal, 313*(7064), 1058–1061.

Bisman, C. D. (2003). Rural aging: Social work practice models and intervention dynamics. *Journal of Gerontological Social Work, 41*(1/2), 37–58.

Bradley, N., & Poppen, W. (2003). Assistive technology, computers and Internet may decrease sense of isolation for homebound elderly and disabled persons. *Technology & Disability, 15*(1), 19–25.

Camberg, L., Woods, P., Ooi, W. L., Hurley, A., Volicer, L., Ashley, J.,...McIntyre, K. (1999). Evaluation of simulated presence: A personalized approach to enhance well-being in persons with Alzheimer's disease. *Journal of the American Geriatrics Society, 47*(4), 446–452.

Campbell, J. A., Robertson, M. C., Gardner, M. M., Norton, R. N., Tilyard, M. W., & Buchner, D. M. (1997). Randomized controlled trial of a general practice program of home based exercise to prevent falls in elderly women. *British Medical Journal, 315*(7115), 1065–1069.

Caplan, G. A., Williams, A. J., Daly, B., & Abraham, K. (2004). A randomized, controlled trial of comprehensive geriatric assessment and multidisciplinary intervention after discharge of elderly from the emergency department: The DEED II Study. *Journal of the American Geriatrics Society, 52*(9), 1417–1423.

Ciechanowski, P., Wagner, E., Schmaling, K., Schwartz, S., Williams, B., Diehr, P.,...LoGerfo, J. (2004). Community-integrated home-based depression treatment in older adults: A randomized controlled trial. *Journal of the American Medical Association, 291*(13), 1626–1628.

Council in Social Work Education (2006, February). Gero-Ed Forum [Abstract]. Chicago. Retrieved from www.Gero-EdCenter.org

Cummings, S. (2003). The efficacy of an integrated group treatment program for depressed assisted living residents. *Research on Social Work Practice, 13*(5), 608–621.

Cummings, S. M., & Kropf, N. P. (Eds.). (2009). Handbook of psychosocial interventions with older adults: Evidence-based approaches. NY: The Haworth Press.

De Leo, D., Buono, D., & Dwyer, J. (2002). Suicide among the elderly: The long-term impact of a telephone support and assessment intervention in northern Italy. *British Journal of Psychiatry, 181*(3), 226–229.

Dipko, L., Xavier, K., & Kohlwes, R. (2003). Advance directive group education in a VA outpatient clinic. *Social Work in Health Care, 38*, 93–106.

Dougherty, M. C., Dwyer, J. W., Pendergast, J. F., Boyington, A. R., Tomlinson U., Coward, R. T.,...Rooks, L. G. (2002). A randomized trial of behavioral management for continence with older rural women. *Research in Nursing and Health, 25*(1), 3–13.

Dunlop, J., & Holosko, M. J. (2006). Technology and evidence-based practice [Special guest edition]. *Journal of Evidence-Based Social Work Practice, 3*(3/4).

Engelhardt, J. B., Toseland, R. W., Gao, J., & Banks, S. (2006). Long-term effects of outpatient geriatric evaluation and management on health care utilization, cost, and survival. *Research on Social Work Practice, 16*, 20–27.

Enguidanos, S. M., Davis, C., & Katz, L. (2005). Shifting the paradigm in geriatric care management: Moving from the medical model to patient-centered care. *Social Work in Health Care, 41*(1), 1–16.

Feit, M. D., & Cuevas-Feit, N. (1991). An overview of social work practice with the elderly. In M. J. Holosko & M. D. Feit (Eds.), *Social work practice with the elderly* (2nd ed., pp. 3–27). Toronto, Canada: Canadian Scholar's Press.

Feit, M. D., & Cuevas-Feit, N. (2004). An overview of social work practice with the elderly. In M. J. Holosko & M. D. Feit (Eds.), *Social work practice with the elderly* (3rd ed., pp. 3–27). Toronto, Canada: Canadian Scholar's Press.

Formiga, F., Chivite, D., Ortega, C., Cassas, S., Ramon, J. M., & Pujol, R. (2004). End-of-life preferences in elderly patients admitted for heart failure. *Quarterly Journal of Medicine, 97*, 803–808. doi: 10.1093/9jmed1hch135

Fries, J. F., Carey, C., & McShane, D. J. (1997). Patient education in arthritis: Randomized controlled trial of a mail-delivered program. *Journal of Rheumatology, 24*(7), 1378–1383.

Gambrill, E. (2006). Evidence-based practice and policy: Choices ahead. *Research on Social Work Practice, 16*(3), 338–358.

Gibbs, L. (2005, October). *Using research to make life-affecting judgments and decisions.* Keynote address at the 17th National Symposium on Doctoral Research, Ohio State University, Columbus.

Gill, T. M., Baker, D. I., & Gottschalk, M. (2002). A program to prevent functional decline in physically frail, elderly persons who live at home. *New England Journal of Medicine, 347*(14), 1068–1074.

Glasgow, R., La Chance, P., Toobert, D., Brown, J., Hampson, S., & Riddle, M. (1997). Long term effects and costs of brief behavioral dietary intervention for patients with diabetes delivered from medical office. *Patient Education and Counseling, 32*(3), 175–184.

Graziano, R. (2003). Trauma and aging. *Journal of Gerontological Social Work, 40*(4), 3–21.

Greene, R. (1988). *Continuing education for gerontological careers.* Washington, DC: Council on Social Work Education.

Groth-Juncker, A., & McCusker, J. (1983). Where do elderly patients prefer to die? Place of death and patient characteristics of 100 elderly patients under the care of a home health care team. *Journal of the American Geriatric Society, 31*(8), 457–461.

Gutheil, I. A., & Heyman, J. C. (2005). Communication between older people and their health care agents: Results of an intervention. *Health and Social Work, 30*(2), 107–128.

Haight, B., & Gibson, F. (Eds.). (2005). *Burnside's working with older adults: Group processes and techniques* (4th ed.). Sudbury, MA: Jones & Bartlett.

Hobart, K. R. (2001). Death and dying and the social work role. *Journal of Gerontological Social Work, 36*(3/4), 181–192.

Holosko, M. J. (1995). The inclusion of gerontology consent into undergraduate social work curricula in Australia and New Zealand. *Gerontology and Geriatrics Education, 15*(4), 5–20.

Holosko, M. J. (2004). Evidence-based practice in Canada. In B. Thyer & M. Kazi (Eds.), *International perspectives: Evidence-based practice in social work* (pp. 61–78). London: Venture Press.

Holosko, M. J., & Feit, M. D. (Eds.). (2004). *Social work practice with the elderly* (3rd ed.). Toronto, Canada: Canadian Scholar's Press.

Holosko, M. J., & Holosko, D. A. (2004). What is unique about social work practice with the elderly? In M. J. Holosko & M. D. Feit (Eds.), *Social work practice with the elderly* (3rd ed., pp. 27–49). Toronto, Canada: Canadian Scholar's Press.

Holosko, M. J., & Leslie, D. R. (2004). Social policies that influence practice with the elderly. In M. J. Holosko & M. D. Feit (Eds.), *Social work practice with the elderly* (3rd ed., pp. 119–151). Toronto, Canada: Canadian Scholar's Press.

Holosko, M. J., White, L., & Feit, M. D. (2004). Gerontological social work practice in 2005 and beyond. In M. J. Holosko & M. D. Feit (Eds.), *Social work practice with the elderly* (3rd ed., pp. 549–557). Toronto, Canada: Canadian Scholar's Press.

Hooyman, N. R., & Kayak, H. A. (2002). *Social gerontology: A multi-disciplinary perspective* (6th ed.). Upper Saddle River, NJ: Pearson Education.

Howard, M. D., McMillan, C., & Pollio, D. (2003). Teaching evidence-based practice: Toward a new paradigm for social work education. *Research a Social Work Practice, 13*(2), 234–259.

Hunkeler, E. M., Katon, W., Tang, L., Williams, J. W., Jr., Kroenke, K., Lin, E. H., . . . Unützer, J. (2006). Long-term outcomes from the IMPACT randomised trial for depressed elderly patients in primary care. *British Medical Journal, 332*(7536), 259–262.

Husaini, B. A., Cummings, S., Kilbourne, B., Roback, H., Sherkat, D., Levine, R., & Cain, V. A. (2004). Group therapy for depressed elderly women. *International Journal of Group Psychotherapy, 54*(3), 295–319. doi 10.1521/ijgp.54.3.295.40340

Inouye, S. K., Wagner, D. R., Acampora, D., Horwitz, R. I., Cooney, L. M., & Tinetii, M. E. (1993). A controlled trial of a nursing-centered intervention in hospitalized elderly medical patients: The Yale Geriatric Care Program. *Journal of the American Geriatrics Society, 41*, 1353–1360.

Kapasi, Z. H., Ouslander, J. G., Schnelle, J. F., Kutner, M., & Fahey, J. L. (2003). Effects of an exercise intervention on immunologic parameters in frail elderly nursing home residents. *Journal of Gerontology: Series A, Biological Sciences and Medical Sciences, 58*(7), 636–643.

Keefe, F. J., Caldwell, D. S., Baucom, D., Salley, A., & Robinson, E. (1999). Spouse assisted coping skills training in the management of knee pain in osteoarthritis: Long-term follow up results. *Arthritis Care and Research, 12*(2), 101–111.

Kochevar, A., Smith, K., & Bernard, M. (2001). Effects of a community-based intervention to increase activity in American Indian elders. *Journal of the Oklahoma State Medical Association, 94*(10), 455–460.

Kolomer, S. (2008). Evidence-based psycho-social treatments for grandparent care-givers. Journal of Gerontological Social Work, 50 (sup. 1), pp 321–334.

Kuhn, D., & Mendes de Leon, C. (2001). Evaluation of an educational intervention with relatives of persons in the early stage of Alzheimer's disease. *Research on Social Work Practice, 11*(5), 531–548.

Leff, B., Burton, L., Mader, S. L., Naughton, B., Burl, J., Inouye, S. K., . . . Burton, J. R. (2005). Hospital at home: Feasibility and outcomes of a program to provide hospital level care at home for acutely ill older patients. *Annals of Internal Medicine, 143*(11), 798–808.

Leon, A. M., Altholz, J. A. S., & Dziegielewski, S. F. (1999). Compassion fatigue: Considerations for working with the elderly. *Journal of Gerontological Social Work, 32*(1), 43–62.

Li, H., & Blaser, C. J. (2003). Rural program planning and development for older adults. *Journal of Gerontological Social Work, 41*(1/2), 75–89.

Lomas, J., Woods, J., & Veenstra, G. (1997). Devolving authority for health care in Canada's provinces: Pt. 1. An introduction to the issues. *Canadian Medical Association Journal, 56*, 371–377.

Lowry, L. (1979). *Social policies and programs on aging.* Lexington, MA: Lexington.

Maisiak, R., Austin, J., & Heck, L. (1996). Health outcomes of two telephone interventions for patients with rheumatoid arthritis or osteoarthritis. *Arthritis Rheumatology*, *39*(8), 1391–1399.

Mazzuca, S. A., Brandt, K. D., Katz, B. P., Hanna, M. P., & Melfi, C. A. (1999). Reduced utilization and cost of primary care clinic visits resulting from self-care education for patients with osteoarthritis of the knee. *Arthritis Rheumatology*, *42*(6), 1267–1273.

McInnis-Dittrich, K. (2002). *Social work with elders: A biopsychosocial approach to assessment and intervention.* Boston, MA: Allyn & Bacon.

Mittelman, M. S., Roth, D. L., Coon, D. W., & Haley, W. E. (2004). Sustained benefit of supportive intervention for depressive symptoms in caregivers of patients with Alzheimer's disease. *American Journal of Psychiatry*, *161*(5), 850–856.

Mo-Kyung, S., Belza, B., LoGerfo, J., & Cunningham, S. (2005). Evaluation of a community-based exercise program for elderly Korean immigrants. *Public Health Nursing*, *22*(5), 407–413.

Mollica, R., & Morris, M. (2005). *Massachusetts supportive housing program.* New Brunswick, NJ: Rutgers Center for State Health Policy.

Morrow-Howell, N., & Burnette, D. (2001). Gerontological social work research: Current status and future directions. *Journal for Gerontological Social Work*, *36*(3/4), 63–79.

Motohashi, Y., Kaneko, Y., Sasaki, H. (2004). Community-based suicide prevention progran in Japan using a health promotion approach. *Environmental Health and Preventative Medicine*, *9*(1), 3–8. doi: 10.1265/ehpm.9.3

Naleppa, M. J., & Reid, W. J. (2003). *Gerontological social work: A task-centered approach.* New York, NY: Columbia University Press.

National Association of Social Workers (2004). *End-of-life care.* Retrieved from www.socialworkers.org

National Association of Social Workers (2006). National study of licensed social workers 2006. Retrieved from http://workforce.socialworkers.org

Otten, A. (1984, July 10). The oldest-old (3 Pts.). *Wall Street Journal*, pp. 1–2.

Padgett, D. K. (2005). The Society for Social Work Research at 10 years of age and counting: An idea whose time had come. *Research on Social Work Practice*, *15*(1), 3–7.

Peck, M. D. (2001). Looking back at life and its influence on subjective well-being. *Journal of Gerontological Social Work*, *35*(2), 3–21.

Pinquart, M., Sörensen, S., & Peak, T. (2004). Helping older adults and their families develop and implement care plans. *Journal of Gerontological Social Work*, *43*(4), 3–23.

Pollio, D. (2002). The evidence-based group worker. *Social Work with Groups*, *25*(4), 57–70.

Pollio, D. (2006). The art of evidence-based practice. *Research on Social Work Practice*, *16*(2), 224–232.

Poon, P., Hui, E., Dai, D., Kwok, T., & Woo, J. (2005). Cognitive intervention for community-dwelling older persons with memory problems: Telemedicine versus face-to-face treatment. *International Journal of Geriatric Psychiatry*, *20*(3), 285–286.

Proctor, R., Burns, A., Powell, H. S., Tarrier, N., Faragher, B., Richardson, G.,...South, B. (1999). Behavioural management in nursing and residential homes: A randomized controlled trial. *Lancet*, *354*(9172), 26–29.

Rich, M. W., Beckham, V., Wittenberg, C., Leven, C. L., Freedland, K. E., & Carney, R. M. (1995). A multidisciplinary intervention to prevent the readmission of elderly patients with congestive heart failure. *New England Journal of Medicine, 333*(18), 1190–1195.

Rich, M. W., Gray, D. B., Beckham, V., Wittenberg, C., & Luther, P. (1996). Effect of a multidisciplinary intervention on medication compliance in elderly patients with congestive heart failure. *American Journal of Medicine, 101,* 3270–3276.

Rosen, A. (2003). Evidence-based social work practice: Challenges and promises. *Social Work Research, 27,* 208–210.

Rowe, J. W., & Kahn, R. L. (1998). *Successful aging.* New York, NY: Pantheon.

Ryan-Woolley, B. M., & Rees, J. A. (2005). Initializing concordance in frail elderly patients via a Medicines Organizer. *Annals of Pharmacotherapy, 39,* 1–6.

Sackett, D. L., Richardson, W. S., Rosenberg, W., & Haynes, R. B. (1997). *Evidence-based medicine: How to practice and teach EBM.* New York, NY: Churchill Livingstone.

Schneider, R., Decker, T., Freeman, J., Messerschmidt, L., & Syran, C. (Eds.). (1984). *Specialized course outline for gerontological social work education.* Washington, DC: Council on Social Work Education Press.

Schonfeld, L., Dupree, L. W., Dickson, F. E., Royer, C. M., McDermott, C. H., Rosansky, J. S., . . . Jarvik, L. F. (2000). Cognitive behavioral treatment of older veterans with substance abuse problems. *Journal of Geriatric Psychiatric and Neurology, 13,* 124–128.

Sharpe, P. A., Jackson, K. L., White, C., Vaca, V. L., Hickey, T., Gu, J., & Otterness, C. (1997). Effects of a one-year physical activity intervention for older adults at congregate nutrition sites. *Gerontologist, 37,* 208–215.

Slaets, J. P., Kauffmann, R. H., Duivenvoorden, H. J., Pelemans, W., & Schudel, W. J. (1997). A randomized trial of geriatric liaison intervention in elderly medical inpatients. *Psychosomatic Medicine, 59*(6), 585–591.

Solomon, P. R., Adams, F., Silver, A., Zimmer, J., & DeVeaux, R. (2002). Ginkgo for memory enhancement: A randomized controlled trial. *Journal of the American Medical Association, 288,* 835–840.

Solomon, R. (2004). The role of the social worker in long-term care. *Journal of Gerontological Social Work, 43*(2/3), 187–202.

Stinson, C. K., & Kirk, E. (2006). Structured reminiscence: An intervention to decrease depression and increase self-transcendence in older women. *Journal of Clinical Nursing, 15,* 208–218.

Tennstedt, S., Howland, J., Lachman, M., Peterson, E., Kasten, L., & Jette, A. (1998). A randomized, controlled trial of a group intervention to reduce fear of falling and associated activity restriction in older adults. *Journal of Gerontology: Series B, Psychological Sciences, 53,* 384–392.

Thomas, G. N., Hong, A. W. L., Tomlinson, B., Lau, E., Lam, C. W. K., Sanderson, J. E., & Woo, J. (2005). Effects of Tai Chi and resistance training on cardiovascular risk factors in elderly Chinese subjects: A 12-month longitudinal, controlled intervention study. *Clinical Endocrinology, 63,* 663–669.

Thyer, B., & Kazi, M. (Eds.). (2004). *International perspectives: Evidence-based practice in social work.* London: Venture Press.

Tsang, H. W. H., Mok, C. K., Yeung, Y. T., & Chan, S. Y. C. (2003). The effect of Qigong on general and psychosocial health of elderly with chronic physical illnesses: A randomized clinical trial. *International Journal of Geriatric Psychiatry, 18*(5), 441–449.

Tse, M. Y., Pun, S. P. Y., & Benzie, I. F. F. (2005). Affective images: Relieving chronic pain and enhancing quality of life for older persons. *CyberPsychology and Behavior, 8*(6), 571–579.

U.S. Bureau of Labor Statistics. (2004). Occupational employment statistics. Retrieved November 21, 2004, from www.bls.gov/OES/

Vourlekis, B., Zlotnick, J., & Simons, K. (2005). *Evaluating social work services in nursing homes: Toward quality psychosocial care and its measurement.* Washington, DC: Institute for the Advancement of Social Work Research.

White, H., McConnell, E., Clip, E., Branch, L. G., Sloane, R., Pieper, C., & Box, T. L. (2002). A randomized controlled trial of the psychosocial impact of providing internet training and access to older adults. *Aging and Mental Health, 6*(3), 213–221.

Wright, L., Hickson, M., & Frost, G. (2006). Eating together is important: Using a dining room in an acute elderly medical ward increases energy intake. *Journal of Human Nutrition and Dietetics, 19*(1), 23–26.

Chapter 9
Assessment of Families

Robyn Munford and Jackie Sanders

> **Purpose:** This chapter provides an overview of the history of assessment within social work practice, a discussion of the current views of assessment and some challenges to these views, as well as the assessment process at the micro-, mezzo-, and macrolevels of practice as related to families.
>
> **Rationale:** To educate readers about the purpose of assessment, its definitions, and where it is located within the helping relationship.
>
> **How evidence-informed practice is presented:** This chapter focuses on evidence-informed assessment of families and what approaches have been predominant in the field by presenting a range of sources such as research and evaluation using a range of methods informed by specific paradigms on the purpose and nature of the research and evaluation task, literature that has documented practice, and information from the field through practitioner and client accounts.
>
> **Overarching question:** Why is assessment an integral component of good social work practice with families?

Historical Background

The ideas just discussed are reflected in a recent history of social work (Johnson & Yanca, 2004) and in the historical accounts of work with families (Lightburn & Sessions, 2006; Maluccio et al., 2011; Thompson, 2002; Warren-Adamson & Lightburn, 2006). The historical debates underpinning social work with families parallel those in other fields of social work practice. Changes in the assessment of families over time have been closely aligned with the way families have been viewed by professionals and with how resources and services have been developed and allocated (Chenoweth & McAuliffe, 2008). Service provision for children with disabilities and their families illustrates this point. There have been dramatic changes to the assessment procedures used with families with children with disabilities. Early services to these families were focused on protection and asylum. Children with disabilities were removed from their families to live in institutions and often had little contact with their family. The focus of social work with the family was often on assisting them to forget about the child with the disability and to channel their energies into taking care of other family members (Ferguson & O'Brien,

2005). Deficit-based assessment that highlighted what people with disabilities were unable or incapable of doing were prominent historically, and one of the most common service interventions involved exclusion and removal from mainstream society. However, challenges from families and from the disability-rights movement has brought about a transformation in perspectives and services, and now assessments typically focus on identifying support and resources so that families can care for their children with a disabilities at home and encourage participation in all community activities. Social work is now focused on providing advocacy, support, resources, and services to families so that their child can fully participate in their community (Sullivan & Munford, 2005), and assessment has accommodated this significant reorientation.

This example demonstrates the complex factors that have influenced the way that social work has been constructed. As will be noted throughout this chapter, changes in the way social work occurs produces fundamental shifts in the nature, focus, and delivery of assessments (Milner & O'Byrne, 2002). Significant changes to social work practice are closely connected to changes in the political and economic context and to societal expectations of the social work role (Dominelli, 1996; Healy, 2000, 2005; Ife, 1997, 2001; Munford & Sanders, 2011). These changes are also linked to the belief systems that define and assess certain populations and groups and determine their rights to have support and to participate in their communities (as is illustrated in the example of families caring for children with disabilities).

Social work began in most Western countries as a voluntary activity, often located within religious and charitable organizations that saw the need to address the consequences of poverty and urbanization (Johnson & Yanca, 2004). There has always been a tension between providing charity, philanthropy, and support and the need for control and protection. There have been consistent debates throughout the profession's history about how the recipients of services are to be identified and defined and about the client's right to determine how services should be delivered. The service user's voice has become stronger in more recent times as social work has continued to reflect on the balance between rights and obligations and on complex issues around matters of risk and safety (Ellis & Dean, 2000).

Alongside the debates of how to organize the delivery of care and support and who should have the responsibility for ensuring the well-being of families, social workers have also debated their role and their knowledge base (Allan, Pease, & Briskman, 2003; Chenoweth & McAuliffe, 2008; Healy, 2005; Stepney & Ford, 2000). Historically, this debate has moved from a benevolent support approach to an approach that focused on professional and expert knowledge where social workers could effectively target assessments and interventions. Although work in the community and neighborhood and the support of self-help groups remained important interventions, casework became a predominant activity for social workers (Johnson & Yanca, 2004). Social workers located their work within agencies and worked with other professionals to provide services to children and families and other client groups (R. W. Roberts & Nee, 1970). Alongside this work (as is evident in most Western nations) were debates about how much the state should intervene to eradicate poverty and to provide welfare services to families (Stepney & Ford, 2000). Social workers, however, have maintained their commitment, through social work education programs and their national associations, to work to enhance human potential and to promote social change, problem solving in human relationships, and the empowerment and liberation of people in order to achieve well-being. As the international definition of social work has asserted: "central to social work practice is an understanding of the principles of human rights and social justice. Indigenous and local knowledge should define the context of social work, and the key social work task is to embrace humanitarian and democratic ideals addressing injustices and inequities through their daily practice" (www.ifsw.org).

The international view that social work should have a primary interest in the principles of social justice and human rights has been comprehensively debated within the profession. The key issues have been concerned with how social work contributes to these principles at what level of practice. The role of social work with all client groups will remain hotly contested (Dominelli, 1998) as will the theoretical frameworks utilized to inform our practice. These debates will also continue to influence the way that assessment processes will be constructed and the types of evidence that will be adopted in order to assess effectiveness in all aspects of social work practice with families.

Current Evidence on the Assessment of Families

The evidence on the assessment of families and what approaches have been predominant in the field comes from a range of sources including research and evaluation using a range of methods informed by specific paradigms on the purpose and nature of the research and evaluation task (Dolan, Canavan, & Pinkerton, 2006), literature that has documented practice, and information from the field through practitioner and client accounts (Parton, 2000). There are many debates about what constitutes robust and sound evidence (Healy, 2005; Maluccio et al., 2011; O'Hare, 2005; Parton, 2000; A. R. Roberts & Yeager, 2006). These often focus on the authenticity of the perspectives and the knowledge paradigms being used to measure this effectiveness (A. R. Roberts & Yeager, 2006). For example, some would argue that tightly controlled and regulated scientific investigations, such as random controlled trials, are best equipped to allow social workers to assess the effectiveness of interventions. Others would argue that these take a too-narrow approach and may not take into account the context of social work practice ignoring the important role of critical thinking in social work practice (O'Hare, 2005). The focus on measuring variables that can be controlled may ignore key aspects such as the processes and contexts that flow through clients' lives. An effective social worker should be aware that the achievement of positive outcomes with clients requires them to respond to uncontrollable events and to know how to make the best use of knowledge from research and evaluation and from the practice domain (Healy, 2005; A. R. Roberts & Yeager, 2006).

Clegg (2005) argues that evidence is a contested domain and that a conceptual shift to a critical realist approach is required where positivist models of evidence are not seen as the only measure of evidence. A critical realist approach defines "evidence as work that can give insight into the structures, powers, generative mechanisms and tendencies that help us understand the concrete worlds of experience" (p. 421). This approach recognizes the transformative nature of social action, such as social work, and the centrality of human agency in change processes. These approaches focus on the need to be sensitive to the realities of practice and to the complexities of the experiences of the participants involved in the practice environment (Clegg, 2005; McNeill, 2001). There is recognition of the dynamic interplay between practice and research (Healy, 2005; A. R. Roberts & Yeager, 2006) and an acceptance that evidence must be derived from multiple sources using multiple methods that can accommodate a wide range of practice situations (O'Hare, 2005).

These ideas on the nature of evidence and the approach taken by authors such as O'Hare (2005) have informed this discussion on assessment and the need to work with multiple information sources across a range of settings. Although one can argue that there are many views on how to classify current frameworks for assessing families, a number of key themes have emerged over time. These are connected to the role of the social worker in the change process and understandings about the nature of the social work task. These are intricately connected to the perspectives held about family life and the complex ways in which wider contexts influence outcomes (Cooper, 2001; Holland, 2004; McCartt Hess, McGowan, & Botsko, 2003; Sanders & Munford, 2010). Dominelli (1998) suggests that the broad categories of social work can be classified as therapeutic helping approaches, maintenance approaches, and emancipatory approaches. Therapeutic helping approaches to assessment and intervention assist individuals, families, and groups to address their life circumstances by exploring strategies for problem solving. In the family therapy field, a number of therapeutic approaches in a range of settings have been adopted including structural family therapy, narrative approaches, multisystemic therapy, just therapy (Sessions & Lightburn, 2006), and psychosocial approaches that connect the inner self to wider environment and systems issues (Dominelli, 1998). Some of these approaches have attempted to locate the family within the community and work with wider issues outside the family system (Waldegrave, 1990); however, most of these remain focused on a therapeutic approach and the interactions within the family (Sessions & Lightburn, 2006). Researchers such as Sessions and Lightburn (2006) are advocating for a stronger connection between the work done within families and the wider systems and propose that the most effective location for this work is within community-based settings.

Maintenance approaches represent another major strand in social work practice and family work. Here, social work is often labeled as practical and pragmatic (Dominelli, 1998), with the focus of the assessment being on the identification of practical and concrete needs; the social worker assists the client to procure resources and to solve problems. This approach is not usually associated with intense therapeutic work, focusing often, instead, on the here and now and the immediate resolution of problems. A range of assessment and intervention strategies are used, including task-centered approaches and behavior management strategies. Ecological and systems perspectives can be included in these approaches and focus on assisting clients to achieve balance in their networks. They can also involve an adaptation of behavior and the development of more effective coping strategies.

There has been criticism of both therapeutic and maintenance approaches by some social workers who argue that neither address power imbalances. That may be the fundamental reason why clients and families are facing challenges (Finn & Jacobson, 2003). Emerging out of this critique has been the development of structural and critical approaches and more recently poststructural perspectives. These newer approaches explicitly focus on power, a critique of systems, and a commitment to achieving personal and social change. Assessment strategies emphasize understanding how the troubles that families face are embedded within structural conditions. Dominelli (1998) classifies these perspectives as emancipatory and includes within this category any approach that has a commitment to social justice and to making explicit work with clients that focuses on exposing power relations and the root causes of conditions such as poverty, abuse, gender inequality, and racism. Clients are encouraged to make links between their personal troubles and public issues. Feminist social work, anti-oppressive practice, radical social work, community work, advocacy and empowerment, and indigenous approaches are commonly found in the emancipatory group (Munford & Sanders, 2011).

Assessment strategies depend on which approach to social work is taken. However, the focus is not always clearly delineated, with theoretical concepts often being utilized in more than one of these approaches. Although it is relatively easy to identify the boundaries between the different approaches on paper, practitioners frequently draw from more than one theoretical approach in their work (Chenoweth & McAuliffe, 2008). For example, the principles and concepts of strengths-based work with clients are present in therapeutic work with families and in emancipatory approaches. In a similar way, the assessment tools used vary across settings and with the mandates held by the social worker. The status of the client as either voluntary or involuntary will have a significant influence on the nature and approach taken to assessment. So, for instance, a family who comes voluntarily to a community-based mental-health setting to address relationship issues will present different assessment challenges and require a different approach than the family who is under investigation by a child protection agency.

Thompson (2002) suggests that social workers need to have a strong repertoire of assessment knowledge, including tools and strategies, and be able to use their knowledge across settings and populations. Working with a young person within a family will require a different focus and understanding than working with the parent of this young person. Thompson asserts that being clear about the key elements of the social work assessment process and one's key role in this process will assist the social worker in being more effective. He argues for a reflective approach that enables the social worker to know how assessment fits within the other aspects of the helping process and to be explicit about the ideas that are informing assessment decisions.

A reflective approach also requires the social worker to know how to use the evidence available and to make informed decisions about problems and possible solutions. It also demands that the social worker use processes such as supervision to evaluate practice and to continually develop their competence and critically reflect on their practice. Thompson (2002) identifies a number of factors to be aware of when reflecting on one's assessment practice. These include: being aware of how to form helping partnerships with clients, knowing how to use a broad range of evidence about assessment, balancing a focus on the problem with a focus on solution finding, being creative in seeking solutions, being explicit about the system and organizational barriers that interrupt the assessment process, and focusing on the holistic needs of the family, not only on the individuals within it.

Assessment of families requires that attention be given to the immediate family needs as well as broader issues. Epistemological issues such as the nature and status of knowledge also need to be carefully considered when thinking about the assessment of families. Assessment is fundamentally about the construction of the official story about a family, its needs and strengths; and decisions are usually made about access to resources, relationship issues, and care of children (Sanders & Munford, 2010). Power relations and issues around the control of knowledge often feature in social work debates about assessment; it is not a neutral, fact-gathering exercise that can be executed by the application of a value-free set of skills. In this connection, Holland (2004) reminds us to be vigilant about the helping role and the way in which knowledge is socially, culturally, and historically constructed within the helping relationship. In terms of approaches to assessment, it is important that social workers seek a range of evidence and work to identify what it is that clients bring to the helping relationship and how this can assist in finding solutions to the problems they bring to social workers (O'Hare, 2005).

Limitations to the Evidence on the Assessment of Families

The failure to take a broad approach to seeking evidence about best practice in assessment constitutes some of the major limitations in this area of practice. The ideas explored in the previous section underline the importance of the use of evidence in assessment processes but focus also on the contested nature of this evidence and encourage the social worker to be constantly aware of how knowledge is constructed and how it will reflect the exigencies of particular contexts. Constructivist approaches attempt to address these issues (Parton & O'Byrne, 2000) and assert the view that social workers should be able to work with the conflicting interpretations of the issues that families bring to the helping relationship and to work with the family to identify solutions that reflect and address the complexities of family life. This requires flexibility, an open approach to your practice, and an ability to continually question the foundational and current social work practice knowledge (Sanders & Munford, 2010).

A key element that has not received due consideration in the evidence on what constitutes good practice in assessment is the way in which the diversity of family life is understood and how this can be incorporated into your practice and inform the strategies used in the assessment of families. Thompson (2002) argues that there are "dangers of adopting an uncritical, reductionist approach to the family as a social institution and the basis of so much social work practice" (p. 45).

Thompson (2002, pp. 45–46) asserts that although the term *family* is regularly used in social work practice "it is often used in a vague and ambiguous way, with little clarity about what we mean by the term or why it is deemed to be so important." To counteract a reductionist and simplistic view of families and family life, the assessment process must explicitly allow for the family to articulate its own sense of family and to identify the key values they have as a family unit. Cultural competence then becomes a core competency for social workers who undertake family assessments. They need to understand the many different ways in which families operate and to be able to differentiate differences from problems. Traditionally some of the literature has failed to identify this diversity and has not situated assessment and intervention strategies within specific historical, social, political, economic, and cultural contexts (Munford & Sanders, 2001, 2005, 2011). This has often resulted in a mismatch between the needs of clients, service provision, and social work interventions. Moreover, this has, at times, resulted in families being blamed for unsuccessful interventions that have failed to recognize that the knowledge systems informing practice have no relevance for the belief systems and contexts of these families (Munford & Sanders, 2005).

This challenge to how family life is perceived is located within wider challenges to dominant paradigms. Writers have argued that the dominant paradigms such as systems and ecosystems approaches construct the social environment as a neutral concept (Finn & Jacobson, 2003). These paradigms do not reveal how "the dominant political and economic order directly contributes to social problems" (p. 61). Diversity is not just about local difference; it also concerns external forces such as globalization, inequality and uneven economic development, advances in communication for selected communities, and the precariousness of human rights (p. 57). Central to these concerns is the need to recognize the diversity of family life from a global perspective and "the multiple constructions of social reality" (p. 60). The social work profession has, in recent times, been challenged to highlight the rights of indigenous populations (Corwin, 2006; Dei, Hall, & Rosenberg, 2000; Munford & Sanders, 2011), and now, with the increasing movement of populations across the globe, social workers are needing to incorporate new knowledge frameworks that challenge previously accepted discourses on practice (Nash, 2005).

When working within families and assessing needs, we need to take a broad approach that recognizes how the family environment and the context in which they live "may open up or restrict life opportunities" (Munford & Sanders, 2005, p. 160). The key challenge here is to recognize how the common themes of making available material and social resources and achieving health and well-being for all family members are constructed within the global economy and have different meanings across different contexts (Parton & O'Byrne, 2000).

The challenges take on a particular character when we consider the way in which assessment of families fits within the wider social work process. Fook (2002) provides an insightful critique of assessment processes and locates this critique within a critical reflective approach to practice that challenges the domination of knowledge systems recognizing multiple and diverse constructions and creates inclusive structures through shared dialogue and knowledge building (pp. 40–41). Fook asserts that the ways we assess problems are "integrally connected with the ways in which we construct knowledge of our world and more generally our place within it" (p. 115).

Fook (2002) suggests that social workers need to build multiple interpretations of issues and problems that include the views of all participants in the change process. Assessment is not a linear process that simply gathers together the facts about a situation. Facts are contested and typically open to multiple interpretations and any information about a family requires careful consideration in order to test out the social worker's assumptions about the family situation. Some of the material on assessment has implied a neutral, systematic process of fact gathering; this view ignores the complexity of the assessment process and its strong connection to the way knowledge and discourses are constructed about family life (Milner & O'Byrne, 2002). Take the earlier example of disability; in order to achieve a comprehensive assessment of the family who is struggling to support a child with a disability, a social worker needs to understand the discourses that have functioned historically to define disabled people and their families. This has included the medicalization of disability as well as perspectives that have pathologized disability and prevented disabled people from participating in their communities. The social worker must be aware of how professionals have contributed to upholding negative practices that have functioned to exclude disabled people. People's experiences often vary across environments (Fook, 2002); they may be active participants in one environment, whereas, in other environments, the entire family may be excluded because their child with disabilities is not encouraged to participate in a community activity. Comprehensive social work assessments take account of the way in which families' experiences differ across contexts and in so doing incorporate understanding of the way in which context shapes both experience and possibilities for change.

Fook's (2002) arguments direct social workers to understand knowledge frameworks that have been previously ignored or misinterpreted. This argument connects with the recognition that family life is diverse. An example from practice in Aotearoa/New Zealand underlines this point and involves the highlighting of indigenous knowledge to inform work with families. Indigenous frameworks and understandings, as well as a desire to develop what it means to practice in bicultural ways, have exerted a powerful influence over the way in which social and community work practice has developed. In Aotearoa/New Zealand for example, this bicultural context has resulted in new ways of working with families. For example, the Whare Tapa Wha model (Durie, 1995) provides an indigenous interpretation of health and well-being. It encompasses spiritual, psychological, physical, and kinship dimensions of family life and can be used to assess families seeking support from state agencies, health services, and community-based services. These models have been used to work with other cultural groups who bring diverse knowledge to the assessment process.

The expansion of social-work-practice frameworks to include new social and cultural understandings of families and the nature of effective support has resulted in improved professional responsiveness and effectiveness in both assessment and intervention. These new understandings have often emphasized the centrality of meaning making and interpretation in the social work task and in the lives of families. Although the opening of social work to these new approaches has not always been smooth, it has resulted in more responsive professional practice and an emphasis on respecting, understanding, and responding directly to diversity at all levels of practice (Munford & Sanders, 2011).

The Assessment Process Within Social Work Practice—Micro-, Mezzo-, and Macrolevels

Social work takes place at a number of levels. All these levels require the social worker to have knowledge and skills to work with "a narrative construction process [where] workers may experiment with different ways of framing a situation, in order to explore multiple perspectives and build up a picture of changing contexts and their influences" (Fook, 2002, p. 124). This process will be facilitated within a values framework that recognizes the strengths and strategies clients bring to the change process (Munford & Sanders, 2005). Context is central to the helping process and, as discussed in previous sections, social workers are being challenged to incorporate previously ignored or misinterpreted knowledge frameworks into their practice (Parton & O'Byrne, 2000). For example, in Aotearoa/New Zealand there is a commitment to embrace new ways of working as part of a search for processes that more effectively support families and communities. The emphasis is on finding local solutions by validating local stories and knowledge in order to build engaged communities that find strength in utilizing their own energy, resources, and local talent (Mataira, 2002, p. 5).

Current social work practice has seen the emergence of new perspectives on family work. A strong influence has been those perspectives informed by critical social work and constructivist approaches (Allan et al., 2003; Finn & Jacobson, 2003; Parton & O'Byrne, 2000). These approaches encourage social workers to interrogate power relations, to appreciate how knowledge is constructed, and to critically examine the relationship between clients and social workers. They provide a foundation for discussion in this chapter on the assessment of families; central to these views is an understanding of how theory and practice interact with each other and contribute equally to knowledge development (O'Hare, 2005; Parton, 2000). The constructivist approach challenges social workers to foreground the authority of clients as "engaged" subjects and to understand that clients "will be undertaking their own active synthesis and interpretation of the social work intervention" (Cooper, 2001, p. 724). This view transforms the way we perceive assessment and intervention processes, where the definition of clients moves from seeing them as passive recipients of help, for whom the social worker as expert controls the change process, to a view that sees clients as active participants in the change process and experts on what will work in their lives (Ife, 2001). Strength-based approaches are encompassed within the constructivist paradigm and emphasize a focus on what it is that enables clients to survive and grow as well as those matters that may stand in the way (Corcoran, 2005; Saleebey, 2002). These approaches focus on hearing stories differently in order to find solutions and create positive change (Munford & Sanders, 1999). Strengths-based approaches to assessment, as with many of the emerging models, move away from a focus on deficits and on the dysfunctional aspects of family life (Corcoran, 2005), opening up new possibilities for finding solutions to the problems clients bring to social workers.

This following consideration of the micro-, mezzo- and macrolevels of assessment practice is informed by the current thinking on assessment that incorporates strengths approaches and that also acknowledges the need for critical thinking around meaning, context, power, history, and possibility for clients (Finn & Jacobson, 2003). Although not minimizing the enormous difficulties families may face, such as abuse, poverty, poor health, and the loss of hope (Dawson & Berry, 2002), the strengths-based approach to assessment focuses on the competencies families have used to overcome and survive difficult circumstances (Munford & Sanders, 2001).

The microlevel is concerned with direct work with the family. The focus is on working with the family system and its networks. Assessment considers the family and includes an exploration of the systems that impact on family life in all its diversity. The mezzolevel expands the assessment process to include organizations, communities, and neighborhoods. The worker pays attention to identifying the capacity of wider systems around the family and developing intervention plans at this level on behalf of families (Alston, 2009). The macrolevel involves an assessment of the structures and policies that impact family life and may involve the social worker in advocacy roles and in policy analysis and critique.

The key themes informing assessment processes with families include:

- A commitment to the belief that families bring strengths and resources to the helping relationship, and these can be harnessed in finding solutions. This means that the assessment can provide opportunities for exploring both problems and resources within the family.

- An understanding that a focus on strengths does not diminish the importance of identifying risk and safety issues and finding ways to protect clients from harm and causing harm.

- A move to a focus on strengths challenges some of the traditional approaches that have focused on deficits and problems (Corcoran, 2005; Saleebey, 2002). These approaches have been criticized for focusing on the dysfunctional aspects of families and holding a narrow view of the family that requires assistance from formal service systems. The competencies of these failed families have often been ignored with the social worker missing key information that will demonstrate how these families have, in fact, survived and managed to achieve success despite the challenges (Gilligan, 2000, 2004; Norman, 2000).

- A consistent challenge to social workers to think about what it is that enables families to survive and grow and how to identify the moments when positive change was achieved. Social workers need to be aware of the impact of service systems that may function to further alienate families and to mask the possibilities for change.

- A focus on help-seeking behavior as a positive event representing the beginning of a process that locates the family as the key agent of change. This will be achieved through the establishment of strong relationships and partnerships between clients and social workers (Sanders & Munford, 2010).

- An understanding that, in the wider environments and networks of clients, there are resources that can assist in the change process. There are informal networks available that can be harnessed as key components of the change process. Social workers need to adopt a perspective that enables them to be creative in seeking out resources (Alston, 2009). This may also require them to understand that they are not the only experts in the change process.

These ideas inform all levels of assessment practice. The goal is to have a wide-ranging repertoire of assessment, planning, and intervention strategies that are developed within an action and reflection cycle that has a strong solution focus. Although the focus in this chapter is on assessment, the strategies outlined are intricately linked to the other phases of the helping relationship. It should be noted that assessment is present in all phases of social work interventions, given the need to continually reflect on intervention strategies and to seek further information and clarification if these strategies are not successful. The evidence on the phases of assessment is vast (Thompson, 2002). The following discussion represents a synthesis of the key ideas and is informed by those perspectives that conceive social work as socially constructed within a relationship between clients and social workers who both have connections with a wider context that impacts on the nature of the helping relationship (Parton & O'Byrne, 2000).

The discussion begins with the microlevel and the assessment processes that are considered to be effective at this level. The knowledge and strategies used at this level will also be present at the mezzo- and macrolevels of practice, such as the importance of understanding context and the way this influences how social work relationships will be constructed (Healy, 2005).

The Microlevel

The key phases to be addressed in working directly with families at the microlevel include: engaging with the family and forming a helping partnership and identifying possible solutions and planning for positive change.

Engaging With the Family and Forming a Helping Partnership

This phase of the assessment process provides a foundation for subsequent phases, and the success of these will depend on how well this first phase can be achieved. When entering the world of a family, the social worker must take the time to understand the broader influences that may determine how families live their lives (Munford & Sanders, 1999). Families are likely to have difficulty identifying their competences and abilities when they are immersed in challenging times. During assessment, the social worker has a central role in assisting families to tell their stories in ways that enables them to identify positive aspects of their experience and to build on this to create a vision for the future. Issues in the wider environment (e.g., the meeting of basic needs such as income and shelter) may have to be addressed alongside other family issues.

Before social workers engage with families, they must be clear about the mandate for the helping relationship and the expectations of their organization. This includes understanding the principles on which the organization is based and the philosophies it holds about work with families (Sanders & Munford, 2010). Although it is expected that the social worker will have the appropriate value base, skills, and knowledge to work effectively with families, it is also expected that social workers will be aware of the practical and material resources they can mobilize to assist the family. Even while in the assessment phase, social workers may need to assist the family in dealing with these issues before they can focus on other issues such as addressing challenges in family relationships, including matters such as parenting issues.

It is important for social workers to engage in context-sensitive work (Healy, 2005). This requires understanding how inclusion of the political, economic, religious, and cultural contexts informs the helping relationship. A key example is that of culture (Corwin, 2006). The beginning phase of the assessment process must take into account the cultural frameworks that underpin family decision making and how these influence the construction of family relationships. If the social worker ignores these influences, he or she is likely to miss key information that will assist in the assessment process. The worst possible scenario would see the social worker unable to form a positive partnership with the family in this crucial first phase of relationship building. The social worker may also miss opportunities to harness informal networks that can assist the family in finding a solution. For example, the use of extended family members to support the care of children and young people may well be an appropriate early support to draw on.

There are some specific strategies social workers can use to facilitate this phase of assessment. The first includes active listening and fully engaging in the stories being presented by the family. This may require social workers to suspend judgment; this is especially relevant for those families who have been labeled as multiproblem families, which have been the focus of many social service interventions from many agencies. The suspension of judgment does not deny the existence of risk and safety issues, but it allows the social worker to see the issues from new perspectives; it is from here that fresh insights may emerge. This is particularly important for families for which social workers have not been able to provide support to address supposedly intractable issues. As Thompson (2002) suggests, we can utilize assessment tools that are focused on information gathering to provide a description of the family and the issues they are facing. However, social workers must also reflect on whether this description leads them to explore different questions so that they can achieve a deeper understanding of the issues, disrupt taken-for-granted assumptions, and assist the family to be creative in their solution finding.

Social workers who are engaged in active listening also work to disrupt notions of the "expert" and to critically examine how they view the knowledge and experience that clients bring to helping relationships (Munford & Sanders, 2003; Sanders & Munford, 2003, 2010). Forming constructive partnerships requires a genuine sharing of ideas and an understanding from the social worker's perspective that clients have critical knowledge that can be harnessed in the change process (Fook, 2003). Social work is facilitative, not directive, and families need to maintain control and identify priorities for what they want to achieve in family life (Cooper, 2001; Egan, 2002). This partnership is based on an understanding that clients may hold narratives that portray themselves as incompetent and without agency over their circumstances. A skilled worker is able to draw out the strengths in these narratives and assist the family to develop alternative meanings and interpretations of their situation.

One of the major challenges in work with families is to identify how a social worker can work with the whole family system and also with individuals within it. One of the challenges is to ensure that the needs of all family members are being addressed. To achieve this goal, social workers may need to change both direction and focus at different times throughout the assessment and intervention processes. The goal is to ensure that the social worker provides many opportunities to explore the multiple interpretations of issues and solutions taking into account the perspective of all family members. Fook (2002) asserts that discovering meaning requires a commitment from the social worker to work with families to construct a narrative about their situation that may change as the helping partnership develops. Given that the issues that families bring to the social worker are likely to be complex, the assessment process will also be complex, and at times interpretations of issues by different family members may be contradictory. The social worker needs to take care to ensure that there are no missed opportunities and that contradictory messages from family members are thoroughly explored because they often contain information that will assist in the finding of solutions.

Some of the assessment tools used in this phase include:

- *Systems assessment:* Here the focus is on the social worker's understanding that what happens in the everyday lives that families face may prevent them from finding solutions (Morison Dore, 1993). For example, many parents struggle to parent their children well, not because they do not desire to, but because there are factors that prevent them from doing so. They may struggle with the daily tasks associated with being a parent. They may be poor, experience ill health, parent alone, or have negative experiences that prevent them from developing effective solution-finding strategies. Here social workers listen to the stories about how families organize their daily lives and what it is that works for them in their daily routines and what it is that gets in the way.

- *Assessment of family history:* Past experiences influence the current everyday experiences of families. For example, parents' negative experiences in childhood may prevent them from developing positive strategies with their own children and with other adults in the family. These past experiences may also prevent them from having aspirations and dreams for their family.

- *Asking questions differently:* The social worker can support the family to tell its story and to reflect on all of the factors that have influenced family life. Many families have not had the opportunity to explore what family life is about for them and how they would like it to be for all family members. Taking time on this enables the family to build trust and confidence in the social worker that will provide a strong foundation for subsequent interactions and interventions.

- *Discovering successful change strategies:* Social workers need to understand how hard it can be for families to believe that change is possible. Families may have internalized the discourses that have labeled them as difficult families and unable to care for each other. Moreover, families who are struggling to find the basic resources for survival often feel marginalized and isolated and unable to fully utilize the resources available to them. This strategy involves working with the family to identify where and in what situations they have been successful. This information is then used to identify strategies for addressing current issues.

These factors remind us that the assessment process is not just about what families are not able to do and what is getting in the way, but it is also a process that enables families to identify what it is that they have achieved despite difficult circumstances. It is important that the assessment does not become a checklist for what has gone wrong in the past but rather that it provides a framework for thinking differently and creatively about what it is that has enabled families to survive despite these difficulties. Many families have been continually assessed, and this has often not resulted in any positive outcomes for the family. Norman (2000, p. 2) challenges social workers to resist working with clients to find "evermore sophisticated formulations of their problems" while ignoring the factors that will be significant for achieving and sustaining positive change.

Identifying Possible Solutions and Planning for Positive Change

In the process of hearing the family's story, the social worker and the family are identifying strengths and finding solutions. Planning takes place throughout the assessment phases and into the intervention phase and through until termination. A reflective approach to practice means that, at times, plans will need to be revised and new strategies identified. Central to the planning process is the focus on analysis and being prepared to explore a range of alternative meanings and interpretations (Milner & O'Byrne, 2002). The supervision of social work practice is critical here, and social workers can use this opportunity to test out interpretations and strategies. Unlike some of the traditional approaches in which clients have not been actively involved in the assessment process, constructivist processes are built on the key principle that assessment involves the development of a shared understanding of issues and solutions and that the client is central in this process (Cooper, 2001). Assessment work is completed together within a strong partnership between worker and client. The success of this phase will have a significant influence on the success of intervention strategies (Milner & O'Byrne, 2002).

Planning involves making short- and long-term goals, outlining a pathway and direction for the change process, and identifying intervention strategies. This process can provide an opportunity for social workers and families to test out possible intervention strategies and the accuracy of assessment observations. For example, families who are unable to see possibilities for change may work with the social worker to try out alternative ways of operating. Take the example of parents who are having difficulty relating to their teenager. The worker may assist the parents to find a moment in the day to be with their teenager when there are no expectations other than to be together for 15 minutes. When this is achieved, the parents may be able to work to find other times when they have been able to relate positively with their teenager. The focus here is on a reframing of a difficult situation in which everything appears to be negative to one in which there are glimpses of what is possible in this relationship. Discovering how and where success has been achieved can disrupt the overwhelming feeling of incompetence felt by many families. The reframing and reinterpretation of everyday activities, routines, and relationships within the family and the achievement of small changes can assist families to find out how seemingly intractable issues can be addressed and long-term positive change achieved.

Planning for positive change must have a realistic focus for families and be connected to what they can manage at any point in time. For example, the parents of children with disabilities often find that the demands of support services are too great and often expect too much of all family members (Hughson, 2003; Saleebey, 2006). Many cite the example of the demands placed on them to ensure that their children are fully involved in a range of educational, recreational, and social activities. In this situation, the needs of family members conflict, and unrealistic expectations may be placed on siblings whose own activities then become disrupted. Although not wanting to abandon the belief that success is possible and solutions can always be found, social workers must also listen to their clients' genuine concerns about balancing the needs of all family members as they seek solutions to their current issues.

As with the first phase in the assessment process, the planning phase also requires the social worker to be creative in supporting the family to explore alternative meanings about the issues presented and to find solutions to these. The themes identified in the previous phases also have relevance for this phase. In addition, consideration must be given to identifying and planning for solutions. This particular aspect has some key characteristics and includes some specific tools and strategies:

- *Understanding context in the planning process:* The social worker needs to reflect on meaning frameworks and context and how this influences planning for solutions. For example, if working with a cultural group other than one's own, alternative-knowledge frameworks must be acknowledged and incorporated in all phases of the helping process. Recognizing the diversity that families bring to the helping relationship is a powerful strategy that allows the social worker to harness different strategies and utilize a wide range of resources.

This may include using interpreters and cultural advisors who can assist the social worker to have fresh perspectives on the issues being presented. Taking care of the traditions that cultures have around important activities such as greeting and welcoming visitors, forming relationships, and acknowledging ancestors and others who are part of extended family networks will bring richness to the helping partnership and enable the social worker to form authentic relationships with clients (Munford & Sanders, 2011).

- *Multileveled interventions:* The previous point is closely connected to social workers' abilities to work on a number of levels. They need to be able to assess the availability of resources both within and external to the family. Often they will work with social workers involved at other levels of practice to ensure that family needs are met, for example, those working in advocacy roles. At other times, they will be working at an organizational level to ensure that services remain relevant for families and can contribute positively to the change process (Sanders & Munford, 2003).

- *Identifying multiple intervention strategies:* In planning for the intervention, social workers need to be familiar with a wide range of strategies and, if necessary, seek assistance from these. For example, in working on parenting issues with a family who is supporting a child with mental-health issues, securing some home support so parents can have some time out may become an important and effective strategy to initiate during the assessment phase. Comprehensive assessments and planning processes incorporate holistic approaches and include: practical assistance (such as organizing child care and home support and transport to support groups), environmental change (arranging for adaptation to the home environment so a child with disabilities can learn to cook), and service provision (arranging for a medical assessment to ensure that a child's challenging behavior is not connected to a health-related issue).

- *Maintaining a reflective stance:* In forming a partnership with the family, the social worker would have responded effectively and sensitively to the factors that contribute to the way in which family life is organized. This continues into the intervention phase. The planning process provides another opportunity to reflect on one's responsiveness to the family and to identify what barriers may emerge in the intervention phase. For example, the social worker may have noticed that tension was developing in the way he or she had related to a young person and to the parents. For example, the parents, given the way they run their household, may want all contact and communication between the social worker and the teenager to be first approved by them. If the social worker makes an assessment that this may create some difficulties in the intervention phase, the planning process can provide an opportunity to address this matter.

- *Evaluation of family support networks:* An effective planning process should include a review of how families are going to be supported to utilize their own networks in the change process. This strongly connects to the principle that social workers must not be seen as central in families' lives and that they must not disrupt the naturally occurring support networks that families have developed over time (Munford & Sanders, 1999). A strategy for the social worker is not to be the replacement for these networks but to support families to reactivate networks that may have become inactive or to develop alternative networks. For example, families may need to establish new networks as their children move through the education system and develop new interests and connections. Families may also need to be assisted to find more productive and nurturing networks if those they currently have are harmful to their well-being, such as gang associations. The central point here for the social worker is to remain focused on the principle that families are at the center of their own change process (Gilligan, 2004) and that one of the social worker's key tasks is to assist families to fully utilize the resources within their own contexts.

This section focused on the microlevel and direct work with families. This work is closely connected to work on the mezzolevel where workers will carry out interventions in the environments that will impact on family life including organizations, communities of interest, and neighborhoods. In the discussion on the microlevel, connections to the mezzolevel were introduced; we now turn to a discussion of the mezzolevel.

The Mezzolevel

This work is often based within community organizations that have a mandate to work alongside families to improve community environments and to develop more effective organizational responses to the needs of families. Many of the factors that are present in direct assessment work with families are also evident at the mezzolevel. For example, the close connection between theory and practice and the way one informs the other is often recognized in work at the mezzolevel, as is the highlighting of local knowledge and the harnessing of the experiences of communities and their past history in resolving issues. Context is also important, and typically this involves social workers recognizing that families live their everyday lives within particular contexts and that these will influence how they can exercise agency over the matters that impact on family life. Social workers must also acknowledge the connections between the local and the global and the way in which global issues impact daily lives within neighborhoods and other communities of interest (Alston, 2009). The key theoretical approaches informing this work have historically been based on critical approaches (Fook, 2003; Ife, 1997); those that focus on empowerment and structural change; feminist and radical approaches; and, in more recent times, indigenous approaches.

There are a number of factors that inform assessment processes within community and organizational settings (Chenoweth & McAuliffe, 2008). These include linking the personal troubles of families to public issues, working with diversity in family and community life, and building strong and nurturing communities.

Linking Personal Troubles to Public Issues

This involves an analysis of the connections between the personal troubles families face and public issues. Structural conditions will have a major influence on family life, either positively or negatively. Take the example of a mother living in public housing, parenting alone, and having difficulty meeting the electricity payments. The community worker, after working with her on an assessment of the situation, discovers that the public housing agency is not meeting its obligations to its tenants. Here the social worker can assist the mother to intervene at this level to effect change. In these circumstances, the client may choose to join the social worker in addressing this immediate need and may also join in working for better conditions for public housing tenants more generally. This will always be a choice on the part of the client. Community workers should have no expectations that clients who are dealing with difficult everyday issues will have energy to give to wider issues. However, for some of these clients, becoming involved in these issues can enhance their self-efficacy and self-determination, as they discover that others are facing similar difficulties as a result of structural conditions and as they begin to see that, through action, they can change some of their material circumstances.

In the process of linking the personal and the political, social workers and clients can develop alternative scenarios for understanding how issues are constructed (Allan et al., 2003). This can provide opportunities for clients to address the factors that have caused them to internalize some of the negative labels (e.g., the assumption that single parents will have parenting challenges and struggle to be good enough parents) and to join with others to gain an understanding of the discourses that have functioned to maintain them in marginalized positions. At this point, they may choose to become actively involved in wider social change processes. It is here that the skilled social worker, working from a community base, is able to assist clients to reexamine the meanings attached to their current positions and to share knowledge as part of the collaborative social change process.

Working With Diversity in Family and Community Life

Assessment at the mezzolevel also involves an understanding of how difference and diversity is constructed within community life. As in direct work with families, social workers must be aware of the different contexts within the community and how these will impact the life events of the family. Take, for example, the position of different cultural groups in the community. It is important for the social worker to know how they are positioned in relation to each other and the way in which different positions may be linked to different resources. This will involve an assessment of historical trends regarding these groups and how the movement of new groups into the community has transformed the cultural and social landscape (Nash, 2005). It will also involve an understanding of the positioning of indigenous groups within dominant structures and how this has influenced the participation of these families in community life and the way in which community level decisions are made (Munford & Sanders, 2011).

Communities are increasingly socially and culturally diverse, drawing people from very different places and with very different backgrounds together. Although, in many ways, this diversification is positive, it does raise some specific issues for social workers who work at the mezzolevel. In particular, the issue of knowing how to build an understanding of the social ecology of neighborhoods and communities and assess the impact of neighborhood characteristics on family life is an essential competency for contemporary social workers (Alston, 2009). For example, migrant families often find themselves unable to participate fully in community life because the dominant cultural frameworks uphold the position of certain belief systems and practices that marginalize their belief systems. Take also the discourses around disability and the inclusion of people with disabilities in community life. Physical environments that do not facilitate easy access are likely to see people with disabilities become increasingly marginalized and isolated. Assessment examines the impacts of these factors on family life, how they may restrict opportunities for families, and how they impact on well-being and quality-of-life issues (Beilharz, 2002).

Building Strong and Nurturing Communities

Social workers operating at the mezzolevel are concerned about how communities enhance or hinder family life. Family life is likely to be enhanced when children are cared for in well-resourced families and communities (in a range of domains such as social, cultural, and economic) and when a range of opportunities are freely available (Munford & Sanders, 2001). Assessment here involves the worker in an examination of how communities are able to provide support to those families who may be isolated and who have restricted informal networks of support. The challenge for social workers in impoverished communities is to identify how formal helping systems can develop innovative strategies that facilitate the establishment of support networks within the local neighborhood. The focus is on providing locally based services and networks that are accessible, identifying and supporting the development of local solutions, and creating local environments that are family friendly.

The building of strong and nurturing communities parallels work with families in that its goal is to strengthen the capacity of communities to respond to issues and to nurture all of their members. It is also strongly connected to approaches that focus on developing strengths within communities (Beilharz, 2002) and strategies that support communities to become self-determining. Many of the major issues confronting families can be addressed on a wider community level (Sanders & Munford, 2001). For example, providing safe environments and community programs for children that underline the importance of nurturing adults being able to participate in children's lives. As Masten and Coatsworth (1998, p. 216) suggest:

> Successful children remind us that children grow up in multiple contexts—in families, schools, peer groups, baseball teams, religious organizations, and many other groups—and each context is a potential source of protective as well as risk factors.

Community strategies that focus on communities and social change combined with family and individual intervention can have a major impact on key issues and can strengthen family and community life.

The assessment tools used at the mezzolevel include:

- *Community profiling:* The social worker carries out an assessment of the naturally occurring networks, local resources, and social ecology of communities and identifies how well these are utilized by community members and how these can be enhanced (Munford & Sanders, 1999). This also includes documentation of changes to the neighborhood over time and how these changes impact family life. Key areas include an evaluation of the physical environment, an analysis of population profiles and changes to this, an analysis of historical changes in the community and their impacts on community life, and an examination of the functioning of community networks and how well these are operating to support families (Munford & Walsh-Tapiata, 2000).

- *Organizational mapping and profiling:* The social worker evaluates the contributions formal organizations are making to family and community life and how well they are working together to support families. It involves tracking service delivery and responsiveness and mapping the interactions and collaboration between organizations. Social workers working within organizations may also use this tool to assess how well their own organization is supporting social work practice with families. Here the social worker may focus on organizational health and well-being (Zunz & Chernesky, 2000) and may facilitate such activities as reviewing how much effort is spent on organizational matters that interrupt direct work with families and the time given to reflective practice.

- *Asset-based inventories:* Emerging directly out of strengths-based approaches (Kretzman & McKnight, 1997), these tools enable the worker to assess the resources, capacities, and strengths of a community. This information is then used to identify intervention strategies that use community capacity and capability to address community-wide issues. The inventory enables the social worker to identify how current capability can be used to address new issues. For example, as part of an initiative to address the needs of young people in the community who are living on the margins of community life, an asset-based inventory can be compiled that identifies the resources available to young people and also considers the acceptability of each of these to specific subgroups. The inventory can also be used as evidence to support the lobbying for changes to existing services or the development of new targeted activities.

- *Structural analysis approaches:* The social worker uses a structured process for bringing groups together to work on a social-change project. The assessment continues throughout the project via a continuous feedback and action and reflection cycle (Munford & Walsh-Tapiata, 2005). The assessment focuses on process and task goals including assessment of group cohesiveness and how to enhance this throughout the project, analysis of the factors contributing to the identified issue, review of possible intervention strategies, and planning for change.

The work carried out at the mezzolevel is closely connected with work at the microlevel. The issues addressed at the community level often emerge out of direct work with families. For example, addressing violence against women and children within direct work often leads to public education and the development of programs designed to involve the community to develop strategies that will respond to the issue from a wider perspective. Organizations may also be involved in contributing to positive change for families more generally as links are made between the personal experiences of clients and the wider contributing factors. Social work organizations can provide valuable information and support to those working on family issues at the community level. Work at the mezzolevel can be closely aligned to the macrolevel, where assessment is concerned with the structures and policies that impact on family life.

The Macrolevel

Work at the macrolevel will connect closely to that done at the mezzolevel (e.g., advocacy typically arises at the mezzolevel, but often targets macrolevel decision makers). However, a key role at the macrolevel involves work in policy analysis and development as well as research and evaluation carried out in a number of key areas in federal, state, regional, and community organizations. For many social workers, this may become the focus of their work, and they may move out of direct practice to engage in these roles. Here, the knowledge they have developed in working directly with families and within communities enables them to critically evaluate the impact of policy development and implementation. Other social workers will remain in direct practice but will be aware that decisions at the macrolevel will have implications for practice and will determine how family services are to be resourced and delivered.

These social workers may take on roles at the macrolevel within their direct delivery roles. This may involve activities such as advocacy for or against policy and practice developments including submission writing and meetings with key stakeholders.

Work at the macrolevel begins with a perspective that acknowledges that what is happening in the daily lives of families is strongly influenced by wider forces (Munford & Sanders, 1999). This work often draws on social justice perspectives (Finn & Jacobson, 2003) that seek to address the needs of the family within a framework that incorporates an understanding of the factors that may prevent families from participation and from finding ways to address their immediate concerns. The work at the macrolevel will be informed by work at other levels. For example, organizations can have a key role in documenting the impact of policy on service provision and delivery, and with this evidence they can demonstrate both positive and negative outcomes of these policies. This work at the macrolevel assists families to see that their issues may not be caused by their actions and relationships, but may, instead, be connected to wider factors. For example, the closure of a key industry in their town, housing policies that increase the rents of public housing, education policies that decrease the support given to children with challenging behavior, and welfare policies that expect mothers and fathers to be in the paid workforce but do not provide enough financial resource for the delivery of quality child-care services. These examples illustrate that changes in local economies and punitive government policies can result in inadequate resources for families and can together, in turn, make it difficult to focus on creating changes in patterns of family relations. The social worker may choose to become part of the process of challenging these policies while assisting families to mediate the effects on family life. Social work is "on the boundary between private lives and public concerns" and what happens within "individual, specific applications" is strongly connected to wider issues (Cooper, 2001, p. 722).

Assessment tools at the macrolevel include:

- *Policy analysis, development, and critique:* Policy development and implementation is assessed for the impact on family life. Those working within organizations charged with developing policy for families must engage in consultation processes that involve the ideas of key stakeholders such as families and social workers. There will be pressure on these workers to assess the costs and benefits of policies from all perspectives often within a tightly constrained fiscal environment. This pressure can make it difficult to retain a focus on what types of policies are beneficial for families.

- *Advocacy:* This is a key role at the macrolevel and may include class advocacy focused on particular issues or case advocacy on behalf of clients. Assessment involves the gathering and synthesizing of information from a range of sources. It will also include historical and comparative investigation so that successful strategies adopted in earlier issues and cases or in other jurisdictions can be used to inform current advocacy processes.

- *Research and evaluation:* Assessment is focused on researching and evaluating the outcomes of programs and services and developing or synthesizing new ideas. Social workers need skills in gathering and investigating information from a range of sources. This will include working with social workers and clients to assist them to present their information on services and programs and to become involved in the evaluation of these. This work can be strongly connected to reflective practice in which social workers are encouraged to make links between their everyday experiences of clients and the factors that enhance or hinder the achievement of well-being (Maluccio et al., 2011).

It can be argued that effective social work assessment will include knowing how to achieve deep understandings of family life in a range of contexts on a range of levels—the micro, mezzo, and macro. Although not all social workers will be involved at all levels, it is essential that they understand how the relationships within these levels and the interactions between them will impact on the everyday experiences of families.

Conclusion

This chapter has taken a broad approach to the assessment of families and has examined social work at the micro-, mezzo- and macrolevels of practice. It began with a discussion of the historical perspectives on the assessment of families. This revealed that, over time, theoretical perspectives informing assessment processes had changed in response to a range of demands, including those from the profession, clients, and the wider society. The discussion on the evidence about what constitutes best practice in assessment demonstrated that practice is influenced by changes in the contexts of family life and in social work practice. An underlying theme in this chapter has been that assessment processes must be sensitive to and respond appropriately to the diversity of family life and be able to accommodate new frameworks of knowledge that will continue to influence the development of social work practice in the future.

Key Terms

Context	Diversity	Partnerships
Strengths based	Relationship building	

Review Questions for Critical Thinking

1. Why is an understanding of the context of family life an important component of effective-assessment processes?

2. Identify three key concepts of strengths-based practice.

3. Why is an understanding of diversity, including culture, an important factor in effective assessment processes?

4. Identify why relationship building and forming partnerships with families is important in creating effective assessment processes.

5. Think of examples from your practice to illustrate the micro-, mezzo-, and macrolevels of assessment processes and identify the evidence for why these are effective.

Online Resources

www.ifsw.org International Federation of Social Workers (IFSW) – This is a very useful website for students to keep informed of developments in social work practice around the globe. It provides an excellent starting point for students to discover what is new in practice at the micro, mezzo and macro levels.

http://ifp.nyu.edu/ This website is a useful resource for those wishing to keep abreast of current developments on practice. Students interested in social work with families can search this website for current information on family research and practice.

http://resilience.socialwork.dal.ca/ This website provides information on cutting-edge research on children, young people, and families. It is based in Canada but includes up-to-date information on research from around the globe.

http://www.parentingcouncil.org.nz/clearinghouse.html This website has connections with international clearinghouses that provide information on research on family life. It is a useful resource for students who are interested in keeping informed of developments in the provision of support for families.

http://www.scie.org.uk/Index.aspx This UK website provides knowledge about what works in practice. It provides practical examples and resources and draws primarily on information from the UK but also from around the globe; its broad approach to social issues and the social services will be of interest to social workers who work in collaboration with other professionals.

References

Allan, J., Pease, B., & Briskman, L. (2003). *Critical social work: An introduction to theories and practice.* Sydney, Australia: Allen & Unwin.

Alston, M. (2009). Working with communities. In M. Connolly & L. Harms (Eds.), *Social work: contexts and practice* (pp. 345–359). Melbourne, Australia: Oxford.

Beilharz, L. (2002). *Building community: The shared action experience.* Bendigo, Australia: St. Luke's Innovative Resources.

Chenoweth, L., & McAuliffe, D. (2008). *The road to social work and human service practice.* Melbourne, Australia: Cengage Learning.

Clegg, S. (2005). Evidence-based practice in educational research: A critical realist critique of systematic review. *British Journal of Sociology of Education, 26*(3), 415–428.

Cooper, B. (2001). Constructivism in social work: Towards a participative practice viability. *British Journal of Social Work, 31,* 721–737.

Corcoran, J. (2005). *Building strengths and skills: A collaborative approach to working with clients.* New York, NY: Oxford University Press.

Corwin, M. D. (2006). Culturally competent community-based clinical practice: A critical review. In A. Lightburn & P. Sessions (Eds.), *Handbook of community-based clinical practice* (pp. 99–110). New York, NY: Oxford University Press.

Dawson, K., & Berry, M. (2002). Engaging families in child welfare services: An evidence-based approach to best practice. *Child Welfare League of America, 81*(2), 293–317.

Dei, G. J. S., Hall, B. L., & Rosenberg, D. G. (2000). *Indigenous knowledges in global contexts: Multiple readings of our world.* Toronto, Canada: University of Toronto Press.

Dolan, P., Canavan, J., & Pinkerton, J. (2006). *Family support as reflective practice.* London, UK: Jessica Kingsley.

Dominelli, L. (1996). Deprofessionalising social work: Anti-oppressive practice, competences, and postmodernism. *British Journal of Social Work, 26,* 153–175.

Dominelli, L. (1998). Anti-oppressive practice in context. In R. Adams, L. Dominelli, & M. Payne (Eds.), *Social work: Themes, issues, and critical debates* (pp. 3–22). Houndmills, UK: Macmillan.

Durie, M. (1995). *Whaiora, maori health development.* Auckland, New Zealand: Oxford University Press.

Egan, G. (2002). *The skilled helper: A problem-management and opportunity-development approach to helping.* Pacific Grove, CA: Brooks/Cole.

Ellis, K., & Dean, H. (2000). *Social policy and the body: Transitions in corporeal discourse.* Houndmills, UK: Macmillan.

Ferguson, P., & O'Brien, P. (2005). From giving service to being of service. In P. O'Brien & M. Sullivan (Eds.), *Allies in emancipation: Shifting from providing service to being of support* (pp. 3–18). Melbourne, Australia: Thomson.

Finn, J. L., & Jacobson, M. (2003). Just practice: Steps toward a new social work paradigm. *Journal of Social Work Education, 39*(1), 57–78.

Fook, J. (2002). *Social work: Critical theory and practice.* London, UK: Sage.

Fook, J. (2003). Critical social work: The current issues. *Qualitative Social Work, 2*(2), 123–130.

Gilligan, R. (2000). Family support: Issues and prospects. In J. Canavan, P. Dolan, & J. Pinkerton (Eds.), *Family support: Direction from diversity* (pp. 13–34). London, UK: Jessica Kingsley.

Gilligan, R. (2004). Promoting resilience in child and family social work: Issues for social work practice. *Social Work Education, 23*(1), 93–104.

Healy, K. (2000). *Social work practices: Contemporary perspectives on change.* London, UK: Sage.

Healy, K. (2005). *Social work theories in context: Creating frameworks for practice.* New York, NY: Macmillan.

Holland, S. (2004). *Child and family assessment in social work practice.* London, UK: Sage.

Hughson, A. (2003). Evaluation research in social programmes: The centrality of families. In R. Munford & J. Sanders (Eds.), *Making a difference in families: Research that creates change* (pp. 171–192). Sydney, Australia: Allen & Unwin.

Ife, J. (1997). *Rethinking social work: Towards critical practice*. Melbourne, Australia: Longman.

Ife, J. (2001). *Human rights and social work: Towards rights-based practice*. Cambridge, UK: Cambridge University Press.

Johnson, L. C., & Yanca, S. J. (2004). *Social work practice: A generalist approach*. Boston, MA: Pearson.

Kretzman, J., & McKnight, J. (1997). *A guide to capacity inventories: Mobilizing the community skills of local residents*. Chicago, IL: ACTA.

Lightburn, A., & Sessions, P. (2006). Community-based clinical practice: Recreating the culture of care. In A. Lightburn & P. Sessions (Eds.), *Handbook of community-based clinical practice* (pp. 19–35). New York, NY: Oxford University Press.

Maluccio, A. N., Canali, C., Vecchiato, T., Lightburn, A., Aldgate, J., & Rose, W. (2011). *Improving outcomes for children and families*. London, UK: Jessica Kingsley.

Margolin, L. (1997). *Under the cover of kindness*. Charolottesville: University Press of Virginia.

Masten, A., & Coatsworth, D. (1998). The development of competence in favourable and unfavourable environments: Lessons from research on successful children. *American Psychologist, 53*(20), 205–220.

Mataira, P. J. (2002). Treaty partnering: Establishment of a charter for Maori community based programmes. *Te Komako, Social Work Review, 14*(2), 5–7.

McCartt Hess, P., McGowan, B. G., & Botsko, M. (2003). *Nurturing the one, supporting the many: The Center for Family Life in Sunset Park, Brooklyn*. New York, NY: Columbia University Press.

McNeill, F. (2001). Developing effectiveness: Frontline perspectives. *Social Work Education, 20*(6), 671–687.

Milner, J., & O'Byrne, P. (2002). *Assessment in social work*. London, UK: Macmillan.

Morison Dore, M. (1993). Family preservation and poor families: When ''homebuilding'' is not enough. *Families in Society*, November 545–556.

Munford, R., & Sanders, J. (1999). *Supporting families*. Palmerston North, New Zealand: Dunmore.

Munford, R., & Sanders, J. (with Andrew, A., Butler, P., Kaipuke, R., & Ruwhiu, L.). (2001). Aotearoa/New Zealand: Working differently with communities and families. In C. Warren-Adamson (Ed.), *Family centres and their international role in social action* (pp. 146–162). Aldershot, UK: Ashgate.

Munford, R., & Sanders, J. (2003). *Making a difference in families: Research that creates change*. Sydney, Australia: Allen & Unwin.

Munford, R., & Sanders, J. (2005). Working with families: Strengths-based approaches. In M. Nash, R. Munford, & K. O'Donoghue (Eds.), *Social work theories in action* (pp. 158–173). London, UK: Jessica Kingsley.

Munford, R., & Sanders, J. (2011). Embracing the diversity of practice: Indigenous knowledge and mainstream social work practice. *Journal of Social Work Practice, 25*(1), 63–77.

Munford, R., & Walsh-Tapiata, W. (2000). *Strategies for change: Community development in Aotearoa, New Zealand*. Palmerston North, New Zealand: Massey University.

Munford, R., & Walsh-Tapiata, W. (2005). Community development: Principles into practice. In M. Nash, R. Munford, & K. O'Donoghue (Eds.), *Social work theories in action* (pp. 97–112). London, UK: Jessica Kingsley.

Nash, M. (2005). Responding to settlement needs: Migrants and refugees and community development. In M. Nash, R. Munford, & K. O'Donoghue

(Eds.), *Social work theories in action* (pp. 140–154). London, UK: Jessica Kingsley.

Norman, E. (2000). *Resiliency enhancement: Putting the strengths perspective into social work practice.* New York, NY: Columbia University Press.

O'Hare, T. (2005). *Evidence-based practices for social workers: An interdisciplinary approach.* Chicago, IL: Lyceum.

O'Neil, D. (2003). Clients as researchers: The benefits of strengths-based research. In R. Munford & J. Sanders (Eds.), *Making a difference in families: Research that creates change* (pp. 113–129). Sydney, Australia: Allen & Unwin.

Parton, N. (2000). Preface. In P. Stepney & D. Ford (Eds.), *Social work models, methods and theories* (pp. v–vi). Dorset, UK: Russell House.

Parton, N., & O'Byrne, P. (2000). *Constructive social work: Towards a new practice.* Houndmills, England: Palgrave.

Roberts, A. R., & Yeager, K. R. (2006). *Foundations of evidence-based social work practice.* New York, NY: Oxford University Press.

Roberts, R. W., & Nee, R. H. (1970). *Theories of social casework.* Chicago, IL: University of Chicago Press.

Saleebey, D. (2002). *The strengths perspective in social work practice.* White Plains, NY: Longman.

Saleebey, D. (2006). A paradigm shift in developmental perspectives? The self in context. In A. Lightburn & P. Sessions (Eds.), *Handbook of community-based clinical practice* (pp. 3–18). New York, NY: Oxford University Press.

Sanders, J., & Munford, R. (2001). *Heart work and hard mahi: A report on the first 18 months of the Highbury Whanau Resource Centre's Alternative Education Programme.* Palmerston North, New Zealand: Massey University.

Sanders, J., & Munford, R. (2003). Strengthening practice through research: Research in organizations. In R. Munford & J. Sanders (Eds.), *Making a difference in families: Research that creates change* (pp. 151–170). Sydney, Australia: Allen & Unwin.

Sanders, J., & Munford, R. (2010). *Working with families: Strengths-based approaches.* Palmerston North, New Zealand: Dunmore Press.

Sessions, P., & Lightburn, A. (2006). What is community-based clinical practice? Traditions and transformations. In A. Lightburn & P. Sessions (Eds.), *Handbook of community-based clinical practice* (pp. 3–18). New York, NY: Oxford University Press.

Stepney, P., & Ford, D. (2000). *Social work models, methods and theories.* Dorset, UK: Russell House.

Sullivan, M., & Munford, R. (2005). Disability and support: The interface between disability theory and support: An individual challenge. In P. O'Brien & M. Sullivan (Eds.), *Allies in emancipation: Shifting from providing service to being of support* (pp. 19–34). Melbourne, Australia: Thomson.

Thompson, N. (2002). *Building the future: Social work with children, young people and their families.* Dorset, UK: Russell House.

Waldegrave, C. (1990). Just therapy. *Dulwich Center Newsletter, 1,* 6–47.

Warren-Adamson, C., & Lightburn, A. (2006). Developing a community-based model for integrated family center practice. In A. Lightburn & P. Sessions (Eds.), *Handbook of community-based clinical practice* (pp. 261–284). New York, NY: Oxford University Press.

Zunz, S. J., & Chernesky, R. H. (2000). The workplace as a protective environment: Management strategies. In E. Norman (Ed.), *Resiliency enhancement: Putting the strengths perspective into social work practice* (pp. 157–176). New York, NY: Columbia University Press.

Chapter 10
Intervention With Families

Cynthia Franklin, Catheleen Jordan, and Laura Hopson

> **Purpose:** This chapter reviews the historical development of family therapy, the existing research evidence on the effectiveness of various approaches, and the importance of family interventions for social work practice at the micro-, mezzo-, and macrolevels.
>
> **Rationale:** To educate readers about evidence-informed family interventions and how this has become a valuable tool in social work practice.
>
> **How evidence-informed practice is presented:** This chapter focuses on evidence about various theories routinely used by practitioners with a variety of families.
>
> **Overarching question:** How would you select and use an evidence-informed intervention with a family you are working with?

The ecological systems perspective that guides social work practice calls for intervention on multiple levels to achieve treatment goals. For this reason, social work practice often engages families in sessions rather than working with an individual alone. Family intervention takes many forms, and the definition of the family may vary widely. The family is the center of attention (Hartman & Laird, 1983). In some cases, family therapy may consist primarily of an individual and his or her spouse or significant other. In others, parents, children, and grandparents may all be involved in sessions. It is helpful to involve any family member who is connected with or influences a client's reason for seeking help. Even when individuals seek social work services for help with an issue that they view as their own individual problem, the ecosystems perspective calls for engaging family members who have an important connection with that individual. In other situations, clients may begin by seeking help as a family unit, involving parents, children, and other family members from the first session.

The ecosystems perspective theorizes that intervening to change dynamics in one part of a system can improve functioning in other parts of the system. Thus, intervening to improve relationships within the family system can improve the functioning of the individual family members (Franklin & Jordan, 1999). Improving the communication between an individual and his or her estranged parent may result in improved communication between the individual and a spouse or child as well. The stress that is alleviated by improving family interactions can result in improvements in school performance and mental-health status. Because social workers understand the importance of working with an individual within their environment, family intervention has become a valuable tool in social work practice. This chapter reviews the development of family therapy, the existing research evidence on the effectiveness of various approaches, and the importance of family intervention for social work practice at the micro-, mezzo-, and macrolevels.

Historical Background

Although understanding family history and characteristics was highly valued among the earliest social workers, family intervention did not become a formal mode of treatment until the 1950s. Before that time, practitioners worked primarily with the individual (Janzen, Harris, Jordan, & Franklin, 2005). Early social workers performing casework, or case management, roles often worked through organizations called "family service" agencies. Yet, the progression from working with individuals to working with families did not occur until later. The emphasis on psychoanalysis and the mental hygiene movement was on rehabilitating the individual. Thus, social workers and other mental health practitioners did not typically focus on the family. Even when practitioners recognized the value of working with the family, the traditional psychoanalytic model did not lend itself well to this practice (Hartman & Laird, 1983).

As social workers began to shift from working with individuals to families, they began to change the way they viewed the presenting problem. A difficulty experienced by the individual was viewed as an issue involving family dynamics. The behavior of a child who was disruptive in school, for example, was no longer viewed as simply a child with disruptive behaviors. Instead the social worker might explore family interaction styles, including household rules, discipline, consistency, and communication styles of the parents in defining the goals for intervention.

The development of systems theory as a general orientation that guided social work practice provided a framework for working with families more effectively. Systems theory is concerned with the social, structural, and interactional foundations of behavior. The focus is on problematic patterns of family communication or interaction rather than deficits of a particular family member. Early practitioners of systemic approaches drew on general systems theory and sociological theories, such as structural functionalism, to guide their interventions. Later theorists incorporated ideas from cybernetics and ecological theory resulting in approaches such as Hartman and Laird's family-centered ecological systems model (Franklin & Jordan, 1999; Hartman & Laird, 1983). Systems theory posits that behavior is a result of interactions with others in the environment. The structure and patterns of interaction within a family will influence the behavior of each family member (Franklin & Jordan, 1999). Practice consistent with systems theory calls for working with the family as well as considering the environmental factors affecting the family (Hartman & Laird, 1983).

Structural family therapy, developed by Salvador Minuchin in the 1970s, and strategic family therapy developed by Jay Haley were among the earliest family intervention models. These perspectives viewed family functioning as a result of structure, subsystems, and boundaries. These structural and interactional components drive relationship patterns between family members. Every family has spoken or unspoken rules that govern these interactions. Family subsystems are defined as family members who are joined to perform particular family functions (Janzen et al., 2005). Parents, for example, are a subsystem whose purpose is to raise the children in the family. Boundaries are conceptual barriers to interactions within the family. A boundary commonly exists between the subsystems of children and parents. A helpful boundary between parents and children may be evidenced by the parents' ability to communicate family rules and feelings of love and support to children while refraining from discussing other topics, such as stress within the parental subsystem resulting from financial difficulties or relationship problems. Structural and strategic models of family therapy greatly influenced social work practice by defining the way presenting problems were conceptualized and guiding techniques used with families.

Other early family therapy approaches that influenced social work family practice include the gestalt approach, developed by Kempler, and the communicative-interactive approach, developed by Satir. These and other influential models view family functioning in terms of connections and separations from various family members (Janzen et al., 2005). When difficulties arise within the family, the practitioner explores whether connections or alliances between family members are contributing to the presenting problem. It may also be that the absence of connections between family members is contributing more to the problem than existing connections. When the mother is estranged from the father in a family, for example, the result may be behavior problems in the children.

Tools that developed from early treatment approaches and are still commonly used to understand family interactions are roles, rules, homeostasis, and triangulation. *Family roles* are the positions each member holds in the family that govern their interactions with the other family members. If the mother's role is that of the caretaker, she may be designated as the family member who takes the children to school and doctor's appointments and is expected to take time off from work when the children are ill. One parent may take on the role of primary decision maker. When important family issues are discussed, the other parent will typically defer to the decision maker, who will make the final decision (Janzen et al., 2005).

Homeostasis refers to a tendency among family members to balance out efforts to change interactions. If a child's behavior problems serve a function within a family system by distracting parents from their own relationship difficulties, they may behave in subtle ways that encourage the ongoing behavior problems because improving the child's behavior would disrupt the family equilibrium. Closely related to the example used earlier, *triangulation* occurs when two people in a family focus energy on a third to relieve tension. In the previous example, the parents relieve tension by triangulating the child and focusing their attention on the child's behavior problems rather than their own relationship difficulties (Janzen et al., 2005).

Rules are spoken or unspoken agreements about the behavior and interactions of family members. A spoken family rule could include a child's responsibility to help prepare a meal or care for a younger sibling after school while the parents are at work. Often, the most powerful rules are unspoken. There may be an unspoken family rule that a grandparent's problem with alcohol abuse is never discussed. This has important implications for family intervention because, often, the intervention will require discussing and potentially changing unspoken family rules (Janzen et al., 2005).

The techniques and concepts developed in the early family intervention models continue to appear in modern family interventions. One primary difference in the current climate, however, is the emphasis on providing evidence for the effectiveness of intervention techniques.

Summary of Current Evidence-Based Intervention With Families

In today's practice environment, social workers and other helping professionals are increasingly called on to demonstrate the effectiveness of their interventions. Many family intervention models have been well researched and are effective in achieving positive outcomes, such as reduced behavior problems and improved family interactions.

In order to obtain funding from state and federal agencies, community-based organizations must demonstrate that they are using evidence-based practices (EBP). In addition, practitioners are often called on to demonstrate that their interventions with clients are resulting in positive outcomes that are tied directly to treatment goals. Often, they are required to deliver interventions that can produce positive change within a brief period of time (Franklin & Jordan, 1999). They may be required to provide explanations for continuing work with a particular family for more than 2 to 3 months, for example.

Because cost containment systems are commonly used to finance health and mental-health care, it has greatly influenced the delivery of services. In order to maximize efficiency and contain costs, managed care companies typically pay only for treatments that are proven to be brief and effective (Franklin & Jordan, 1999). Cost containment and the demand for evidence-based practices has changed the practice of family therapy by encouraging the use of practices grounded in research, the use of outcome measures in evaluating interventions with clients, group rather than individual interventions, goal-oriented treatment planning, and time-limited, rather than long-term, therapy (Franklin & Jordan, 1999).

Evidence-Based Practices

Though many definitions of EBP saturate the literature, we offer two definitions that most closely define our understanding of the concept and serve to explicate our vision of EBP:

> The use of the best available scientific knowledge derived from randomized controlled outcome studies, and meta-analyses of existing outcome studies, as one basis for guiding professional interventions and effective therapies, combined with professional ethical standards, clinical judgment, and practice wisdom.
>
> —(Barker, 2003, p. 149)

> ...the integration of the best research evidence with our clinical expertise and our patient's unique values and circumstances.
>
> —(Strauss, Richardson, Glasziou, & Haynes, 2005, p. 1)

We realize that the debate about EBP is sometimes polarized, but we offer definitions of EBP broad enough to take into account its limitations. For example, critics have charged that there is not enough available evidence to guide practice; therefore, the few available evidence-based micro- and macrolevel interventions would be too limited to be of use to clients. However, we take this into account and agree with Gray (2001) who says, "the leading figures in EBP...emphasized that clinicians had to use their scientific training and their judgment to interpret (guidelines) and individualize care accordingly" (p. 26).

Though there is some disagreement in the literature regarding the definition of EBP, the field of family treatment is informed by rigorous standards. According to the most rigorous standard, an intervention is considered evidence-based if it has been evaluated in a well-controlled experimental design in which participants were randomly assigned to treatment and control conditions, and the intervention resulted in statistically significant positive outcomes for participants. Often, the designation requires that the positive outcomes have been replicated in other well-controlled research. Because such a design is often difficult or impossible to achieve in community organizations that provide mental-health services to families, less well-controlled research, quasi-experimental designs have been deemed as acceptable for defining an intervention as evidence based. Quasi-experimental designs are often used when it is not possible to randomly assign families to intervention and control conditions due to agency rules and standards for treatment. The evidence-based interventions described next include those that have been evaluated using well-controlled experimental designs, and those evaluated using strong quasi-experimental designs.

Evidence-based interventions have many common characteristics regarding the format in which services are delivered and the content included in the curricula. A list of these elements include the following:

Format of Effective Practices

- Use of group and/or family sessions rather than relying on individual sessions alone.
- Brief in duration, lasting approximately 6 weeks.
- Limited number of sessions (10–15).
- A written manual that provides step-by-step guidelines for each session.
- Use of multiple approaches to changing behavior (i.e., instructional and skill building components).
- Intervening on multiple ecological levels (i.e., child, parent, teacher).
- Family approaches that have foundations in cognitive behavioral, structural, or strategic therapy.

Content Included in Effective Practices

- Program content addresses general life skills or knowledge and skills related to drug use.
- Opportunities to practice newly learned skills such as modeling and practicing behaviors and completing homework assignments, such as practicing skills at home with family members.
- Emphasis on the importance of family, school, and community support to create a culture that promotes shared accountability for change.
- Programs promoted a consistent prevention message that is communicated by families, schools, and community members.
- Student strengths rather than deficits as the program's focus.
- Programs that serve ethnically and culturally diverse youth tailored materials for the target group and often used bicultural facilitators. Simply translating a curriculum into another language was insufficient in promoting intervention effectiveness with minority youth (Schinke, Brounstein, & Gardner, 2002).
- Communication and problem-solving skills.
- Behavioral goal setting.
- Target changes in different systems (e.g., family, school, peer group).
- Providing feedback about behavior (Roans & Hoagwood, 2000; Schinke et al., 2002).

Before discussing family interventions with solid research support, we will identify clinical assessment techniques, as well as treatment-planning techniques, that help us to arrive at the correct intervention. These concepts—assessment, treatment planning, and intervention—are necessarily linked and cannot stand alone. Following a discussion of each, we discuss the final element of a complete approach to family treatment, treatment monitoring.

Family Assessment

Assessment techniques inform treatment planning and selection; these techniques may be qualitative, quantitative, or a combination of the two approaches. Levine (as cited in Jordan & Franklin, 2003) identifies common features of social work assessment models:

- *Social work assessment emphasizes both individuals and their social environments*: Viewing clients in their contexts of families, groups, and communities is the preferred approach to assessment.

- *Social work assessment includes the strengths and resilience of clients*: It is equally important to assess competencies and strengths as it is to address problem areas and pathologies. The goals of most approaches include increasing the self-efficacy of clients, restoring or supporting their inherent problem-solving capacities, and returning clients to their best adaptive functioning.

- *Most social work assessment models are integrative and rely on more than one underlying theory*: The theory base of social work practice is extremely eclectic. Social work models combine multiple theories in their assessment and practice focuses. Social work is interprofessional by nature, and social workers usually are employed in host settings. Knowledge from several fields is also integrated into social work assessment and practice.

- *Assessments de-emphasize long history taking*: Overall, history for the sake of history taking has been de-emphasized, even in models such as the psychosocial that traditionally focused on this information. Instead, only relevant history is used in a more strategic manner to understand presenting problems and needed interventions.

- *Assessments are organized around task-centered planning or goal orientations*: The purpose of assessment across models is to resolve presenting problems or to move clients toward desired goals. Assessments across social work models focus mostly on the present contexts and future behaviors that client's desire.

- *Social work assessments share common types of information*: Even though different tools and methods are used across models for gathering information from clients, social work models appear to share in common the types of information that are valued in constructing assessments. All models share problem definitions, identified strengths, specific goals, intervention planning or solution building, and outcome monitoring.

- *Social work assessments use a collaborative process between client and practitioner*: Social work models all show a preference for collaborative work with clients in gathering information and goal construction. Shared power and client-centered perspectives are important to the clinical assessment process. This stands in contrast to more authoritative approaches in which the practitioner is seen as the only expert on the client and his or her problems.

- *Assessments in social work emphasize brief, time-limited perspectives*: The preference for brevity and short-term assessments and interventions is acknowledged by all practice models reviewed. This is perhaps driven by the current-day realities of the practice environments in which practitioners work as well as the applied and human problem-solving nature of social work practice. (pp. 37–38)

Assessment as we have described it fits in nicely with an EBP approach. Assessment using this approach is integrative and follows theoretically, with Lazarus's technical eclecticism that "assumes that practice methods from different underlying theoretical models may be used together [and] . . . choice is based on research support for the technique or the best available practice wisdom" (Jordan & Franklin, 2011, p. 29).

Franklin & Sanchez (2011) provide a rationale for using quantitative measurement in assessment and identify assessment techniques that inform treatment planning and intervention selection, as well as provide guidelines (Jordan & Franklin, 2003, pp. 71–96). Quantitative assessment methods are used because they (a) help practitioners improve treatment by providing feedback about treatment progress, (b) enable practitioners to contribute to the clinical research literature, (c) provide information to ensure practice evaluation and accountability, and (d) allows social workers to increase their repertoire of skills and compete with other helping professionals in doing independent client assessments.

Seven types of quantitative measures helpful for family work are discussed here. First is *client self-recording and monitoring*. These measures are used by the client to collect and record his or her thoughts, feelings, or behaviors. Self-recording refers to retrospective data collected (i.e., remember the number of arguments you had with your dad last week) versus monitoring that refers to data collected on the spot (i.e., record information about an argument when it occurs). The format of this type of recording can be in the form of a log or diary as seen in Table 10.1. Note that more than one family member can independently complete such a log so that the social worker obtains the differing members' perspectives.

Self-anchored and rating scales are a second type of measurement technique. These measures are constructed by the social worker and client

Table 10.1   **Client Log—Completed by Teenage Son**

Date	Time	Duration	Situation	Thoughts
Sunday	11:00 P.M.	1 hour	Dad yelled at me when I came home after curfew.	Very angry. Wanted to hit him. Thought about running away.

Table 10.2   **Client Self-Anchored Scale for Communication—Completed by All Family Members**

Instructions: Circle the number that applies every day after dinner.

Family communication good.	1 2 3 4 5 6 7
Family communication broke down.	1 2 3 4 5 6 7
Pleasant conversation at dinner.	1 2 3 4 5 6 7
One or more members did not participate in the conversation or were angry, rude, etc.	1 2 3 4 5 6 7
Everyone was respectful to others.	1 2 3 4 5 6 7

family together when a standardized scale is not available. They are brief and use the client's own behavioral indicators as the "anchors." Table 10.2 shows an example of a log used to assess family members' communication at dinnertime. Each family member fills out a self-anchored scale after dinner to rate the level of communication that took place.

Third, *questionnaires* can be used to collect various types of information. Questionnaires may be obtained from publishers or may be designed by the practitioner to obtain information of a specific or of a global nature, depending on the information needed. For example, questionnaires exist to measure children's behavior problems, marital and family relationship quality, and so forth. These questionnaires are helpful in providing a systemic view of family problems that informs treatment planning rather than monitoring change.

A fourth type of quantitative measure is *direct behavioral observation*. The specific behavior in question is observed and recorded in this type of measurement. Direct observation is mostly used in residential or institutional settings due to the expense and time required to do it. In family treatment, a child's school problems might be operationalized and measured by the teacher. For example, if the child is disruptive in the classroom by talking and getting out of his seat, the teacher can record these incidents.

Related to behavioral observation, *role-play and analogue situations* are a fifth type of quantitative measurement. These are enactments of the families' problems allowing the practitioner to observe the problem (e.g., family arguments) as they are reenacted. As the practitioner observes the scene, she may record the number of sarcastic remarks versus the number of appropriate requests for feedback, for instance.

Table 10.3   Goal Attainment Scale—To Measure Teenager's Staying at School

Scale Attainment Level	Scale: Staying at School
Most unfavorable (−2)	Left school, picked up by police
Less than expected (−1)	Left school
Expected level (0)	Stayed at school all day
More than expected (+1)	Stayed at school all day, did homework
Best anticipated success (+2)	Stayed at school all day, did homework, participated in a group

Sixth is *goal-attainment scaling* measure. This is a measurement of client change as defined by the treatment goals. For instance, a teenage family member's school avoidance problem might be the focus of treatment. Table 10.3 gives an example of how the goals would be used to collect information in this way.

Finally, a seventh type of quantitative measure is *standardized measure*. A standardized measure is not only ready made and available for most family problems, it has uniformity of scoring and interpreting. The best ones have cutoff scores so that problems may be compared with a reference group of clinical and/or nonclinical individuals. For example, several standardized measures measure family satisfaction using various indicators of satisfaction. One measure might focus on the behavioral indicators of satisfaction (i.e., "My family members always treat each other with respect"), whereas another measure might focus on the family members' feelings (i.e., "I feel like no one in my family really loves me"). It is important to match the standardized measure with the family's way of viewing the problem. Jordan and Franklin (2003) provide more information about these and other types of assessment techniques.

Guidelines for developing a measurement system include:

- *Use of multiple methods to measure client behavior*: Ideally, both a self-report and a report of another rater should be used. Multiple clients are available to observe or record information in family work.
- *Development of a baseline indicator*: Baseline refers to the information collected before treatment begins. The baseline information should establish the need for intervention and indicate the seriousness of the problem. It can be used as a comparison with treatment data collected in order to monitor treatment progress.
- *Use of at least one repeated measure*: This refers to collection of data several times during assessment and intervention in order to track progress. More will be said about this approach later in this chapter.
- *Incorporate both specific and global measures*: Using this approach, you will be more likely to capture both the breadth and depth

of the client's problem(s). In sum, an ideal measurement system might include: (a) a self-report measure, (b) a behavioral observation measure, and (c) a report measure filled out by a significant other. To illustrate, a family with communication/anger problems might have each family member (a) complete a self-anchored scale on his or her own communication, (b) be observed in a communication role-play situation, and (c) complete a rating scale of their family members' communication attempts.

Ultimately, assessment is the link between research and practice. It informs treatment planning.

Treatment Planning

Jordan and Franklin (2003, pp. 59–68) review the treatment planning process, or moving from assessment to intervention. Steps are assessing client readiness, assessing alternative interventions, and using a treatment-planning framework. Finally, treatment monitoring is an essential aspect of the approach.

Client readiness may be assessed by considering the quality of the relationship between the family and the practitioner. If barriers to open communication exist, these must be addressed before intervention begins. Also, baseline information should be collected before intervention begins so that the nature and extent of the problem is known.

Several *alternative interventions* may exist to treat a particular family problem and the practitioner must choose in which direction to proceed. An important consideration is the evidence base of the particular treatments. Which treatments have the most evidence to support their use with the type of family and type of family problem that is the focus of interventive efforts. If more than one treatment meets this critical evaluation of evidence, practitioner and client preference may then help to determine the best choice. For instance, some treatments may be outside the training of the practitioner and would not be the appropriate choice until the practitioner has the appropriate supervision, certification, and so forth to perform the treatment. Or one treatment may appeal to the client family more than alternative treatments, so clients should be given a choice whenever possible. For example, one family may prefer an educational approach, whereas a second family would be happier with an experiential approach.

Use of a *treatment planning framework* provides the final linkage between assessment and intervention. Steps are problem selection, problem definition, goal development, objective construction, intervention creation, and diagnosis determination (if appropriate). Table 10.4 provides a basic treatment-planning framework.

We mentioned *treatment monitoring* earlier in this chapter. In this section, we describe this process, also sometimes called single-subject design, as described by Jordan and Franklin (2003, pp. 57–59). This

Table 10.4   Treatment Plan—Family With Communication Problems

Problem Selection

1. Poor communication

Problem Definition

Poor communication equals communication style characterized by angry arguments with yelling and
   screaming; disagreements remain unresolved.

Goal

1. Improve couple's communication.

Objectives

1a. Improve communication as measured by an improvement on the Primary Communication Inventory
   (Navran, 1967).

1b. Improve communication skills as measured by practitioner in role-play.

Intervention

Communication training: The therapist will focus on teaching the couple both verbal and nonverbal
   communicating skills. Verbal skills include the use of ''I'' statements to communicate needs, active
   listening, correct timing of message delivery, expression of feelings, and editing of unproductive
   communications. Nonverbal tools include appropriate facial expressions to match verbal content,
   posture, voice, and physical proximity to partner. In addition, anger-control techniques like recognizing
   escalating anger, taking a time-out, admitting one's own part in the argument, and problem solving will
   also be taught.

From *Clinical Assessment for Social Workers: Quantitative and Qualitative Methods* (pp. 66–67), by C. Jordan and
C. Franklin, 2003, Chicago, IL: Lyceum Books. Adapted with permission.

approach assumes repeated measures of the targeted problem in order to
track progress of the intervention. The steps of single-subject design are:

1. Measures are administered repeatedly, usually weekly or daily.

2. Baseline data is collected before the formal intervention begins.

3. Data is collected in phases, usually baseline, intervention, and follow-
   up. These phases are graphed, and data is compared across the
   phases. The intervention must be clearly defined. It is important to
   know when the intervention is being applied and when it is not so
   that its success or failure may be assessed.

4. The data is analyzed. Success or failure of the intervention can be
   determined by looking at the slope and trend of the data in each
   phase or using statistical procedures, such as the acceleration line or
   Shewhart chart approaches.

Single-subject designs have other uses in addition to tracking client
problems. They may be used by supervisors to help improve the interventive efforts of their staff. Data from caseloads may be aggregated and
provided to funders in order to show success and obtain funding for
services or further research.

The linkage has now been made from the beginning assessment, through client readiness, treatment selection, planning, and monitoring. Let's turn to an examination of some of the interventions with the strongest evidence base.

Family Interventions With Solid Research Support

The following section describes some of the *family interventions* that have research support for their effectiveness. Not every family approach that has solid research support can be covered, but this section summarizes several of the prominent approaches. Treatment manuals are available for all the approaches described in this section, making it easier for social workers to learn and achieve adherence to the practices. In addition, the results of outcome research using experimental, and quasi-experimental designs have suggested that each approach may be effective with various clinical populations.

Brief strategic family therapy (BSFT) was developed by Jose Szapocznik to address conduct and behavior problems, including drug use in families with an adolescent between the ages of 12 and 17. Families typically meet for 12 –15 sessions, which focus on building communication and problem-solving skills. The practitioner works to promote parental leadership; mutual support between parents; effective communication; problem solving; clear, consistent rules and consequences; nurturing; and shared responsibility for family problems (Substance Abuse and Mental Health Services Administration [SAMHSA] Center for Substance Abuse Prevention, 2005). BSFT has been found to be effective in multiple well-controlled studies with minority and nonminority youth (Robbins et al., 2011, Santisteban et al., 2003).

The Incredible Years is an intervention for families with younger children developed by Carolyn Webster-Stratton. The intervention employs three curricula for parents, teachers, and children. Facilitators use videotaped scenes to structure the content and stimulate group discussion. Sessions focus on improving communication and social skills and reducing behavioral and emotional problems in children between the ages of 2 and 8. The Incredible Years has been evaluated in multiple randomized control group studies with children diagnosed with oppositional defiant disorder or conduct problems. Findings demonstrate that over half of the children diagnosed with oppositional defiant disorder before the intervention no longer carried this diagnosis after participation (SAMHSA Center for Substance Abuse Prevention, 2005). Recent research also points to the importance of targeting multiple settings (i.e., intervening in the school and home) in implementing the Incredible Years to treat and prevent conduct disorder (Foster, Olchowski, & Webster-Stratton, 2007).

Family psychoeducation may be offered to individual families or to multiple families meeting as a group. The model has demonstrated effective outcomes with families affected by mental illnesses, such as depression, bipolar disorder, and schizophrenia (Anderson et al., 1986; Brennan, 1995; Holden & Anderson, 1990; Schwartz & Schwartz, 1993). The approach was influenced by structural family therapy, which emphasized joining with the family and enhancing boundaries. The practitioner begins by building a strong working alliance with the family and discussing resources as well as past attempts to cope with the illness. Early in the course of the intervention, the practitioner provides current information about the illness and treatment, including information about symptoms, medication, warning signs of relapse, and coping strategies (Anderson et al., 1986).

Psychoeducation also focuses on understanding and building a support network for families. Other families, church groups, family members, or friends who are affected by mental illness may be included in the concept of a family's social network. Through modeling and rehearsing social skills, the practitioner assists the family in learning skills that will help them maintain strong support networks (Franklin & Jordan, 1999).

Multifamily psychoeducational groups include the members of multiple families and their social support network in the intervention. Research demonstrates that this approach effectively helps families manage negative symptoms of Schizophrenia (Voss, 2003). Other studies have found that the approach results in reduced emotional distress (Katsuki et al., 2011), improved knowledge about mood disorders, and more positive family interactions (Fristad, Goldberg-Arnold, & Gavazzi, 2003; Hoagwood, 2005). The group allows different families to share their stories and find commonalities among families' experiences. The practitioner encourages positive interaction between families in which they share their feelings and can offer each other suggestions (Janzen et al., 2005; McFarlane, 2002). Research on multifamily psychoeducation groups indicate that the positive clinical outcomes of families coping with a first psychotic episode make it a cost-effective intervention (Breitborde, Woods, & Srihari, 2009).

Multisystemic therapy (MST), developed by Scott Henggeler, is another well-researched family intervention. This home-based intervention aims to decrease delinquency, antisocial behavior, and substance abuse among juvenile offenders between the ages of 12 and 17. The intervention works with the parents to provide guidance and intervenes on multiple system levels to effect changes in adolescents' behavior within their own environment. Multiple well-controlled studies evaluating MST demonstrate that it is effective in reducing substance use and antisocial behavior among juvenile offenders. It is also effective in improving the functioning of parents by reducing their psychiatric distress, reducing parenting behaviors associated with maltreatment, and improving their social supports (Swenson, Schaeffer, Henggeler, Faldowski, & Mayhew, 2010).

The practitioner aims to empower parents and help them develop structure and discipline needed for effective parenting while increasing family connectedness. Children are encouraged to reduce contact with peers who exert a negative influence through drug use or delinquency. Practitioners also work to establish collaboration between parents and school staff. The approach is characterized by a comprehensive approach that addresses issues on multiple environmental levels, although practitioners tailor the intervention to meet the specific needs of each family

(Randall & Cunningham, 2003). The following are the nine principles of MST (Multisystemic Therapy Services, 1998):

1. Understanding the fit between problems and their systemic context.
2. Emphasizing strengths.
3. Designing interventions that promote responsible behavior and decrease irresponsible behavior.
4. Focus on the present, remain action-oriented, and target problems that are well-defined.
5. Target behaviors that maintain identified problems.
6. Choose interventions that meet youths' developmental needs.
7. Require effort from family members on a daily or weekly basis.
8. Continuously evaluate the effectiveness of intervention.
9. Promote treatment generalization and long-term maintenance of positive changes by empowering caregivers.

Multidimensional family therapy, developed by Howard Liddle, aims to reduce substance use and delinquency among adolescents. The approach combines individual sessions with the adolescent and parents as well as family sessions. Studies have been conducted with ethnically diverse youth between the ages of 11 and 18 in a wide variety of settings. Research demonstrates that adolescents in families that receive the intervention reduce marijuana use, depression, anxiety, and delinquent behaviors compared with families who receive another form of intervention.

Multidimensional family therapy (MDFT) has demonstrated effective outcomes related to substance abuse and delinquent behavior for adolescent substance abusers in multiple controlled studies and has been named as an effective program by the U.S. Department of Health and Human Services, the National Institute on Drug Abuse (NIDA), and the Substance Abuse and Mental Health Services Administration (SAMHSA; Dennis et al., 2002; Henderson, Dakof, Greenbaum, & Liddle, 2010; Liddle et al., 2001, 2002). Multidimensional family therapy tends to be more effective than individual cognitive behavior therapy among youths who indicate more severe substance use (Henderson et al., 2010).

Multidimensional family therapy consists of five core components:

1. Intervention with the adolescent to address developmental issues, such as identity formation, peer relations, and drug use consequences.
2. Intervention with the parent(s) to improve monitoring and limit setting.
3. Intervention to change the parent-adolescent interaction to encourage the parents' participation in the teen's life.
4. Interventions with other family members to develop the motivation and skills to interact in more positive ways.

5. Interventions with systems external to the family to develop collaborative relationships among all other systems in which the adolescent is involved, such as school or the juvenile justice system.

Cognitive Behavior Therapy With Parent Component

Functional family therapy (FFT) is a prevention/ intervention approach that aims to decrease behavior problems for youth between the ages of 11 and 18. Practitioners work individually or in two-person teams with clients in their homes and in clinical settings (Center for the Study and Prevention of Violence, 2006). The model aims to reduce risk factors and promote protective factors, and it includes the following processes:

- Engagement, to prevent dropping out of treatment before completion.
- Building motivation for working toward sustained behavior change.
- Assessment, to clarify relationships among family members and with larger systems.
- Behavioral change, through communication training, behavioral tasks, parenting skills, contracting, and evaluating costs and benefits of communication patterns.
- Generalization, which includes case management to assist the family in addressing environmental constraints and accessing resources. (Center for the Study and Prevention of Violence, 2006)

Functional family therapy has been evaluated in multiple clinical trials and has been found to be effective with adolescents diagnosed with conduct disorder, oppositional defiant disorder, disruptive behavior disorder, and those who abuse substances. The approach has also been effective in preventing placement in more restrictive settings (Alexander et al., 1998; Center for the Study and Prevention of Violence, 2006). Recent research indicates that the model is effective for youths involved with the juvenile justice system when therapists adhere to the treatment model as it was designed. In these cases, youths receiving FFT are significantly more likely to experience a reduction in behavior problems and involvement in criminal behavior, in comparison to youths receiving probation services (Sexton & Turner, 2010).

Parent–child interaction therapy was developed by Eyeberg and colleagues for children with conduct disorder and their families. The approach is based on the assumption that, by improving the interactions between parents and children, children's behavior will improve. Parents are taught skills to interact with children in a warm, responsive manner. The parents learn to praise positive behaviors, ignore negative behaviors, and provide consistent consequences (Child Anxiety Network, 2006). Multiple studies evaluating the model demonstrate that the outcomes of the approach include positive changes in interaction styles, increased compliance from children, and reduced behavior problems (Child Anxiety Network, 2006; Eyberg & Robinson, 1982; Foote, Eyberg, & Schuhmann, 1998).

Parent management training (PMT) aims to train parents to manage problem behaviors in the home and at school. Practitioners provide information about social learning principals and techniques and models the techniques for parents. Parents learn to define behaviors through observation and recording and to change behavior through reinforcement of prosocial behaviors and punishment of negative behaviors (Feldman & Kazdin, 1995). Through numerous studies evaluating the effectiveness of PMT, it has demonstrated effectiveness in decreasing oppositional and aggressive behaviors and increasing prosocial behaviors (Feldman & Kazdin, 1995; Hautman et al., 2011). The approach has demonstrated therapeutic change for both children and parents and reduced barriers to parent's success in treatment (Hoagwood, 2005; Kazdin & Whitely, 2003). For example, parents receiving PMT report improved disciplinary practices, and greater compliance from their children (Ogden & Amlund Hagen, 2008).

Emotionally focused therapy (EFT) was developed by Greenberg and Johnson (1988). Problems in the relationship are defined as a failure to provide a secure attachment base for one or both of the partners. Emotionally focused therapy assumes that negative patterns of interaction cycles result from fear of losing one's primary object of attachment. The resulting communication is often characterized by withdrawing, attacking, being overly rational, discounting the partner's concerns, or criticizing. The intervention often begins with individual sessions before moving on to couple or family sessions. The practitioner helps couples identify and communicate their own emotions, understand how they evoke negative responses in their partners, and change their interactions to be more genuine and positive (Greenberg & Johnson, 1988; Janzen et al., 2005) Although there is only limited research on the effectiveness of EFT, a few studies demonstrate that it improves the quality of relationships (Dunn & Schwebel, 1995; Janzen et al., 2005; Lebow, Chambers, Christensen, & Johnson, 2012). For example, individuals receiving EFT report improvement in forgiveness of those who have inflicted emotional injury and a reduction in emotional distress (Greenberg, Warwar, & Malcolm, 2008).

Solution-focused brief therapy (SFBT) is another intervention that has a growing body of research support and has recently been evaluated in numerous well-controlled research studies. Solution-focused brief therapy evolved out of brief family therapy in the early 1980s and in clinical work with clients with multiple problems in which practitioner/researchers used qualitative research method to try and discover what worked best in brief family therapy (Lipchik, Derks, LaCourt, & Nunnally, 2012). Since that time, solution-focused brief therapy has been widely applied in community organizations and in the past 10 years has been more rigorously evaluated by researchers. Solution-focused brief therapy is a strengths approach, and the assumption is that clients have the knowledge, strength, skills, and insights to solve their own problems (Berg, 1994). Four underlying assumptions guide solution-focused therapy sessions:

1. Each client and family is unique.
2. Clients already possess the strength and resources to achieve their goals.
3. Change is constant, and a small change in one part of a client or family system can produce bigger change or changes in another part of the system.
4. Sessions should focus on the present and future because it is impossible to change the past. (Lipchik, 2002)

Throughout the intervention, the therapist defines the situation and goals using clients' perceptions and language. The practitioner continuously emphasizes clients' strengths and compliments them for every success.

The outcome research on SFBT has been growing to the point that there are currently 48 experimental outcome studies on its effectiveness, two independent meta-analyses of all the studies to date, and one systematic review on its effectiveness with children in schools (Gingerich, Kim, Stams & MacDonald, 2012; Kim & Franklin, 2009). Overall, these studies show small to moderate effect sizes demonstrating that solution-focused brief therapy gets the same results as other interventions. Overall, the research has also shown that solution-focused brief therapy gets the same results as longer therapies in a much shorter amount of time (Franklin, Trepper, Gingerich & McCollum, 2012). For example, in the meta-analysis completed by Kim (2008), most SFBT interventions took place in eight or fewer sessions.

Studies have also suggested that solution-focused brief therapy studies demonstrates good results with important clinical and socially significant problems. For example, solution-focused brief therapy has shown positive outcomes for clients on improving depressive symptoms, self-esteem, and coping (Kim, 2008); reducing behavior problems (Corcoran & Stephenson, 2000; Franklin, Biever, Moore, Clemons, & Scamardo, 2001; Franklin, Corcoran, Nowicki, & Streeter, 1997; Newsome, 2002); attaining goals (LaFountain & Garner, 1996; Littrell, Malia, & Vanderwood, 1995; Newsome, 2002); and improving social skills (Newsome, 2002). Research links SFBT with improved behavior and academic outcomes, with participants demonstrating improved academic performance and motivation (Daki & Savage, 2010; Kim & Franklin, 2009). Among criminal justice populations, solution-focused brief therapy has demonstrated efficacy in reducing recidivism (Lindforss & Magnusson, 1997) and externalizing behaviors, such as decreasing conduct problems and substance abuse in schools and in other institutional settings (Kim & Franklin, 2009; Seagram, 1997, as cited in Gingerich & Eisengart, 2000). Some research has also demonstrated that SFBT results in positive outcomes for improving parenting skills (Zimmerman, Jacobsen, MacIntyre, & Watson, 1996).

Limitations of Evidence-Based Family Interventions

Overall, there are a number of rigorous studies evaluating the effectiveness of family treatments and, as a field, family therapy has made great strides in developing a research base for its interventions. Additional research is always needed to further support the effectiveness of clinical interventions and to demonstrate the effectiveness of other approaches that are widely used in the community. Over the past decade, the research designs for family therapies have been improving, and there are currently ongoing research programs on the family interventions discussed earlier. Even though much more work is needed to produce larger clinical trials on the efficacy of the interventions, social work practitioners can have confidence that the family interventions have considerable empirical support when compared to other psychotherapies.

Producing strong outcome studies does not, in itself, bridge the gap between social work practice and research and assure that the most effective family interventions will be implemented. Even in fields that have a strong record of evaluating their interventions, the research does not adequately demonstrate that effective interventions will remain effective in naturalistic settings. Much of the psychology research on psychosocial interventions for children has been conducted in clinical settings. Because successful outcomes of research in such settings often do not result in consistent effects when applied to naturalistic settings, there is a great need to evaluate the interventions in the real world (Brestan & Eyberg, 1998). Despite the availability of family treatment approaches that have demonstrated positive outcomes in methodologically strong research studies, for example, these interventions sometimes have limited impact on work with families in the community. Family practitioners have a multitude of evidence-based practices from which to choose, and organizations such as SAMHSA provide information on these interventions, outcomes of efficacy trials, target population, and training requirements, among other things. Even though the field has the availability of effective programs and clearinghouses of information, few practitioners that work in community organizations consistently use evidence-based practices and this is a major limitation for EBP (Franklin, 1999).

Implementation of family interventions with empirical support may be circumvented for ideological, practical, and environmental reasons. A lack of effective and sustainable ways for practitioners to learn new family interventions may also hinder effective implementation. When considering research-based family interventions, for example, practitioners may be concerned that the intervention was not tested with clients similar to those seen in community settings. Some family studies evaluate family interventions on clients that meet the criteria for a particular diagnosis, but social workers more typically work with families who have multiple problems or co-occurring disorders. Families served by community organizations may be more diverse than study samples with respect to culture, ethnicity, and socioeconomic status. Clinicians may perceive that the family interventions under study do not adequately address complex problems that their clients face, such as abuse, neglect, poverty, or parental drug use (Robbins, Bachrach, & Szapocznik, 2002). Such ideological objections may exist despite the fact that several of the family interventions have been evaluated with difficult populations in the community and have been found to be at least moderately effective. Solution-focused brief therapy, multisystemic therapy, and functional family therapy are examples of interventions that have been evaluated in the community and have researchers and trainers who have worked to increase their fidelity and appropriate use with community practitioners (Franklin et al. 2012; Henggeler, 2004; Sexton & Turner, 2010).

Practical and environmental barriers also make it difficult to use the family interventions that are grounded in research. The success of any EBP in the community may depend greatly on characteristics of community-based organizations and the resources provided clinicians (Franklin & Hopson 2007). Organizational characteristics that may impact use of EBPs include the size of the organization, staff turnover, salary level, caseload size, and availability of resources (Chillag et al., 2002; Miller, 2003; Schoenwald & Hoagwood, 2001). Lack of supervision and support and high caseloads may affect the time and energy a practitioner can devote to learning and implementing a new approach, for example (Hutchinson and Johnston 2004; Schoenwald & Hoagwood, 2001). Often, implementation of an EBP family approach (i.e., multisystemic therapy) may call for coordinating services within a team of service providers. This can become difficult for community organizations because they may have to devote disproportionate resources to implementing one program and devoting fewer resources to other important programs. Working with a team of service providers requires skills in collaboration. These skills require training in order to collaborate successfully, and many social workers may not be accustomed to working within a team to plan treatment goals, for their clients, for example (Corrigan, Steiner, McCracken, Blaser, & Barr, 2001).

Inadequate funds for purchasing training services and materials may also serve as a barrier. Family interventions, such as multisystemic therapy and brief strategic family therapy, often have high costs for training and ongoing consultation services (e.g., Henggeler, Melton, Brondino, Scherer, & Hanley, 1997; Henggeler, Schoenwald, Liao, Letourneau, & Edwards, 2002). Many community-based organizations may have difficulty obtaining the necessary funds (Aos, Phipps, Barnoski, & Lieb, 2001). Staff turnover and the need to train new therapists in a short time period may further complicate these issues.

Improving the Implementation of EBP

Myers and Thyer (1997) recommend that social workers be trained in techniques that are based on research evidence to the fullest possible extent suggesting that continuing education for practitioners should also consist of empirically based knowledge, and this would possibly improve professional development. Including ongoing consultation in addition to didactic training for practitioners may facilitate the sustained use of EBPs (Corrigan et al., 2001; Kelly et al., 2000; Marinelli-Casey, Domier, & Rawson, 2002). Supervision and personal consultation also helps motivate clinicians to learn and use effective interventions (Corrigan et al., 2001; Kelly et al., 2000; Proctor, 2003), but these types of practices are often underfunded. Combining training and consultation with treatment manuals may be an effective strategy for encouraging the sustained use of EBPs in the community (Kelly et al., 2000; McFarlane, McNary, Dixon, Hornby, & Cimett, 2001). Incentives, such as monetary bonuses or vacation time, can also encourage practitioners to learn and implement a new intervention (Corrigan et al., 2001).

Family interventions also have to be implemented with a great amount of clinical acumen and skill to get the same results that they were able to achieve in the research studies that were described in this chapter. There is no doubt that family interventions are less effective when practitioners do not implement the intervention with strict adherence to implementation instructions and do not have the adequate training to carry out the intervention (Franklin et al., 2012; Henggeler, 2004; Sexton & Turner, 2010). Funding agencies (i.e., NIH, SAMHSA) are currently devoting considerable resources to translational and implementation sciences to create new ways of learning and to help practitioners implement the evidence-based practices with high adherence. To assure success in implementation social work, administrators, researchers, and program developers usually collaborate actively with practitioners and other key agency staff. Researchers also consider the staff who will be responsible for conducting the intervention, the conditions under which the intervention will be implemented, and the effect the intervention is likely to have on the target population.

Finally, choosing an EBP practice that has a good organizational and community fit may help improve implementation of the family interventions. The family intervention must be a good fit for the organizational setting, practitioners within the setting, and those whom the intervention is intended to benefit. If a family intervention requires specialized training and particular skills, the researcher considers how practitioners in the setting can be realistically trained to provide the intervention and whether they are likely to conduct the intervention as the researcher intended (Schoenwald & Hoagwood, 2001).The philosophy of the organization and the culture of the surrounding community also influence whether a family intervention can be implemented successfully. Before organizations adopt an intervention, they evaluate the intervention's compatibility with the organization's philosophy and with values of the local community. Organizations usually prefer to adopt family programs that fill an unmet need in the community (Miller, 2001). The family intervention must also be relevant to the organization's mission, feasible within the agency setting, and compatible with the opinions of agency consumers (Miller, 2003). Evidence-based family practice requires careful planning, taking all these factors into consideration, as well as the evidence base of the intervention for client populations.

Implications for Social Work Practice

Family intervention has implications for social work practice at multiple ecological levels. The ecological systems perspective defines an individual's environment using three systemic levels: the microsystem, the mesosystem, and the macrosystem (Bronfenbrenner, 1979). The levels exist along a continuum defined by the amount of direct interaction between the individual and the systems within each level. The microsystem is defined by influential others with whom an individual has regular face-to-face contact, such as family and friends (Heffernan, Shuttlesworth, & Ambrosino, 1992). Microsystem interventions work with the individual directly and may include those with whom the individual has direct contact, such as family members or teachers (Hepworth, Rooney, & Larson, 1997). The mezzosystem is defined by relationships between the microsystems that do not include the individual but affect the individual's behavior. The mezzosystem includes interactions between a child's parents, between parents and teachers, or between a child's peers (Heffernan et al., 1992). It may also include schools, school boards, community organizations, and local government. Mezzosystems interventions aim to change systems, such as family or peer group, that affect the individual (Hepworth et al., 1997). The macrosystem is defined by societal factors, such as cultural values and social policy. Macrolevel interventions include social planning and community organization (Heffernan et al., 1992).

Newer perspectives on ecological approaches propose that ecological theory is inherently limited by its emphasis on understanding social processes within different ecological levels with few implications related to altering these dynamics. Newer models propose the use of ecological principals to inform interventions that alter suboptimal social processes in the interest of promoting positive outcomes and, more broadly, social justice (Ungar, 2002; 2011).

In line with these newer models of ecological practice, family interventions aim to foster interactions between individuals and their environments that promote the development of healthy relationships and behavior. The practitioner is concerned with characteristics of individual family members, such as a child's behavior in school, or a parent's diagnosis of depression. These issues may be explored with an individual member of the family. However, the family practitioner always takes the next step of understanding how the characteristics of individual family members are influenced by family dynamics and how they influence the family system. Much of the work occurs on the mezzosystems level.

The mezzosystems level of the ecological systems framework involves interactions among those with whom an individual has closest contact (Heffernan et al., 1992). Family therapy interventions are consistent with interventions that aim to affect change at the mezzosystems level because they aim to change patterns of interaction among family members. Family practitioners work to improve family relationships and communication patterns. These improvements in the dynamics of a family system can change individual behavior. Family interventions, for example, have been associated with reduced risk behavior among adolescent family members (Borduin, Henggeler, Blaske, & Stein, 1990; Santisteban et al., 2003).

The mezzosystem also consists of settings in which an individual does not participate directly but which affect the individual or those who directly interact with the individual. These systems include schools, school boards, community organizations, and local government. Interventions work to affect change on a systems level by changing the culture within an organization or school, for example (Heffernan et al., 1992). Although family interventions focus primarily on changing family dynamics, practitioners may have to also address organizational factors that influence the effectiveness of their practices. In order to be successful, interventions need to be compatible with the organization's philosophy and with values of the local community. Organizations prefer to adopt programs that fill an unmet need in the community, but they also consider the feasibility of introducing a program given the available money and personnel (Miller, 2001). This is relevant for promoting the use of effective family interventions in the community because organizations need to feel that the intervention meets the needs of their community and clients before investing in the training and resources required for many evidence-based interventions.

It is important that practitioners acknowledge the mezzosystem factors that influence family functioning. The stress resulting from poor housing conditions or difficulty paying utility bills can greatly affect how family members relate to each other. A school's disciplinary practices may affect family dynamics. If a child diagnosed with ADHD is sent to the principal's office every day for disruptive behavior, a parent may feel that the school is insensitive to the needs of the child and that the child is missing out on important educational experiences. This can create a great deal of tension between the school and the parents in a family system that can affect the functioning of the family as a whole. A parent's place of employment often affects the amount of time that the parent can spend interacting with children and providing consistent care. Mezzosystem factors may also determine the resources available to the family. If a family belongs to a church or community organization that provides a network of supportive friends, they may be better able to cope with stressors.

The macrosystem is defined by societal factors, such as cultural values and social policies (Heffernan et al., 1992). Family practitioners need to be aware of macrosystem factors that affect their work with families. As discussed earlier, the influence of managed care means that social workers are often expected to use EBPs and time-limited interventions. Social policies may play a large role in family functioning. Families served by social workers may be affected by welfare legislation, policies on subsidized housing, and education policies. Social workers may have to help families understand policies and advocate on behalf of families that are negatively affected by policies.

If a social worker focuses only on the micro- and mezzolevel issues, the therapeutic relationship may suffer greatly. Practitioners need to be constantly aware of cultural issues that can affect the process of family intervention. Families from one particular ethnic group may have a negative view of seeking mental-health services and may experience shame in meeting with a social worker. Those from other cultural backgrounds may feel no shame at all. Cultural factors often determine the roles that family members take. On some cultures more than others, older siblings may assist in caretaking for younger siblings. Cultural factors may influence the father's level of involvement in child rearing. Culture influences the approach to raising children and disciplinary practices.

Social work researchers are uniquely qualified to affect change at multiple systemic levels, given the profession's grounding in the ecological systems perspective. They can intervene to change organizational systems in which they work or those with which their clients interact. A social worker can educate school administrators about the importance of school culture for student success, for example, or work to change an organizational policy that makes it difficult to serve families living in poverty, such as billing rules.

Conclusion

Family intervention has grown in importance during the past 50 years and has become integral to social work practice. This chapter has reviewed the historical background of family interventions and the growing need to demonstrate the effectiveness of interventions. The growing body of research on evidence-based family intervention has the potential to greatly improve social work services with families, but the interventions can only benefit families if community organizations put them into everyday use. This next step is critical for improving services delivery. Yet, it will require a great deal of collaboration and communication among practitioners, researchers, and program developers. This collaboration can result in evidence-based practices that are more relevant for community organizations and user-friendly for practitioners.

Key Terms

Evidence-based practice

Family psychoeducation

Assessment

Treatment planning

Intervention

Ecological systems theory

Review Questions for Critical Thinking

1. What is the definition of evidence-based family practice? Describe how you would select evidence-based interventions for one of your clients/client problems.

2. Define family assessment, treatment planning, and intervention. Discuss the relationship between these three concepts.

3. Explain how a family intervention can affect change at the micro- and mezzosystems levels. Use specific examples in your answer.

4. Identify organizational factors that can serve as barriers to implementing a family intervention with fidelity.

Online Resources

http://store.samhsa.gov/product/Family-Psychoeducation-Evidence-Based-Practices-EBP KIT/SMA09-4423 SAMHSA: Family Psychoeducation Evidence Based Practice

http://www.childwelfare.gov/famcentered/casework/assessment.cfm U.S. Department of Health and Human Services, Administration for Children and Families

http://www.nrepp.samhsa.gov/ SAMHSA: National Registry of Effective Programs and Practices (NREPP)

http://www.childwelfare.gov/ U.S. Department of Health and Human Services Administration for Children and Families: Child Welfare Information Gateway

References

Alexander, J., Barton, C., Gordon, D., Grotpeter, J., Hansson, K., Harrison, R., . . . Sexton, T. (1998). *Blueprints for violence prevention: Book three. Functional family therapy*. Denver: Colorado Division of Criminal Justice.

Anderson, C. M., Griffin, S., Rossi, A., Pagonis, I., Holder, D. P., & Treiber, R. (1986). A comparative study of the impact of education versus process groups for families of clients with affective disorders. *Family Process, 25*, 185–205.

Aos, S., Phipps, P., Barnoski, R., & Lieb, R. (2001). The comparative costs and benefits of programs to reduce crime (Version 4.0). Olympia: Washington State Institute for Public Policy. Retrieved from www.wa.gov/wsipp/

Barker, R. L. (2003). *The social work dictionary*. Washington, DC: National Association of Social Workers Press.

Basen-Engquist, K., O'Hara-Tompkins, N., Lovato, C. Y., Lewis, M. J., Parcel, G. S., & Gingiss, P. (1994). The effect of two types of teacher training on implementation of smart choices: A tobacco prevention curriculum. *Journal of School Health, 64*, 334–339.

Berg, I. K. (1994). *Family-based services: A solution-focused approach*. New York: Norton.

Borduin, C. M., Henggeler, S. W., Blaske, D. M., & Stein, R. (1990). Multisystemic treatment of adolescent sexual offenders. *International Journal of Offender Therapy and Comparative Criminology, 35,* 105–114.

Breitborde, N. J. K., Woods, S. W., & Srihari, V. H. (2009). Multifamily psychoeducation for first-episode psychosis: A cost-effectiveness analysis. *Psychiatric Services, 60,* 1477–1483.

Brennan, J. (1995). A short-term psychoeducational multiple family group for bipolar clients and their families. *Social Work, 40*(6), 737–743.

Brestan, E. V., & Eyberg, S. M. (1998). Effective psychosocial treatments of conduct-disordered children and adolescents: 29 years, 82 studies, and 5,272 kids. *Journal of Clinical Child Psychology, 27,* 180–189.

Bronfenbrenner, U. (1979). *The ecology of human development: Experiments by nature and design.* Cambridge, MA: Harvard University Press.

Center for the Study and Prevention of Violence (2006). *Blueprints model programs: Functional family therapy.* Retrieved from www.colorado.edu/cspv/blueprints/model/programs/FFT.html

Child Anxiety Network (2006). *Specialized programs: Parent–child interaction therapy.* Retrieved from www.childanxiety.net/Specialty_Programs.htm

Chillag, K., Bartholow, K., Cordeiro, J., Swanson, J. P., Stebbins, S., Woodside, C.,...Sy, F. (2002). Factors affecting the delivery of HIV/AIDS prevention programs by community-based organizations. *AIDS Education and Prevention, 14*(Suppl. A), 27–37.

Close-Goedjen, J. L., & Saunders, S. M. (2002). The effect of technical support on clinician attitudes toward an outcome assessment instrument. *Journal of Behavioral Health Services and Research, 29*(1), 99–108.

Corcoran, J., & Stephenson, M. (2000). The effectiveness of solution focused therapy with child behavior problems: A preliminary report. *Families in Society, 81,* 468–474.

Corrigan, P. W., Steiner, L., McCracken, S. G., Blaser, B., & Barr, M. (2001). Strategies for disseminating evidence-based practices to staff who treat people with serious mental illness. *Psychiatric Services, 52*(12), 1598–1606.

Daki, J., & Savage, R. S. (2010). Solution-focused brief therapy: Impacts on academic and emotional difficulties. *Journal of Educational Research, 103*(5), 309–326.

Dennis, M., Titus, J. C., Diamond, G., Donaldson, J., Godley, S. H., Tims, F. M.,...C.Y.T. Steering Committee. (2002). The Cannabis Youth Treatment (CYT) experiment: Rationale, study design, and analysis plans. *Addiction,* (Suppl. 1), 16–34.

Dunn, R. L., & Schwebel, A. I. (1995). Meta-analytic review of marital therapy outcome research. *Journal of Family Psychology, 9,* 58–68.

Eyberg, S. M., & Robinson, E. A. (1982). Parent–child interaction training: Effects on family functioning. *Journal of Clinical Child Psychology, 11,* 130–137.

Feldman, J., & Kazdin, A. E. (1995). Parent management training for oppositional and conduct problem children. *Clinical Psychologist, 48*(4), 3–5.

Foote, R., Eyberg, S. M., & Schuhmann, E. (1998). Parent–child interaction approaches to the treatment of child behavior disorders. In T. H. Ollendick & R. J. Prinz (Eds.), *Advances in clinical child psychology* (pp. 125–151). New York, NY: Plenum Press.

Foster, E. M., Olchowski, A. E., & Webster-Stratton, C. H. (2007). Is stacking intervention components cost-effective? An analysis of the incredible years program. *Journal of the American Academy of Child & Adolescent Psychiatry*, *46*(11), 1414–1424.

Franklin, C. (1999). Research on practice: Better than you think? [Editorial]. *Social Work in Education*, *21*, 3–10.

Franklin, C., Biever, J., Moore, K., Clemons, D., & Scamardo, M. (2001). The effectiveness of solution-focused therapy with children in a school setting. *Research on Social Work Practice*, *11*(4), 411–434.

Franklin, C., Corcoran, J., Nowicki, J., & Streeter, C. (1997). Using client self-anchored scales to measure outcomes in solution-focused therapy. *Journal of Systemic Therapies*, *16*(3), 246–265.

Franklin, C., & Hopson L. (2007). Facilitating the use of evidence-based practice in community based organizations. *Journal of Social Work Education*, *43*(3), 377–404.

Franklin, C., & Jordan, C. (1999). *Family practice: Brief systems methods for social work*. Pacific Grove, CA: Brooks/Cole.

Franklin, C., & Sanchez, K. (2011). Quantitative clinical assessment methods. In C. Jordan & C. Franklin, (Eds.) *Clinical assessment for social workers: Quantitative and qualitative methods* (3rd ed., pp. 51–79). Chicago, IL: Lyceum.

Franklin, C., Trepper, T. S., Gingerich, W. J., & McCollum, E. E. (2012). *Solution-focused brief therapy: A handbook of evidence-based practice*. New York, NY: Oxford University Press.

Fristad, M. A., Goldberg-Arnold, J. S., & Gavazzi, S. M. (2003). Multi-family psychoeducation groups in the treatment of children with mood disorders. *Journal of Marital and Family Therapy*, *29*(4), 491–504.

Gambrill, E. (2006). Evidence-based practice and policy: Choices ahead. *Research on Social Work Practice*, *16*(3), 338–357.

Gingerich, W. J., & Eisengart, S. (2000). Solution-focused brief therapy: A review of the outcome research. *Family Process*, *39*, 477–498.

Gingerich, W. J., Kim, J. S, Stams, G. J.., & MacDonald, A. J. (2012). Solution focused brief therapy outcome research. In C. Franklin, T. S. Trepper, W. J. Gingerich, & E. E. McCollum, *Solution-focused brief therapy: A handbook of evidence-based practice* (pp. 3–19). New York, NY: Oxford University Press.

Gray, J. A. M. (2001). The origin of evidence-based practice. In A. Edwards & G. Elwyn (Eds.), *Evidence-informed client choice* (pp. 19–33). New York, NY: Oxford University Press.

Greenberg, L., & Johnson, S. (1988). *Emotionally focused therapy for couples*. New York, NY: Guilford Press.

Greenberg, L. S., Warwar, S. H., & Malcolm, W. M. (2008). Differential effects of emotion-focused therapy and psychoeducation in facilitating forgiveness and letting go of emotional injuries. *Journal of Counseling Psychology*, *55*(2), 185–196.

Hartman, A., & Laird, J. (1983). *Family centered social work practice*. New York, NY: Free Press.

Hautmann, C., Stein, P., Eichelberger, I., Hanisch, C., Plück, J., Walter, D., & Döpfner, M. (2011). The severely impaired do profit most: Differential effectiveness of a parent management training for children with externalizing behavior problems in a natural setting. *Journal of Child & Family Studies*, *20*(4), 424–435.

Heffernan, J., Shuttlesworth, G., & Ambrosino, R. (1992). *Social work and social welfare: An introduction*. Minneapolis, MN: West.

Henderson, C. E., Dakof, G. A., Greenbaum, P. E., & Liddle, H. A. (2010). Effectiveness of multidimensional family therapy with higher severity substance-abusing adolescents: Report from two randomized controlled trials. *Journal of Consulting & Clinical Psychology, 78*(6), 885–897.

Henggeler, S. W. (2004). Decreasing effect sizes for effectiveness studies—Implications for the transport of evidence-based treatments: Comment on Curtis, Ronan, and Borduin. *Journal of Family Psychology, 18,* 420–423.

Henggeler, S. W., Melton, G. B., Brondino, M. J., Scherer, D. G., & Hanley, J. H. (1997). Multisystemic therapy with violent and chronic juvenile offenders and their families: The role of treatment fidelity in successful dissemination. *Journal of Consulting and Clinical Psychology, 65,* 821–833.

Henggeler, S. W., Schoenwald, S. K., Liao, J. G., Letourneau, E. J., & Edwards, D. L. (2002). Transporting efficacious treatments to field settings: The link between supervisory practices and therapist fidelity in MST programs. *Journal of Clinical Child Psychology, 31,* 155–167.

Hepworth, D. H., Rooney, R. H., & Larson, J. A. (1997). *Direct social work practice: Theory and skills* (5th ed.). Pacific Grove, CA: Brooks/Cole.

Hoagwood, K. (2005). Family-based services in children's mental health: A research review and synthesis. *Journal of Child and Family Psychiatry, 46*(7), 690–713.

Holden, D., & Anderson, C. M. (1990). Psychoeducational family intervention for depressed clients and their families. In G. I. Keitner (Ed.), *Depression and families: Impact and treatment* (pp. 57–84). Washington, DC: American Psychiatric Press.

Hutchinson, A. M., & Johnston, L. (2004). Bridging the divide: A survey of nurses' opinions regarding barriers to, and facilitators of, research utilization in the practice setting. *Journal of Clinical Nursing, 13*(3), 304–315.

Janzen, C., Harris, O., Jordan, C., & Franklin, C. (2005). *Family treatment: Evidence-based practice with populations at risk* (4th ed.). Belmont, CA: Thomson Learning.

Jordan, C., & Franklin, C. (2003). *Clinical assessment for social workers: Quantitative and qualitative methods* (2nd ed.). Chicago, IL: Lyceum.

Jordan, C., & Franklin, C. (2011). *Clinical assessment for social workers: Quantitative and qualitative methods* (3rd ed.). Chicago, IL: Lyceum.

Katsuki, F., Takeuchi, H., Konishi, M., Sasaki, M., Murase, Y., Naito, A.,...Furukawa, T. A. (2011). Pre-post changes in psychosocial functioning among relatives of patients with depressive disorders after Brief Multifamily Psychoeducation: A pilot study. *BMC Psychiatry, 11*(1), 56–62.

Kazdin, A. E., & Whitley, M. K. (2003). Treatment of parental stress to enhance therapeutic change among children referred for aggressive and antisocial behavior. *Journal of Consulting and Clinical Psychology, 71,* 504–515.

Kelly, J. A., Somlai, A. M., DiFranceisco, W. J., Otto-Salaj, L. I., McAuliffe, T. L., Hackl, K. L.,...Rompa, D. (2000). Bridging the gap between the science and service of HIV prevention: Transferring effective research-based HIV prevention intervention to community AIDS service providers. *American Journal of Public Health, 90,* 1082–1088.

Kim, J. S. (2008). Examining the effectiveness of solution-focused brief therapy: A meta-analysis. *Research on Social Work Practice, 18*(2), 107–116.

Kim, J. S., & Franklin, C. (2009). Solution-focused brief therapy in schools: A review of the literature. *Children and Youth Services Review, 3*(4), 464–470.

LaFountain, R. M., & Garner, N. E. (1996). Solution-focused counseling groups: The results are in. *Journal for Specialists in Group Work, 21*(2), 128–143.

Lebow, J. L., Chambers, A. L., Christensen, A., & Johnson, S. M. (2012). Research on the treatment of couple distress. *Journal of Marital & Family Therapy*, *38*(1), 145–168.

Liddle, H. A., Dakof, G. A., Parker, K., Diamond, G. S., Barrett, K., & Tejeda, M. (2001). Multidimensional family therapy for adolescent drug abuse: Results of a randomized clinical trial. *American Journal of Drug and Alcohol Abuse*, *27*(4), 651–688.

Liddle, H. A., Rowe, C. L., Quille, T., Dakof, G., Sakran, E., & Biaggi, H. (2002). Transporting a research-developed adolescent drug abuse treatment into practice. *Journal of Substance Abuse Treatment: Special Edition on Transferring Research to Practice*, *22*, 231–243.

Lindforss, L., & Magnusson, D. (1997). Solution-focused therapy in prison. *Contemporary Family Therapy*, *19*(1), 89–103.

Lipchik, E. (2002). *Beyond techniques in solution-focused therapy*. New York, NY: Guilford Press.

Lipchik, E., Derks, J., LaCourt, M., & Nunnally, E. (2012). In C. Franklin, T. S. Trepper, W. J. Gingerich, & E. E. McCollum (Eds.), *Solution-focused brief therapy: A handbook of evidence-based practice* (pp. 3–19). New York, NY: Oxford University Press.

Littrell, J. M., Malia, J. A., & Vanderwood, M. (1995). Single-session brief counseling in a high school. *Journal of Counseling and Development*, *73*, 451–458.

Marinelli-Casey, P., Domier, C. P., & Rawson, R. A. (2002). The gap between research and practice in substance abuse treatment. *Psychiatric Services*, *53*, 984–987.

McFarlane, W. R. (2002). An overview of psychoeducational multifamily group treatment. In W. R. McFarlane (Ed.), *Multifamily groups in the treatment of severe psychiatric disorders* (pp. 71–103). New York, NY: Guilford Press.

McFarlane, W. R., McNary, S., Dixon, L., Hornby, H., & Cimett, E. (2001). Predictors of dissemination of family psychoeducation in community mental health centers in Maine and Illinois. *Psychiatric Services*, *52*, 935–942.

Miller, R. L. (2001). Innovation in HIV prevention: Organizational and intervention characteristics affecting program adoption. *American Journal of Community Psychology*, *29*(4), 621–647.

Miller, R. L. (2003). Adapting an evidence-based intervention: Tales of the hustler project. *AIDS Education and Prevention*, *15*(Suppl. A), 127–138.

Multisystemic Therapy Services (1998). MST treatment model: Multisystemic therapy at a glance. Retrieved from www.musc.edu/fsrc/overview/atreatment model.htm#treatmentmodel/

Myers, L., & Thyer, B. (1997). Should social work clients have the right to effective treatment? *Social Work*, *42*(3), 288–298.

Navran, L. (1967). Communication and adjustment in marriage. *Family Process*, *6*, 173–184. doi: 10.1111/j.1545-5300.1967.00173.x

Newsome, S. (2002). The impact of solution-focused brief therapy with at-risk junior high school students. Unpublished doctoral dissertation, Ohio State University, Columbus.

Ogden, T., & Amlund Hagen, K. (2008). Treatment effectiveness of parent management training in Norway: A randomized controlled trial of children with conduct problems. *Journal of Consulting & Clinical Psychology*, *76*(4), 607–621.

Proctor, E. K. (2003). Evidence for practice: Challenges, opportunities, and access. *Social Work Research*, *27*(4), 195–196.

Randall, J., & Cunningham, P. B. (2003). Multisystemic therapy: A treatment for violent substance-abusing and substance-dependent juvenile offenders. *Addictive Behaviors, 28*, 1731–1739.

Roans, M., & Hoagwood, K. (2000). School-based mental health services: A research review. *Clinical Child and Family Psychology Review, 3*(4), 223–241.

Robbins, M. S., Bachrach, K., & Szapocznik, J. (2002). Bridging the research-practice gap in adolescent treatment: The case of brief strategic family therapy. *Journal of Substance Abuse Treatment, 23*, 123–132.

Robbins, M. S., Feaster, D. J., Horigian, V. E., Bachrach, K., Burlew, K., Carrion, I., . . . Szapocznik, J. (2011). Brief strategic family therapy versus treatment as usual: Results of a multisite randomized trial for substance using adolescents. *Journal of Consulting & Clinical Psychology, 79*(6), 713–727.

Rohrbach, L. A., Graham, J. W., & Hansen, W. B. (1993). Diffusion of a school-based substance abuse prevention program: Predictors of program implementation. *Preventive Medicine, 22*, 237–260.

Rowe, C. L., Liddle, H. A., & Dakof, G. A. (2002). Classifying adolescent substance abusers by level of externalizing and internalizing symptoms. *Journal of Child and Adolescent Substance Abuse, 11*(2), 41–66.

Santisteban, D. A., Coatsworth, D., Perez-Vidal, A., Kurtines, W. M., Schwanz, S. J., LaPerriere, A., . . . Szapocznik, J. (2003). The efficacy of brief strategic family therapy in modifying Hispanic adolescent behavior problems and substance use. *Journal of Family Psychology, 17*, 121–133.

Schinke, S., Brounstein, P., & Gardner, S. (2002). *Science-based prevention programs and principles.* Rockville, MD: U.S. Department of Health and Human Services.

Schoenwald, S. K., & Hoagwood, K. (2001). Effectiveness, transportability, and dissemination of interventions: What matters when? *Psychiatric Services, 52*(9), 1190–1197.

Schwartz, A., & Schwartz, R. (1993). *Depression: Theories and treatments.* New York, NY: Columbia University Press.

Sexton, T., & Turner, C. W. (2010). The effectiveness of functional family therapy for youth with behavioral problems in a community practice setting. *Journal of Family Psychology, 24*(3), 339–348.

Strauss, S. E., Richardson, W. S., Glasziou, P., & Haynes, R. B. (2005). *Evidence-based medicine: How to practice and teach EBM* (3rd ed.). New York, NY: Churchill Livingstone.

Substance Abuse and Mental Health Services Administration Center for Substance Abuse Prevention (2005). *SAMHSA Model Programs.* Retrieved from www.modelprograms.samhsa.gov/matrix_all.cfm

Swenson, C. C., Schaeffer, C. M., Henggeler, S. W., Faldowski, R., & Mayhew, A. M. (2010). Multisystemic therapy for child abuse and neglect: A randomized effectiveness trial. *Journal of Family Psychology, 24*(4), 497–507.

Ungar, M. (2002). A deeper, more social ecological social work practice. *Social Service Review, 76*(3), 480–497.

Ungar, M. (2011). *The social ecology of resilience: A handbook of theory and practice.* New York, NY: Springer.

Voss, W. D. (2003). Multiple family group (MFG) treatment and negative symptoms in schizophrenia: Two-year outcomes. *Dissertation Abstracts International: Sciences and Engineering, 63*(11B), 5541.

Zimmerman, T. S., Jacobsen, R. B., MacIntyre, M., & Watson, C. (1996). Solution-focused parenting groups: An empirical study. *Journal of Systemic Therapies, 15*(4), 12–25.

Author Index

Grant, R., 28
Gray, J. A. M., 217, 219, 269
Gray, M., 154
Graziano, R., 202, 204
Greenbaum, P. E., 279
Greenberg, L., 281
Greene, G., 125
Greene, G. J., 72
Greene, R., 199
Greenley, R. N., 45
Greif, G. L., 6
Gresham, F. M., 21
Grogan-Kaylor, A., 12, 18
Groth-Juncker, A., 212
Guerra, N., 57
Gutheil, I. A., 207
Gutierrez, L., 12
Guttman, C., 183
Guyatt, G., 152, 154

Hagen, K., 53, 281
Haggerty, R. J., 116
Hagopian, 180
Haight, B., 202
Haley, J., 18
Haley, W. E., 207
Hall, B. L., 244
Hall, G. S., 71
Hall, P., 139
Hamilton, G., 5, 10
Hamilton, M., 137
Hanley, J. H., 284
Hanna, M. P., 215
Hansen, W., 104
Harrington, R., 18
Harris, M. B., 111, 266
Harrison, M., 112
Hart, S. L., 5
Hartman, A., 7, 128, 130, 265, 266, 267
Hautman, C., 281
Haw, S., 97
Hawkins, J. D., 46, 79
Haynes, R. B., 152, 199, 269
Healy, K., 238, 239, 240, 248, 249
Heck, L., 217, 220

Heffernan, J., 286, 287
Hegedus, A., 80
Henderson, C. E., 279
Henggeler, S. W., 53, 54, 107, 108, 113, 130, 278, 284, 285, 287
Hepworth, D. H., 4, 5, 12, 14, 135, 141, 286
Hersen, M., 149, 161
Hervis, O. E., 55
Heyman, A., 137
Heyman, J. C., 207
Hibbs, E. D., 98, 107, 110
Hickerson, J., 79
Hicks, T. V., 109
Hickson, M., 206, 211
Hoagwood, K., 43, 44, 98, 270, 281, 284, 285
Hobart, K. R., 201, 203
Hodges, K., 81
Holden, D., 277
Holland, S., 240, 242
Holleran, L., 127
Hollis, F., 5, 127, 147
Holmbeck, G. N., 45
Holosko, M. J., 198, 210, 221, 222, 223, 225
Holtgrave, D. R., 17
Hooyman, N. R., 199
Hops, H., 106, 107
Hopson, L., 284
Hornby, H., 285
Howard, M., 157, 160
Howard, M. D., 199
Howard, M. O., 157
Howden-Chapman, 156
Huang, L., 45
Hudson, W. W., 14, 77, 78
Hughson, A., 252
Hui, E., 213, 219
Hulac, D., 133
Hunkeler, E. M., 213, 219, 220
Hunsley, J., 15, 71, 86, 151
Husaini, B. A., 219
Hutchinson, A. M., 284

Ialongo, N. S., 18
Ife, J., 238, 246, 254
Inouye, S. K., 209
Ivens, C., 17

Jabine, T. B., 24
Jackson, B. A., 182
Jackson, C., 97
Jackson, R., 15
Jacobsen, M., 11
Jacobsen, R. B., 282
Jacobson, M., 241, 243, 246, 259
Jaffe, M. W., 182
Jagannathan, R., 28
Jankowski, L., 182
Janzen, C., 266, 267, 268, 278, 281
Jefferson, K. W., 105
Jemmott, J., 105
Jemmott, L., 105
Jensen, J., 160
Jensen, P. S., 88, 98, 107, 110
Jenson, J., 88, 157
Jobe, J. B., 24
Johnson, C., 103
Johnson, L. C., 237, 238
Johnson, S., 281
Johnson, W., 27
Johnston, L. D., 97, 100, 284
Jordan, C., 72, 79, 126, 127, 129, 131, 138, 265, 266, 268, 269, 271, 272, 274, 275, 276, 278
Joshi, P., 135

Kamata, A., 77
Kane, M. T., 113
Kapasi, Z. H., 208, 211
Karls, J., 7, 136, 141
Katz, L., 213, 215, 219
Katz, S., 182
Katzman, R., 181
Kauffmann, R. H., 217, 219
Kaufman, J., 30
Kavanagh, K., 113, 114, 115

Subject Index